"Seldom have I read a book by assorted authors from cover to cover, yet this particular volume in Tom Singer's worthy and wide-reaching series on varieties of cultural complexes was compelling for its breadth and depth of focus. I feel better informed about sensitive issues that are still unresolved and that bear the marks of intergenerational trauma, passed on from the colonization, conflicts, and cross-cultural influences of previous centuries, both within Asia and between West and East. Just as it is a 'must-read' for the Westerner desirous of knowing more intimately the Easterner, it will be a valuable aid for intra-Asian cultural understanding."

– **Jean Kirsch**, Jungian analyst, USA

"The essays gathered in this beautifully designed and edited collection, most written by Asian Jungian psychoanalysts, present a brilliant display of psychological insight into the cultural histories and complexes of the nationalities under consideration. The broad diversity in perspective and content among these reflections is unified within the framework of Jungian theory. For the curious Westerner and Easterner they bring the soul of the Far East closer."

– **Murray Stein**, author, *Jung's Map of the Soul*

"In *Cultural Complexes in China, Japan, Korea, and Taiwan: Spokes of the Wheel*, an amazing collection of contributors provide profound insights into cultural complexes. Far East Asia has never been so broadly represented in the Jungian literature. This unique text, drawing upon the Tao Te Ching, links a multitude of cultures into a coherent vision of the collective psyche at its most dynamic. Tom Singer, as maestro of the cultural complex in this collection, creates a polyphonic harmony—it will be a treat for any reader interested in the Far East. The gateway east is open; this is a psychological guide to its riches."

– **Joe Cambray**, PhD, President/CEO,
Pacifica Graduate Institute, USA

CULTURAL COMPLEXES IN CHINA, JAPAN, KOREA, AND TAIWAN

● ● ● ● ● ●

Thomas Singer presents a unique collection which examines cultural complexes in four parts of East Asia: China, Japan, Korea, and Taiwan.

From ancestor worship in China to the "*kimchi*-bitch" meme of South Korea, the search for the father in Taiwan and *hikikomori* in Japan, the contributors take a Jungian lens to aspects of culture and shine a light on themes including gender, archetypes, consciousness, social roles, and political relations.

This insightful and timely book will be essential reading for academics and students of Jungian and post-Jungian ideas, politics, sociology, and Asian studies. It will also be of great interest to Jungian analysts in practice and in training.

Thomas Singer, MD, is a psychiatrist and Jungian psychoanalyst, practicing in San Francisco, USA.

CULTURAL COMPLEXES IN CHINA, JAPAN, KOREA, AND TAIWAN
• • • • •

Spokes of the Wheel

Edited by
Thomas Singer

LONDON AND NEW YORK

First published 2021
by Routledge
2 Park Square, Milton Park, Abingdon, Oxon OX14 4RN

and by Routledge
52 Vanderbilt Avenue, New York, NY 10017

Routledge is an imprint of the Taylor & Francis Group, an informa business

© 2021 selection and editorial matter, Thomas Singer; individual chapters, the contributors

The right of Thomas Singer to be identified as the author of the editorial material, and of the authors for their individual chapters, has been asserted in accordance with sections 77 and 78 of the Copyright, Designs and Patents Act 1988.

All rights reserved. No part of this book may be reprinted or reproduced or utilised in any form or by any electronic, mechanical, or other means, now known or hereafter invented, including photocopying and recording, or in any information storage or retrieval system, without permission in writing from the publishers.

Trademark notice: Product or corporate names may be trademarks or registered trademarks, and are used only for identification and explanation without intent to infringe.

British Library Cataloguing-in-Publication Data
A catalogue record for this book is available from the British Library

Library of Congress Cataloging-in-Publication Data
Names: Singer, Thomas, 1942– editor.
Title: Cultural complexes in China, Japan, Korea, and Taiwan : spokes of the wheel / edited by Thomas Singer.
Description: 1 Edition. | New York : Routledge, 2020. | Includes bibliographical references and index.
Identifiers: LCCN 2020038160 (print) | LCCN 2020038161 (ebook) | ISBN 9780367441043 (hardback) | ISBN 9780367441050 (paperback) | ISBN 9781003007647 (ebook)
Subjects: LCSH: Jungian psychology—East Asia. | Social psychology—East Asia. | Psychoanalysis and culture—East Asia.
Classification: LCC BF173.J85 C87 2020 (print) | LCC BF173.J85 (ebook) | DDC 155.8/951—dc23
LC record available at https://lccn.loc.gov/2020038160
LC ebook record available at https://lccn.loc.gov/2020038161

ISBN: 978-0-367-44104-3 (hbk)
ISBN: 978-0-367-44105-0 (pbk)
ISBN: 978-1-003-00764-7 (ebk)

Typeset in Times New Roman
Layout, Design, and Cartography by Northern Graphic Design & Publishing

DEDICATION

● ● ● ● ● ●

The book is dedicated in loving memory to **Thomas B. Kirsch** who was "a man for all seasons," which included being a pioneer in building a bridge between the East and the West.

PERMISSIONS

• • • • • •

In Chapter 1, Figure 1.3, Bixia Yuanjun; Figure 1.4, The main temple for Bixia Yuanjun at the top of Mount Tai; Figure 1.5, Xi Wang Mu—a brick with picture of the Queen Mother of the West (Han Dynasty); and Figure 1.6, Nüwa, shown on stone coffin, Shandong Province, appear by permission of Nora Liu.

In Chapter 2, Figure 2.2, Hongtong Daihuaishu Ancestor Memorial Garden (root carved door); Figure 2.3, Scheme of Hongtong Dahuaishu migration routes during the Ming Dynasty; Figure 2.4, The scenes of migration under the Grand Chinese Scholar Tree; and Figure 2.5, The site of the Grand Chinese Scholar Tree (screen wall with root character), appear by permission of Hongtong Dahuaishu Ancestor Memorial Garden, Ltd.

In Chapter 6, Figure 6.1, Paul Cezanne, *The Bay of Marseilles seen from L'Estaque*, is in the public domain; Figure 6.2, Paul Cezanne, *Rocks at L'Estaque*, appears by permission of Museu de Arte de São Paulo Assis Chateaubriand; and Figure 6.3, Li Cheng, *A Solitary Temple Amid Clearing Peaks*, appears by permission of Nelson-Atkins Media Services.

In Chapter 7, Figure 7.1, Underwater scene from Masuda and Nisbett's experiment, appears by permission of Takahiko Masuda and Richard Nisbett.

In Chapter 8, Figure 8.3, Gunko-Zu, Tanyū Kanō, seventeenth century, appears by permission of the Kyoto National Museum.

TABLE OF CONTENTS

• • • • • •

Acknowledgements ....*xiii*
List of Illustrations...*xv*
Foreword
  John Beebe *1*
Introduction
  Thomas Singer.. 7

China

Chapter 1
  Femininity in Chinese Culture:
    Archetype and Complex
  Gao Lan and Shen Heyong..25
Chapter 2
  Ancestral Worship:
    A Cultural Complex of the Chinese
  Zhang Lei, Hou Yingchun, and Li Xianghui 49
Chapter 3
  Single Mothers in Marriage:
    Cultural and Individual Complexes in
    Displacement of Immigrant Mothers
  Gong Xi..77
Chapter 4
  The Animus Archetype in Chinese Culture
  Xu Jun...97

Japan

Chapter 5
  Postmodern Consciousness in the
  Novels of Haruki Murakami:
    An Emerging Cultural Complex
  Toshio Kawai *123*

SPOKES OF THE WHEEL

Chapter 6
Japanese Landscape and the Subject:
On the Old and New States of Consciousness
Yasuhiro Tanaka *139*
Chapter 7
Agency, a Japanese Cultural Complex:
Transformation of Jungian-Oriented
Psychotherapy in an Age of Weaker Agency
Chihiro Hatanaka *163*
Chapter 8
Voices from Nature and Withdrawal
(*Hikikomori*) in Japanese Culture
Nanae Takenaka *181*

Korea

Chapter 9
Seeking *Hieros Gamos* on the Korean Peninsula:
Understanding the Political Situations
of Two Koreas from a Jungian Perspective
Nami Lee *201*
Chapter 10
The *Kimchi*-Bitch Cultural Complex:
Modern Misogyny, Memes, and Millennial
Men in South Korea
Amalya Layla Ashman *227*

Taiwan

Chapter 11
The History of the Search for the Father in Taiwan:
A Cultural Complex
Hao-Wei Wang *261*
Chapter 12
An Orphan of the Patriarchy:
A Cultural Complex in Taiwanese History
Su-chen Hung and Hung-Chin Wei *291*
Chapter 13
The Wounded Feminine in Chinese Culture
Liza J. Ravitz *311*

Index *331*

ACKNOWLEDGEMENTS

• • • • • •

Nancy Cater of Spring Journal Books has been a wonderful publisher. I am most grateful for her consistent and deep support of my work over the years.

Dr. John Beebe has unfailingly shared his extraordinary knowledge of things both Asian and Western with a truly generous spirit.

LeeAnn Pickrell has made it all happen once again. This book would simply not exist without her diligence, skill, and real care.

And, finally, all the contributors have given selflessly and enthusiastically in a spirit of exploration and discovery.

LIST OF ILLUSTRATIONS
• • • • • •

Chapter 1

Figure 1.1: Ji (left), Jiang (center), and Si (right).
Figure 1.2: Xing.
Figure 1.3: Bixia Yuanjun.
Figure 1.4: The main temple for Bixia Yuanjun at the top of Mount Tai.
Figure 1.5: Xi Wang Mu—a brick with picture of the Queen Mother of the West (Han Dynasty).
Figure 1.6: Nüwa, shown on stone coffin, Shandong Province.
Figure 1.7: Sandtray of thirteen-year-old girl: feeling the mother's embrace.
Figure 1.8: Sandtray of twenty-three-year-old woman: regaining her lost feminine.
Figure 1.9: Sandtray of thirty-six-year-old woman: using the feminine image.
Figure 1.10: Ci-Bei.
Figure 1.11: The archetypal image of love in oracle bone script form.
Figure 1.12: Hui.
Figure 1.13: Weaving.

Chapter 2

Figure 2.1: 艮 (*Gen*) hexagram (*Gen* means "mountain").
Figure 2.2: Hongtong Daihuaishu Ancestor Memorial Garden (root carved door).
Figure 2.3: Scheme of Hongtong Dahuaishu migration routes during the Ming Dynasty.
Figure 2.4: The scenes of migration under the Grand Chinese Scholar Tree.
Figure 2.5: The site of the Grand Chinese Scholar Tree (screen wall with root character).

xvi SPOKES OF THE WHEEL

Chapter 4

Figure 4.1: Pangu in the cosmic egg.
Figure 4.2: Pangu created Yang and Yin.
Figure 4.3: Hexagram 11 Tai.
Figure 4.4: Ding, the vessel.
Figure 4.5: Marshal Peng Dehuai disgraced in the Cultural Revolution.
Figure 4.6: Scholars beaten in public in Tiananmen Square.
Figure 4.7: City dwellers sent to the Great Northern Wilderness.

Chapter 6

Figure 6.1: Paul Cézanne, *The Bay of Marseilles seen from L'Estaque.*
Figure 6.2: Paul Cézanne, Aix-en-Provence, França [France], 1839–
1906. *Rochedos em L'Estaque* [Cliffs in L'Estaque],
1882–85. Óleo sobre tela [Oil on canvas], 73 × 92 cm.
Acervo [Collection] Museu de Arte de São Paulo Assis
Chateaubriand. Doação [Gift] Edward Marvin, 1953
MASP.00087. Foto [Photo] João Musa.
Figure 6.3: Attributed to Li Cheng, Chinese (919–967 C.E.). *A
Solitary Temple Amid Clearing Peaks*, Northern Song
Dynasty (960–1127). Hanging scroll, ink and slight color
on silk, 14 × 22 inches (111.8 × 55.9 cm). The Nelson-
Atkins Museum of Art, Kansas City, Missouri. Purchase:
William Rockhill Nelson Trust, 47–71. Photo courtesy of
Nelson-Atkins Media Services / John Lamberton.
Figure 6.4: Li Cheng, *High Pines, Level Distance.*
(https://aras.org/spokes-of-the-wheel).
Figure 6.5: Guo Xi, *Early Spring.*
(https://aras.org/spokes-of-the-wheel).
Figure 6.6: Sesshu, *Splashed-Ink Style Landscape* (1495).
(https://aras.org/spokes-of-the-wheel).
Figure 6.7: Sesshu, *Long Scroll of Landscapes* (1469).
(https://aras.org/spokes-of-the-wheel).

List of Illustrations xvii

Figure 6.8: Sesshu, *Autumn Landscape*.
 (https://aras.org/spokes-of-the-wheel).
Figure 6.9: Sesshu, *Winter Landscape*.
 (https://aras.org/spokes-of-the-wheel).
Figure 6.10: Sesshu, *View of Ama-no-Hashidate* (1501–1506).
 (https://aras.org/spokes-of-the-wheel).
Figure 6.11: Fan Kuan, *Travelers Among Mountains and Streams*.
 (https://aras.org/spokes-of-the-wheel).

Chapter 7

Figure 7.1: Underwater scene from Masuda and Nisbett's experiment

Chapter 8

Figure 8.1: Ryoan-ji Kyoto Zen garden May 2007.
Figure 8.2: Étienne Dupérac (1525–1604), bird's-eye plan view of the gardens at Villa d'Este (Tivoli) Italy between 1560 and 1575.
Figure 8.3: Gunko-Zu, Tanyū Kanō, seventeenth century.

Chapter 10

Figure 10.1: Meme of the *kimchi*-bitch by a cartoonist under the pseudonym Na-neun Aegukja (I am a Patriot).
 (https://aras.org/spokes-of-the-wheel).

Chapter 11

Figure 11.1: Taiwan independence versus unification with the mainland.

Chapter 12

Figure 12.1: Mudan incident map.

Foreword

• • • • • • • •

John Beebe

No analytic process, including the reading of a pioneering contribution to analytical psychology like this one, can avoid evoking a counter-response. A reader who has spent any time in East Asia may be forgiven for saying to him- or herself, "I thought so!" when confronted by the cultural complexes that in this book are so precisely identified and carefully surveyed by Jungian psychotherapists living and working in Mainland China, Japan, Korea, and Taiwan at the present time. The reader may be quick to applaud the unmasking of lingering prejudices toward, for instance, the worth of female children, which reveal intergenerational blinders that continue to limit the psychological vision of the citizens of these countries that have become in other ways so cognate with the Western world.

But it would, of course, be a mistake to regard East Asians as exceptional in failing to review and discard outmoded psychological ideas. Can any American reader of this book, for example, be unaware of how hard it has proven for the present-day United States to shake off the dismissive presumptions of its founding fathers toward Native Americans, Africans, and women? Can a reader in Europe (or, again,

---

John Beebe, a past president of the C. G. Jung Institute of San Francisco, is the author of *Integrity in Depth* and of *Energies and Patterns in Psychological Type: The Reservoir of Consciousness*. He is co-author, with Virginia Apperson, of *The Presence of the Feminine in Film*. John was founding editor of the *San Francisco Jung Institute Library Journal* (now called *Jung Journal: Culture & Psyche*) and was the first American co-editor of *The Journal of Analytical Psychology*.

2   JOHN BEEBE

in the United States) overlook the shadow projections on immigrants? An attitude of superiority toward the complexes described in this book cannot seriously be sustained.

Nor can the tendency to become too grateful to Asia for its inspiring qualities be entirely wise. A reader might cherish the ways matriarchal consciousness has been kept alive as an underground tradition in these overtly patriarchal countries—in Chinese conceptions of yielding to the *Tao* as a way of furthering it, in the Buddhist notions of interdependence that make Japan cohere when its citizens are threatened by natural disasters, and in the extraordinary culture of sincerity, grace, and integrity that Korean Confucianism has fostered. The tradition of taking responsibility for the personal impact of any communication upon others that so informs the I Ching was singled out by C. G. Jung as a key to prudence in managing personal affairs; he did not hesitate to recommend it to Western readers. Perusing the present book in the light of its own powerful ancestors, the rich legacy of East Asian psychology that has made, for instance, Lao Tzu's *Tao Te Ching* a perennial favorite in the present-day West, may sway some readers to assume that a similar ethic of care has already emerged through the practice of analytical psychology sweeping Asia today.

Neither feeling ahead of Asian attitudes nor assuming that Western countries need to catch up with them will help the reader to hear accurately the voices of the authors of these thoughtful chapters. I would rather recommend the attitude Jung first described in the Commentary he wrote to introduce Richard Wilhelm's translation of "The Secret of the Golden Flower," a text that we now know was as Buddhist as it was Taoist, and essentially East Asian in recommending *wu wei,* an attitude of letting a phenomenon happen. A willingness on the part of the reader to simply let this book happen page by page will enable the discovery that all of its authors have struggled to listen without presuppositions to the psyches of Asians themselves. They have actually picked up the drift of the East Asian psyche, in therapy dialogue, in sandplay, and in East Asian works of art that dramatize issues of the soul.

Their subjects voice their own struggles to reconcile the duty to take up self-cultivation with an inbred cultural obligation to serve the collective well-being of the group self of their countries of origin. Asian readers will immediately recognize this tension. I would advise

FOREWORD

Western readers, rather than feeling superior to this effort just because our Renaissance humanism has taught us for over five hundred years to individuate the personal self, to let Asian psychotherapists tell us what emerging personhood looks like in East Asia today. Both Eastern and Western readers should allow themselves to notice what happens to individuals in Asian countries when they do not relegate the notion of a transpersonal Self to Jungian theory but take its needs up as a duty, only to discover that their own traditions come alive in the process to help them.

Whether we regard reading this book as a window on how the traditional practice of personal self-cultivation is undertaken in East Asia today or as a reminder that thinking in terms of an objective group Self is a social duty for all psychologically minded people, we can join the East Asian authors who bear witness to a moving human effort to represent both "little *s*" personal self and "big *S*" transpersonal Self freshly. With the help of the dedicated new band of psychological interpreters that are applying Jung's ideas to the lives of their patients and the records of artists and religious figures who have moved them, we can recognize how often East Asians have mined their traditional complexes for consciousness, even without the assistance of the analysts they can find in Asia today. This book offers a unique opportunity to contemplate and distill stories from that humbling tradition.

Asia

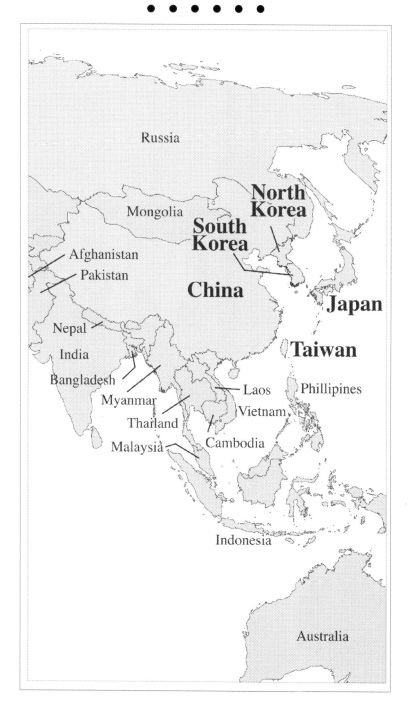

Introduction

• • • • • • • •

Thomas Singer

The goal of this book is to expand the ways in which we can use the insights of analytical psychology to understand how the psyche lives in the broader world of group life and its many unique local and regional conflicts. In particular, the series of books of which this is a part has been using the Jungian concept of the cultural complex as a vehicle to navigate an exploration of the psyche in its collective expression. And, of course, the collective psyche plays many roles in the psyche of the individual. This need for a broader exploration has encouraged its contributors to include history, sociology, geography, economics, and religious history as well as depth psychology in considering how cultural complexes live in the psyche of individuals, groups, nations, and larger regional areas.

As an analogy, we might think of the exploration of cultural complexes as the creation of a vehicle that is equipped with a Jungian GPS, or global positioning system. This Jungian GPS provides psychological navigation, with one axis oriented toward the "spirit of

---

Thomas Singer, MD, is a psychiatrist and Jungian psychoanalyst who trained at Yale Medical School, Dartmouth Medical School, and the C. G. Jung Institute of San Francisco. He is the author of many books and articles that include a series of books on cultural complexes that have focused on Australia, Latin America, Europe, the United States, and Far East Asian countries, in addition to another series of books featuring Ancient Greece, Modern Psyche. He serves on the board of ARAS (Archive for Research into Archetypal Symbolism) and has edited *ARAS Connections* for many years.

the depths" and a second axis oriented toward "the spirit of the times." This cultural complex vehicle is designed to provide a balanced perspective that honors both the profound inner archetypal insights of analytical psychology and a sophisticated approach to compelling outer realities, such as the social, cultural, and political events that also beckon for psychological attention and analysis. Most important to this tool's biaxial orientation is its emphasis on specific locations of intense interest. Just as any retail merchant knows that "location, location, location" is the key to success, so the application of Jungian theory to the complexes of the collective psyche requires "specificity, specificity, specificity" in its attention to where collective psychic energy is bubbling over in intense arousal.

The original Jungian tradition tended to be inner oriented, even esoteric and abstract. Its spirit was compensatory to the overweening material ambitions of the time leading up to World War I, which Jung saw as a conflict that in many ways emerged from the neglect of spirit. Even today, Jungian insights, which seem so natural to those of us who travel in and are comfortable with the living reality of archetypes and complexes, are often incomprehensible to most people because of the highly intuitive and abstract nature of our perspective. To make our tradition relevant to the world, we need to give up our exclusive emphasis on spirit and psyche found in private and sensitive spaces and speak simply, clearly, and directly. We need to more fully connect our theory with the social, political, and cultural realities of the day-to-day world. Exploring cultural complexes in particular regions is one way of accomplishing this.

The cultural complex theory is a vehicle built to travel on wheels equipped with such a bi-directional capacity, designed to find ground for a psychological orientation, and able to bring Jungian theories into a living relationship with everything in the world that might welcome and find exciting this psychological vehicle's arrival.

The cart: spokes of the wheel

Thinking of the cultural complex theory as a vehicle built for the exploration of psychological ground in Far East Asian countries has led me to consider an image from one of this region's most revered ancient texts, the *Tao Te Ching*. Its author, Lao Tzu, wrote in Chapter 11 of his classic book:

INTRODUCTION 9

> Thirty spokes share one hub.
> Adapt the nothing therein to the purpose in hand, and
> you will have the use of the cart.

We can think of this book about cultural complexes as a Far East Asian cart that carries the many insights harvested by its Jungian-oriented authors. And we can also think of the wheels of this cart as having their own structure, which we might also liken to the notion of the cultural complex. "The nothing therein" that is at the center of each wheel of our cart would be an openness to what culture teaches that is as free as possible from presuppositions. The spokes of each wheel represent the solidly ventured analysis of individual cultural complexes that have become evident to Jungian analysts working in Far East Asia. The complexity that arises from realizing that there are four such wheels, each a bit different in its localization of the energy to be applied, reminds us that there are Southern and Northern as well as Eastern and Western regions of "Far East Asia." It is the ambition of this volume that the complexity of Far East Asia will come across with an appropriately comprehensive diversity of points of view, so the reader might get a glimpse of how cultural complex theory is used by Far East Asians themselves to cover psychological ground in their own countries. Those used to Far East Asian texts will notice how much not only Lao Tzu but also Confucius, the Buddha, and the I Ching are drawn on by Asians today to approach the problem of cultural analysis of their countries' psychology. Perhaps these traditions are the four wheels of the cart that the Far East Asians have constructed to orient themselves over the centuries. Putting these pieces together, we can think of cultural complex theory as being one spoke, one wheel, one cart, and one vehicle all at the same time and for anyone to use.

At different times in his life, Jung allowed himself to depend one after another on each of these supporting wheels of Asian philosophy (he read the I Ching, commented on both Confucian and Buddhist philosophy, and in his "Psychological Commentary on 'The Secret of the Golden Flower,'" showed how much he shared the Taoist perspective of Lao Tzu).[1] That he allowed himself to turn each of these wheels around so that it could offer a new orientation to Western psychology is impressive, but Jung was not in a position to build the cart they have become for studying the deep psychological complexes that continue to live in contemporary Far East Asia. This book offers

10   THOMAS SINGER

some of the first reports available from authors who have only recently been studying Jung seriously in China and Taiwan and for some decades more in Japan and Korea. This book draws its contributors from both the newly emerging Jungian groups as well as from the established groups in all these regions.

As the convener and editor of the book, I have been struck by how foreign and "other" the contributions to this book have felt to me. In a way, this should not be unexpected. Other than a week in Japan and three weeks in Southeast Asia, I am virtually a stranger to the many forms that the Asian mind, collective psyche, and culture have taken. But I have learned enough through working with the authors of this volume to know that they live in vastly different cultures from our Western world. This raises interesting questions: How will the Eastern mind/psyche adapt to notions of Western psychology, generally, and analytical psychology, in particular? Given the huge differences in culture, is it suitable to apply a Western psychological container, a concept such as the cultural complex theory, to the many particular complexes Jungians have so far been able to identify in the Far East Asian countries? Is there a potential meeting between East and West in the application of such an idea? Separate and interrelated themes should also be acknowledged at this point:

- People in Far East Asia (China, Japan, Korea, Taiwan) relate to one another and to being part of a family, clan, greater community, and nation in very different ways than the people of the post-industrial, postmodern Western world. For instance, in Chinese cultures, the wife customarily leaves her own family and takes on the responsibilities of becoming part of and caring for the husband's family.
- Far East Asians relate to the difference that exists between being an individual and being a member of a group in a way that is quite distinctive from how Western people regard themselves as autonomous centers of agency when they are mature enough to think and act for themselves. The Western emphasis on the development of the individual as separate from the family and community is much less important in the East than in the West. Another way of saying this is that the identity of the individual as separate from

INTRODUCTION

11

the group is not the highest value in the East; group identity is much more treasured.

These great divides between the East and the West do not negate the reality that Far East Asians have a rich collective psyche that expresses itself in group complexes, even as they have quite different relationships with the groups to which they belong than those from the West have. This volume demonstrates that the rich collective psyche of Far East Asian people, both conscious and unconscious, often expresses itself in cultural complexes. In fact, the emphasis in the cultural complex theory on "specificity" of person, group, place, and time creates the space to learn about the vast differences between Eastern and Western cultural complexes. And the part of the cultural complex theory that has its eye both on "the spirit of the depths" and on "the spirit of the times" can also point to how cultural complexes, although at times vastly different in content from one culture to another, are a basic structure of the psyche wherever there are groups in the world.

Collective psyche

Before delving into the contents of this book, I would like to step back a bit to make sure the reader is properly introduced to the notions of the collective psyche and complexes, both personal and cultural.

Jung was intensely curious about the differences between groups of people and their varying cultures. He was keenly attuned to what we now call the cultural level of the psyche. He traveled to the Americas, to Africa, to Asia, and he was constantly exploring the sacred traditions and *mores* of other peoples. Certainly, Jung and his followers have taken note of different cultural types, which is evident, for example, in Jung's discussion of national personality characteristics.[2] On the other hand, Jung was so suspicious of the life of groups and the danger of archetypal possession in collective life that he tended to divorce the development of the individual through the individuation process from the individual's life in groups.

Clearly, a substantial part of Jung's genius was his sensitivity to the perils of the individual's falling into the grips of a possession by the collective psyche. Like all who lived through the twentieth century, Jung witnessed the terrible side of collectivity. Beginning with the deadening effect of collective religious life on his father's spirit, Jung went on in October 1913—just prior to outbreak of the

Great War—to have vivid, anticipatory visions of Europe suffering massive destruction, which he later reported as follows: "I realized that a frightful catastrophe was in progress, towns and people were destroyed, and the wrecks and dead bodies were tossing about on the water. Then the whole sea turned to blood."[3] In the later part of his life, he shared in the nightmare horror of imagining nuclear holocaust. It is, therefore, easy to see why Jung had such a dread of the individual and group psyche falling into possession by collective and archetypal forces.

For these reasons, collective life more often than not has fallen into the Jungian shadow—so much so that it can feel, within the Jungian tradition, as if the life of the group and the individual's participation in it exists in a no man's land, suspended in the ether somewhere between the much more important and meaningful individual and/or archetypal realms. This tendency for collective life to fall into the Jungian shadow has done a great disservice to the tradition of analytical psychology and its potential to contribute to a better understanding of group forces in the psyche.

Jung's natural introversion (and his appeal to other introverts) and his fundamental focus on individuation had an unacknowledged tendency to set the individual up against or in opposition to the life of the group. In the Jungian tradition (as in the more general Western tradition), the individual has been given the heroic task of slaying the group's devouring hold on him or her. Individuation and wholehearted participation in the life of the group do not fit together easily or naturally. There is something in the tension between the individual and the group that is wholesome and natural, but the Jungian tradition has magnified that tension beyond perhaps what is healthy for either the individual or the group. Maybe this is, in fact, a "cultural complex" of the Jungian tradition. Whether true or not, it is my hope that the notion of a "cultural complex" will lead to an enhanced capacity to see the shadow of the group in its cultural complexes more objectively, rather than the Jungian tendency to see the group itself as the shadow.

Perhaps we may even become more aware of the positive value of living in the "collective." We may also get better at differentiating cultural complexes from individual complexes. The point I want to make here, however, is that, although Jung and the analytical

Introduction 13

psychologists he trained spoke at length about the nature of the collective psyche, including discussions of different national, ethnic, and religious characteristics, Jung's theory of complexes was never systematically extended beyond its fundamental relevance in the development of individual psychology to include its application to group life or the study of how complexes shape collective experience. Complexes clustered around archetypal cores have been at the heart of the understanding of individual psyche but only peripheral to the study of the collective psyche. A Jungian psychology of group complexes as distinct from, independent of, and yet interrelated with, personal complexes is only now beginning to be elaborated in the specificity of all its different global manifestations.[4]

Personal complexes

Jung's theory of complexes grew out of his early word association tests, which were first published in 1902 and 1903. In these experiments in which he timed responses to long lists of words, Jung noted that certain trigger words would cause significantly delayed responses. He hypothesized that the delayed responses were caused by the interference of unconscious, autonomous contents that he named *complexes*:

> [The complex] has a sort of body, a certain amount of its own physiology. It can upset the stomach. It upsets the breathing, it disturbs the heart—in short, it behaves like a partial personality. For instance, when you want to say or do something and unfortunately a complex interferes with this intention, then you say or do something different from what you intended. You are simply interrupted, and your best intention gets upset by the complex, exactly as if you had been interfered with by a human being or by circumstances from outside.[5]

Interestingly enough, three decades after his initial complex theory researches when the group that had formed around Jung in the 1930s was considering a name separate from the founder's, Jung himself thought it should be called "complex psychology." For many analytical psychologists, Jung's theory of complexes remains a cornerstone of the day-to-day work of psychotherapy and analysis. Like the Freudian theory of defenses, Jung's notion of complexes provides a tool for understanding the nature of intrapsychic and interpersonal conflict.

The cultural unconscious

In the 1960s, Joe Henderson, one of Jung's most creative students, introduced the notion of the *cultural unconscious.* He postulated that a separate layer of the psyche existed between that of the personal unconscious and what Jung called the collective unconscious. Henderson's model of a layered psyche consisting of personal, cultural, and archetypal levels represented a significant advance in the refinement of Jungian theory. It enabled envisioning separate but interrelated layers of psychic contents. The personal unconscious could be imagined as the home of personal complexes as originally conceived of by Jung. The collective unconscious could be imagined as the home of the archetypes, also as conceived of by Jung. In Henderson's newly imagined intermediary zone, the cultural unconscious sitting between the personal and collective unconscious, one could begin to imagine contents that were unique to specific cultures that were neither personal nor archetypal but had their "feet" potentially in both the personal and collective unconscious. It is here that Sam Kimbles and I imagined the home of what we called *cultural complexes.* As personal complexes are the building blocks of the personal unconscious and the archetypes are the building blocks of the collective unconscious, cultural complexes became the building blocks of the cultural unconscious.

Cultural complexes

Today, we can say that a cultural complex can interfere with the rational center of consciousness of a culture, what we might think of as the *group* or *cultural ego,* in the same way that Jung wrote about personal complexes: "You are simply interrupted, and your best intention gets upset by the complex."[6] When a cultural complex possesses the psyche and soma of an individual or a group—it causes us to think and feel in ways that might be quite different from what we think we should feel or think, or, as Jung put it, "We say or do something different from what we intended."[7] In other words, cultural complexes are not always "politically correct," although being "politically correct" might itself be a cultural complex.

The basic premise of the cultural complex theory is that another level of complexes exists within the psyche of the group (and within individuals at the group level of their psyche). We call these group complexes *cultural complexes,* and they, too, can be defined

Introduction

as emotionally charged aggregates of ideas and images that tend to cluster around an archetypal core and are shared by individuals within an identified collective.

As personal complexes emerge out of the level of the personal unconscious in its interaction with deeper levels of the psyche, cultural complexes can be thought of as arising out of the cultural unconscious in its interaction with both the archetypal and personal realms of the psyche and with the broader outer world arena of schools, work and religious communities, media, and all the other forms of group life. Elizabeth Osterman, a senior Jungian analyst of an earlier generation, liked to say that she had learned that her complexes would never completely disappear, but a life-time of struggling with them had resulted in their debilitating effects, including foul moods, lasting only five minutes at a time rather than decades at a time. Some of the cultural complexes that we are exploring have caused uninterrupted foul moods in cultures for centuries, if not millennia, at a time.

Characteristics of cultural complexes

Personal complexes and cultural complexes are not the same, although they can get all mixed up with one another. I've suggested that personal and cultural complexes share the following characteristics.

- *Cultural complexes are autonomous.* They have a life of their own in the psyche that is separate from the everyday ego of an individual or group. Sometimes they are dormant. Sometimes, as when activated by trigger words, they come alive in the psyche and take hold of one's thoughts, feelings, memories, images, and behavior.
- *Cultural complexes are repetitive.* The ongoing life of a cultural complex continues uninterrupted in the psyche of an individual or group, sometimes for generations and even millennia. When they are activated, they are surprisingly unchanged, in the sense that they are recurring, repetitive, and expressive of the same emotional and ideological content over and over again.
- *Cultural complexes collect experiences and memories that validate their own point of view.* Once a cultural complex has established itself, it has a remarkable capacity—like a virus replicating—not only to repeat

itself but also to make sure that whatever happens in the world fits into its pre-existing point of view. Cultural complexes are extremely resistant to facts. Everything that happens in the world is understood through their point of view. Cultural complexes collect experiences and self-affirming memories.

- *The thoughts of cultural complexes tend to be simplistic and black and white.* Although they form the core cognitive content of a cultural complex, the thoughts themselves are not complex. They are unchanging and without subtlety. They are rigid and impervious to modification. Indeed, they seem to be impermeable to any outside influence.
- *Cultural complexes have strong affects or emotions by which one can recognize their presence.* Potent knee-jerk affectivity or emotional reactivity is a sure sign that one has stepped on a cultural complex.
- *Not all cultural complexes are destructive; not all cultural complexes are ego-dystonic to the cultural identity of a group or individual.* Indeed, some cultural complexes can form the core of a healthy cultural identity and provide an essential sense of belonging to individual members of the group.

Another parallel set of criteria that I have developed as a way of identifying a cultural complex involves a series of questions about the various types of mental activity that are recruited when a cultural complex is triggered. A good way to think about a particular cultural complex is to ask the following questions:

- What feelings or affects go along with this complex?
- What images tend to appear with this complex?
- What memories come to mind when this complex is activated?
- What behaviors are triggered by a particular complex?
- What stereotypical thoughts recur with a particular complex?

Attending to the personal, cultural, and archetypal levels of complexes requires respect for each of these realms without condensing or telescoping one into the other, as if one realm were more real, true, or fundamental than another. Cultural complexes are based on

INTRODUCTION

repetitive, historical experiences that have taken root in the collective psyche of a group and in the psyches of the individual members of a group, and they express archetypal values for the group. As such, cultural complexes can be thought of as the fundamental building blocks of an inner sociology. But this inner sociology does not claim to be objective or scientific in its description of different groups and classes of people. Rather, it is a description of groups and classes of people as filtered through the psyches of generations of ancestors. It contains an abundance of information and misinformation about the structures of societies—a truly inner sociology—and its essential components are cultural complexes.

Cultural complexes/cultural identity/national character

"Cultural complexes" are not the same as either "cultural identity" or what Jung called "national character," although at times cultural complexes, cultural identity, and national character can seem impossibly intertwined. For instance, those groups emerging out of long periods of oppression through political and economic struggle must define new identities for themselves, which are often based on long-submerged traditions. This struggle for a new group identity can get all mixed up with underlying potent cultural complexes that have accrued experience and memory over centuries of trauma and lie slumbering in the cultural unconscious, waiting to be awakened by the trigger of new trauma. In the fierce and legitimate protest for a group identity freed up from the shackles of oppression, groups and individuals within the groups can easily get caught up in cultural complexes. And for some people, their complexes—cultural and personal—are their identity. But, for many others, there is a healthy cultural identity (or *cultural ego*) that can clearly be seen as separate from the more negative and contaminating aspects of cultural complexes.

The bipolarity of cultural complexes

Another way to make this most important distinction between cultural complex and cultural identity and/or national character is to use the idea of the *bipolar complex* that John Perry introduced in his seminal paper on complexes in the individual psyche.[8] Perry spoke of the everyday ego as being quite different from the ego that has been taken over by a complex. When a complex is activated in the unconscious (for instance, rebellious son and authoritarian father), one-half of its bipolar content (the rebellious son) with its

18 Thomas Singer

potent affect and one-sided perceptions of the world takes hold of the everyday ego and creates what Perry called "the affect-ego." The other part of the bipolar pair (the authoritarian father) is projected out onto the person with whom one is caught in the complex, and they, in turn, become what Perry labeled an "affect-object." Hence, you get the ragged and highly charged interactions between an "affect-ego" and an "affect-object." Neither party in this unholy pair usually fares very well. This same notion of "affect-ego" and "affect-object" can be carried over into the discussion of cultural complexes to help make the distinction between cultural identity and cultural complex clearer. An individual or group with a unique cultural identity that is not in the grips of a cultural complex is much freer to interact in the world of people from other groups without being prey to the highly charged emotional contents that can quickly alter the perception and behavior of different groups in relation to one another. Once the cultural complex is activated in an individual or a group, however, the everyday cultural identity can be overtaken by the affect of the cultural complex. At that point, the individual and/or the group has entered the territory of what Perry called "affect-ego" and "affect-object"—but at the level of the cultural complex rather than the personal complex.

Structure of this book

Many contributors to this book do not make specific reference to the characteristics of cultural complexes that I have outlined in the introduction. I urge the reader to keep these characteristics in mind as you read these essays. This exercise will allow you to understand more fully what constitutes a cultural complex. In addition, this book does not claim to be an exhaustive study of Far East Asian cultural complexes. Rather, it is a sampling of how cultural complexes manifest themselves in this region of the world. This is the first volume devoted exclusively to the study of cultural complexes in Far East Asia by colleagues from China, Japan, Korea, and Taiwan. The book's chapters are organized in sections by country.

China

In "Femininity in Chinese Culture: Archetype and Complex," Gao Lan and Shen Heyong explore the loss of connection to the archetypal image and meaning of the feminine in modern China as a result of a century of wars, revolutions, and political movements. The authors

INTRODUCTION

19

argue that this disconnection has contributed to psychospiritual damage to the heart and soul of Chinese culture.

In "Ancestral Worship: A Cultural Complex of the Chinese," Zhang Lei, Hou Yingchun, and Li Xianghui explore the ancient and continuing tradition of ancestor worship practiced by people at every level of Chinese society. This worship is practiced with piety and the expectation that the ancestors can be accessed. It constitutes a unique phenomenon that distinguishes Chinese civilization.

Gong Xi from Vancouver contributes a report on how "Single Mothers in Marriage" adapt to life as immigrants. An increasing number of affluent people from mainland China are migrating to North America and resettling their families. Often the wife and children live without their husbands who remain in China to run businesses. Adaptation to this displacement is difficult and has generated its own form of a cultural complex.

In "The Animus Archetype in Chinese Culture," Xu Jun explores the image of the masculine in its long cultural and historical development in China. This masculine image has both its ideal and more negative aspects, which the author explores in clinical studies, historical contexts, and in the famous Chinese tale of "Madame White Snake."

Japan

Toshio Kawai studies "Postmodern Consciousness in the Novels of Haruki Murakami: An Emerging Cultural Complex." Professor Kawai argues that the Japanese soul is caught between postmodern consciousness and a lost mythological world, leading to a dissociation because modern consciousness, in the Western sense, has never been established in Japan.

Yasuhiro Tanaka's essay on "Japanese Landscape and the Subject: On the Old and New States of Consciousness" conducts an exploration of the traditional style of Chinese-style landscape painting in Japan in relation to perspective and especially to the place of the subject or person in the painting. He compares this traditional style of painting to how modern Japanese people with Autism Spectrum Disorder (ASD) represent themselves in Landscape Montage Technique (LMT), a type of art therapy in which patients are encouraged to draw a landscape.

Chihiro Hatanaka argues in "Agency, a Japanese Cultural Complex" that a cultural complex has been developing in Japan that indicates a weakening of a sense of individual personality. This

20 THOMAS SINGER

is reflected in a diminished sense of personal agency, a weakening ability to make stories, and a loss of the sense of the flow of time.

Nanae Takenaka investigates in "Voices from Nature and Withdrawal (*Hikikomori*) in Japanese Culture" the uniquely Japanese condition of *hikikomori* in which hundreds of thousands of young adults are in a state of profound social withdrawal. There is a dissolution of the "I," which Takenaka likens to the short story *Sangetsuki*.

Korea

Nami Lee takes on the difficult task of explaining differences between North Korea and South Korea with particular emphasis on the historical emergence of the Kim clan in North Korea in "Seeking *Hieros Gamos* on the Korean Peninsula." From a Jungian perspective, she argues: "Without mutual understanding of the deep-rooted origin of the disputes between capitalism and communism or between South and North Korea, there can be no real understanding of the opposites."

Amalya Layla Ashman presents an exposition of a Korean cultural complex that promotes, without any regard to political correctness, the hatred of women among young Korean males who face a culture and economy in which they see little hope for their futures. "The *Kimchi*-Bitch Cultural Complex: Modern Misogyny, Memes, and Millennial Men in South Korea" uncovers how misogyny promotes itself through social media to a millennial audience that is ripe for such a possession.

Taiwan

Anchoring his essay in a clinical vignette, a review of modern Taiwanese history, and a novel about a Taiwanese man seeking a better life for himself, Hao-Wei Wang describes "The History of the Search for the Father in Taiwan: A Cultural Complex." Personal identity, ethnic identity, cultural identity, and national identity get all mixed up in this uniquely Taiwanese story about being caught between conflicting historical and psychological forces in the search for the father.

Su-chen Hung and Hung-Chin Wei continue the theme of Hao Wei's chapter in their focus on Taiwan as an "orphan" in search of recognition by its adoptive parents. "An Orphan of the Patriarchy: A Cultural Complex in Taiwanese History" describes a pivotal historic event, the so-called Mudan incident, which offers a context for

INTRODUCTION

understanding how Taiwan has been caught between its identifications with both China and Japan, while simultaneously seeking to give birth to its own unique identity.

Liza Ravitz, an American Jungian analyst, spent two years living in Taiwan. She provided Jungian analysis and taught Jungian theory to the emerging Taiwan group. In the course of her time in Taiwan, she observed "The Wounded Feminine in Chinese Culture." She argues that the wounded feminine is a shadow complex in the cultural unconscious of the Taiwanese hierarchical patriarchy.

Dear reader

Because there is a limitation on the number of images that can be included in the print text, we have created a special arrangement with ARAS (the Archive for Research in Archetypal Symbolism) that permits us to link the reader to more images than we can include in the book. These images are integral to the written text. Simply go to the URL site (https://aras.org/spokes-of-the-wheel) indicated in the text with the image caption. All the images for the book are included in one place on the ARAS site.

Notes

[1] C. G. "Commentary on "The Secret of the Golden Flower'" (1929), in *The Collected Works of C. G. Jung,* vol. 13, ed. and trans. Gerhard Adler and R. F. C. Hull (Princeton, NJ: Princeton University Press, 1968).

[2] C. G. Jung, *Memories, Dreams, Reflections* (New York: Vintage Contemporary, 1989), pp. 238–288.

[3] *Ibid.,* 175.

[4] Thomas Singer, "The Cultural Complex: A Statement of the Theory and Its Application," *Psychotherapy and Politics International* 4 (3, 2006):197–212. https://doi.org/10.1002/ppi.110.

[5] C. G. Jung, "The Tavistock Lectures" (1935), in *The Collected Works of C. G. Jung,* vol. 18, ed. and trans. Gerhard Adler and R. F. C. Hull (Princeton: Princeton University Press, 1976), § 149.

[6] *Ibid.*

[7] *Ibid.*

[8] John W. Perry, "Emotions and Object Relations," *Journal of Analytical Psychology* 15 (1, 1970): 1–12.

China

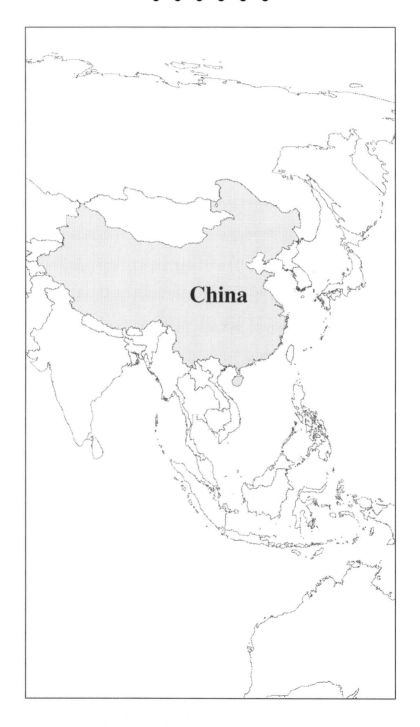

1

• • • • • •

Femininity in Chinese Culture
Archetype and Complex

Gao Lan and Shen Heyong

Chinese culture, in a foundational sense, is essentially a culture of femininity. Ku Hweng-Min has characterized the national personality of China that arose from this feminine core as being "gentle," and Richard Wilhelm also saw "gentleness and calm" as the main qualities of the Chinese people.[1] These "feminine" virtues are reflected in the Daoist philosophy laid down by Lao Tzu and are also reminiscent of what C. G. Jung called "introverted

---

Gao Lan, PhD, is a professor of psychology at the City University of Macao (CityU) and South China Normal University (SCNU). She is a Jungian analyst and sandplay therapist. In addition to her work as president of the Chinese Society of Sandplay Therapy, she serves as CEO of the Oriental Academy of Analytical Psychology (Guangdong, China) and the Garden of the Heart & Soul Project.

Shen Heyong, PhD, is a professor of psychology at the City University of Macao (CityU) and South China Normal University (SCNU). He is a Jungian analyst and sandplay therapist, as well as founding president of the Chinese Federation for Analytical Psychology and Sandplay Therapy. In addition to being the main organizer of the International Conference of Analytical Psychology and Chinese Culture (1998–2015), Shen Heyong has presented at the Eranos Conferences (1997/2007) and the Fay Lecture Series (2018) and served as chief editor for the Chinese translation of *The Collected Works of C. G. Jung*.

intuition" in both his psychological types and also in the Beebe Model of Typology.

Unfortunately, after more than a century of wars and revolutions and then pressure from extreme political movements, such as the Cultural Revolution (1966–1976), the Chinese people have lost their connection to the archetypal image and meaning of the feminine. Because the archetype of the feminine serves as the basic container for the psyche and the heart and soul of a culture, when the connection to it is lost or damaged, psychological problems are bound to increase. This loss of connection to the feminine contributes to various seemingly unrelated symptoms.

As Chinese people, once we know that something vital has been lost, we should search to find it again. We should seek to rebuild the connection to our lost cultural "container"—the archetypal feminine. The Garden of the Heart & Soul project is one such effort, founded on a yearning for kindheartedness.

Three archetypes of femininity: their images and meanings

Almost all of the original Chinese surnames incorporate script that shows a maternal influence. In their original oracle bone script forms, names such as Ji, Jiang, and Si (Figure 1.1) combine images for female and femininity in their makeup.

Figure 1.1: Ji (left), Jiang (center), and Si (right).

The fact that Xing (Figure 1.2), the very term for surname itself, is created by combining "female" and "life" also indicates the primacy of the feminine.

FEMININITY IN CHINESE CULTURE

The cultural archetype of Chinese femininity is mainly reflected through three historical supernatural images: *Bixia Yuanjun* (Goddess of the Tai Mountain), *Xi Wang Mu* (Queen of the West), and *Nüwa* (Empress Wa).

Bixia Yuanjun

Figure 1.2: Xing.

The holy mountain of Mount Tai, which Richard Wilhelm described as the "Olympus of China," was believed to belong to the goddess Bixia Yuanjun. People commonly refer to her as "Lady of Mount Tai," "Mother of Mount Tai," or "Master of Bixia." Mount Tai is known as the easternmost of the Five Great Mountains of China and is associated with sunrise, birth, and renewal. It is often regarded as the foremost of the five. Mount Tai has been a place of worship for at least three thousand years and served as one of the most important ceremonial centers in China during its long dynastic history.

According to Ge Hong, a famous Daoist of the Jin Dynasty (265–420 CE), the name *Yuanjun* means great immortal, the unity of Yin and Yang; and even though the common people worship Bixia Yuanjun as the "Mother of Mount Tai" or "Grandmother of Mount Tai," her image, as shown in Figure 1.3, is always that of a young lady.

In the Bixia temple at the top of Mount Tai (Figure 1.4), several stelae record various scriptures related to the worship of Bixia Yuanjun. She is described as the fundamental representation of femininity and motherhood. Worshiping her produces life in abundance. She personifies great compassion, caring, and kindness, the containment of harm and protection from pain, comfort in suffering, healing in illness. During the Song (960–1279), Yuan (1271–1368), and Ming (1368–1644) Dynasties, there were many thousands of Bixia Yuanjun temples all over China, testifying to the power of the Yuanjun image.

Xi Wang Mu

The next important image of the Chinese feminine emerged from the legendary Kunlun Mountains, one of the most enduring places

Figure 1.3: Bixia Yuanjun.

FEMININITY IN CHINESE CULTURE

Figure 1.4: The main temple for Bixia Yuanjun at the top of Mount Tai.

in Chinese mythology. Worship of Xi Wang Mu, meaning "Queen of the West," or literally, "Queen Mother of the West," formed during the Warring States period (475–221 BCE), with the golden age of her cult in the Han Dynasty (202 BCE–220 CE). She is the first "human-shaped" goddess to be widely worshipped and remains an important goddess in the Chinese mythological system. Academic researchers generally agree that the Queen Mother of the West is the representative figure of the matrilineal system widely existing in China about three thousand years ago. In a matrilineal community, women not only played a main role in production and politics, but also were the center of spiritual life in these tribes. The Feminine was deified as a hybrid creature, both human and Universe.

In Figure 1.5, we see the typical characteristics related to the Queen Mother of the West. She sits on a throne with a dragon and a tiger on each side. A giant toad dances below (in front of) her (the symbol of the toad relates to the goddess of the moon). At the lower left of the picture stands the jade hare, holding a *Lingzhi* (*ganoderma lucidum*), a woody mushroom and special spiritual healing herb. To the right of the toad is a three-legged crow (representing the Sun principle and Yang energy); beside the crow is the legendary warrior *Da Xing Bo* standing with his weapon. Above the hare, there is the nine-tails fox.

Figure 1.5: Xi Wang Mu—a brick with picture of the Queen Mother of the West (Han Dynasty).

And at the bottom of the image, a person kneels with a scepter in his hands, facing two people who may be Xi Wang Mu's attendants.

Although human in appearance, Xi Wang Mu was clearly not human. In the *Shan Hai Jing* (*Legend of Mountains and Seas*), a Chinese classic compilation of mythic geography and stories, Xi Wang Mu is described as having a human face with a leopard's tail and a tiger's teeth. Versions of the text may have existed as early as the fourth century BCE. According to her legend, the Queen Mother of the West takes charge of disease and healing, justice and penalty, production and destruction, life and death. The worship of the Queen Mother of the West has influenced culture across many regions and within most of the various ethnic groups of China. She was warmly worshiped by the poor who could not find what they needed in reality and prayed for release. Ironically, she was also worshipped by the wealthy, who prayed for long lives and immortality. She is the Golden Mother who protects people, the beautiful and passionate goddess, and

FEMININITY IN CHINESE CULTURE

the Iron Mother who punishes the evildoer.

The Chinese fairytale version of the Kunlun Mountains is a spatial reality where magic is a containable object. Unlike Mount Tai where worship took place at its peak, the mythological symbol of the power of Kunlun is a cave. The cave is the material representation of the uterus, the vaginal orifice, even the whole womb. The image of Kunlun and Xi Wang Mu who rules there is inextricably related to fertility.

A famous quotation from Chuang-tzu is "Kunlun Mountain is where the Yellow Emperor rests." Cheng Xuanying who interpreted Chuang-tzu in various commentaries concluded that "Kunlun means human body."[2] The fertility worship practiced at "Kunlun corresponds to the basic human prototype," and working to contain vitality, fertilizing new life, the Queen Mother of the West is the "Great Mother!"

Figure 1.6: Nüwa, shown on stone coffin, Shandong Province.

Nüwa

The third great symbol of the Chinese feminine is Nüwa. The Chinese creation myth begins with Nüwa who is credited with creating humankind and repairing the Pillar of Heaven to prevent the destruction of material existence. Her reverential name is *Wa Huang,* meaning literally "Empress Wa." The Chinese character for the name *Wa* features the image of the feminine and was defined in the Han dynasty Imperial Dictionary as "The sacred woman of ancient times, who transformed all things." According to Daoist tradition, Nüwa is the Mother of the planet Earth and in charge of the cycles of yin and yang and also fertility.

Figure 1.6 is an image of Nüwa from a stone coffin that dates from the Han Dynasty. Nüwa is shown holding the *Ju* (square) in her right hand and the moon in the left hand. Her lower body is like a snake, and she flies on flexible and elegant wings.

32   GAO LAN AND SHEN HEYONG

In traditional Chinese culture, Nüwa was esteemed as the highest goddess. Her legend begins before any recording by the known historical books, and almost all traditions recognize Nüwa as the one responsible for creating human beings by using yellow clay to make the flesh of the people. Because the clay was not strong enough, she put ropes in the clay to make the bodies erect, forming the skeleton. In addition to giving birth to humanity, Nüwa is also credited with repairing the Pillars of Heaven. Chapter 6 of *Huainanzi* tells the story of how Nüwa came to the rescue during the time when Heaven and Earth were in disruption:[3]

> Going back to more ancient times, the four pillars were broken; the nine provinces were in tatters. Heaven did not completely cover [the earth]; Earth did not hold up [Heaven] all the way around [its circumference]. Fires blazed out of control and could not be extinguished; water flooded in great expanses and would not recede. Ferocious animals ate blameless people; predatory birds snatched the elderly and the weak. Thereupon, Nüwa smelted together five-colored stones in order to patch up the azure sky, cut off the legs of the great turtle to set them up as the four pillars, killed the black dragon to provide relief for Ji Province, and piled up reeds and cinders to stop the surging waters. The azure sky was patched; the four pillars were set up; the surging waters were drained; the province of Ji was tranquil; crafty vermin died off; blameless people [preserved their] lives.

These catastrophes were supposedly caused by the battle between the deities Gonggong and Zhuanxu (an event that had been mentioned earlier in the *Huainanzi*). The five-colored stones symbolize the five Chinese elements (wood, fire, earth, metal, and water). The black dragon was the essence of water and thus caused the floods. Ji Province serves metonymically for the central regions (the Sinitic world). Following this, the *Huainanzi* tells how the sage-rulers Nüwa and Fuxi set order over the realm by following the Way (道) and its potency (德).

In Chinese mythology, Nüwa is not only a remote deity responsible for creating human beings and saving people from disaster in ancient times, but also an intimate goddess of love and beauty. She is prayed to as a matchmaker and is credited with creating courting etiquette and the customs of the marriage ceremony. She taught people how to carry on the ancestral line properly. An ever hands-on "Mother," she is the

FEMININITY IN CHINESE CULTURE

one who taught the Chinese the secret connection between mulberry leaf and the rearing of silkworms, sparking the creation of silk. She started the crafts of spinning and weaving and also inspired some of the ancient musical instruments of China.

After the Han Dynasty, people's conception of Nüwa primarily as the ancestor goddess shifted to her role as the mate of the god Fuxi and how they created the world together. The deeper meaning in this shift was the implicit lowering of the status of maternal influence and the ascendency of paternalistic power.

The Daoist goddesses

It is interesting to note that all three of the foundational Chinese cultural images of the feminine—Bixia Yuanjun, Xi Wang Mu, and Nüwa—are Daoist goddesses. The Daoist archetypal image of femininity is envisaged as the "Great Mother," but its meaning is not limited to maternity. In the Dao De Jing by Lao Tzu, for instance, the quality of *mother* is synonymous with *feminine, Yin, tenderness,* and even *water*—all qualities Lao Tzu called "valuable qualities through which one can get closer to the Dao."

Praise for cultivation of these qualities is replete in Daoism's foremost classic. In Chapter 6 of the Dao De Jing, we read: "The Valley Spirit never dies. It is named the Mysterious Female. And the Doorway of the Mysterious Female is the base from which Heaven and Earth sprang." In Chapter 25: "There was something formless yet complete, that existed before heaven and earth; without sound, without substance, dependent on nothing, unchanging, all pervading, unfailing. One may think of it as the mother of all things under heaven." In Chapter 28: "He who knows the male, yet cleaves to what is female. Become like a ravine, receiving all things under heaven." And in Chapter 52: "That which was the beginning of all things under heaven, we may speak of as the mother of all things. He who apprehends the mother, thereby knows the sons. And he who has known the sons, will hold all the tighter to the mother, and to the end of his days suffer no harm."[4]

For C. G. Jung, the Dao is the "primordial condition of things, and at the same time a most ideal achievement, because it is the union of elements eternally opposed."[5] From this perspective, the proper "union of elements eternally opposed" in the individual is at the heart of all clinical work, all therapy, and all healing. Jung continues in the next quote.

> Conflict has come to rest, and everything is still or once again in the original state of indistinguishable harmony. You find the same idea in ancient Chinese philosophy. The ideal condition is named Tao, and it consists of the complete harmony between heaven and earth.[6]

The difficulties of fully describing his vision of the conflicts between the conscious and the unconscious that is so crucial to Jungian analysis and depth psychotherapy seems to have led Jung to turn to Chinese culture for support, and he tried to bring the concept of Dao into depth psychology:

> The idea of a middle way between the opposites is to be found also in China, in the form of *tao*. The concept of *tao* is usually associated with the name of the philosopher Lao-tzu, born 604 B.C. But this concept is older than the philosophy of Lao-tzu. It is bound up with the ancient folk religion of Taoism, the "way of Heaven," a concept corresponding to the Vedic *rta*. The meanings of *tao* are as follows: way, method, principle, natural force or life force, the regulated processes of nature, the idea of the world, the prime cause of all phenomena, the right, the good, the moral order. Some translators even translate it as God, not without some justification, it seems to me, since *tao*, like *rta*, has a tinge of substantiality.[7]

In a letter to Herr Dass (July 12, 1947), Jung wrote the following:

> As regards the "centre" you are quite right: the pairs of the opposites in German psychology have flown to extremes because the centre has got lost ... Only in this spiritual centre is there any possibility of salvation. The concept of the centre was called by Chinese Tao, which the Jesuits in their day translated as Deus. This centre is everywhere, i.e., in everybody and when the individual does not possess this centre he infects all the others with this sickness. Then they lose the centre too.[8]

In "The Development of Personality," Jung wrote deeply and beautifully about the image and meaning of Tao:

> The undiscovered vein within us is a living part of the psyche; classical Chinese philosophy names this interior way "Tao," and likens it to a flow of water that moves irresistibly towards its goal. To rest in Tao means fulfillment, wholeness, one's destination reached, one's mission done; the beginning, end, and perfect realization

FEMININITY IN CHINESE CULTURE

35

of the meaning of existence innate in all things. Personality is Tao.[9]

For Jung, "Tao" is the "the oldest and most central idea" of Chinese philosophy.[10] "The concept of Tao pervades the whole philosophical thought of China."[11] He shows his appreciation to Richard Wilhelm who introduced him to Daoism, when he writes in "Richard Wilhelm: In Memoriam" (1930):

> We must continue Wilhelm's work of translation in a wider sense if we wish to show ourselves worthy pupils of the master. The central concept of Chinese philosophy is tao, which Wilhelm translated as "meaning." Just as Wilhelm gave the spiritual treasure of the East a European meaning, so we should translate this meaning into life. To do this—that is, to realize tao—would be the true task of the pupil.[12]

Losing the connection:
the missing women of China

As we wrote at the beginning of the chapter, Chinese culture, in its foundational sense, is essentially a culture of femininity. For the Chinese people, the land, the hills, and the rivers have always been referred to as the "mother-land" and "mother-river." The holy mountains, such as Mount Tai and the Kunlun Mountains, are envisioned as earthly places where female deities live. We can see how revered the feminine once was. This unique intersection of the physical land, rivers, and mountains, with the myths and legends, the archetypal images and their meanings, historically cultivated by the Chinese people, is what we refer to as China's national cultural container. This container is badly damaged and missing important elements.

This damage is created by and reflective of damage to the psychological health of the individuals who collectively create the culture to which they belong. By ensuring that one's individual cultural container is filled with the required elements, one can not only lay the groundwork for psychological harmony, promoting the effect of therapy and healing, and even open the way for individuation, but also serve to repair the national cultural container.

Unfortunately, based on our research and the clinical experiences and observations of others in the field, most Chinese have almost completely lost touch with the symbols that lead to connection with their cultural container, the archetypes of femininity. The overreliance on ideology today and the related issue of limited education in the humanities has worsened issues left over from repeated rounds of extremist political movements such as the Cultural Revolution and the campaign to destroy the Four Olds.

The perpetrators of the Cultural Revolution and Destroy the Four Olds had a clear purpose: to destroy old customs, old culture, old habits, and old ideas. One cannot imagine now that the "Olds" they wanted to destroy included everything related to Bixia Yuanjun, Xi Wang Mu, and Nüwa, and anything related to Confucianism, Daoism, and Buddhism, the entire unique history of Chinese culture! In the West, there is the saying "to throw the baby out with the bathwater." In China we can add to this, "to throw out the treasure due to the dust on it."

When the Red Guards destroyed the home of Confucius, a temple dedicated to him, and his grave in Qufu, they smashed more than a thousand stone tablets, burned more than one-hundred-thousand books, felled thousands of old pine trees, and dug up more than two thousand tombs. These acts emerged from intense mania and have caused deep cultural trauma. For many Chinese this cultural trauma is alive in their personal complexes and lies behind a wide variety of symptoms we see in our practices today.

Femininity, motherhood, traditional culture, including Confucianism, Daoism, and Buddhism, are all important elements in the making of the Chinese psyche. This "national psyche" or what we are calling the "cultural container of a nation," has old elements because the container is ancient. When this psychic container is missing important elements, or when it is damaged and destroyed, the people have no place to heal their hearts and find solace for their souls.

When a people's cultural container is destroyed, they will make mistakes that will lead to more experiences of deep psychological suffering. The mass decision to gender-select males and abort females is such a mistake. To highlight this issue, we used the title "The Missing Women of China" for our presentation at the second Analysis and Activism Conference in Rome. When the Chinese government took the national Population Census in 2012, it found that there were 37 million more men than women in China. The extent of the problem is shown in the *British Medical Journal* study issued in 2009 using data from the 2005 national census.[13] In nine provinces of China between 160 and 190 boys were delivered for every 100

FEMININITY IN CHINESE CULTURE

37

girls born. However, "The Missing Women" of our presentation are not just aborted female fetuses. We are more concerned about what is being lost behind the horrible statistics; it is not only the loss of female lives, but also the loss of femininity and connection to motherhood itself that is slipping away.

This kind of deep psychic loss can lead to an increase in social problems and psychosomatic diseases. Behind the various psychological symptoms we commonly see today lies the effects of this loss of cultural connection. We have encountered in our work many clients who have been trying very hard, in the process of analysis, to find the "missing women," their "inner femininity," and the "lost mother" in their lives.

The sandtray in Figure 1.7 was made by a thirteen-year-old girl who lost her mother at age ten when her father, psychotic and drunk, killed her mother and her younger sister and brother. After three years of working very hard with her, she produced this tray reflecting her desire to have "the mother" back.

In the sandtray, this girl made a careful mother image with her heart. She used the colored stones, like jade, to decorate the mother's braids and as earrings. The process was vivid, when the image emerged, her mother was there. Finally, she put a doll on the mother's chest, as if to feel the mother's embrace.

The sandtray in Figure 1.8 was made by a twenty-three-year-old female patient who tried to take her own life four times and often self-harmed. At first glance, it appeared that, at a behavioral level, she could not accept her female body, but later it emerged that behind the alienation to her body was a traumatic history of sexual abuse and the loss of her femininity. After a long process of therapy, she realized that the inner femininity she had lost could be regained, and she reached a turning point in her therapy. Following this change, she made the tray shown here. In this sandtray, the client created high ground in the upper-left corner. She put a nest there, with eggs and birds, representing incubation of the femininity. The lower-right corner, with its plentiful trees and plants, also represented femininity. Before the end of our work together, the client got married and had a baby.

The sandtray in Figure 1.9 was made by a thirty-six-year-old female patient who was hospitalized in a mental hospital for about one year before we started working with her. The hospital diagnosed her as having obsessive compulsive disorder (OCD) with social withdrawal

Figure 1.7: Sandtray of thirteen-year-old girl: feeling the mother's embrace.

Figure 1.8: Sandtray of twenty-three-year-old woman: regaining her lost feminine.

Figure 1.9: Sandtray of thirty-six-year-old woman: using the feminine image.

behavior. In the process of Jungian psychotherapy using dream analysis, drawing, and sandplay, we worked to rebuild the connection with her inner femininity. This rebuilding is the continuing theme of our therapy. After some time, the client began to use the feminine image. In the sandtray shown here, the symbol, while still isolated, began to show signs of a divine nature and connections to eternity.

As collectively more and more individuals go "crazy" from loss of connection to cultural and psychic anchors, so too will the nation suffer. As we survey the national landscape, we witness another kind of loss of femininity and fertility. An overemphasis on economics has changed the entire condition of the natural environment. The mountains, rivers, and land suffer from pollution. Desertification is on the rise. The most important rivers in China, the Yellow River and the Yangtze River—our mother rivers—have suffered reduced flow for the past thirty-five years. When a large earthquake hit Yushu in the Tibet Autonomous Zone in 2010, we went there with volunteers from the Garden of the Heart & Soul. The headwaters and source for the Yellow River, the Yangtze River, and the Lancang River are located there.

As introduced previously, according to Chinese legend, this area is home to the Queen of the West, *Xi Wang Mu,* who in addition to carrying the image of the goddess of healing is also the source for the waters of life. With the loss of our connection to the feminine, we have also lost sight of how to manage our natural environment. China's major rivers now face ecological and environmental degradation. Other worrying signs include glacial recession, shrinking of swamps, and lowering of groundwater tables.

Zhang Yihe, an important female writer in China today reported the following dream in her weibo (similar to Twitter):

> *I dreamt my loving mother was lying on a bed, talking to herself, saying: "cold, so cold" from time to time. I looked around and could not find anything to cover her. The thin quilt she had on her body was so flimsy; it was more like a piece of paper. I woke up suddenly, sweating and crying.*

Our interpretation of the dream was that the mother in the dream may not be the personal mother of the dreamer. As the dreamer is well versed in the problems resulting from the loss of connection to the feminine in our culture, her dream could reflect that our collective Mother is now lying in bed with nothing to keep her warm. She may even be very ill. I wrote to Zhang that what was urgent was that "We need to do something for our mother, the mother of the culture, and the inner femininity."

Behind the plethora of clinical symptoms we see in Chinese people are the cultural complexes and common cultural trauma we share, but even deeper than these causes is the damage to the Chinese cultural container and the loss of connection to the feminine aspects of the psyche. In China today, mental illness statistics are startling. According to the data announced in 2009 by the Mental Health Center of the China Center for Disease Control and Prevention, there were more than 100 million people suffering from all kinds of mental illness (roughly defined), 16 million of whom were considered seriously ill (this number is rapidly increasing).

In the eyes of many social commentators, mental illness is often seen as being rooted in the social system and life style of the population. It is a reflection of and a projection of material social problems. Arthur Kleinman's book *Social Origins of Distress and Disease: Depression, Neurasthenia, and Pain in Modern China* was the first by a psychiatrist to try to explain how this works in the lives of Chinese people.[14]

FEMININITY IN CHINESE CULTURE   41

Although the material causes of mental illness should not be ignored, its cultural and archetypal aspects are even more foundational. China's cultural container is badly damaged, and we must do something to repair it. If we have lost our connection to the archetypal feminine in ourselves, then we should find it again and rebuild the connection.

The Garden of the Heart & Soul:
a yearning for kindheartedness

We started the project of the Garden of the Heart & Soul in 2007 in various orphanages in Mainland China. The mission of the project was to build safe and protected spaces within the orphanages where Jungian analysis, sandplay, and depth psychology would be available to support the orphans' psychological development. When the massive 8.1 earthquake hit the southwest of China in 2008 (the Wenchuan Earthquake), our volunteers expanded our mission and were there from the first week to offer psychological relief work. Later we shifted to providing continued psychological support for recovery, and we continue to work there today. In 2010, there was another big earthquake at Yushu, Tibet, and our team went to that earthquake zone to set up several workstations for the Garden of the Heart & Soul. Now, after eleven years, we have set up seventy-six workstations in Mainland China. We work in more remote areas such as Lhasa (capital of Tibet), Ürümqi (capital of Xinjiang Province) Hohhot (capital of Inner Mongolia Province), Yinchuan (capital of Ningxia Hui Autonomous Region), as well as the major cities of Beijing, Shanghai, Guangzhou, and so on. After many years of hard work, the project is starting to gain momentum.

Our therapeutic process includes three primary steps. First, we build an effective relationship within a contained, safe, and free and protected space. The cultural unconscious, rituals, and archetypal images are considered in building the relationship with our clients. Second, we enhance therapeutic containment by "being with" and actively listening "with the heart." Sandtrays, drawing, music, and archetypal drama are all brought into play. We also bring other kinds of Jungian approaches such as embodied expression and depth psychotherapies into the practice. Finally, we offer sustained psychological support using my psychology of the heart approach,

42   GAO LAN AND SHEN HEYONG

employing the principles of *Ci-bei* (empathetic grief), and *Gan-ying* (heartfelt influence) to promote healing and to activate the transforming function of the cultural archetypes.

We provide the following description and introduction to the cultural archetypes and their related practical activities.

Dayu: naming and initiating

From Dayu (2200 BCE) who is famous for his victory over the floodwaters and the naming of the mountains and rivers, we have obtained and explored the cultural archetypal image and meaning of naming and initiating. *Naming* in Chinese has two characters: *Ming* (fate, order from the Heaven, to make) and *Ming* (name, self-destiny, self-enlightenment). The initiating imagery we use carries the significance of awakening and initiating the heart nature inside of things.

From our understanding of the "Talking Cure," a joint work published by Josef Breuer and Sigmund Freud in 1895 about Anna O's case, "revealing" through talking can lead to a cure. This kind of "talking" is similar to what we mean when using the terms *naming* and *initiating*. Jung's active imagination can mean "imagery naming," or "the naming of imagery." Naming-initiating is an important principle in the Jungian practices used in the Garden of the Heart & Soul projects and in our application of Jungian sandplay and embodied imagination and dream work, including the interpretation of the initial dream and the initial sandtray.

The way of Dayu to control water was to "dredge rivers and direct stagnate." We found symbolic meaning for our work in this. We use therapy and analysis (naming-initiating) to enlighten ritual behaviors (dredge rivers), and arouse and collect the healing factors inside of clients (direct stagnate). Thus the imagery for "naming," and the transformative function of "naming," became the first fundamental part of our Jungian practice at the Garden of the Heart & Soul.

Shennong: taming, nurturing, and healing

From Shennong (4300 BCE) who started farming, agriculture, and Chinese herbal medicine, we have taken the cultural archetypal image and meaning for taming, nurturing, and healing. Also known as Yan-di (the Emperor Yan), Shennong is best known as the "Divine Farmer," the literal translation of his name. Aside from his titles, the actual character used for his family name, Jiang, includes the image of the

FEMININITY IN CHINESE CULTURE

43

female and the sheepherder. As the Chinese god of medicine and also the god of agriculture and farming, he in charge of all things related to the cultivating of plants and the taming of animals. Shennong's archetypal images are those of nurturing and taming.

The Shennong way of taming is reflected in the Chinese character for *Xun* (taming). It is a combined image of a horse and a river. According to the Imperial Dictionary, the word means "following and kindness," including the alternative meaning of "adjust and adaptation of heart-nature and behavior." We use *taming* to mean "yield to the right way." Or, as the second Hexagram of the I Ching puts it, "Through taming one can get to the Dao." Another Chinese character for taming is *Mu* with the combined image of an ox and a whip. This image is used in the famous Chinese Chan story called "Ten Pictures of Ox." In the story, it first seems as if force is the way to discipline an ox, but then the core of the story reveals itself to be about taming the heart.

Fuxi: timing and transforming

From Fuxi (4700 BCE), founder of the I Ching, we have explored and obtained the cultural archetypal image and meaning for *timing* and *transforming*. According to his legend, Fuxi taught his subjects to cook, to fish with nets, and to hunt with weapons made of bone, wood, or bamboo. He instituted marriage and offered the first open-air sacrifices to heaven. Traditionally, Fuxi is considered the originator of the I Ching. According to this tradition, the arrangement of the trigrams (八卦 *bāgùa*) of the I Ching was revealed to him in the markings on the back of a mythical dragon horse (sometimes said to be a tortoise) that emerged from the Luo River. This arrangement precedes the compilation of the I Ching during the Zhou dynasty.

This discovery is said to have been the origin of calligraphy. It is said that "Fuxi drew the first Yang line to start Chinese civilization," and with the eight hexagrams, he was able to "communicate with the virtue of heaven, and express the feelings of all things."[15] I Ching literally translates as the *Book of Changes,* but the more profound meaning that it conveys is a deep wisdom on timing and changing and the meaning of transformation. In the Chinese cultural tradition, the sages use the I Ching as a way to connect to divine wisdom.

As we have discussed previously, Fuxi and Nüwa were worshipped as co-creators of humankind, and their images both shared the same human upper body and snake lower body formation. In the I Ching of

Fuxi, the most important principles are "timing," "trend," "opportunity," "changes," and "transforming." In the West, there is the saying "Timing is everything." In China there is the old song of Shun (2200 BCE), one of the oldest Chinese proverbs: "The order from Heaven pertains only to timing and the opportunity."

The Jungian principle of synchronicity conveys the same meaning as "timing and transforming" does in our use of them. I saw a sign linking these Chinese terms and Jung on the desk of Dr. Joseph Henderson while visiting him. On his desk was a small card with two Chinese characters: *Shi-Ji* (*Timing* and *Transforming*), and Dr. Henderson wrote some small English letters beside the Chinese characters for his *thinking* and *reflection*.

To best serve the Chinese patients we encounter, we use the cultural archetypes that most pertain to them. Through meditation on these archetypes we developed the following principles. The first principle of our practice is *heart-meaning,* establishing a deep emotional connection to what the work means. The second principle is *naming-initiating,* allowing clients to define their own process and outcome. The third principle is *taming-nurturing,* or fellowship and mentoring that model desired characteristics. The last principle is *timing-transforming,* seizing opportunities for transformation as they present themselves. These are the basic principles of our Jungian practice in China. They have proven especially helpful in our work during the May 12, 2008, Wenchuan and April 14, 2010, Yushu earthquakes, and continue to guide our work in orphanages across mainland China.

The volunteers working with the Garden of the Heart & Soul have inspired some people to call our work healing by *Ci-bei,* a form of empathetic catharsis. This Chinese term is most often applied to healings performed by the Guanyin bodhisattva, so we are humbled by the comparison.

The ancient Chinese script for *Ci-Bei,* shown in Figure 1.10, is an image of "from heart to heart loss." The first character *Ci* means love associating with the heart; and the second character *Bei* means grief, literally loss of the heart. When we can hold

Figure 1.10: Ci-Bei.

FEMININITY IN CHINESE CULTURE 45

the emotions of love (heart) and grief (loss of the heart) together in harmony, then we can experience the transcendent function arising from their union—compassion. Compassion can be called *Ci-Bei* in Chinese, but it also can be translated as *Great Love*.

In this portion of the oracle bone script character for love we see the combined symbols of *trust* and *sincerity* (this portion is also the image for I Ching hexagram 61, Inner Truth); in the middle is a symbol for protection, its image coming from the Great mother's womb. The lower part is the image for "hand in hand," suggesting support and harmony; and at the center, or core of the character, is the image of the heart. In the one image of the archaic Chinese character for love (Figure 1.11), we find the deep meaning of all the elements that go into creating love. Implicit in the entire character is an abiding connection with the archetypal feminine.

Figure 1.11: The archetypal image of love in oracle bone script form.

If, as I argue, the cultural container of the Chinese people has been damaged due to having lost its connection to the archetypal feminine, then experiencing "love" for many Chinese people will prove to be a complicated and conflicting experience. Until the Chinese people individually and then collectively re-find and rebuild this connection, kindness, love, and compassion could remain something people believe in but do not "know" much about.

At the 2018 Chinese New Year, we used a four character phrase, *Wei Hui Suo Huai*, to express our new year's wish. This phrase translates as "yearning for kindheartedness." The key word being *Hui* (kindheartedness), or kindness that comes from the heart. According to the Han Dynasty dictionary, *Shuo-Wen*, kindheartedness is synonymous with love, wisdom, peacefulness, and benevolence. This last aspect was especially valued by Confucius.

The Chinese character for kindheartedness, *Hui*, is made by combining the image of a spinning brick (above) and a heart (below).

Figure 1.12: Hui.

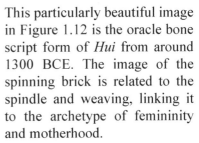

This particularly beautiful image in Figure 1.12 is the oracle bone script form of *Hui* from around 1300 BCE. The image of the spinning brick is related to the spindle and weaving, linking it to the archetype of femininity and motherhood.

The character for weaving (Figure 1.13) relates to the ideas of love and wisdom, also linking it to the feminine archetype. The Chinese character for weaving is also associated with silk and silkworms, mulberry and "picking mulberry." There was a time in China when the natural division of labor in the culture was that men hunted and women wove. In those days, mulberry sericulture, silkworm stripping, silk spinning, and weaving were viewed as the essence of femininity. These activities required qualities such as gentleness, caring, yielding quietness (patience), sensitivity, sufferance, and perseverance, all seen as feminine ideals. Today we can see that these qualities are not only important for women, but also vital for anyone wishing to develop inner harmony, inner beauty, wisdom, and integrity.

Figure 1.13: Weaving.

One of the more mysterious archetypal images found in the human mind, "Fate," is often depicted as a woman weaver. This is the case in Chinese mythology as well as in Africa and in Europe. For instance, the goddesses Clotho, Lachésis, and Atropos, responsible for spinning and weaving cloth, also spin the thread of human life and make the weave of history. It is only by finding the thread of our own heart and following it back to the completed weave, a cultural container made whole again, that we can find fulfillment.

FEMININITY IN CHINESE CULTURE   *47*

In closing, we would like to quote from the book *Soul of China* by Richard Wilhelm: "In the old and in the new there was, nevertheless, a common element: the soul (and the heart) of China in the course of evolution; that soul (and the heart) which had not lost its gentleness nor its calm, and will, I hope, never lose them."[16]

Notes

[1] Ku Hweng-Min (Thomson) is author of *The Spirit of the Chinese People,* which was originally published in 1915. Accessed Feb. 28, 2019, at https://en.wikisource.org/wiki/The_Spirit_of_the_Chinese_People.

[2] Guoxiang and Cheng Xuanying, "Chuang-tzu," in *A Thorough Understanding of Life* (Beijing, Zhonghua Book Company, 2011), Chapter 19.

[3] The Huainanzi is an ancient Chinese text that consists of a collection of essays that resulted from a series of scholarly debates held at the court of Liu An, King of Huainan, sometime before 139 BCE.

[4] Arthur Waley, trans., *Laozi* (Chuangsha: Hunan People's Publishing House, 1999).

[5] C. G. Jung, "The Tavistock Lectures" (1935), in *The Collected Works of C. G. Jung,* vol. 18, ed. and trans. Gerhard Adler and R. F. C. Hull (Princeton, NJ: Princeton University Press, 1976), § 262.

[6] *Ibid.*

[7] C. G. Jung, *Psychological Types* (1921), vol. 6, *The Collected Works of C. G. Jung,* ed. and trans. Gerhard Adler and R. F. C. Hull (Princeton, NJ: Princeton University Press, 1971), § 358.

[8] C. G. Jung, *Letters,* selected and edited by Gerhard Adler and Aniela Jaffe (Princeton, NJ: Princeton University Press. Princeton, 1973), pp. 470–471.

[9] C. G. Jung, "The Development of Personality" (1934), in *The Collected Works of C. G. Jung,* vol. 17, ed. and trans. Gerhard Adler and R. F. C. Hull (Princeton, NJ: Princeton University Press, 1954), § 323.

[10] C.G. Jung, "Synchronicity: An Acausal Connecting Principle" (1952), in *The Collected Works of C. G. Jung,* vol. 8, ed. and trans. Gerhard Adler and R. F. C. Hull (Princeton, NJ: Princeton University Press, 1969), § 917.

[11] *Ibid.*

[12] C. G. Jung, "Richard Wilhelm: In Memoriam" (1930), in *The Collected Works of C. G. Jung,* vol. 15, ed. and trans. Gerhard Adler and R. F. C. Hull (Princeton, NJ: Princeton University Press, 1966), § 89.

[13] Wei Xing Zhu, Li Lu, and Theresa Hesketh, "China's Excess Males, Sex Selective Abortion, and One Child Policy: Analysis of Data from 2005 National Intercensus Survey," *British Medical Journal* (338, 2009): doi: https://doi.org/10.1136/bmj.b1211.

[14] Arthur Kleinman, *Social Origins of Distress and Disease: Depression, Neurasthenia, and Pain in Modern China* (New Haven, CT: Yale University Press, 1988).

[15] *The Comprehensive Chinese Word Dictionary* (Bejing: The Commercial Press, 2015), p. 88; Fu Huisheng, trans., *The Zhou Book of Changes II* (Bejing: Hunan People's Publishing House, 2008), p. 411.

[16] Richard Wilhelm, *Soul of China* (Maple Shade, NJ: Lethe Press, 2007), Preface.

2

• • • • • •

Ancestral Worship
A Cultural Complex of the Chinese

Zhang Lei, Hou Yingchun, and Li Xianghui

Zhang Lei is a doctoral candidate at the City University of Macau, majoring in applied Jungian analytical psychology and Chinese culture. He serves as a national second-level psychological consultant, specializing in adolescent psychological counseling and treatment. His research is focused on mental health and education and his interests include culture, religion, archetypes, and Jungian analytical psychology. He is currently applying for IAAP and ISST certification.

Hou Yingchun is a doctoral candidate at the City University of Macau, majoring in applied Jungian analytical psychology and Chinese culture. He serves as a psychological therapist in the psychic trauma department of the psychology hospital in China, at the college counseling educators, and has been engaged in psychological education work for many years. He is an English-Chinese translator of psychology and is currently applying for IAAP and ISST certification.

Li Xianghui is a doctoral candidate at the City University of Macau and also works in the school of psychology, Nanjing Normal University. He serves as an associate researcher, master tutor of applied psychology and mental health education, a national second-level psychological consultant, and sandplay counselor. His research is focused on psychological counseling and treatment for children and adolescents, and he is currently engaged in theoretical and practical research on children and adolescents' psychological analysis, combining psychoanalysis, Jung's analytical psychological, and Chinese culture.

50   ZHANG LEI, HOU YINGCHUN, AND LI XIANGHUI

For the Chinese, the most traditional virtue is to pay respect to their ancestors. Sincere grief in death and deep affection in life toward one's ancestors is the cultural standard. Among the ruling elite, commemoration of their ancestors' meritorious service, graciousness to others, and dedication to the nation cemented their legitimacy. For thousands of years, Chinese people at all levels of society have literally worshiped their ancestors at ancestral altars, with piety and an expectant attitude that the ancestors can be accessed. The *ancestral worship cultural complex* is a unique cultural phenomenon that distinguishes Chinese civilization from other civilizations.

The ancestral worship cultural complex has two components: a collective one and an individual one. The collective component is the *national spirit* that represents the collective ancestors, and the individual component, which is passed down from generation to generation via one's familial line, is the *soul* of the complex. An individual's "blood bond" with other citizens from the same "nation" is determined by the strength of the national spirit component of this complex. In modern-day China, the influence of this complex has centered on its collective component, leading to an emphasis on the "national spirit that will never die."

This chapter investigates the following three areas of the ancestral worship cultural complex: the historical meaning of the Chinese words *ancestral root* and their significance to the ancestral worship cultural complex; the meaning of the complex for Chinese nationalism; and the mythic symbolism of the *Hongtong Dahuaishu,* or *ancestral tree.* This chapter examines aspects of ancient ancestral worship and how this practice has changed in modern times. If it were possible to truly follow in the footsteps of the ancestors and give life once again to the rituals that allowed access to their archetypal power, then it might restore balance to the ancestral worship cultural complex of the Chinese nation. A tree will grow as tall as its roots run deep, and a nation can only rise as high as the depth of its embrace of its cultural heritage.

Part I: The significance
of the *root* and *ancestor*

The origin of the Chinese word for root

The meaning of the word *root* comes from the image for *roots of vegetation*. In the small seal script, the left part of the character 槷 is

ANCESTRAL WORSHIP

木, which means "wood" and resembles the shape of a tree, and the right is 艮 (*gen*), which means "heel." The root of the tree is the part of the tree that grows into the ground and makes it steadfast. *Root* also refers to the foundation of things or a matter's background. Because a tree's roots are the tree's support, the word also can be extended to the origin of things. The Chinese character for *root* is identified with various meanings that encompass a range of definitions: the *Shuowen Jiezi* defines it as the sustaining part of a plant; the *Kuan Tzu* says that the "root of all things" is the land upon which everything rests.[1]

In the *Book of Changes*, or I Ching, the Gen hexagram is based on the image of two mountains with the divinatory meaning of *cease* (Figure 2.1). Both the *Tuan Zhuan, Shuo Gua* (*Understanding Hexagrams*), and *Xu Gua Zhuan* (hexagram order) have same interpretation of *cease*.[2] *Cease* is linked to the image of a toe, which is further linked to the mountains. For people, the toes appear separate, but they are connected at their roots to the foot. The image of the toes is thus connected to the image of a range of mountains. In *Da Xiang* (*Greater Reality*) it is written that *Gen* means multiple mountains that are interconnected, and thus, there are "mountains in the mountains."

Gen also refers to the ways in which life is like climbing a mountain—life contains ups and downs, and one must keep one's gaze firmly on one's "toes," or he or she will "stumble and be wrestled to the ground."[3] *Da Xiang* clarifies that this example implies that a gentleman (君子) should keep his thoughts to matters that are within his ability and area of responsibility. In other words, know your limits. According to an explanation of the sixth line of the *Gen* hexagram, if one keeps an eye on one's toes and keeps one's foot firmly rooted in place, one will not make mistakes or encounter accidents.

Figure 2.1: 艮 (*Gen*) hexagram (*Gen* means "mountain").

52   ZHANG LEI, HOU YINGCHUN, AND LI XIANGHUI

The origin of the Chinese word for ancestor

The word 祖 (pronounced *Zu*) means "ancestor." The left portion 示 (*Shi*) is its radical part, and the right 且 (*Qie*) is its phonetic part.[4] Combining the *Shi* radical with *Qie,* the co-constructed word *Zu* reflects the high esteem given to the ancestors through which the beginning of the human race can be traced. According to later literature, the basic meaning of the word *Zu* is "the beginning" and "the origin."

According to *Shuowen Jiezi,* the *Shi* radical refers to "signs in the sky responding to prayers to foretell of good or bad things."[5] The ancient image for 示 shows the image 二 (*heaven*) supported by three verticals that stand for the sun, the moon, and the stars. The image refers to the use of astronomy to detect when things will change in the human sphere. Therefore, *Shi* stands for "revealing the matters of the gods." According to the *Xu Yue* (*Collected Thoughts of Xu Daofu of the Tang Dynasty*), *Shi* is an ancient word, with the stroke of the sun on the left, the moon on the right, and the star in the middle.[6] The three verticals represent the light descending from them. As *Shi* stands for matters of the gods, it is closely related to ancient shamanistic forms of "nature worship." In Chinese characters, *Shi* is linked to a unique divine color. It symbolizes the ancient ancestors' knowledge of the heavens and the earth (*divine nature*) and their people (*human nature*).

In small seal script form, 且 (*Qie*) is a single structural pictogram, and its shape resembles the memorial tablet offered to the gods and the ancestors. From the time of the oracle bone inscriptions in the Shang Dynasty (1600–1046 BCE), *Qie* was already used to represent the ancestors. In the oracle inscriptions, Qie (且) is the same as *Zu* (祖), and the former is "the ancient body" of the latter. *Qie* became *Zu* with the addition of the *Shi* radical, and the evolution of the word *Zu* not only reflected the social function of Chinese characters, but also captured a unique moment in cultural linguistic psychology.

Exploring the significance of "ancestral worship culture"

Nowadays *roots* and *ancestors* seem to be irrelevant totems of a distant past. "Ancestral worship" as a genuine cultural practice is rarely performed by modern Chinese people. Unfortunately, most have thrown out the "baby" of psychic connection to one's roots with the "bathwater" of empty ritual handed down from a bygone age. However, history has shown that abandoning one's roots and identification with one's ancestors hinders individual personality growth and social development.

ANCESTRAL WORSHIP

53

Jung pointed out that

> our souls as well as our bodies are composed of individual
> elements which were all already present in the ranks of our
> ancestors. The "newness" in the individual psyche is an
> endlessly varied recombination of age-old components.
> Body and soul therefore have an intensely historical
> character and find no proper place in what is new, in things
> that have just come into being. That is to say, our ancestral
> components are only partly at home in such things. We
> are very far from having finished completely with the
> Middle Ages, classical antiquity, and primitivity, as our
> modern psyches pretend. Nevertheless, we have plunged
> down a cataract of progress which sweeps us on into the
> future with ever wilder violence the farther it takes us from
> our roots. Once the past has been breached, it is usually
> annihilated, and there is no stopping the forward motion.
> But it is precisely the loss of connection with the past, our
> rootlessness, which has given rise to the "discontents" of
> civilization and to such a flurry and haste that we live more
> in the future and its chimerical promises of a golden age
> than in the present. This is a state of being that our whole
> evolutionary background has not yet caught up. We rush
> impetuously into novelty, driven by a mounting sense of
> insufficiency, dissatisfaction, and restlessness.[7]

Jung further pointed out that "The less we understand of what our
fathers and forefathers sought, the less we understand ourselves, and
thus we help with all our might to rob the individual of his roots and
his guiding instincts, so that he becomes a particle in the mass, ruled
only by what Nietzsche called the spirit of gravity."[8]

The Taoist sage Lao Tzu said that the "Tao is vast, boundless,
far-flung, and finally returning to its roots as a whole, which is the
Tao—the source of all changes in the universe."[9] When the Tao is
imaged as a unified whole, it is usually shown as interpenetrating Yin
and Yang symbols. The Yin and Yang areas merge and diverge to form
areas of all Yin, all Yang, and a line where *He* (*harmony*) exists. It is
said that everything carries *Shade* on its back and *Shine* in its arms, the
opposites tending to harmony. Only Yin and Yang together can make
everything grow. *Lao Tzu* wrote that

> when things in the world have displayed their luxuriant
> growth, we see each of them return to its root and origin
> from dynamic to static state. The root and origin is
> supremely vacant and still, but, the still and vacant origin

> gestates new, huge life and motive power. The above report
> of that process is the regular, unchanging rule. To know
> that unchanging rule is to be intelligent and become wise.[10]

In Lao Tzu's final analysis, death is a return to the original state, and even as all things in the world change and evolve, regardless of their "luxuriant growth," in the end, all must return to their roots. For example, as people grow older, they will eventually get into a psychological state where they return to their childhood period. The same is true for vegetation, which is always growing upward. When plants reach the end, their flowers and leaves fall onto the soil to feed the roots.

If the individual is seen as a seed, then when the seed germinates, downward growth symbolizes the attribute of rooting into one's cultural soil, and upward growth represents the attribute of reaching for maximum future development. The two attributes must somehow combine to form a harmonious state. Only when "Yin, Yang, and He" are all available will "everything" be produced. Individuals are the foundation of social development; therefore, only individuals who are aware that "root-seeking" is the vital balance to "future seeking" can pave the needed road toward the foundation of social harmony. Can we reclaim the collective unconscious energy and vitality once transmitted through the ancestral worship cultural complex without its paternalistic cultural baggage? We can if "root" energy is activated and absorbed; then we will see improved personality and harmonious development in society.

Part II:
Ancestral worship cultural complex
and Chinese nationalism

China's unique cultural and historical circumstances have created an ancestral worship cultural complex rather particular to the Chinese people. This cultural complex has, as previously discussed, inner and outer aspects. On the one hand, it derives meaning from the blood bond shared by the same family line. Deceased elders were literally "deified" and placed on a list of the honored dead. Extending this logic into imagined racial history, the Chinese claim to be descendants of mythic ancestors such as the Yan and Yellow Emperors. This powerful bond uniting the Chinese nation began with the ancient system of totemic worship shared by the people in the area. This system was inherited and adapted into the

ANCESTRAL WORSHIP   55

Chinese ancestral worship system, which was further influenced by the patriarchal imperial hereditary system and integrated into the surnames inheritance system.

In its collective aspect, the ancestral worship cultural complex draws power from the *national spirit* that has been passed down over many eras, that is, the people's recognition and pursuit of the unique spirit of the Chinese nation. This *unique spirit* is founded on the ancient teachings of the *creators of humanity,* the ancestral gods, to always seek to strengthen the community and dedicate itself to self-improvement. Later, Confucian thinkers upheld *rituality* as the highest *benevolence* and eventually transformed rituality philosophy into a system based on blood relationships called the *filial piety* system. These ethical and cultural ideas form the backbone of the Chinese national spirit.

The popular slogan "love in the family, loyalty in the country, and peace will be in the world" is derived from farming culture and is essentially an extension of ancestral worship culture. The Chinese failed to adopt their rituals to the arrival of secularism and atheism, however, leading to the decline of the personal, or soul, aspect of the ancestral worship cultural complex. Therefore, most of the psychic energy in the complex has been directed to the collective aspect of the complex in support of the national spirit.

In the next sections, we discuss the historic roots of the ancestral worship cultural complex.

Totem worship of the ancient Chinese people

The English word *totem* is borrowed from the Native American tribes in North America and is used by some of the Aboriginals in Australia. It generally means "of the same kin" or "same clan." *Totems* are the emblems or signs used by these Indigenous ancestors to differentiate the various tribes and clans who lived together. Furthermore, they believed that their totemic animal or object was in psychic kinship with them. *Totem worship* is a form of mystical unification of nature and the human bloodline. It reflects the idea of general kinship with natural forces beyond human nature and the kinship among the ancient peoples themselves. Totem worship formed the original conceptual basis of ancestral worship by solving the problems of clan origin.[11] The likely fact that totemic worship was prevalent among the ancient Chinese can be verified from a large number of myths and legends corroborated by archaeological artifacts.

56   ZHANG LEI, HOU YINGCHUN, AND LI XIANGHUI

In much of Chinese mythology, the male gods or male heroes only know their mothers and don't know much about their fathers.[12] Often their births are related to their mothers' encounters with a mysterious power from nature, usually in the form of divine intercourse. The heroes then develop a kinship with the totemic objects related to their paternal link to the natural world. The appearance of this kind of heroic myth is often related to the founding legend of a particular system of totemic worship. For example, in the legend of Huaxu (one of the reputed ancestors of the ancient Chinese), after a mystical encounter in Leize (a place in Shandong Province), she gave birth to Fuxi (the Blue Emperor). Nujie (one of the wives of the Xuanyuan Emperor) had an encounter with "floating stars" and later gave birth to Shaohao (the White Emperor). In the legend of Jiang Yan, she steps on the footprint of the King of Heaven, and later gives birth to Hou Yi (the founder of the Zhou Dynasty). In another tale, the mother of the founder of the Shang Dynasty reportedly conceived him after swallowing the egg of a divine blackbird.

Archaeological artifacts unearthed in many parts of China testify to the extensive traces of totem worship from these ancient times, indicating that China had, indeed, embraced totemic worship during its formative stage as a cultural entity. A famous artifact, "Painted Stork fishing, Stone Axe Pattern Pottery," is from the Neolithic Age. The height of the artifact is 47 cm (18.5 inches); its diameter is 32.7 cm (12.9 in.); and the bottom diameter is 20.1 cm (7.9 in.). In 1978, it was unearthed in a village located in Lincang County, Henan Province. The painted pottery is the work of the Neolithic Yangshao culture and it depicts a stork catching a fish on one side and a stone axe on the other side. This pot is considered to be a burial article of a clan leader. The white stork is most likely a totem of the clan to which the leader belonged, and the fish is probably the totem of a rival clan. The stone axe is a sign of power and possibly a portrait of the tool used by the chief. The painted vessel tells the story of a leader of the White Stork clan fighting desperately against the Fish clan and achieving a decisive victory. In commemoration of this leader and his deeds, his tribe used the totemic image to incorporate living memory into symbolic pictures and recorded it on the leader's own burial urn.[13]

Ancestral worship of the ancient Chinese

Totemic worship gravitated toward two kinds of internal orientations: one was the totem became a god and its worship tended

ANCESTRAL WORSHIP 57

toward religious organization; and the other was the totem became identified with all the ancestors and worship then tended to be identified with an ethical system. The latter system directed the people's attention to the divinity within human kinship, the physiological inheritance across time, the persistence of kinship leading to a form of human immortality, and the importance of cultural inheritance. This system tended to be matrilineal and could trace its origins to female ancestors rather than male ancestors. Over time, the totemic social systems that focused on blood inheritance from a distant divine origin were replaced by the worship of clan ancestors that fell within written records. Reinforced by beliefs that the ancestors could intervene in the lives of the living to express their desires, the Chinese social system shifted its focus from worship of a totemic symbol that connected to nature and the divine, to one that made the departed ancestors themselves the totemic symbol. Property and rules of inheritance became intertwined with worship of family ancestors.

Gradually totemic worship in ancient China transformed into ancestor worship. The ancestor worship of the ancient Chinese was originally expressed as worship of the clan itself as a collective. This collective identity can be traced back to the period of the Three Sovereigns and Five Emperors—the mythic ancestors of *Huaxia* (the ancient name for China). Among the elite, ancestral worship combined the honoring of blood relationships and clan worship. The official genealogy of the royal families of the Xia, Shang, and Zhou Dynasties all traced back to the Yellow Emperor, and *Yanhuang Zisun* (*Descendants of the Yellow Emperor*) have become synonymous with the Chinese people.

The ancestral worship cultural complex of the Chinese relates to three types of ancestors: the earliest ancestors, the near ancestors, and the remote ancestors.[14] The *earliest ancestors* refer to national heroes known in myths and legends. These heroic ancestors are often portrayed as semidivine and able to use magical powers to achieve various significant contributions to their clans. *Near ancestors* refer to the last three generations of ancestors of the same clan, and *remote ancestors* refer to the ancestors past that of great-great-grandfather. The near ancestors and remote ancestors are familial ancestors.

The ancient mythic ancestors were generally believed to have become powerful spirits that could influence events in this world, including vital matters such as victory in war, success in hunting,

58   ZHANG LEI, HOU YINGCHUN, AND LI XIANGHUI

and even reproduction, illness, and death. Therefore, people sincerely prayed for the ancestors to bless important clan activities. Familial ancestors were mainly influenced by the idea of ghosts, and people worshiped their familial ancestors for shelter and protection. The power of the ancestral worship cultural complex derives from its support from both the nonphysical (the idea of ghosts and gods) and the physical (blood relations). It also draws strength from its ancient origin within the totem belief system. Its persistence in China despite decades of modernization and secularization is indicative of its ability to give a sense of wisdom, strength, and ancestral spirit to people who can still manage to tap into that "root" of subconscious knowledge in a balanced way.

The patriarchal "imperial hereditary system" and ancestral worship

The Xia Dynasty (2070–1600 BCE) was the first one in ancient China to fully embrace slavery as their social system. After the death of Xiayu (founder of the Xia Dynasty), his son, Qi, abolished the *abdication* system (a form of meritocracy) and implemented a hereditary system. Around this same time, Chinese culture ceased to hold the "primitive" outlook of the commons belonging to everyone to one where there was no "the commons" as the whole world belonged to the Emperor and, by extension, his descendants. Even when the Xia Dynasty's centralization of power was fully established, however, clan and family organizations did not collapse. In fact, the new feudal system of government strengthened and preserved the importance of clan organizations, which provided the conditions necessary to implement the patriarchal clan system that dominated China for many thousands of years after.

The linkage of ancestors and gods is made explicit in the character *Zong* (宗). According to the *Shuowen Jiezi*, *Zong* originally meant the temple in which to sacrifice to the ancestors.[15] The image of offering respect to the ancestral tablets within the ancestral halls is where the form of the word *Zong* came from. The patriarchal lineage system became dominant during the Shang Dynasty (1600–1046 BCE) and shaped the development of the influential Western Zhou Dynasty (1046–771 BCE). The patriarchal lineage system connected blood bonds with political relationships and closely integrated "noble families" with the national leadership. Respect for the ancestors

ANCESTRAL WORSHIP

59

became the top tier of a psychic hierarchy that justified the distribution of political power and served to maintain the clan's unity.

This patriarchal ancestral worship system was inherited and maintained by later rulers until the end of imperial rule in China (1912). Offering sacrifice at the national temple became the duty of the royal family and was made on behalf of the whole country. Whereas the common man and his family performed the sacrificial rituals for their clan, the Emperor performed his ritual activities for "all under heaven."

The traditional rites of ancestral worship involved a detailed elaboration of family history, rules, and principles for living family members. Activities undertaken during ancestral worship played an important role in strengthening family consciousness and maintaining family unity. Ancestral worship had the highest value in traditional Chinese society, and it remains a powerful influence today. For most of Chinese history, all the major festivals were related to ancestral worship: Ching Ming Festival (Tomb Sweeping Day), Mid-July Festival (Ghost Month), and Winter Festival (first day of lunar October). These festivals were collectively called the *Three Ghost Festivals* because they were all closely related to ancestor worship and the belief that the ancestors' spirits were "closer" to the physical realm at these times.[16]

Surnames, inheritance, and ancestral worship

The character for the surname *Xing* (𤱓 in small seal script), according to the *Shuowen Jiezi,* means the "people who gave birth." The image of the word contains the legend of the sacred virgin who felt a mysterious power from nature and gave birth to a son, who became the emperor. This word has 女 (*women*) as its radical part, and 生 (*birth*) as the phonetic part while also meaning the name of the father. In ancient oracle bone form 𤲟 contains 女 (*a lady*) as the radical part and 生 (*initial birth of a plant*) as the phonetic part. The two parts combine to create *Xing,* indicating a high likelihood that the word originally connoted a matrilineal society that established the bloodline through birth by women.

China is the first country in the world known to have used surnames. The establishment of surnames and a family name further personalized human relations and the individualization of each member of society. In clan society, the surname and the family name were separated. The *surname* referred to the people who had the same ancestor and common kinship. The surname was the corresponding identification mark created by the ancient Suiren Mouz in order to distinguish between bloodlines and prevent those of the same bloodlines from mating. The earliest surname in China originated in the Fuxi era (7774–7707 BCE). *Wind* was an ancient surname, known as the earliest surname of the Chinese nation.[17] *Family name* referred to certain people within a clan.

In the ancient legends there are literally hundreds of family names, such as the Pangu, Heaven Sovereign, Earthly Sovereign, Suiren, and Nuwa. After the First Emperor of the Qin Dynasty unified ancient China (221–206 BCE), surnames and family names began to be integrated into one another without distinction, with the surname evolving into a textual symbol indicating family origin and kinship.[18] After several thousand years of development and evolution, the surnames of modern Chinese people have gradually become a unique cultural system. From simple lineage markers, Chinese surnames still show hints of their origins in the period of totemic belief during a more matrilineal era.

The first name was *Wind,* and then that tribe divided into ten branches, and the branches divided into the thousands of surnames used in China today. Modern Chinese surnames not only relate information about where one's family is from, but also imply certain virtues or character. What is in a name? The Chinese answer would indicate how a name touches deep universal truths and is part of the mysterious harmony between being human and being of nature.[19]

Chinese surnames with the same root and origin can be traced back through Chinese civilization for thousands of years. The Chinese surname is not just limited to a social title; it also embodies the ancestral worship cultural complex in a personal way. Knowing the history of one's Chinese surname establishes a sense of belonging and identity to blood ancestry in some significant way. Often this is where the Chinese who grow up outside China begin when they start looking for their roots.

The ancestral worship cultural complex as a call to constantly strive for self-improvement and self-sacrifice

Mythology naturally expresses the most stable and constant part of the national spirit.[20] The main gods in ancient Chinese myths and legends possessed the mythic quality of having god-like powers— whether they were the cosmic eternal gods like Pangu who created

ANCESTRAL WORSHIP 61

the world by separating the heaven from the earth, or the gods of human origin like Nuwa who created the lesser humans from mud, or the semi-historical ancestor gods like the Three Emperors and Five Sovereigns. In other words, Chinese people have long believed that their ancestors were capable of all kinds of miracles whether or not they were personally accomplished by their ancestors.[21]

The traits of these ancestors were the epitome of wisdom and strength, their spirit and beliefs guided by a philosophy of respecting heaven and earth and maintaining harmony between heaven and human beings. In the *Book of Changes,* the "superior man," or the mythic ancestor, is described as "The movement of heaven is full of power. Thus the superior man makes himself strong and untiring.[22] The earth's condition is receptive devotion. Thus the superior man who has breadth of character carries the outer world."[23]

The image of the ancestor with "god-like virtue" has penetrated into the Chinese subconscious by means of widely referenced symbolism. Chinese ancestors had a strong self-improving spirit. Their stories all tell of courage, risks, and perseverance in the face of overwhelming odds, and of overcoming all hardships and dangers to achieve their aims. A quick summary illustrates the level of their accomplishments: Pangu created the world by dividing the heaven from the earth; Nuwa patched a hole in the sky and created mortal men; Fuxi invented the Eight Trigrams of the *Book of Changes;* Suiren first drilled wood to make fire; Youchao first built houses with wood; Shen Nong (the god of agriculture) tasted hundreds of plants to find useful herbs; the Yellow Emperor became the first medical practitioner; Cang Jie invented the written Chinese characters; Tang Yao formulated the calendar; and Gun Yu prevented floods with water control.

These mythic ancestors were considered "real" and regarded as exemplars for balancing reality and pragmatism with optimism and compassion. They were also noted for their spirit of devotion and sacrifice for the greater good. For example, the primordial god, Pangu, used his own body to support the heavens for 18,000 years in order to stabilize the earth. When the earth was strong enough to stand on its own, he collapsed and his body turned into the natural world. For a more relatable example, consider the historic ancestral figure of Dayu who led the people in their fight to control the flood waters for thirteen continuous years, exhausting all his energy and health. His burden was so heavy that he could not even visit his family while passing by his house as he rushed from one flood point to another. This quality of self-sacrifice was common to the ancestral gods, and its roots are still present in the Chinese national spirit. Finding a meaningful way to reinterpret ancestral worship for our modern age can bring it forth again in the hearts and minds of the people.

Using emotion to reinterpret ritual and establishing filial piety culture under confucianism

Han Feizi in his work *Five Vermin* wrote: "Men of remote antiquity strove to be known as moral and virtuous; those of the middle age struggled to be known as wise and resourceful; and now men fight for the reputation of being vigorous and powerful."[24] "Now" in this quote, refers to the end of the Spring and Autumn period and "fight for the reputation of being vigorous and powerful" refers to a time when common courtesy was uncommon. During the Spring and Autumn period (722–476 BCE) and the Warring States period (475–221 BCE), the patriarchal system of the Western Zhou Dynasty (1046–771 BCE) collapsed; even the clan system and kinship relations collapsed. The "aura" of the ancestral worship system itself was in question.

Conservative thinkers lead by Confucius realized that the collapse in the patriarchal system of ancestor worship was due to an over reliance on ritual. They saw the need to reconnect to the source of the power that drove sincere forms of *filial piety* and *fraternal duty*— genuine emotional attachment. Without emotional attachment, the blood bond was meaningless. Therefore, the Confucian basis for proper worship of the ancestors was "filial piety" and "fraternal duty" in daily life and the standard for behavior was "respect for the people who are worthy of it."[25]

Confucianism's model of using benevolent emotions to inform ritual replaced the feudal paternalistic model that emphasized external kinship and courtesy with one that focused on *inherent moral ethics* and *inner benevolence*. In practice, Confucius stipulated that the nature of filial piety was built on the common love between parent and child. His system of thought helped to replace the rigid rules of the paternalistic model with a more conscious concept of life. Ancestral worship was transformed from a religious mystery into a natural human action that integrated the social need for rituals with the personal psychological desire to connect to one's "roots." This way of living—respect for elders, cooperation with peers, and love toward children, all motivated by genuine emotions—creates a space where

ANCESTRAL WORSHIP

ancestral worship can become psychologically real. This is the *Tao,* which exists in daily ethics.

China still upholds filial piety as one of its core cultural values. For thousands of years, the concept of filial piety has been deeply engrained into Chinese consciousness, and it has become a major cultural phenomenon that distinguishes Chinese civilization from other civilizations. The concept of filial piety naturally flows from the originating concept of ancestor worship. From the time of our ancient ancestors to present day, the idea is to return the kindness of those who begot us and not to forget our origins.

The patriarchal system in the Western Zhou Dynasty (1046–771 BCE) enshrined five cardinal relationships: the primary one being the monarch to subject relationship, followed by the parent-child relationship, the husband and wife relationship, fraternal relationships, and finally the relationships between friends. Under the filial piety system, each side of the relationship had duties and responsibilities. If one side abused its privileges and abdicated its responsibilities, the system would collapse. Although the people of the Zhou Dynasty (1046–256 BCE) knew the concept of ethical behavior within the spirit of filial piety in the period of Confucius (551–479 BCE), both rituals and principles collapsed during times of political crisis and moral confusion. Confucian scholars separated filial piety in the family from ancestor worship in the religious sense and introspected and humanized the formalized ritualized behavior of the past, developing a moral, universal, and ethical filial piety culture synonymous with Confucianism.

Ancestor worship, for a time, found a balance between its personal and universal aspects. The universal psychology of filial piety culture linked the first "ancestor" to "Heaven" and its principles (natural law), and "Zu" was the ancestor god of the temple. Following the Qin and Han Dynasties, Chinese culture has used the common image of heaven and earth as the primal ancestors while regarding ancestral worship within the home as a natural form of emotional sustenance.

"Love in the family, loyalty in the country, brings harmony to the world!"—The morality of China's farming culture

Historically, China was defined by its farming culture. Fuxi, the legendary head of the first three emperors, taught the people to fish and hunt and grew the farming economy; Shen Nong is revered mainly for teaching the people how to sow and reap, creating agricultural abundance; Dayu dredged the rivers to promote the development of water-control and irrigation for farming. The Yellow River Basin is widely acknowledged as the "cradle of Chinese Civilization" because of its agricultural riches.

The ancient ancestors lived by rivers, built water conservancy systems, and cultivated intensively, forming a self-sufficient lifestyle and cultural tradition that remained unchanged for thousands of years. This self-sufficient farming culture formed a restrictive social model where the moral imperative of "taking care" of one's parents became a rule: "While the parents are alive, the son may not leave the village" ("父母在, 不远游").

Farming culture esteemed "being self-sufficient without handouts or favors." Under this restrictive social environment, when few individuals would ever move away from their native land for any lengthy period of time, the idea of *home* became the most powerful ethical value for Chinese peasants. Farming culture valued the idea of home in the kinship of blood relations, the closeness of coming from the same hometown, and a deep nationalism for the home country. It is a home-centric culture rooted in the land.

The symbol 𩰠 (from ancient bronze inscriptions) meant "Home" and contains the symbol 宀 as its radical part and 豕 (*shi*, meaning "pig") as its phonetic part. This character represents the place where one has settled down and become prosperous enough to have pigs under a shelter. The Chinese term for nation is a compound term of the words *country* and *home*. The underlying reasoning behind the term illustrates that thriving families are the basis for the strength of the state, and the strong state is the protective barrier for the continuation of the family.

Based on this deeply accepted concept of interdependence of home and country, the highest value of Chinese farming culture can be summed up in this popular saying: "Love in the family, loyalty to the country, brings harmony to the world." This natural nationalism is activated by the ancestral worship cultural complex, and attachment to the home country, in turn, strengthens the complex. If this kind of nationalism becomes more universal in outlook, it could well contribute to world harmony.

Shi Bo, a famous ideologist of the Western Han Dynasty (202 BCE–8 CE), said that "Harmony fosters new growth."[26] As China has transformed from a peasant majority country and shed its traditional

ANCESTRAL WORSHIP 65

cultural influences, harmony has been retained as a stated national goal for internal development as well as for China's international relations. The Chinese people have embraced the government's diplomatic efforts calling for a harmonious world through mutual respect between countries and its internal policies under the slogan "harmony brings wealth."

China's ancestral worship cultural complex has a collective aspect that can become universal and support and promote thoughts such as "all nations living side by side in perfect harmony." When "ancestors" are not restricted to one's nation, "good neighborliness" becomes easier. Pride in one's nation and its historic achievements is healthy and, indeed, vital for psychological stability and development on the path of individuation. However, if that pride becomes excessive and the complex is triggered in a negative way, it can engender a quite dangerous form of jingoism.

The Chinese often refer to China as *Zu Guo* (ancestral country), even if they never lived in another country. The common usage of the term indicates that the collective "ancestors" have become the nation-state. However, there is a deep danger in the nation-state absorbing the collective aspect of the ancestral worship cultural complex. "Historic enemies" will tend to loom larger as political leaders and the general population fall sway to collective emotions.

Meanwhile the personal aspect of the cultural complex has been "freed" from its historical straitjacket and left to individual choice. On this level, the Chinese are now free to worship their ancestors in novel ways that, psychologically speaking, reactivate the possibility of giving life to the ancestors in the very real sense of them being "present" in the minds of their descendants. Through Jungian psychology, it is possible to understand the ancestral worship cultural complex as a way to access the deeper levels of one's personal unconscious and encounter the archetypal ancestors through direct experience.

The following table summarizes the reasons why ancestral worship developed into a cultural complex for the Chinese. On the one hand, it is related to the development of Chinese history and culture. On the other hand, it is related to the unique spiritual beliefs of the Chinese people.

ZHANG LEI, HOU YINGCHUN, AND LI XIANGHUI

Table 2.1: The Connotation Frame of the Ancestral Worship Cultural Complex

The ancestral worship cultural complex of the Chinese	Reasons related to history and culture	Totem worship of the ancient people
		Ancestor worship of the Chinese nation
		The patriarchal system of "imperial family" (a hereditary system)
		Surnames inheritance and ancestor worship
	Reasons related to for spiritual beliefs	Ancestral worship cultural complex as a call to strive for self-improvement and self-sacrifice
		Using emotion to inform ritual and establishing filial piety culture under Confucianism
		Culture

Part III:
The "sacred ancestral tree" culture of Hongtong Dahuaishu

For hundreds of years, a popular folk song from Shanxi Province has been the unofficial anthem for Chinese who had to move from their hometowns. Its wistful lyrics are known widely across the vastness of China and even among the Chinese overseas: "Where did my ancestors come from? O' Hongtong Dahuaishu! What was the former residence of the ancestors? The old stork nests on the Dahuaishu." *Dahuaishu* is a type of tree called the "Grand Chinese Scholar Tree" indigenous to Hongtong County. The place where the Dahuaishu grows is home to millions of descendants of emigrants from the Ming Dynasty (1368–1644) who left their hometown because of forced mtigration.[27]

It was once said that "Wherever there are Chinese migrants, there will be descendants of Hongtong Dahuaishu." The Grand Chinese Scholar Tree as well as the "old stork nest" have become symbols of "Hometown" in the hearts of hundreds of millions of Chinese forced from their ancestral villages. The symbolic power of the tree whose roots represent culture itself created an almost spiritual bond, combining nationalistic emotions and authentic feelings for one's ancestral home.

ANCESTRAL WORSHIP

In the following section, we will elaborate on three aspects of the history and development behind the symbolic ancestral tree of the Dahuaishu legend: the forced emigration involved in the rise of the legend, the cultural reaction to the emigration in the form of popular ballads and stories, the holy land with the theme of "roots" and "ancestral worship"—Hongtong Daihuaishu Ancestor Memorial Garden (Figure 2.2).

Figure 2.2: Hongtong Daihuaishu Ancestor Memorial Garden (root carved door).

The emigration history of Hongtong Dahuaishu

The legend of the Dahuaishu begins with the forced movement of vast numbers of people. The Chinese character for *Move,* according to the *Shuowen Jiezi,* is related to the idea that "Dense seedlings need to be moved transplanted."[28] The Chinese Characters Dictionary (written by Dai Tong using six-script theory to interpret the Chinese characters) says: "Move also means transplant. If you want to grow rice, you should cultivate seedlings first and then move them."[29] The symbol for the word *Move* originates from an image of agricultural production.

The phenomenon of forced migration in Chinese history is also closely related to the extension of arable territory and the development of the farming economy. The first wave of forced mass migration took place under the Ming Dynasty (1368–1644). This became the largest politically decreed migration up to that time in history. In order to achieve the goal of transplanting vast populations and to multiply the nation's territory by cultivating deserted places, the Ming government (1371–1417) organized eighteen large-scale migration campaigns from the area that is home to the Grand Scholar trees. These migrants were moved to more than five hundred counties in eighteen provinces across the country (Figure 2.3), and the imperial records number those moved at more than one million, involving 1230 surnames.[30]

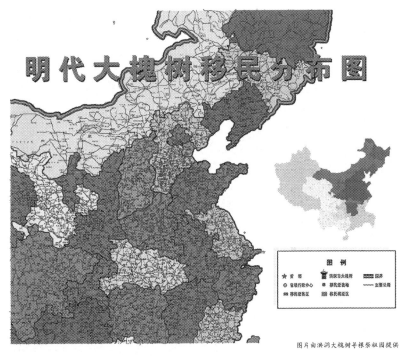

Figure 2.3: Scheme of Hongtong Dahuaishu migration routes during the Ming Dynasty.

After the overthrow of the Mongol-imposed Yuan Dynasty (1271–1368), Zhu Yuanzhang (1328–1398, founding emperor of the Ming Dynasty) implemented forced emigration as a policy for social stability and sustained economic development. Shanxi had the densest population in the empire, with Pingyang (now Linfen City)

ANCESTRAL WORSHIP

ranking first and Hongtong County being the largest county in terms of population. Therefore, the forced migration policy naturally started with Hongtong County.[31] Hongtong, named after the Hongya Ancient Cave, was known as Yang Hou County. In Hongtong County, there was an ancient Grand Chinese Scholar Tree with a girth of 13 meters (almost 43 feet). The mating storks from nearby Fenhe Beach always came to nest in it. This Grand Chinese Scholar Tree and its stork nests were the symbols of Hongtong County.

As the Chinese saying goes, "Even if the family is poor, it still is hard to leave one's own home." People did not want to leave their hometown and the relatives who they loved, so the Ming government took a deceptive approach to implement forced migration.

According to local legend, the first call for migration was largely ignored. The government then posted a deceptive notice saying that anyone who did *not* want to be displaced must report in person to the Grand Chinese Scholar Tree within three days and be registered, whereas those who sat at home would be forced to leave. Entire villages, including the elderly and children, rushed to the Grand Chinese Scholar Tree. Within three days, more than 100,000 people were clustered around the area. Soldiers of the imperial army arrived, blocking off all routes out of the area, and the commanding official loudly declared: "According to the command of the Ming Emperor, those who came to the Grand Chinese Scholar Tree will be moved to new towns."

The people had been deceived, and the pain of separation and their fear of an unknown future made the migrants feel like uprooted trees. The elderly picked branches from the Scholar Trees as souvenirs for their family members and told them not to forget their hometown and the Grand Chinese Scholar Tree. Young people put the branches on their palms and cried. At the urging of officials and under threat of the soldiers, the migrants could only move slowly as tears ran down their faces. They left their hometown and moved far away, which in those days meant they would never again see their relatives again (Figure 2.4).

As the migrants departed, they looked back to see the dotted stork nests and the Grand Chinese Scholar Tree in the distance. The elders pointed to that ancient tree, saying to their children and grandchildren: "Remember, this is our hometown!" At that moment, the Grand Chinese Scholar Tree and the stork nests became symbols of home, branded on the collective hearts of the migrants.

Figure 2.4: The scenes of migration under the Grand Chinese Scholar Tree.

Ballads and stories spread the legends of the Grand Chinese scholar tree

In Suizhou City in Hubei Province, there is a lullaby that goes:

> Mountains of Shanxi, waters of Shanxi, Hongtong of Shanxi is our home; the tree is big, the Grand Chinese Scholar Tree, we live under the Grand Chinese Scholar Tree; two toenails on the little toe and hands in the back, we walk far away from the Grand Chinese Scholar Tree in Shanxi; oh my baby, please don't cry, there are Grand Chinese Scholar Tree in Shanxi, the ancestors lived in Shanxi, when you grew up you can go back.

In Baixiang County there is also a widely circulated ballad that sings of the "six villages named Shanggeng in Hebei Province, and they are all from the Grand Chinese Scholar Tree."

In addition to these songs, there are ballads about the full moon, the crescent moon, children sleeping in their mother's arms, the fragrant flowers, and the old storks coming to bring them back to their hometown. These folk songs, with their lively vitality, tell the story of the Dahuaishu migrants' homesickness. The forced migration of Dahuaishu residents separated many millions of Shanxi people from their own flesh and blood over the centuries, and the cultural response that this separation spawned speaks to their sadness and their deep attachment to their hometown.

The legend of two toenails on the little toe

In yet another well-known ballad, the lyrics ask and answer how to tell if someone is a Hongtong migrant: "Who is the emigrant of the Grand Chinese Scholar Tree, just take off the shoe and see two toenails on the little toe." This is a reference to the story of how government

ANCESTRAL WORSHIP

officials registered the migrants. According to regulations, when a person was registered, they would take off their shoes and the toenails of the little toes would be cut in two to prevent attempts to run away. The story suggests that all the descendants of migrants from Hongtong have two toenails on the little toe.

The origin of the term "loosen hands"

In many parts of China, going to the toilet is still called "loosening hands." It is said that this is a remembrance of a phenomenon that occurred during the forced migrations. Government officials were afraid that the migrants would try to escape during their forced relocation, so they tied the arms of the migrants, but this proved inefficient for the long journey. Subsequently, they used a rope to connect several dozen people together so that no one could escape without the whole troupe going. If someone wanted to go to the toilet, he or she would have to ask the guards to untie the rope. Initially, the request was detailed: "Please loosen my hands as I need to go to the toilet." But over time, this sentence was simplified to the two words "loosen hands." Eventually, "loosen hands" became a generic name for using the toilet. As an example of the power of the Hongtong diaspora to affect Chinese culture, the phrase "loosen hands" is still widely used in many parts of China today.

The custom of planting Chinese scholar trees and hanging lucky charms

In Shandong, Henan, and Hebei Provinces, people regard the Chinese Scholar Tree as an auspicious tree and like to plant them in their courtyards or at their gates. This custom comes from the story of migrants carrying "folded twigs" of the original Hongtong Chinese Scholar Tree on their exodus. According to the legend, when the migrants were forced to leave their native lands, many latched onto the Grand Chinese Scholar Tree and would not let go. The officers ordered the soldiers to chop off the branches that the people were clinging to and the people held on to their branches and twigs as they were driven away from the tree. The migrants clung to the scraps of wood with tears in their eyes as they were forced onto the road.

After arriving at their new places of residence, the migrants planted the branches and twigs in their village squares, at their main gates, and at the local crossroads. According to the legend, these pieces of the original Grand Chinese Scholar Tree miraculously took root in the new land, growing with tenacious vitality. Soon the landscape was dotted with magnificent large trees. The migrants regarded these trees as symbols of their hometown and used them in their ancestral worship ceremonies. Soon the Chinese Scholar Trees themselves became sacred. At certain festivals, the people would hang "wish knots" on the tree and pray for the ancestors' blessings. Today, the custom of planting Scholar Trees and hanging lucky items on them has spread beyond the descendants of the Hongtong migrants and is prevalent throughout most of China in places where the climate allows the tree to grow. It is believed that having a Grand Chinese Scholar Tree in one's home blesses the whole family and is an invitation for the ancestors to come and visit often.

The holy land with the theme of "roots" and "ancestral worship"

The original Grand Chinese Scholar Tree in the Hongtong legend has a history of more than eighteen hundred years. When the Fenhe River flooded (1652), the tree was destroyed by the floodwaters. A historical commemoration hall was built on the original site of the Grand Chinese Scholar Tree in the third year of the Republic of China (1914).[32] The second-generation Grand Chinese Scholar Tree was born from the same roots as the first-generation Grand Chinese Scholar Tree and is over four hundred years old. It experienced the vicissitudes of life and gradually dried up after China's liberation. The third-generation Grand Chinese Scholar Tree, born from the second-generation Grand Chinese Scholar Tree's roots, is nearly one hundred years old. This third-generation Grand Chinese Scholar Tree is flourishing. After China was liberated by Communist forces and the opening up policy was adopted, economic development sped up in China. Descendants of the Grand Scholar Tree migrants began to formulate a unique "root-seeking culture" that led them to visit Hongtong in large numbers, which positively impacted the local economy.

Hongtong County, where every year thousands of people participate in "root-seeking" cultural activities held under the giant trees, is now synonymous with traditional ancestor worship. The Hongtong Daihuaishu Ancestor Memorial Garden has become a holy land, with "roots" and "ancestral worship" as its theme (Figure 2.5). In the Ancestor Worship Hall of this Memorial Garden, the memorial tablets of 1,230 surnames from the migrant families are enshrined. Almost everyone who returns to Hongtong to find their ancestors can at least find traces of their presence at this place.[33]

ANCESTRAL WORSHIP

Figure 2.5: The site of Hongtong Daihuaishu (screen wall with root character).

The migrants who were forced from their homes took on a slogan in their new homes: "*luo di sheng gen*" ("touch ground grow roots"). But they also carried their old slogan with them: "*ye luo gui gen*" ("fallen leaf returns to roots"). The fallen leaf is someone who dies away from their ancestral home; it was considered the duty of the migrant family to return the remains for burial. Although the main focus was to physically "return" the dead, the sentiments of the migrant's descendants continue to give life to the ancestral worship cultural complex among these populations. Mainland China is seeing the return of traditional ancestral worship as well as nontraditional embodiments of the spirit of "paying respect to ancestors." The Chinese ancestral worship cultural complex is deeply embedded with China's overall culture, and like the filial piety culture, its deep roots make it relevant to anyone who wishes to understand China's future.

It is said that a tree can only grow luxuriant leaves if it has deep roots to support it, and only a river that knows its source can reach the sea. This chapter is an attempt to illustrate the connection between the pursuit of ancestral identity by the Chinese in the midst of change and modernization and the psychological need that we all have for "origin" as we mature. It is also an argument that the key to the peaceful evolution of the "Chinese national spirit," as well as the recovery of the individual Chinese "soul," lies in the proper psychological understanding and interpretation of the Chinese people's ancestral worship cultural complex.

Sadly, at the moment, we are seeing more signs that the Chinese people have not found ways to reconnect to their "roots." Amid rampant complaints from the elderly that they feel abandoned by their children, the government is considering a law that would require adult children to visit their parents a certain number of days a year. Areas with historical significance continue to fall to the spread of "redevelopment." Popular interest in history is dominated by and focused around fictional romances. Recognition of the non-material power of the "collective ancestors" to psychologically influence events in the present remains weak and even controversial in the public sphere. Imaginary heroes need a moving "origin story" to make them interesting. How much more do real people need to know their origins to give meaning to their lives?

Notes

[1] Xu Shen (58–148 CE), *Shuowen Jiezi,* volume 6. Xu Shen was a Chinese scholar-official and philologist of the Eastern Han Dynasty (25–189 CE). His compilation *Shuowen Jiezi* ("Explaining Graphs and Analyzing Characters") was an early second-century Chinese dictionary. *Kuan Tzu* is a collection of the sayings and deeds of Guan Zhong, a statesman and reformer of State Qi in the Spring and Autumn period and the Kuan Tzu School. *Kuan Tzu* is one of the longest early Chinese philosophical texts.

[2] Chapter Tuan Zhuan 彖传，"艮，止也。"; Chapter Shuo Gua 说卦，"艮为止。"; Chapter Xu Gua Zhuan 序卦传，"艮者，止也。", I Ching, or *The Book of Changes* (1965).

[3] Jin Chunfeng, *The Book of Changes and New Interpretations of the Thoughts of the Bamboo Texts of Guodian* (Taiwan: Taiwan's Ancient Books Publishing co., LTD, 2003), p. 14.

[4] A Chinese radical part (Chinese: 部首, section header) is a graphical component of a Chinese character under which the character is traditionally listed in a Chinese dictionary.

[5] Xu Shen, *Shuowen Jiezi,* volume 1.

[6] Chapter Xu Yue 徐曰, *KangXi Dictionary,* p. 839.

[7] C. G Jung, *Memories, Dreams, Reflections,* trans. Richard and Clara Winston (New York: Vintage Books, 1989), pp. 235–236.

[8] *Ibid.,* p. 236.

[9] Lao Tzu, *Tao Te Ching,* Chapter 25.

ANCESTRAL WORSHIP

[10] Lao Tzu, *Tao Te Ching*, Chapter 16.

[11] Wang Xiaodun, *Original Beliefs and Ancient Chinese Gods* (Shanghai: Shanghai Ancient Books Press, 1989), p. 59.

[12] *Ibid.*, p. 127.

[13] Yu Lu and Wang Yueqian, *Painted Squid Stone Axe Pattern Pottery*, National Museum of China. Retrieved Jan. 17, 2019, at http://www.chnmuseum.cn/tabid/212/Default.aspx?AntiqueLanguageID=444.

[14] Ma Fuzhen, *Cultural Beliefs—Chinese Traditional Culture Lecture (Revised Version)* (Beijing: People's Publishing House, 2017), p. 15.

[15] Xu Shen, *Shuowen Jiezi·radical⌐*, volume 7.

[16] Ma Fuzhen, *Cultural Beliefs*, p. 17.

[17] Wang Dayou, *Seeking Roots for Thousand Years of China: The Origin of Chinese 100 Family Names Totem* (Beijing: Chinese Times Economic Publishing House, 2005), p. 8.

[18] Guan Yongli, *The Culture of Chinese Surnames* (Nanchang: Baihuazhou Literature & Art Press, 2012), pp. 8–9.

[19] Wang Dayou, *Seeking Roots for Thousand Years of China*, p. 220.

[20] Yuan Ke, *Ancient Chinese Mythology* (Beijing: HuaXia Publishing House, 2006), p. 17.

[21] Min Changhong and Shen Wei, "The Value Orientation Difference between 'God with Person Virtue' and 'Person with God Virtue,'" *Journal of Yancheng Normal College* 30 (2010): 52–55.

[22] *The Book of Changes*, The Qian Hexagram, Xiangzhuan.

[23] *Ibid.*, The Kun Hexagram.

[24] Han Fei Zi (280–233 BCE), *Five Vermin (Wu Du)*. Han Fei Zi was a Chinese philosopher in the Warring States period and a leader of the Legalist school. He is often considered to be the greatest representative of Chinese Legalism for his eponymous work *Wu Du* (Chinese: 五蠹, literally "five kinds of pests"). The five kinds of "pests" of the state were, namely, Confucians, Elocutionists, Mohists, and the spoiled dependents of noblemen and rich merchants.

[25] Li Zehou, *On the History of Chinese Ancient Thoughts* (Tianjin: Tianjin Academy of Social Sciences Press, 2003), pp. 12–16.

[26] The quotation is from *Guo Yu·Zheng Yu*. It is a simple dialectical view on the origin of the world put forward by Shi BO at the end of the Western Zhou Dynasty.

[27] For social stability and sustained economic development, the Ming government (1371–1417) organized eighteen large-scale migration campaigns from the area that is home to the Grand Chinese Scholar Trees. People who lived in Hongtong County were forced to leave their hometowns (moving from Shanxi province to other provinces of China). Nowadays, millions of descendants of emigrants return to Hongtong Dahuaishu to seek their "roots."

[28] Xu Shen, *Shuowen Jiezi·radical* 禾, volume 7.

[29] Dai Tong (1200–1285), *The Chinese Characters Dictionary*.

[30] Zhang Qing, *Hongtong Dahuaish Emigration Chronicle* (Taiyuan: Shanxi People's Publishing House, 2000), p. 47.

[31] Li Guangjie and Zhang Qing, *Three-Jin Culture* (Taiyuan: Shanxi People's Publishing House, 2007), p. 17.

[32] Hu Shixiang, *The Grand Scholar Tree and Guangji Temple*, local pamphlet, p. 40.

[33] Zhang Xingjian and Dong Aimin, *Remembered Homesickness: Hongtong Dahuaish* (Beijing: Chinese Federation of Literary Press, 2016), p. 127.

3

• • • • • •

Single Mothers in Marriage
Cultural and Individual Complexes in Displacement of Immigrant Mothers

Gong Xi

Don't ask from where I have come
My home is far, far away
Why do I wander so far?
For the little bird free I wander
For the brook clear and limpid
For the meadow green and wide
I wander, wander so far
And yes, for the olive tree in my dream
Don't ask from where I have come
My home is far, far away
Why do I wander?
For the olive tree in my dream[1]

Popular in the 1980s in China, the melancholy and euphemistic lyrics of this folk song fully express the wanderer's sense of wandering, loneliness, sadness, as well as hopefulness. As I wrote this chapter, its melody echoed in my mind. By such response and guidance from the unconscious, I was brought into a kind of light but pervasive nostalgia.

Gong Xi is a Ph.D. candidate at Macau City University for Applied Psychology. She is a registered professional counselor (RPC) in Canada and has a private practice in Vancouver, British Columbia.

78   GONG XI

As a psychotherapist with a private practice in Vancouver, British Columbia, I have worked with many women who, like myself, are newly immigrated to Vancouver from mainland China. Here, I use the phrase *newly immigrated* to distinguish them from Chinese immigrants who arrived before the twenty-first century. This new generation of immigrants is significantly different from the previous ones. In the past, people migrated mainly for work, study, and family reunions; today, with the rise of China's economy in recent years, many wealthy families in mainland China have chosen to emigrate abroad to educate their children, for financial security, asset allocation, or better social welfare and living environments, and so on. Most families choose an arrangement whereby the wife attends to the children and takes care of the overseas assets while the husband stays in China attending to business development. They reunite regularly or irregularly with the family, a phenomenon called *family of flyer*. Facing the difficulties of parenting alone, cultural adaptation, and marital crisis, many women have suffered, referring to themselves jokingly as "single mothers in marriage." Hereafter, I will also call them "immigrant mothers."

In this chapter, I discuss the phenomenon of the "single mother in marriage" from the perspective of Jungian analytical psychology, exploring the challenges these women face in the process of displacement and individuation. I will cite two cases as examples that represent the phenomenon of "single mothers in marriage"; however, these are not presented as analytic case studies. These two cases are typical from the perspective of analytical psychology. Anne has a negative mother complex and a somewhat over-developed animus, whereas Wendy is possessed by a strong father complex and her animus is underdeveloped. For privacy reasons, no real names are used and no identifying details about the clients and their families are disclosed.

The stories of Anne and Wendy

"Repeating routines every day, I hardly have time for myself." Anne, forty-six years old, moved to Canada with her two daughters (one aged eighteen and the other nine) six years ago. She is a typical immigrant mother. Anne's husband runs a successful company in China, which guarantees them a rich life. Anne and her husband founded the company. As the company developed, their management styles began to conflict, and they quarreled frequently about the company as well as family affairs. Anne thinks her husband is

SINGLE MOTHERS IN MARRIAGE

79

stubborn, naive, immature, and illogical, whereas her husband regards her as controlling, judgmental, and although good at execution, unkind. After Anne moved to Canada with their daughters, her husband took full control of the company. To put it in Anne's words, "He sent me and our children away to Vancouver. Tired of arguing with him, I simply leave everything to him and stay faraway." But life post-immigration has not been as easy as she imagined. Face-to-face quarrels between the couple have been replaced by disputes over the phone or via video links. The conflicts cover a broad range of topics: their daughters' education, company development, and even trivial things like the garden trimming and after-school study programs for the children. They may not contact each other for weeks after a quarrel. According to Anne, "I don't know what he is doing in China and have no idea if he has done anything bad to the marriage, while he can figure out my every move according to the children's schedules and I'm almost transparent to him." After immigrating, she says, "I have no income of my own and all the money comes from my husband. I feel insecure. I don't buy luxuries and have to live a frugal life." And due to language problems, she has no local friends but has made only casual acquaintances with several other immigrant mothers in the Chinese community. When their children's classes are over, these women return to their role as mother, driving the children to and from school and managing household chores. "Everyone thinks we are leading an extravagant life, but actually, I'm only a senior nanny free of charge in this family. Men deem it good enough to earn money to support the family, but they don't know how tedious and hard it is to raise kids alone." Still in her rebellious period, the elder daughter is strong minded. She was admitted to a university in another city and left home in spite of Anne's opposition. "We cannot beat or scold our children here." The daughter once called the police after being beaten by Anne in a quarrel. Anne said, "In China, it's common to be beaten by the parents in our childhood, while here in Canada, the police will intervene." She was stunned when a police car arrived with sirens blaring, and for a long time after that, she didn't know how to discipline the girls.

Speaking about her family of origin, Anne describes her mother as highly anxious and negative. Her mother, who was fragile, grievous, and needed company all the time, has been hard to please ever since Anne was a child. Her mother neglected looking after her, but she was also keen on controlling her. Their relationship is filled with not only entanglements, conflicts, and complaints, but also a deep attachment. Anne's symptoms reveal themselves in her body: chronic pains and a shadow area on her left breast that was discovered recently. She doesn't feel afraid, but she has been learning about breast cancer, and she feels isolated. Now she is actively taking a course of Chinese medicine therapy. After the shadow areas on the breast were discovered, *she had a dream in which she was taking a science examination in English. She was quite anxious as she could not understand the questions in English at all.* Anne did not breastfeed her daughters, but she did have a large number of estrogen injections for a failed in-vitro fertilization.

Wendy, forty-seven years old, is also a mother of two children. Her father was a senior official in China and her mother a schoolmistress with a strong character. All her grandparents suffered political persecution. Wendy's parents rarely exchanged feelings with their children and apparently preferred their son to their daughter, so she has been making sacrifices for her younger brother since she was a little girl. A telling memory from her childhood is that her brother had an apple but she only got the apple peel to eat. Her parents quarreled, casting a great shadow over her. With little attention and compassion from her father, she could not feel his love. He physically beat her, even after she graduated from university. Feeling unloved and with her needs unsatisfied, she has faced obstacles and lived with frustration her whole life. She doesn't know how to get along with a man or how to develop a good relationship. Every time she quarreled with her ex-husband, she would protect her head unconsciously as she did in childhood when being punished physically by her father.

She had hoped to escape her father's control and live and work independently after graduating from university, but her father did not allow it. He arranged a job for her that kept her under his influence. After she married, she wanted to get a new job, but found herself pregnant instead and became a mother. After that, she worked at her husband's company. He was a successful entrepreneur whose father had also suffered political persecution during the Cultural Revolution. Having experienced extreme poverty and riddled by powerful insecurities, he was a workaholic who enjoyed no pleasures in life. She and her husband had little in common. He blamed her and ordered her around, showing her little respect. She and her ex-husband divorced in 2016, six years after she immigrated. Wendy lacks self-confidence and

Single Mothers in Marriage 81

regrets not being able to live her own full life. Instead she still submits to her father's and ex-husband's rules. She and her ex-husband quarrel frequently about their children's education.

Immigrant mothers' phenomenon and displacement anxiety

Anne's and Wendy's stories are commonplace for Chinese immigrant mothers in Vancouver. The problems they face are typical. There have been a large number of research studies on immigrants, but few in-depth studies on a particular group over a specific period of time. In the past twenty years, most of the immigrants in Vancouver are families from mainland China. Most of the attention on these families has been focused on the purposes of immigration and the flow and allocation of their assets. Hardly any research has been done on the adaptation of these Chinese immigrants and their living status after immigration. For those Chinese mothers in Vancouver who bring up their children alone, their worries in life and emotional distress have not raised enough concern from the local community, their families of origin, or even among themselves due to their sound financial condition. However, we know from the study of psychology that immigration is one of the major separation traumas. These immigrant mothers are not only in the midst of midlife crises but also experiencing profound displacement anxieties. Although they are not economically vulnerable, their emotional adjustment to a new society and culture in a foreign land deserves the attention of the community, their families, and themselves.

Living environment

In comparison with previous immigrants, the new immigrants who moved from mainland China after 2000 are lucky. Earlier immigrants had few financial resources. They had to study hard to learn English and Cantonese to find a job to support themselves and their families, because most of the immigrants from the Chinese mainland did not speak Cantonese, whereas Cantonese had been the first language for many of the earliest immigrants who were already in Vancouver. If the pre-2000 immigrants wanted to work at a local company or in a small business such as a restaurant or travel agency owned by previous groups of immigrants, they would have to speak English or Cantonese. They also faced more exclusion and racial discrimination than more recent immigrants have. They even suffered exploitation at the hands of Chinese who came before them.

82 GONG XI

The new immigrants have come with enormous wealth to ensure a good material life. The wives don't need to work to support their children financially. Moreover, life in Vancouver is quite accommodating to new immigrants from mainland China, as Mandarin, which is the official language of China, has replaced Cantonese since 2000 as the most common language in many Chinese-speaking communities. As a result, Mandarin-speaking Chinese don't have to learn Cantonese to survive anymore. Even English is no longer necessary because social service agencies employ Chinese-speaking staff and signs written in Chinese can be seen everywhere. Financial abundance and living conveniences make learning English an entertainment rather than a requirement for most new immigrants. There are quite a few immigrants who have lived in Vancouver for a dozen years but speak only limited English. This is common in many immigrant communities nowadays.

Family environment

To the casual observer it might seem that immigrant mothers have a relaxed life in Vancouver. This is not exactly the case. They experience many hardships that are invisible to strangers. As the majority of single mothers who move to Vancouver arrive when their children are young, they have to take care of them most of the time because school hours are much shorter in Canada than they are in China. On the other hand, these mothers deal with everything around the home alone, and they don't have much time for themselves, especially those mothers whose children are younger than ninth grade. They sarcastically call themselves "manly women."

Language barrier

Because many services in Vancouver are available in Chinese, mothers have few opportunities to improve their English and most of them stay away from local life. They meet friends who speak Chinese, eat at Chinese restaurants, and receive services in Chinese. They live in a Chinese culture to a large extent, and their involvement with local culture is not as extensive as those technical immigrants who need a job to survive. Most immigrant single mothers live a relatively isolated life. However, language skills still matter if a new immigrant wants to integrate into society in a real sense. It is far more difficult for a rich immigrant to find a satisfying job or set up his or her own business without knowing English. The inability of these immigrant mothers to

SINGLE MOTHERS IN MARRIAGE

speak English has made it hard to adapt to society, preventing them from getting involved in local affairs where English is dominant. Facing critical moments in their lives can be a source of great anxiety. For example, in the dream Anne had after an x-ray revealed a shadow on her breast, raising the fear of breast cancer, *she was required to take a science exam in English. She was quite anxious as she could not understand the questions in English at all.*

Marriage crisis

Without the daily support and company of their husbands, many women feel empty and helpless. The absence of a sexual life also unconsciously elevates their anxiety. They call themselves "single mothers in marriage" and "nannies free of charge." Meanwhile, long-time separation inevitably raises concerns about husband-wife relationships. I have observed twenty-three new immigrant families in which marital crises occurred in different forms and to varying degrees within two to four years after immigration. These cases involved increasing communication difficulties between the couple, conflicts about educational ideas, and short- or long-term extramarital affairs. The wives are fearful and uneasy about divorce. To maintain their marriages, they endure the isolation and lack of support. Some of them have new babies in late middle age to strengthen the family bond. Among the twenty-three families I observed, two of them engaged surrogate mothers.

Cultural conflicts in family values

In Canada, husbands and wives are more equal in family affairs than in China. Canadian fathers spend much more time accompanying their kids on outings and taking care of the family than a common Chinese man does. Canadian fathers often take their children to after-school classes or exercise with them, and few would want to live separately from their wives. Observing this difference between Chinese and Canadian husbands has a great impact on those Chinese "single mothers in marriage," making them feel more lonely. Nevertheless, it is quite rare for women to take the initiative to end their marriages.

There are also communication problems between parents who have had a Chinese education and their children who are being educated in North America. Chinese families have stronger family bonds, and parents are generally more controlling than Caucasian parents. Encouraged by what they learn at school, children become more independent and ask for more autonomy. Mothers often lament that their children enjoy Chinese care but Western freedom.

To illustrate the confusion in parenting between cultures, here is a dream of a Chinese mother, aged forty-five, *who dreamed of a beautiful Western enamel porcelain cup with poison powder inside it.* The dreamer's association to the beautiful cup is her image of a good mother because she tries to be close with her twenty-year-old daughter, and the poison powder is a symbol of her control of the daughter in the name of love. She doesn't want her daughter to have sex before she graduates from university. The girl agrees. In Chinese culture, this is a normal requirement, whereas in North America, a girl often begins to have sexual relationships during her teenage years. The mother's unconscious shows her inner guilt under the influence of Western culture. She is fond of Chinese tea sets rather than Western ones. The dream, then, also symbolizes the conflict caused by cultural differences, or, you could say, a shadow cast by Western culture over traditional Chinese culture. Classic oriental elements also appear frequently in the dreams of other single immigrant women such as the Chinese red color, traditional Chinese food, yellow earth, classic furniture, and scenes of traditional holidays.

Racial discrimination

Although Canada advocates multiculturalism and a warm openness to immigrants, racial discrimination does occur. However, some immigrant mothers are prone to be sensitive and sometimes overreact to signs of discrimination. For example, when they meet a shop assistant with a cold face, they are likely to attribute his or her attitude to racial discrimination rather than to other unrelated factors such as the assistant being unhappy due to personal reasons. This might lead to a complaint. Such situations might also occur in parents' meetings or in public service organizations such as a bank or a police station. Inevitably, these experiences intensify the mothers' anxiety and sense of insecurity.

Loss of self-value

Most immigrant mothers have received a good education and had a decent position at work in China. Becoming full-time mothers after immigrating, many of them feel devalued. Although financially affluent, the mothers feel they are "economically dependent on their husbands and inferior in family life." Some lead a surprisingly frugal

SINGLE MOTHERS IN MARRIAGE

life, especially during the first two to five years; some have to tolerate their husband's affairs in China and even accept their husband's illegitimate children. They are confused about what to do with their lives and possible careers after their children grow up. Regardless of their participation in various social activities, for most women it takes a long time to establish solid social relationships in a foreign country in midlife.

Psychoanalytical perspectives of "couple separation" in the context of a cultural complex

In this context, *couple separation* does not mean divorce or breakup; it refers to a situation in which the husband and wife live in a different city or country. Such separations seem to go against human nature and are quite rare in Western culture but not so unusual in Chinese culture. Immigrant couples accept separation for practical reasons. New Chinese immigrants to Vancouver are generally the families of successful businessmen, entrepreneurs, government officials, people from cultural and art circles, scholars, and so on. For a man with a thriving career back in China, it's difficult to adjust to the sharp decline in income and social status that goes along with immigrating to a foreign land with a language barrier and unfamiliar customs. So it is quite understandable why husbands stay in China to maintain their families' economic wellbeing while wives (husbands in rare cases) accompany the children abroad. Needless to say, in Chinese culture, the children's education is always the family's highest priority.

However, other factors contribute to the phenomenon of couple separation. Throughout China's long history, a man's fulfillment comes from success in social life and making money for the family. It has long been normal for a Chinese man to leave his family behind and set out for fame and fortune. Evidence of this can be found in many ancient poems. Bai Juyi, a poet of the Tang Dynasty (618 CE–907 CE), wrote in the "Lute Player" about a wife's distress because her husband left home for business: "My merchant husband thinks only of profit and left me two months ago to do business"; and poetess Zhu Wenjun (175 BCE–121 BCE) also expressed her sadness in a poem to her husband who was an official living elsewhere: "Instead of 3 or 4 months as originally planned, it has been 5–6 years since we parted." In "Farewell," written by Lu Guimeng, another poet of the Tang dynasty (?–881 CE), a man who left home in search of success and fame was described as a decisive hero: "Be it a shame to be unable to part as a wanderer, a true man never sheds tears to say goodbye and will cut off his wrist if bitten by a viper without fear. Why should I sigh for parting if I can win success and fame?" The first two poems document the grievances of solitary wives, whereas the third one expresses the heroic sentiment of a fearless man. Full of the beauty of poetic romance, these poems demonstrate the cultural background and historical custom of couple separation in China.

From 1600 to 1700, there were several emigrant tides from China to places overseas where men could find work. Young men, often forced by natural disaster and war, left their families and were displaced to South Asia, Europe, North America, and Australia. A large portion of them never returned to China due to maltreatment, illness, or death. During that time, *Emigration Songs* were created, a type of music that describes in detail the hardship and sufferings of these labor workers.[2] They advise later generations to stay at home and be with the family. Obviously, to migrate is not the same as just "leaving home" for fame and career. It is a serious deviation from the traditional "sedentary lifestyle" cherished by Confucian culture, which stressed the attachment of consanguinity.

Since the 1950s, the household registration system and a series of political movements in China have led to numerous cases of couple separation. For example, from the 1950s to the 1970s, the government encouraged and/or forced educated young people from the city to settle in the remote countryside. When that movement ended, many people returned to the cities where they were born and left their spouses whom they married in the country because the household registration system didn't allow peasants to live in the city. Also if two young people fell in love when they were serving in the army, they had to return to their birthplaces after their service was terminated, even if they had gotten married. So it was quite common in China for couples to live separately before the end of the 1980s.

Children born during this period grew accustomed to separations between their parents and other elders. Although this phenomenon decreased gradually as these children grew up, the impact of separation was unconsciously powerful and long lasting. Many clients I have worked with recalled that their parents lived and worked in different cities for many years when they were children, and I can sense the unseen compulsive desire to repeat this familiar pattern. It is like an

Single Mothers in Marriage

87

invisible hand pushing them unconsciously to accept the fact that they will live separately from their spouse. However, they are not well prepared for the consequence of repeating this pattern.

Because the phenomenon of couple separation has such a long history in Chinese culture, the drive for the husband and wife to separate may be an archetype in the psyche. In China there is a myth about a girl in heaven who weaves beautiful clouds for the heavenly palace every day. She falls in love with a cowherd on earth and comes down to man's world and marries him. They live a happy life with their son and daughter. However, her grandmother, the Queen Mother who is the hostess of the heavenly palace, cannot accept the marriage of her favorite granddaughter to an ordinary man. She sends divine troops to bring the girl back. And to stop the cowherd and their children from chasing her all the way back to heaven, the grandmother cuts out a galaxy with her golden hairpin and separates the cowherd and girl weaver forever. Later, moved by the cries of the sad family, the Queen Mother allows them to meet on a bridge erected by magpies on July 7 every lunar year. This date became the Chinese Valentine's Day. This may be one of the oldest and most influential love stories in Chinese culture. The image of the cowherd and girl weaver who are separated by a galaxy can be seen as an archetypal image of couple separation.

From the perspective of analytical psychology, in the myth the girl's mother is absent, and her fate is dictated by her grandmother, her mother's mother, a devouring image of the great mother archetype. The girl weaver's conscious ego, her animus that was symbolized by the cowherd and the inner child represented by her children, are absolutely powerless in the face of this immense and devouring authority. Except for the rebellious spirit that the girl displays when she comes to earth at the beginning of the story, she has to submit to the power of the great mother in exchange for a reunion once every year on July 7. She is kept in a stage of *self-conservation* by the devouring female power and loses any opportunity to develop an independent ego and Self.[3]

Self-identity in displacement and cultural complex

Joseph Henderson proposed the idea of a cultural unconscious:

> The cultural unconscious is an area of historical memory that lies between the collective unconscious and the manifest pattern of the culture. It may include both these modalities, conscious and unconscious, but it has some kind of identity

arising from the archetypes of the collective unconscious, which assists in the formation of myth and ritual and also promotes the process of development in individuals.[4]

The notion of the *cultural complex* was proposed by Thomas Singer and Samuel Kimbles in 2004, which combined the essential building blocks of Jung's original complex theory and Henderson's "cultural unconscious."[5]

Migration as a human activity can be traced back to ancient times. Perhaps given a long enough time, each clan will naturally spread to every corner of the world, like mercury falling to the ground, to use a Chinese metaphor. Emigrants overseas shine like scattered pearls within different regions and cultural backgrounds. However, in contradistinction to the ancient history of emigration, for centuries China was a self-sufficient, small-scale peasant economy, emphasizing the dependence of people on the land. The ethical principles of the Confucian tradition accentuated the attachment of kin to one another. Living and dying abroad deviates from the traditional cultural values of the Chinese people.

Migration is a major psychological trauma that shakes a person's entire psychic structure. Like a tree that is uprooted and transplanted, immigrants leave the soil and living environment they are familiar with, losing everything that is important, precious, and meaningful, such as interpersonal relationships, domicile, language, cultural customs, climate, and social status.[6] More significantly, immigrants also lose the part of their being that dwells in the people and objects with which they identify. This results in a crisis of self-identification. The migrant loses the containing mother and possibly the containing mind and containing skin-country, which, drawing on Amanda Dowd's ideas, symbolizes one's country.[7]

Anne had a dream during her early years in Vancouver in which *she is running to look for a locked box with the state secrets of China. She cannot remember the password after finding it and this makes her very anxious.* People always compare the homeland to the mother. Nothing makes a child feel more uneasy and vulnerable than the idea of "I don't know who my mother is." The loss of language intensifies the feeling of loss of both the object and subject, making it the most direct and obvious source of trauma in displacement anxiety. Even the partial loss of protection by the "motherland" leads to a profound sense of homelessness and loss of identity in the deep psyche.

Single Mothers in Marriage 89

Losing the containing mind of language increases the sense of loss of identity suffered by immigrant mothers. One's first language is called the *mother tongue*. A mother language contains personal and cultural identity. Difficulties encountered in learning a foreign language can imply a problem in re-establishing one's identity as well as anxiety about "betraying the mother." Culture and language are the soil and basis for human existence. They establish and sustain indivisible ties between an individual and the group to which the individual belongs. Such ties are indispensable, especially during immigration when the immigrant is attaining a new social identity at a time of great psychic vulnerability. The cost of losing a sense of having a stable self-image is incalculable and makes establishing a solid identity in a foreign country all the more challenging.[8]

Immigrant mothers who are free from economic pressure usually choose to avoid integrating into local society as a way to protect themselves from feeling isolated, frustrated, and dis-eased. I disagree with encouraging immigrant mothers to merge into society as soon as possible. They should allow themselves some period of time to encounter the fear of losing their sense of security and the frustration of adapting to a new culture rather than suppressing these experiences by simply choosing to "live a positive life." As long as they are able to perform basic functions, they should be able to experience and embrace their sadness, fear, and fragility. Only then can the hopefulness of life in a new world take hold and truly settle them down, both physically and mentally. I have discovered in my private practice that though previous immigrants have better language skills, they are generally thriftier and less trusting of others, which is the result of having suppressed traumatic feelings brought about by their experience of displacement. Even after many years, they still feel insecure and inferior despite having a stable job and making a decent living. Displacement difficulty can be resolved gradually over a period of two to five years, whereas long-term neglect of physical and mental stress may cause neurosis such as depression or anxiety.

Amanda Dowd states that an individual who lives in a different culture will interact with the environment even if she chooses to keep a distance from the mainstream culture and then "becomes a part of the local culture."[9] What matters is how much the individual allows this change to happen in a natural way. It may take time and patience to grieve the loss, accept the psychic trauma, and reconstruct self-identity. Although immigrant mothers may be less motivated to learn a language or to integrate rapidly into society, they do have the chance to go through the initial hardships of adaptation in a more natural and relaxed way.

In Greek mythology, there are two archetypal images of sorrowful wanderers who are lovers of Zeus. One is Demeter, the goddess of agriculture, the most beautiful, kind-hearted, and diligent among the gods and a mother full of love. Her daughter Persephone is forced by Hades, the chthonic god of the underworld, into a marriage. As a result, Demeter leaves everything unattended every winter as she wanders looking for Persephone. The other sorrowful wanderer is Io. Hera, Zeus's queen, hates her out of jealousy. Io is forced to wander along the Nile in Egypt with her son. Both of these two archetypal images of female wanderers are castoff lovers as well as mothers raising their child alone. In contrast to Chinese men who leave home for success and fame as heroes, Chinese immigrant mothers have to swallow the loneliness of their involuntary wanderings under the influence of a strongly patriarchal culture. "Single mother in marriage" is a perfect description of their experience of being cast out into solitary distress.

Throughout Chinese history, women have been asked to obey the rules of the Three Obediences and Four Virtues.[10] They are required to be loyal and obedient to men, namely, the father before marriage, the husband after marriage, and the son after the husband's death. Thousands of years of cultural influence cannot be radically changed in a few decades, despite the wave of equality between men and women that has swept through modern society. Indeed, this wave may only serve to increase the tension that women experience as they seek their identity.

Though utterly different in personality, both Anne and Wendy are well educated and successful in their husbands' companies. Anne still holds an important position in the company by monitoring its business. Nevertheless, they both admit that moving to Vancouver was more or less a resolution for avoiding conflicts that they had with their husbands. Both of them feel as if they were cast out. With such feelings lingering inside, identifying themselves in the family in a foreign country becomes even more challenging: What kind of wife, mother, and person am I? What is my value? All these questions have to be redefined in a new environment. Identity is the source of self-value, providing a stable foundation for an adaptive personality.

SINGLE MOTHERS IN MARRIAGE

However, identity in the family is affected not only by cultural values and complexes but also by individual complexes. Jung defines complexes as "splinter psyches, and the aetiology of their origin is frequently a so-called trauma, an emotional shock or some such thing, that splits off a bit of the psyche."[11] When individuals are dominated by complexes, they see no real object in a relationship, but a self-object representation. Complexes evoke powerful emotions. Cognition and behavior can become distorted and malfunctioning, which can be destructive to relationships.

The most powerful complexes in the individual psyche are the father complex and the mother complex. Remarkably, there is another rarely known version of the story of the cowherd and girl weaver in which they are punished by the girl's father—the Heavenly Emperor rather than the great mother—because the girl has indulged in love after marriage and drops her work of weaving clouds for the heavenly palace. As work and duty can be seen as originating in the animus, the girl weaver is actually punished by the paternal principle.

This reminds me of Wendy. Weak and timid, Wendy came to Vancouver under her husband's arrangement. He was demanding and criticized her all the time. She tried hard to maintain her marriage with humbleness. Even in quarrels with her husband over the phone, she behaved like a blamed child rather than a wife. Feeling wronged, she retorted and sometimes complained about his absence just to relieve her pain. In her view, he had been a successful man who could be relied upon for her entire life. It was not until after their divorce that she found out he had been in a long-term relationship with another woman in China for many years. Wendy was broken and suffered a deep depression. She experienced her husband as being like her picky father who never accompanied her but always degraded and neglected her. She longed for her father's love, but this need was sadly unfulfilled. Sometimes she also appeared to be bewildered when taking care of her children. Experiencing herself as the "girl who is only allowed to eat the apple peel" she always felt neglected and inferior. If a woman is unable to work through the father complex and develop a mature animus, her projection of the negative father image onto the husband will inevitably cause chaos and disruptions in the relationship, causing her to suffer from separation and deprivation, just like those women being oppressed by the devouring mother complex and archetype.

92 GONG XI

Quite different from Wendy, Anne's negative mother complex led her to make "so long as it is not like mother" the fundamental principle for big decisions in her life.[12] As a result, her animus became overdeveloped. She is independent, rational, good at execution while emotionally detached, controlling, and obstinate. Her relationships with her husband and daughters are imbued with her need to dominate.

She values herself and others by "positive thinking and effective action," but can neither feel the emotional needs of her husband and children nor realize her repressed feelings and the resulting distorted cognition. Dissatisfied with her father, she is inclined to regard her husband as incompetent, careless, and unreliable. That's why she shows little respect or understanding. Her suppressed unconscious conflicts can only be expressed by somatic ailments. According to Jung, a female who rebels against her mother is more at risk than one who rebels against her father. Maybe she seems more rational, but she runs a risk of hurting her instinct, as negation of her mother also means negation of those ambiguous, instinctive, and unconscious elements in her nature.[13] A woman like this, who is rational, resolute, and powerful, can be cherished by a man, however. In spite of inadequate emotional communications between Anne and her husband, he trusts her in company affairs and relies on her judgements and decisions. She is a troublesome wife but also a "spiritual guide and counselor for man."[14]

There is a long history in Chinese families of mothers being anxious while fathers are absent. The absence of a father results not only from the father leaving home for fame and career success or physical absence due to war, disease, death, or divorce, but also from the father not being emotionally responsive. In a way, the father's absence is more about emotional unavailability than physical absence. A kind mother and a strict father are the standard parental images in Chinese culture. Consciously or unconsciously, the son often becomes the mother's emotional support, whereas the daughter may get married with regret about the absent father. Though both will project their ideal anima or animus onto their partners, Jung wrote "the one who is grounded on a positive relationship to the parents will find little or no difficulty in adjusting to his or her partner, while the other may be hindered by a deep-seated unconscious tie to the parents."[15]

In my experience with clients, women, compared to men, tend to project more of the ideal father image or animus onto their partners.

Single Mothers in Marriage 93

This doesn't mean a man won't project the ideal mother image or anima onto his wife, but a man is relatively stable in the marriage because of masculine rationality and a stronger connection established between him and his mother, although sometimes this connection destroys the nuclear family. Unfortunately, the bond between father and daughter is weaker, and a woman's sentimental and ambiguous nature will leave her with more distress in marriage.

Single mother in marriage vs. female individuation

In Jungian analytical psychology, individuation is a concept of particular importance that denotes "a process that one eventually becomes himself, an integrated and integral process of development different from everyone else."[16] The individuation journey of Chinese women is filled with conflicts and hardships. Throughout history Chinese women have been encouraged to seek lifelong dependence through marriage in exchange for which they need to be loyal and submissive to husbands and their families. Men were not expected to be loyal and could have more than one wife, yet they must take life-long care of them. Like the Chinese preference for boys over girls, these values reflect a profound disregard for women, which is why many Chinese females experience an inner voice saying, "I wish I were the boy of the family." Monogamy in modern society has made it possible to get a divorce. With the increasing divorce rate, women have had to learn more than ever to be independent spiritually and financially. This calls for strong animus development. It has become increasingly risky and impossible for women to get married for the purpose of seeking ever-lasting protection as women of previous generations did. Today, the growing tension between cultural customs and the reality of modern society have stimulated the identity problems faced by Chinese women, especially at times of profound transition such as immigration, divorce, or death, which simultaneously offers great opportunities for individuation.

Displacement anxieties of single immigrant mothers are usually accompanied by midlife crises, as most of them emigrate between the ages of thirty-five and forty-five. According to Jung,

> the middle period of life is a time of enormous psychological importance. ... instead of looking forward one looks backward, most of the time involuntarily, and one begins to take stock, to see how one's life has developed up to this point. The real motivations are sought and real discoveries

are made. The critical survey of himself and his fate enables
a man to recognize his peculiarities. But these insights do
not come to him easily; they are gained only through the
severest shocks.[17]

Li Mengchao pointed out that China is a patriarchal society under
the shadow of the great mother archetype.[18] Man's heroic journey
starts with confronting the mother complex. I believe the couple
separation phenomenon in the immigrant family could be regarded
as a man's unconscious effort to be separate and independent from
the great mother; at the same time a woman's individuation process
requires her to work through the complex that originates in the
absence of the father. She has to care for the inner child, say goodbye
to the eternal virgin, and liberate herself from the devouring power
of the mother archetype in order to develop a stable self-image and a
healthy psychic structure.

When Anne starts to enjoy cooking, allows her family to have
different ideas about life than her own, and begins to accept uncertainty
and ambiguity as part of life, she finds herself less anxious. This
suggests a growing comfort with a feminine principle that is nourishing,
containing, and holding. Wendy says, "I know it's a long way to
grow up but I am looking forward to a healthy intimate relationship,
becoming a friend-like mother, and finding a job which can bring me
a sense of achievement several years later." This is also her process of
becoming a whole woman, which includes being a real wife, a wise
mother, and a social woman. Their words resonate with what Jung
described: "Individuation has two principal aspects: in the first place it
is an internal and subjective process of integration, and in the second it
is an equally indispensable process of objective relationship."[19]

If the remoteness and hardship of individuation are a lifelong
process, immigrant mothers have to realize that they are propelled by
the hand of fate to embark on a journey during which they have to
survive loneliness and struggle, to give up and rebuild old psychic
structures, and most of all, to explore ways out of the negative impact of
living under such a powerful patriarchal society. Like the lyrics of the
song at the beginning of the article, these "single mothers in marriage"
are wandering in a strange place far away from the homeland, and they
are on a journey of discovering an inner home with great loneliness
and courage.

Notes

[1] Written in 1979, by Li Tai-Hsiang, a Taiwanese composer and folk songwriter.

[2] Chaohong Lin and Lunlun Lin, "A Comparative Study on Emigrant Songs in South China," *Cultural Heritage Magazine* 5 (2014).

[3] Eric Neumann, *The Fear of the Feminine* (1951), trans. Qinying Hu (Beijing: World Books, 2018), pp. 7–14.

[4] Joseph L. Henderson, "The Cultural Unconscious," in *Shadow and Self: Selected Papers in Analytical Psychology* (Asheville, NC: Chiron Publications, 1990), p. 103.

[5] Thomas Singer and Samuel L. Kimbles, eds., *The Cultural Complex: Contemporary Perspectives on Psyche and Society* (New York: Brunner Routledge, 2004).

[6] Leo and Rebecca Grinberg, *Psychoanalytic Perspectives on Migration and Exile* (New Haven and London: Yale University Press, 1989), p. 26.

[7] Amanda Dowd, "Finding the Fish: Memory, Displacement Anxiety, Legitimacy, and Identity," in Craig San Roque, Amanda Dowd, and David Tacey, eds., *Placing Psyche: Exploring Cultural Complexes in Australia* (New Orleans, LA: Spring Journal Books, 2011).

[8] Li Mengchao, "Sensing, Responding, Transformation, and Integration" (Ph.D. diss., Macau City University, 2017), p. 465; Dowd, "Finding the Fish," p. 139.

[9] Dowd, "Finding the Fish," p. 124.

[10] The term *Three Obediences* was first seen in the Confucian classics of the Zhou and Han Dynasties, *Rites, Mourning Clothes and Biography of Zi Xia,* and later joined with the *Four Virtues* to become the standard for women's morality, behavior, ability, and accomplishments. The Four Virtues are morality, proper speech, modest manner, and diligent work. The term *Four Virtues* appears in *Zhou Li, Tianguan, Inner Slaughter.*

[11] C. G. Jung, "A Review of the Complex Theory" (1934), in *The Collected Works of C. G. Jung,* vol. 8, ed. and trans. Gerhard Adler and R. F. C. Hull (Princeton: Princeton: University Press, 1969), § 204.

[12] C. G. Jung, "Psychological Aspects of the Mother Archetype" (1938/1954), in *The Collected Works of C. G. Jung,* vol. 9i, ed. and trans. Gerhard Adler and R. F. C. Hull (Princeton: Princeton: University Press, 1968), § 170.

[13] *Ibid.,* § 186.

96 GONG XI

[14] *Ibid.*

[15] C. G. Jung, "Marriage as a Psychological Relationship" (1925), in *The Collected Works of C. G. Jung,* vol. 17, ed. and trans. Gerhard Adler and R. F. C. Hull (Princeton: Princeton: University Press, 1954), § 331b.

[16] Heyong Shen, *C. G. Jung & Analytical Psychology* (Beijing: CPU Press, 2012), p. 77.

[17] Jung, CW 17, § 331a.

[18] Li Mengchao, *Sensing, Responding, Transformation, and Integration.*

[19] C. G. Jung, "The Psychology of the Transference" (1946), in *The Collected Works of C. G. Jung,* vol. 16, ed. and trans. Gerhard Adler and R. F. C. Hull (Princeton: Princeton: University Press, 1966), § 448.

4

• • • • • •

The Animus Archetype in Chinese Culture

Xu Jun

The animus archetype in Chinese culture has evolved throughout its history—from the god Pangu (approximately 4000 BCE), the mythic creator of the universe, to the semi-historical yet legendary figure of the Yellow Emperor (2717–2599 BCE) to the modern era. The purely mythic images of Pangu and other male gods have come together with the "true" historical stories of heroic males to form the ancestral basis and content of the Chinese cultural animus. The positive aspect of the Chinese cultural animus is clearly grounded in divine creative power. On a human scale, it is the image of a sage or a savant with innate knowledge. The negative counterpart of the Chinese animus is a submissive man, carrying with him the image of the "ordinary man" who is a materialistic fool.

During the late Qing Dynasty (1840–1912 CE), the positive cultural animus of the Chinese was deeply wounded as a result of the national disgrace brought on by the Opium Wars, and it was not until after World War II and the end of the Chinese civil war that followed, that China reemerged as a unified political entity. After the establishment of the People's Republic of China, further turmoil

---

Xu Jun lives in Nanjing, China, and is in private practice as a Jungian analyst. He is an accredited member of the International Association of Analytical Psychology (IAAP).

98   XU JUN

erupted, deepening the damage to the animus in the collective Chinese mind. Political differences among leaders eventually led to the well-known decade of chaos called the Cultural Revolution. The total disruption of social norms and destruction of the formal educational system exacerbated the disconnection between cultural memory and social knowledge. The attempt to erase everything "old" about China was ultimately a disaster. Many who survived the turmoil felt like lost souls in a material world.

After the opening up and reform policies that began in 1979, the Chinese attempted to compensate for the damage to the cultural animus by returning to the traditional emphasis on formal education. This response has led to other issues, however, and has not improved the state of the cultural animus very much. Instead of children who are self-assured and creative, the emphasis on conformity and competition has led to overwhelming amounts of school work and endless hours of tutoring and test preparation.

After following the evolution of the cultural animus into the present day, this chapter concludes with a case study of a mother who is raising a young son in modern Chinese society. Her attempt to bring forth positive aspects of the Chinese animus despite the drastic severing from her cultural legacy is both inspiring and a hopeful sign that we will witness a rebirth of the Chinese cultural animus from the unconscious in the years to come.

Part I: The cultural heritage

Forming the Chinese animus: myth and man, Pangu and the yellow emperor

In Chinese legends, Pangu is the initiatory male creation God.[1] His effect on the development of the Chinese cultural animus image cannot be underestimated. As the primordial male image in the Chinese mind, even today Pangu continues to exert a powerful influence on the subconscious of Chinese people and on Chinese culture.

According to the legend of Pangu, the "world" as we know it now, originally existed as pure chaos in the form of an egg, and Pangu was inside (Figure 4.1). After ten thousand years, the egg broke open and separated into heaven and earth. The *lucid Yang* ascended to the sky and formed the heaven while the *turbid Yin* descended to earth and formed the realms below (Figure 4.2). Pangu transformed his

Figure 4.1: Pangu in the cosmic egg.

body during this creation process nine times a day to help stabilize the transition and prevent heaven and earth from colliding. "His mind was more than heaven, his glory was more than earth. The heaven grew a Zhang each day (about 3.3 meters). The earth grew a Zhang each day. Pangu was the same. Thus, they grew another ten thousand years."[2]

After describing this expansionary period, the legend tells the secret of creation using the following formula: "The Creation begins from one, and is stable in three, achieves in five, blooming in five, and lying in nine. Thus, the distance between heaven and earth is 9 thousand Li."[3] The essence of this myth is that Pangu, through his innate knowledge of the chaos that precedes heaven and earth (that is, Pangu as the core of the world egg) and his self-sacrificing willingness to destroy and re-create his being (nine transformations a day), created and stabilized the "world" that we enjoy today. Psychologically, it is the story of the Self breaking from the Unconscious, the chaos egg, using its "lucid Yang

Figure 4.2: Pangu created Yang and Yin.

energy," its awareness, to create time space—what we could also call *conscious experience*.

When Pangu separated heaven and earth, Yang and Yin immediately comingled and transformed to become all things on earth. Pangu also transformed himself. His head became Mount Tai, the most famous of China's holy mountains. The Chinese character *Tai*, meaning "exceedingly," is featured in the ancient Taoist text, the *I Ching*, as Hexagram 11 (Figure 4.3):[4]

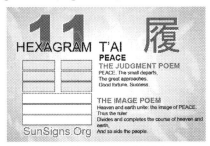

Figure 4.3: Hexagram 11 Tai.

TAI, Co-penetration
Meaning, the Small going, the Great coming. Significant Growing. The situation of Hexagram 11 is characterized by an auspicious conjunction of heaven and earth bringing expansion, harmony, and peace. Heaven and earth mingling. Co-penetration.
Image, The crown prince uses his property to accomplish the Tao that belongs to heaven and earth. And he braces the reciprocity properly belonging to heaven and earth. And he uses the left and right to settle the commoners.

The legacy of this widely held creation story meant that from the most ancient semi-mythical time of the "Three Emperors and Five Sovereigns" to the era of the last Qing emperor (1644–1911/12), each "Son of the Heaven" who aspired to rule the vastness of China was expected to and did go to Mount Tai every year to perform the ceremony of the worship of heaven to pray for peace and prosperity in the land. Symbolically, this ceremony connected the "Son of Heaven" to the "head energy" of Pangu, his intelligence and knowledge.

In this way, the foundational image of the animus for the Chinese people became intellectual brilliance. Mental excellence was held to be the highest value in all of society. *Enlightened wisdom* came to life in images of the Scholar and the Philosopher. *Teacher* became a high

THE ANIMUS ARCHETYPE IN CHINESE CULTURE 101

honorific, and knowledge as a worthy lifelong pursuit was etched into the Chinese psyche. The ultimate spirit of Pangu is symbolized in the final transformation of his total personal being into all of the things we see in the world today. This core universalism from China's ancient past is subconsciously reflected in the internationalism of today's socialist Chinese culture. Of course, no one in China "believes" in the story of Pangu, but everyone knows the story and is affected by it.

The most revered ancient human figures in Chinese history are Yandi, the Yan Emperor and leader of the Shennong tribe in mid-China on the Henan Plain, and Huangdi, the Yellow Emperor and legendary ruler in Western Sichuan Basin. Yandi is known for testing hundreds of plants on himself, creating the foundation for Chinese herbal medicine. Later, Huangdi organized doctors from all over the country to compile and edit the famous *Huangdi's Canon of Medicine*. Even now, *Huangdi's Canon of Medicine* is used as a basic introduction text in modern Chinese medical schools. Huangdi experimented with sowing all kinds of seeds and developed new plants for cultivation. He gave impetus to developing new means of production and to improving people's everyday lives. In addition to being credited with creating cloth making and sewing, he is said to have invented concrete, wheeled machines, and the art of tempering metals as well as advances in construction, medicine, and science.

Huangdi personally coached people on how to plant and farm, using a deep knowledge of water, minerals, and the soil. He designed and produced various household utensils from smelting metal and forged "magical" weapons from alloyed metals. His ability to work metals is likely what led to the selection of the *Ding* (a copper vessel) as his symbolic image. Later generations came to revere the Ding itself as a symbol of imperial power. Credited with being the main ancestor of all Chinese and because of the vast list of accomplishments attributed to him, Haungdi has had a disproportionate influence on the makeup of the Chinese cultural animus. To understand this influence, we will examine how the image of Huangdi has been suffused through Chinese culture over the centuries.

In the *I Ching*, Ding, "the vessel," is Hexagram 50 (Figure 4.4):[5]
DING, The Vessel
Meaning, The situation described by this hexagram is characterized by the alchemical image of a sacred vessel which transforms its content into spiritual nourishment, an offering to higher powers.

Figure 4.4: Ding, the vessel.
Image, The vessel. Spring. Significant growing. Wood becomes fire. Above the vessel. A gentleman uses correcting the positions of things to solidify the welfare of people.

The transposing of the values of Huangdi, the person, into Ding, the vessel for transformation, transforms the archetypal animus from a kind of pure being into being a method capable of changing the world based on intelligence. In a way, it brings form to formlessness.

Of course, the historical foundations of the Chinese cultural animus is much greater than the contributions of just Pangu and Huangdi, but for clarity and simplicity, I will focus my consideration on them in this chapter. Their combined influence is so vast, in my opinion, that readers will be able to apprehend the mythical foundation of the Chinese cultural animus. These are the main features of the Chinese cultural animus influenced by Pangu and Huangdi:

- The animus is a fully conscious being, aware of the Yin and Yang in his being.
- The animus is able to transform all difficulties into positive developments by use of his intellectual excellence.
- The animus is an inspiring and civilizing influence on all around him.
- The animus is aware of historical time and lives for posterity.

These positive features of the Chinese cultural animus are still held closely by the Chinese, but they are not used for day-to-day life. For adapting to the present highly secular, materialistic social reality, people have retreated to formal education, socially approved beliefs, and popular opinions to give meaning to their lives. The values of the positive animus are eternal, and at various points in Chinese history they have been recognized and upheld by heroic men in chaotic times. For such men, "achievement" was not about pursuing fame or fortune

THE ANIMUS ARCHETYPE IN CHINESE CULTURE 103

to get to the top of one life incarnation, but about going down in history as a heroic figure, a *Jun Ji* (a knight or gentleman), or as a famous poem said:

> Everyone must die;
> Let me but leave a loyal heart shining in the pages of history[6]

Positive cultural animus—the sage: Kong Fuzi and Zhu Xi

The Spring and Autumn era in Chinese history (771–476 BCE) was a time of relative peace and prosperity in ancient China. Hundreds of schools of thought contended for attention like flowers blooming together. Among these many contenders, Kong Fuzi (Confucius, 551–479 BCE) and his school emphasizing benevolence and humanism emerged as the dominant philosophy underlying Chinese ethics. The development of the three cardinal guides and the five constant virtues in Confucianism concretized social behavior for generations and established a generally accepted system of ethics. There is no doubt that there were many remarkably wise philosophers during the time of Kong Fuzi, and yet he alone is held above all the others to be revered as a sage, an honor close to what more religious societies would term a saint. The recognition of Kong Fuzi as a sage was emphasized by an imperial decree issued by Han Wudi (156–187 BCE), the second emperor of the Han Dynasty.[7] We get a powerful impression of the way people projected the Chinese cultural animus onto Kong Fuzi, whatever his real qualities were in life. It is also highly possible that he lived in such a way that he was consciously close to the archetypal image of the Chinese cultural animus.

In ancient China, there were at various times many sages in different professions. Although these men reached the clarity of their sagely vision through various means, the essence of their enlightenment was the same. Through the heights they brought to their respective fields of endeavor, they contributed greatly to Chinese culture. There were famous sages of cursive writing, sages of wine making, sages of swordsmanship, and even sages of ceramics.

A comprehensive survey of Chinese history reveals that it was the political policy of all the major states to create educational systems that cultivated the emergence of professional sages, wise men who would render service to the nation. The sage was known as the treasure of the nation. The title of *sage* was not lightly given, however, and although many in the intelligentsia, men of both literary

104   XU JUN

and military capacity, strove for recognition in their professions, few were ever considered sages in their own time. The various dynasties spent considerable amounts of money to train scholars for imperial service. Year after year, these academies taught their students to strive for harmony between human beings and nature. The most famous of these places of learning was the Yuelu Academy established under the Song Dynasty (976 CE). During the Song period, Confucianism experienced a strong revival. "Confucian teachings became central to the civil service examination system, the identity of the scholar-official class, the family system, and political discourse."[8]

> Confucianism had naturally changed over the centuries since the time of its founding (ca. 500 BCE). The original teachings, recorded by his followers in the Analects, were still a central element, as were the texts that came to be called the Confucian classics, which included early poetry, historical records, moral and ritual injunctions, and a divination manual. But the issues stressed by Confucian teachers changed as Confucianism became closely associated with the state from about 100 BCE on, and as it had to face competition from Buddhism, from the second century CE onward. Confucian teachers responded to the challenge of Buddhist metaphysics by developing their own account of the natural and human world.[9]

Beginning in the late Tang Dynasty, Confucianism thrived in the Northern and Southern Song periods, continuing into the Yuan (1270–1368), Ming (1368–1644), and Qing (1644–1911) Dynasties. "The revived Confucianism of the Song period (often called *Neo-Confucianism*) emphasized self-cultivation as a path not only to self-fulfillment but also to the formation of a virtuous and harmonious society and state."[10] Teachers and scholar-officials revived Confucianism by giving the teachings new relevance and providing compelling examples of men who put service to the state above their personal interest.

Traditional Chinese education as taught in academies had three basic features: they operated as a place for giving lectures; they selected the classic books that comprised the cannon of educated learning; and they taught the proper performance of sacrificial ceremonies. The leader of an academy would be a scholar of some renown and would normally be independent from politics. But some sages influenced society way beyond academia. The Southern Song philosopher Zhu

THE ANIMUS ARCHETYPE IN CHINESE CULTURE 105

Xi (1130–1200) was one such sagely academic. During his lifetime, Song high society closely followed his wisdom. His ideas and thoughts also affected the government policies of his time. Renowned for synthesizing Neo-Confucian philosophy, Zhu wrote "commentaries to the Four Books of the Confucian tradition, which he extolled as central to the education of scholars. He was also active in the theory and practice of education and in the compiling of a practical manual of family ritual."[11] Educated by his father in the Confucian tradition, he held several government posts, although he preferred the life of a teacher and scholar. In addition to his commentaries on the *Lunyu* (Analects of Confucius), he also published commentaries on the works on Meniscus and a text on moral government titled *Daxue,* or *Great Learning.* Zhu Xi's commentary on the Doctrine of the Mean (Zhongyang) was central to its acceptance as one of the Four Confucian Classics that scholars hoping to pass civil service examinations were required to have studied.[12] His opinions kept him from achieving greater acclaim in his lifetime, however:

> His uncompromising attacks on corruption and political expediency each time brought his dismissal or his transfer to a new post conveniently distant from the capital. On the last of these occasions, near the end of his life, his enemies retaliated with virulent accusations concerning his views and conduct, and he was barred from political activity ... Zhu Xi's reputation was rehabilitated soon after his death ... culminating in the placement of his tablet in the Confucian Temple in 1241.

Zhu Xi is a classic example of the traditional Chinese cultural animus in action. From birth—or perhaps even before his birth—he was expected to become the *Zhuangyuan,* the very best student in the Chinese world.[13] The socially accepted idea that "a good scholar will make a good official" is also rooted in the cultural animus complex, and so Zhu Xi naturally becomes a government official. His exceptional intelligence gave him the ability to transform difficulties into positive developments and he created a civilizing influence wherever he went. He put aside worldly recognition to work on teachings that would last the ages. In the end, he was recognized by all as a great sage.

Negative cultural animus—the selfish smart fool

Some people pursue education because of the famous saying, "To be a scholar is to be the top of society. Learning is the noblest of human

106   XU JUN

pursuits." The negative aspect of the Chinese cultural animus only focuses on the first part of the saying, belittling the second part. The negative aspect of the cultural animus brings with it an overemphasis on the material realm. Successful men who have neglected the welfare of society have not been treated well by history. In ancient times, the best example might be Lü Buwei, a prime minister during the Qin Dynasty (221–207 BCE) during the Warring States period. Lü achieved amazing feats of political and military conquest—which he compiled in *Lu Shi Chun Qiu* (*The Springs and Autumns of Master Lü*), the most important historical literature of the Qin—by helping a weak prince to become the Qin emperor, contributing to the eventual unification of China under a centralized authority. His unmatched intelligence was rewarded with death by the emperor, however, and he is derisively remembered by the common people as the man who coined the phrase "keep goods back to raise the price." The original price gouger!

Another example would be Cao Cao, a warlord and the penultimate Chancellor of the Eastern Han Dynasty (25–220 CE) who rose to great power during its final years in ancient China. His poem "Vie with the Sea" shows off his linguistic brilliance. He was also a quick witted and decisive politician. Although he governed directly as prime minister and was in a position to order the emperor around behind the throne, he never actually usurped the emperor's position. Despite this, Chinese historiographers still call him "the thief who usurped the nation." His story is recorded in literature famously as "hold the emperor in hand and order the dukes about in his name."

In the realm of the negative animus, Yin energy is depressed. Thus when the negative aspects of the Chinese cultural animus are manifest, it affects the social system in ways that are harmful to the feminine. Paternalistic customs and attitudes develop. Kong Fuzi's thoughts on family order were later developed into a philosophic system by Zhu Xi that Chinese rulers made the sole orthodox creed until the end of the nineteenth century. However, these high achievements had a negative aspect. When neo-Confucianism treats order and harmony as the most valuable things for humanity, it goes against human welfare by making life too inflexible. It does, however, make it easier for those who have to execute the sovereign's rules. Over a long period of time, this way of thinking damaged the value of the Yin aspect of humanity; the feminine was reduced. Women were

THE ANIMUS ARCHETYPE IN CHINESE CULTURE   107

considered empty wombs to be made pregnant, valued only for the male children they might produce.

The negative cultural animus in the ming and qing dynasties (1368–1911)

Under the influence of the negative cultural animus, positive injunctions toward learning, such as the popular phrase, "Reading helps us learn so much about beauty and truth. Reading brings us wife and big house," are turned into negative commands that women have to sacrifice their own will and life so men have a chance to *du shu* (literally "read books") in order to achieve their "dream life." The principle of du shu as the best path for men implied that women were too stupid to do it. Reading (learning in general) was considered a man's provenance. Women had to do the hard work, to earn money, in order to support men to "read" since that was the best chance to improve the family's fate.

The well-known works of fiction produced in the late Ming Dynasty by Pu Songling (1640–1715) present many stories highlighting this aspect of Ming society. The book *The Strange Tales of Liao Zhai* is a classic work of Chinese literature and its collection of about five hundred stories continues to be endlessly retold in Chinese movies and television today. The tales of *Liao Zhai* center on human males who encounter female ghosts, female fox demons, or other supernatural female beings that are moved by the male's studiousness. The fox beauty or ghost beauty is attracted by the intelligence and diligence of the "hard-reading" scholar. The men get supernatural help from the cultural anima in the form of a supernatural feminine power and accomplish their life dream quickly. Those poor men who fail to return the love of their supernatural helper or betray her trust get punished and have a very bad life. Those who are true to the cultural anima despite the obstacles in the story get to live happily through an entire natural life span.

The wounded cultural animus—war, revolution, chaos

In the Taoist practice of Tai Chi, when energy achieves the highest level possible and reaches its extreme, it will undergo decay and then turn into its opposite—a revolution. This archetypal dynamic can be seen in historical trends, and it has powerfully affected the Chinese cultural animus. By the time of the late Qing Dynasty, the influence of paternalistic neo-Confucianism had peaked and began to decline significantly. The defeat of the imperial army in the Opium Wars with Britain led to a major loss of prestige for the government. Politically, the throne was taken over by the Dowager Empress Cici, who after an unsuccessful palace coup attempt, ordered the emperor poisoned and replaced with her nephew Puyi, who would become the last emperor of China.

After the disgrace of the Opium Wars, China was further humiliated by the invasion of the Eight-Country Alliance (八國聯軍) in 1900. The eight nations in the alliance were Italy, the United States, France, the Austro-Hungarian Empire, Japan, Germany, Russia, and England. The Alliance routed Chinese forces on the way to Beijing, following the Qing-inspired uprising called the Boxer Rebellion. Upon reaching Beijing in the summer of 1900, where the international legations of the alliance were being besieged by Boxer rebels (supported by the Qing government), coalition forces massacred the rebels and then looted and burned many of the wealthy households in their path. To the outside world, everything was reported as being done in the name of humanitarian intervention and to defend their citizens as well as a number of Chinese Christians who had taken shelter in the legations.

The incident ended with a coalition victory and the signing of the Boxer Protocol, which ceded territory and called for massive indemnity payments to be paid in silver. The defeat also signaled the end of imperial rule and the decline of neo-Confucianism. Years of war, revolution, and chaos were still in store for the suffering masses. The Chinese cultural animus retreated to its most negative aspects. Men did what they could to survive the Japanese invasion and the Chinese civil war that followed. With the establishment of a "new China" under the banner of the People's Republic in 1949, a semblance of stability seemed to have returned, but it was not to be. The lasting trauma of war and revolution had caused deep wounds to the cultural animus, but the worst was yet to come.

Beginning around 1966, political struggles within the Chinese Communist Party boiled over, and what began as an intra-party (meaning the interactivity inside a party, not with the enemy or opposition) fight over policy was whipped into a national "Great Proletarian Cultural Revolution." The fall of Marshal Peng Dehuai (Figure 4.5), a Communist military leader who was known as one of the Ten Great Marshals, was a signal of massive upheaval to follow. The campaign began as a call for the fall of government officials

Figure 4.5: Marshal Peng Dehuai disgraced in the Cultural Revolution.

Figure 4.6: Scholars beaten in public in Tiananmen Square.

deemed too tied to the old ways, but quickly morphed into a crazed drive to destroy all things related to "old knowledge." Soon it became clear that the scholar-official system itself was to be destroyed. The dictum of the Cultural Revolution was "Knowledge is useless." To the young "Red Guards," empowered and emboldened by the chaos, the more scholarly someone was, the more suspect they were. Formerly respected officials were beaten in public and told they were now the lowest class (Figure 4.6). Many professionals were "sent down" to the rural countryside to be reformed by doing hard labor. Often these untrained city dwellers were sent to remote border areas or to work on reforming wastelands (Figure 4.7).

Figure 4.7: City dwellers sent to the Great Northern Wilderness.

During the ten years of the Cultural Revolution, millions of lives were lost. Many famous scholars, artists, and cultural icons were persecuted. Among the many thousands who suffered, the writers Wu Han (1909–1969), Lao She (1899–1966), and Qian Zhongshu (1910–1998) were singled out for attack simply because their works were found to have unacceptable ideas. Meanwhile, the "gloriously uneducated" cadres with "pure proletarian" blood were appointed to positions as university presidents and education bureau directors. At its most extreme, the Cultural Revolution began to damage the power of the negative animus when the campaign took to disparaging specialized knowledge in any form. Universities were closed. Ancient wisdom and knowledge were treated as superstition and myths. Materialistic science became the fetish that would protect and guide people.

By 1979, the excesses of the Cultural Revolution had been widely recognized, and with Mao Zedong, the man who had launched the

THE ANIMUS ARCHETYPE IN CHINESE CULTURE

chaos, now dead, the Chinese government moved to repair the damage that had been done. Within a short period of time, the physical harm was repaired, and China launched itself into an extended period of economic growth and an opening of society. As the reform movement continued to grow, new ideas were allowed into China. In 2002, the first internationally recognized Jungian psychology doctoral program was launched at South China Normal University. Since then interest in Jung's ideas has grown rapidly, yet the number of people who could be helped by analytical psychology but lack access to it remains large. The following quote from C. G. Jung has guided me in my journey, and I hope the reader will also find meaning in his words, "But man's task is the exact opposite: to become conscious of the contents that press upwards from the unconscious."[14]

Part II: Today's situation

The animus strikes back—compensation through education

As political stability returned to Chinese society, the cultural focus on education as the means for advancement also returned with a vengeance. Beginning in the early 1980s, the whole of mainland China became caught up in the infamous Cram School Craze. Millions of families, driven by the fear of being left behind if they didn't, blindly pushed their children into afterschool study programs. Getting into a good school became the only thing a child should focus on. Happiness in life, the family's future, and even marriage prospects all depended on "hard studying" as a way of life. The mentality that one's very survival depended on studying harder than others became widespread among parents and children.

Hence, children could no longer be children; first, they were students. Parents lived by the mantra: "Pass the examinations and go to the best school." Family time, having fun, friends, every aspect of life was sacrificed to "get to the best school." As it became "normal" for children to not play or relax, psychological symptoms began to emerge.

When Deng Xiaoping introduced the "Opening Up and Reform Policy" in 1980, he also created the "One Child Policy." Almost four decades later, the policy was revised, but it is apparent how these two developments have proven to be huge blows to the Chinese cultural animus. On the one hand, economic reforms led to an attitude that more material possessions would bring happiness and security, and on the other hand social reforms brought in Western culture, which began to supplant and suppress the remnants of authentic Chinese culture that still remained after the decades of war and chaos had just ended. An increase in wealth also brought an increase in greed and grievance. Western culture, once forced on China and vigorously rejected, now returned in a more appealing form, and the new "reformed" China ate it up.

In the midst of this cultural onslaught, the imposition of the One Child Policy exacerbated the rise of the negative Chinese cultural animus. Forcing the Chinese of that time to have only one child meant that an overwhelming number of them wanted a male. The number of legal (and illegal) abortions of female fetuses rose significantly, signaling that the unintended consequences of China's population control policy had not been fully considered. As families adjusted to this new reality—that all of the hopes and dreams for their future were concentrated on the one and *only* child they would be allowed to have—that "one child" had to take on the burden of carrying the weight of the Chinese cultural animus. Without any way to access the power of the whole cultural animus, most people had an all-encompassing drive to achieve the highest educational level possible. "Get into a college" was the battle cry of the millions of parents who hovered over their children to make sure they were doing all their homework.

This simpleminded yet overwhelming urge by the parental masses continues to deform the Chinese education system. Institutionally, China has some of the longest class hours in the world, and the amount of homework given leads to endless nights and even weekends of school work. Parents and other adults unconsciously withhold love and affection from children who don't fit the mold. The universality and love of learning that derive from the positive Chinese cultural animus is mostly absent among Chinese students today. In my own experience growing up in a poor family, I could see that the only time my mother showed joy was when she witnessed her children studying hard and achieving academically. All of her emotional energy was focused on increasing our chances for higher education. Unfortunately, most of the students I met in college seemed to be fully entangled within the self-focused materialism and status consciousness that arose from the influence of the negative cultural animus. In my imagination, I can see the Chinese cultural animus split into pieces. The wounds are so profound that I wonder if the pieces will ever be reunited again. It is my sincere hope that depth psychology can help the Chinese people

THE ANIMUS ARCHETYPE IN CHINESE CULTURE 113

come to recognize the severity of harm that has been done to their collective psyche.

In 2016, when I was invited to host a research project at a private middle school in Nanjing, to show clearly how families influenced students' learning, I found that even among the relatively affluent group that I was interviewing, the power of the negative cultural animus held sway. In the group I studied (twelve- to fifteen-year-olds), the images that arose during our sessions revealed their inner reality. When asked to come up with images for *Home,* the most common and most often repeated among the children were

- Dark, cold, a room without light
- Sitting in front of a desk, mother watching me do homework
- Leaving home in a car to go to school or cram school

Very few children came up with more positive and traditional family images:

- Smoke rising from cooking in the kitchen
- Parents and children doing housework together
- Father coming home after work
- Family sitting together around the dinner table

I believe it is not an exaggeration that the power of the negative cultural animus to demand academic achievement is the single most dominant psychological force in mainland China today. Its influence on all aspects of what it is to be masculine obviously has a strong effect on men, and in my clinical cases, I've seen this develop in the following ways:

- Men are anxious about their economic success.
- Men are willing to take shortcuts even if these are immoral.
- Men have difficulty in intimate relationships and see marriage as an obligation.
- Men see "wife" as the mother of their children and otherwise as almost a stranger.
- Men face severe midlife crises when affairs usually happen.
- Men face decreasing sexual libido over time and an inability to see women as equals.
- Men experience difficulties in the father-child relationship.

And women are also affected. In my clinical experience working with women, the following are sources of inner conflicts:

114   XU JUN

- Women pursue higher educational degrees in competition with men.
- Women have increased desire for economic independence.
- Women show a preference for social engagement rather than family life.
- Women lack the desire to become a wife and mother.
- Women are more likely to initiate a divorce than previously.
- Women experience an increase in miscarriages and difficulty in conceiving.
- Women resent the perceived obligation to take on the role of wife and mother.
- Women use negative emotions as means of control in relationships.

We are in a difficult situation for the survival the positive cultural animus.

Love of the white snake—a case study

When men and women live unconsciously, it seems like events just happen to them without their conscious participation. Even when they pursue what they love, things never work out. When a woman lives under the sway of the negative cultural animus, she might sacrifice everything for the man she loves and fail to see why this is causing her own suffering. There is a famous Chinese story that illustrates this type of situation, the tale of "Madame White Snake."

In the legend, a powerful white snake had practiced self-cultivation for five hundred years and had achieved the ability to take on the appearance of a beautiful woman. She names herself *Bai Suzhen* (literally, in Chinese, "white plain paste") and begins living in the human world. Eventually, she falls in love with Xu Xian, a scholar studying for the imperial exams. She keeps her identity a secret, but with her healing powers, she opens a pharmacy to help ordinary people. Soon after Bai marries Xu Xian, she becomes pregnant. But before she can give birth to their son, a Monk intervenes and tricks Bai into revealing her true form. Shocked and fearing for his life, Xu Xian follows the monk and hides. In order to get her husband back, Bai enters a magical battle with the Monk, and weakened from her pregnancy, she is defeated and locked up under the tower of Jinshan Temple.

"Madame White Snake," also known as "The Legend of the White Snake," is a Chinese legend that has been presented in Chinese operas, films, and television series. The earliest attempt to fictionalize the story

THE ANIMUS ARCHETYPE IN CHINESE CULTURE 115

in printed form appears to be "The White Maiden Locked for Eternity in the Leifeng Pagoda" (白娘子永鎮雷峰塔) in Feng Menglong's *Stories to Caution the World* (警世通言), which was written during the Ming Dynasty (1368–1644). The story is now counted as one of China's Four Great Folktales.

From my perspective, the story reflects how Ming society legitimized the behavior of women who were willing to submit to the requirements of the negative cultural animus. They sacrificed themselves for the men in their lives. Bai Suzhen falling in love with Xu Xian can be seen as symbolic of her anima falling in love with the negative cultural animus. Xu is a symbol of the animus, and for him, she sacrifices her own identity.

I have selected one particular case study of a female patient to present in order to show how Chinese women still suffer from this age-old submission to the negative cultural animus and how they can recover with depth psychology. I will call the patient *Feng* (not her actual name). Feng is thirty-three and works as an illustrator. She came to analysis for two main reasons. First she needed help dealing with her five-year-old son who had been diagnosed with Asperger's syndrome. Second, she suffered from what the Chinese call "fish memory." She would forget what just happened minutes ago, enduring frequent memory lapses during her daily life. As part of my initial observation, I noted that she looked beautiful and well-kept in terms of her clothes and appearance. But I sensed that some of her living energy had been sealed off in another space. She was like a creature living in a glass bottle. Her way of speaking was quite direct, but without breath or intonation. There was little feeling in the words flowing from her mouth. She looked at me, but her eyes did not move at all. I could not say whether she was gazing at me or staring at me. When she walked, her body was stiff like a tree trunk. From head to toe, she looked like a beautiful woman, but she was a wooden beauty.

As we consulted on the issue of her son, I wondered if her son could relate to this wooden woman before me as a human mother. Meanwhile, I was curious at her lack of feeling about her son. Where was the anxious mother? Although I could see she had made efforts to establish a warm relationship with her son, it was not working. In my mind, I imagined the boy looking at his mother's unmoving eyeballs; I could hear the fearful screaming from the boy's psyche. I could sense a deep resistance in her.

Our work was slow and often we sat in silence. Because she did not share her interior world very much, we had little material to work with. Only my curiosity and my respect for the analytical space kept me from ending our work out of frustration. She chose to continue for her own reasons, and so we waited for the "magical moment."

Slowly she was able to share her feelings about her daily experiences and to answer sensitive questions that I asked her. Around this time, we experienced strong issues with transference and she tried to project her identity onto me as her doctor. Sometimes she would say, "How will you remember me? Will I become like a stone again if you forget me?" We weathered this tempestuous period as I sensed that soon the memory of a traumatic event would emerge from her deep unconscious. Would it be a suppressed memory of abuse? Or something to do with her own mother?

After our twentieth session, Feng began to recall some things from her girlhood. Negative feelings for her mother emerged. Memories of a fearful childhood where conflict and violence between her mother and father were very common. A main theme was that her mother demanded that she study hard and get into university. Although helpful, these revelations did not adequately relieve most of her symptoms.

When we began to explore her marriage, her story took an unexpected turn and became more complex. I was shocked that she had almost no memories about her married life. When I invited her to describe her son's father, she disassociated. For the next two weeks, she was physically ill and could not come to our usual sessions. In my experience it was unusual for her to get sick, but this time the illness persisted. The sore throat and other respiratory complications lasted for weeks. I knew this was a physical manifestation of repressed fear and anger that was clearly constellated around her husband. Was she in some sort of hellishly abusive marriage?

After she returned to our regular schedule, she reported a vivid dream. She rarely shared dreams so I considered it a precious contribution. This is the dream she related that day:

I am walking between a modern-looking university building and an ancient-style academy. The space is very narrow. It is so narrow I have to will my body to become as thin as a leaf to get past. I then enter a classroom. The teacher has not arrived yet and the students are waiting for a drawing or painting

THE ANIMUS ARCHETYPE IN CHINESE CULTURE 117

class. Suddenly, a loud noise can be heard from above the ceiling. At the same time a large hole silently appears in the middle of the floor. I immediately know there is a man hiding under the floor; he wants to rob me.

The vivid dream was a catalyst. Quickly she could see that she had been blinding herself to the truth about her husband. She came to recognize that she did this because on a very deep level she believed that doing so was the only way to keep the marriage going and that it was the "way of heaven" for women to be long suffering to enable men to do what they want.

The facts of her marriage are not uncommon in China. First, her husband didn't pay for any family expenses, even the son's kindergarten tuition. Second, he was not responsible for the boy's education and rarely played with him. Third, he did not do housework. Fourth, he was not only cold to but also verbally abused his parents-in-law. He would become suddenly violent, losing his temper, or be suddenly emotional. Her son was afraid of his father, literally shivering in fear when they stayed together. The boy tried not to be noticed by his father, but the father still used any excuse to punish the boy.

Feng was now confronted with the questions of why she married this man and how the marriage survived in this condition for nine years. Why was she so blinded? Finally, she confronted her husband about their marriage and what it meant to him. The man's answer was as direct as it was crude. He told Feng, "Sex. Regular sex." But what about their child? The man answered, "Leave those issues to the mother-in-law or some nanny."

This confrontation opened Feng's eyes for good. Though at that moment she felt abused and disgusted, she decided to file for divorce. When she told her son that she would separate from his father, the five-year-old boy was overjoyed. "Do you mean father will not beat me after the divorce? He will not stand behind me and suddenly beat me? That's wonderful!"

After this breakthrough, we were able to delve deeper into her past to assess the fundamental causes of her actions. What followed was difficult but revealing work that showed Feng how she had created the sad situation she was in. Suppressed in her memory were disappointments from not finding the man she had wanted, which led her to pursue the "next best" young man on her own initiative. She recalled that she was the one who encouraged them to live together before they were engaged. She had agreed he did not need to use his money for their living expenses after their marriage. She submitted to his demand for "regular sex" whether she desired it or not. And she slowly began to push her resentments and fears away so it would not disturb their "happy marriage."

Then she had another vivid dream:

I am in a wilderness next to a huge tree that seems to stretch between heaven and earth. Thunder crashes and a bolt of lightning tears across the sky and hits the tree. The tree is separated into two. A black python appears from inside the tree. I know that it is the python. The python slithers up a hill. At the top of the hill, it transform into a mermaid with a black tail.

In her associations to the dream, Feng connected the mermaid with being an artist. The word *artist* triggered something in her mind. The magic word *artist* answered Feng's question about why she had married this man. When her husband was a student in art school, he was thought to have the potential to be a great artist. Feng was attracted by the title of *artist*. And she was proud of him. After graduation, she took on everything to help him be a successful artist. After he achieved some success, he took it for granted that she wanted to continue to sacrifice herself for him. Since she "allowed" him to behave badly at home and to their son, that was just "normal." I could see that beyond the personal dynamics of this couple, larger cultural and archetypal forces were also at work, particularly with regard to the negative cultural animus.

It was her son's Asperger's diagnosis that had brought her into therapy. The energy from the mother archetype within her anima helped her remove the blinders that had unconsciously buried her individuality. Her actual mother, however, also played a role in putting these "blinders" on to begin with. Feng's mother nearly married an artist, but due to the Cultural Revolution, the romance ended. Fang's mother married a laborer for financial security, but was never satisfied with this choice. She devoted all her attention to her daughter, pushing her to be an artist. When Feng was a little girl, she got rewarded for drawing and punished if she didn't draw. Feng knew not only love from her mother but also rejection.

I hypothesized that her mother most loved the negative cultural animus image of her lost artist lover. With her mother "married" to

THE ANIMUS ARCHETYPE IN CHINESE CULTURE 119

that animus image, Feng, the poor little girl, lost her mother a long time ago. When she grew up, Feng knew she didn't want to be an artist, as she was not gifted in that way. Like her mother, however, her first choice for a husband eluded her, but in her case, the man she married, not the one she didn't, was the perfect carrier for the negative cultural animus. He was a gifted "scholar" who needed a chance to hone his skills. She had to make a "sacrifice" to help him find success. Even better, he was an artist, so she could marry her mother's unfulfilled fantasy.

Feng asked me, "Why do I fall for the title of 'artist' like a fatal attraction?"

I, silent for a period, then said, "Well, I have to tell you a story."

She asked, "Which one?"

I answered, "A date on the Broken Bridge. White Snake is attracted by Xu Xian's umbrella since the umbrella is the symbol of a scholar. You know this story by now. But this might be an opportunity for you to write your own story. I believe in 'Self'-help. And as Jung said, 'Man's task is to become conscious of the contents that press upward from the unconscious,' and of course, he meant women too."

I believe we must explore the unconscious with all our consciousness. For the Chinese, an invaluable path lies in accessing the positive cultural animus as illuminated by the images of Pangu and Huangdi. The positive is not in conflict with the negative aspect of the cultural animus; rather the negative is lacking and the positive is in wholeness and contains both the light and the dark and knows both the male and the female.

Make what is unconscious in yourself conscious. That is the spirit of the Chinese cultural animus!

Notes

[1] Pangu was the creator of the universe in Chinese mythology.

[2] Yan You, *Zhu Shen Ji* [The myth of Ancient China] (Beijing: Beijing University Publishing, 2017), pp. 14–17.

[3] Xu Zheng, Three Kingdoms Period (220–280 CE), Kingdom Wu. He is the author of *The 3 and 5 Calendar.* See Yan You, *Zhu Shen Ji.*

[4] Rudolf Ritsema and Shantena Augusto Sabbadini, *The Original I Ching Oracle: The Pure and Complete Texts with Concordance,* trans. The Eranos Foundation (London: Watkins Publishing, 2007), p. 171.

[5] *Ibid.,* p. 539.

[6] From *Passing by Lindingyang (Crossing the Lonely Ocean)* by Wen Tianxiang (1236–1283) who lived during the Song Dynasty. He wrote literature and was a political figure.

[7] Han Wudi was known as the Martial Emperor; his fifty-four-year reign is considered the most expansionist of the Han Dynasty.

[8] "The Song Confucian Revival," Asia for Educators, Retrieved Jan. 16, 2019, at http://afe.easia.columbia.edu/songdynasty-module/confucian-neo.html.

[9] *Ibid.*

[10] *Ibid.*

[11] *Ibid.*

[12] Philip Wolny, ed., *The 100 Most Influential Religious Leaders of All Time* (New York: Britannica Educational Publishing, 2017), pp. 107–108.

[13] Zhuangyuan, title conferred on the one who came first in the highest imperial examination.

[14] C. G. Jung, *Memories, Dreams, Reflections* (New York: Random House, 1973), p. 326.

Japan

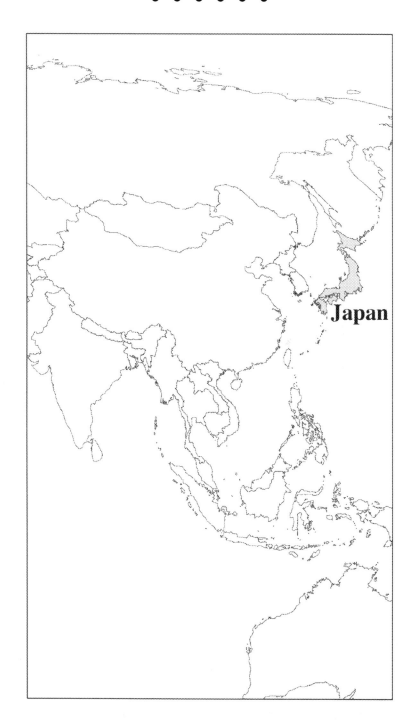

5

• • • • • •

Postmodern Consciousness
in the Novels of Haruki Murakami
An Emerging Cultural Complex

Toshio Kawai

Commentary and psychology

In this chapter I would like to approach the novels of Haruki Murakami.[1] Four of his most famous novels are *Norwegian Wood, The Wind-up Bird Chronicle, Sputnik Sweetheart,* and *Kafka on the Shore*.[2] These are stories with deep psychological and philosophical dimensions, and, at the same time, they have sold millions of copies. In this sense, they seem to reflect the collective in modern Japan and grasp its depth. In terms of cultural comparison and encounter it is also advantageous that the works have been translated into sixteen languages. Most of Murakami's works are available in English.

First I would like to discuss the methodological question regarding the psychological interpretation of novels. The first, and most common, method is to ask which aspects of psyche appear in the

---

Toshio Kawai, PhD, lives and works as a Jungian analyst in Japan. He is president of the International Association of Analytical Psychology. His interests include the cultural and historical background of psychotherapy, with a particular concern about how consciousness today is reflected in psychotherapy with the emergence of new symptoms such as dissociation, developmental disorders, and psychosomatic disorders. As a Jungian analyst Dr. Kawai works with images and has published not only case studies but also investigations of consciousness as reflected in literature.

novel and what kinds of personalities are shown. One of the favorite questions to consider is pathology. The Oedipus complex (*Kafka on the Shore*) or dissociation (many of Murakami's novels) is responsible for the development of events, or behaviors of the persons, in novels. Trauma theory might be summoned up to explain the behaviors of certain persons in stories. This way of seeing tends to reduce the world of a novel to the personal psychology of its hero, or other persons, and then to that of its author, who might have the same psychological problems. This seems to me to be too personal and narrow.

The second way is to see novels as the unfolding process of individuation—union with the anima, processes of initiation, and so on. Murakami's novel *Dance, Dance, Dance* might be interpreted as a process of union with the anima. In this way we might avoid entirely personalistic reduction. However, we still reduce the story to a psychological model and development. In this way the world of each novel is not grasped in its own right.

The third approach goes the other way round. Novels become models for psychology and psychotherapy. In the novels of Haruki Murakami, there are very interesting relationships among people. The hero of *The Wind-up Bird Chronicle* has lost his wife and made an acquaintance with a unique teenage girl named Mei Kasahara. Such a relationship might be understood as a model for the psychotherapeutic relationship.

My position is different from these three approaches that always see the novel and psychology as two separate entities. My understanding of psychology consists in commentaries, that is, the novel as such is psychology, if it is reflected upon, elucidated, and unfolded.[3] Actual psychotherapy or case studies are not enough to qualify as psychology or psychotherapy. Psychology is based on psychological thinking, viewing, and attitude. In this sense, psychology is a commentary. Whatever material psychology has to do with, it is psychology if the way of seeing the material is psychological. Jung's work on alchemy is a typical example of psychological thinking. So I would like to see Murakami's novels from and toward a psychological point of view.

Interpretation of contemporary novels is different from that of myths and fairytales, which are favorite themes in Jungian psychology. In this sense, we are not coping with an eternal "archetypal structure" but rather with historical consciousness, which I would like to call *postmodern consciousness*.

POSTMODERN CONSCIOUSNESS

125

Whenever an actual situation and consciousness are discussed, there is a tendency to try to resolve the actual situation and problem and to heal the actual consciousness. But as Jung said, "We do not cure it [the neurosis]—it cures us."[4] It is important to be immersed in the actual consciousness and to catch up with it. The problem lies not in the content of consciousness as such, but in the discrepancy between the collective consciousness or the soul of the times and our own individual consciousness.

Among the many interesting novels written by Haruki Murakami, I would like to concentrate mainly on *Sputnik Sweetheart* (2001) and refer to other novels in connection with specific points.[5] The reason for this choice is that the work shows the position of the author in a relatively cohesive way. *The Wind-up Bird Chronicle* is surely a quite important work but is extremely long and difficult to discuss in a limited space. *Kafka on the Shore* could also be good material, but was not chosen because at the time there was no English translation.

Sputnik Sweetheart

"In the spring of her twenty-second year, Sumire fell in love for the first time in her life. … The person she fell in love with happened to be seventeen years older than Sumire. And was married. And, I should add, was a woman. This is where it all began, and where it all wound up. *Almost.*"[6] The novel starts in this way. Sumire, who was a unique and somehow unrealistic girl, wanted to become a novelist. The woman she fell in love with was called "Miu." Originally Korean, but born and raised in Japan, Miu studied music in France. She worked as a kind of international agent for organizing concerts, importing wine, and so on.

The person who narrates this novel in the first person singular, identified only as K, a school teacher, was in love with Sumire. He met her by chance in a bookshop as both loved reading novels. She was irreplaceable for him. "Without even trying, we grew close. Like a pair of young lovers undressing in front of each other, Sumire and I exposed our hearts to each other."[7] They are, so to speak, soulmates. Because Sumire could not understand his sexual desire —as she told him clearly, she could not understand sexuality in general—he did not dare tell her of his feelings and dated two or three girlfriends. Most recently, his girlfriend was the mother of one of his pupils.

126 TOSHIO KAWAI

In comparing this situation with the lives of young people in Japan today, we might say that many live in the style of the narrator of this novel, but probably without noticing the dimension Sumire held for him. This is an indication that this novel not only reflects the collective in Japan superficially, but also grasps its depth, its unconscious dimension.

The word *Sputnik* was coined for the love for Miu when Miu called a literary movement *Sputnik* instead of *beatnik*. But this might be an important "Freudian slip" because *Sputnik* not only means "lonely journey," but also "traveling companion." Sumire met Miu at a wedding party and was asked to become a kind of secretary for her. In the moment that Miu touched her hair, Sumire fell in love, which was, for her, a totally new experience.

Sumire and Miu went to Europe on business and afterward took a vacation on a small Greek island. There, Sumire disappeared suddenly. Miu called K and he came to the island to help her look for Sumire. Miu explained that Sumire was in a panic one night and wanted to have sexual relations with her. Miu wanted to and tried to respond to her, but her body did not move at all. Sumire disappeared afterward without saying anything. K discovered a floppy disk, with two documents, in Sumire's suitcase. In one document her repeated dream was reported: "Sumire went up a long staircase to see her mother, who was about to leave this world."[8] The other document was about a strange experience that befell Miu fourteen years ago:

> She was accidentally caught in a Ferris wheel for a night while in a small Swiss town, and observed herself in her own apartment, through binoculars, from the gondola. The person, Miu herself, in her apartment had sexual relations with Ferdinando, a Latin type man, about fifty years old, whom she had met in the town. It was dirty and obscene. Miu lost consciousness. After this one night, Miu became white-haired and stopped playing the piano. She married her husband with the promise of having no sexual relations.

In spite of an intensive search, Sumire was not found. K came back to Japan. On one Sunday, after summer vacation, K had to go to a supermarket because the pupil, whose mother was his lover, was caught shoplifting. K told his pupil what he had experienced in Greece and decided to leave his lover. K caught a glimpse of Miu once again. She was driving her Jaguar beside his taxi. She was white-haired and

POSTMODERN CONSCIOUSNESS 127

passed by without noticing him. At the end of the novel there was a phone call from Sumire, which seemed to be like a vision.

Dissociation and sense of lack

In this novel the narrator, called only K, loved Sumire who liked him, too, but was not sexually interested in him. Sumire loved Miu who could not have any sexual relationship or respond to her. K had a lover with whom he could not feel a deep connection. "For whatever reason, that unconditional, natural intimacy Sumire and I had just wasn't there. A thin transparent veil always came between us."[9] Everyone was like a Sputnik going around and passing by. At the end of the novel Sumire disappeared, a motif that can be seen in many of Murakami's stories.

These difficulties should not only be understood in terms of problems in human relationships. A discrepancy in one's own attitude and personality is also rather noticeable. To take the narrator K as an example, he had an unrealizable love for Sumire and a sexual relationship with another woman, although without love. He had a deep soulful relationship with Sumire, but no bodily relationship with her. He had sexual contact with his lover, but no soulful relationship with her. In this sense we can speak about a dissociation that is situated in one's own personality and requires a feeling of internal unity first; something is missing.

Miu said, "What happened in Switzerland fourteen years ago may well have been something I created myself."[10] This statement implies that what happened to her was not a pure accident, but rather a creation, a neurotic dissociation.[11] The dissociation of Miu was reflected on Sumire and K. Sumire said, "I am in love with Miu. With the Miu on this side... . But I also love the Miu on the other side just as much. The moment this thought struck me it was like I could hear ... myself splitting in two."[12]

From the expression "on the other side" we can hear a nuance which is different from that of a personal dissociation. Sumire's second document said that Miu lived as a mere shadow of her true self; her body was on the other side. After Sumire had suddenly disappeared in the Greek Islands, K concluded that "Sumire went over to the other side." The dissociation is not about human relationship, not about personal splitting, but the dissociation of the world, "the loss of great relationship" (*Verlust des großen Zusammenhangs*).[13]

128   TOSHIO KAWAI

There is no connection between this world and the other world. The dissociation of the world into two sides is a theme that can be seen in many of Murakami's novels. In the novel *Dance, Dance, Dance,* there is another world on the other side of the wall or in the other hotel.[14] *In Hard-Boiled Wonderland and the End of the World* and *Kafka on the Shore* two different parallel stories go on; in one chapter one story, in the next chapter the other one.[15] The other world has the clear implication of a mythological world, the world of Gods and of the dead. The connection to and dissociation from the other side is an important theme in Murakami's novels. As Sumire, the narrator's soulmate, had gone over to the other side, it symbolizes that something essential is lacking.

Sumire said, "Maybe I'm lacking something. Something you absolutely must have to be a novelist."[16] Miu said, almost in the same words, "I understood that something was missing from me. Something absolutely critical, though I did not know what. The kind of depth of emotion a person needs to make music that will inspire others."[17] These words do not mean that they have a dissociated, depersonalized, and pathological personality. They refer to a fundamental understanding of modern being and consciousness as it is shown in Murakami's novel. Something essential is lacking and is probably on the other side. Because of the missing essential, this side is not complete; literature, music, and love are not true. And reality, as such, is not complete. This is the central understanding shown in our novel for the present world and, especially, for present-day Japan. One can think of this as the cultural complex that Murakami is exploring.

Mythological world, modern consciousness,
and postmodern consciousness

In *Sputnik Sweetheart* the connection to the other side is sought. In the mythological world there was great connection. The other side was the world of the Gods and the dead and had its own reality. People could be related with the other world by way of rituals and symbols and were embraced by the mythological world. The shaman could even have direct access to the other world.[18]

In this novel K told a story in replying to Sumire, who was in search of "something for a true novelist." He explained how the ancient Chinese built a gate. At the entrance of the city they'd construct a huge gate and seal in bones that had been gathered in old battlefields. "When the gate was finished they'd bring several dogs

POSTMODERN CONSCIOUSNESS 129

over to it, slit their throats, and sprinkle their blood on the gate. Only by mixing fresh blood with the dried-out bones would the ancient souls of the dead magically revive."[19] He added, "Writing novels is much the same … a story is not something of this world. A real story requires a kind of magical baptism to link the world on this side with the world on the other side."

Owing to sacrifices, Gods and novels can appear with full reality. It is not a mere idea or belief. Through sacrifices things become ensouled; novels become real. Connecting to the other world makes things in this world real and complete first. This moment is real because it has the mythological world in the background. Persons are united to their dead ancestors. The emperor is real, a real ruler, if he is truly rooted in mythology and the Gods.

We can observe many motifs and images of the mythological world, and those of initiation, in the novels of Haruki Murakami. There are many motifs, such as "the other side of the wall," "being in the well," "the killing of animals," and "the skinning of living persons." In his early novel *Pinball in 1973* there is the funeral of a switchboard.[20] The funeral is necessary because each thing has its own soul. It is also important to mention that the other world does not exist objectively. An act is needed to open up and to be linked with the other world. The ritual for the construction of a gate in ancient China is a good example. As is also the case in this example, the blood very often plays a definitive role. In *Kafka on the Shore* the other world opens up through the blood of menstruation and the drawing of blood.

But these novels are not advocating a return to the mythological world. They allude, rather, to the sense that the mythological world is already over; they describe it as something already gone. In the novel *A Wild Sheep Chase* a special sheep with the sign of a star was sought. It might be regarded as a totem or guardian spirit.[21] But the sheep was not found and was totally lost. In our novel, Miu could not reach her other half on the other side. Sumire went over to the other side and did not return. The mythological world is always described as something lost.

The loss of the mythological world does not mean that this world has become only rational and boring. Because rituals and sacrifices, which are full of violent images, do not link us with the other world, naked violence without meaning appears. Some call the characteristic of Murakami's novels "detachment." But we can notice violence as

130   TOSHIO KAWAI

well. I have already mentioned the Chinese ritual in the novel *Sputnik Sweetheart*. In the long novel *The Wind-up Bird Chronicle* a living Japanese soldier was skinned until he died.[22] A slaughter in a Chinese zoo was reported. The outburst of violence has to do with the loss of the mythological world. The violence is not connected to the mythological world. It does not lead to it. The dissociation can also be noticed in this regard. The role of sexuality in Murakami's novel is similar to the role of violence. It appears almost as the last attempt at being real and being linked to the other world, although in vain.

In some of Haruki Murakami's novels we might get the impression that the other side could be rediscovered and reunited. But most of Murakami's novels suggest that the mythological way of being is over for the present world. If the mythological way were still possible, we could look for and find a suitable image, symbol, ritual, and story for ourselves. This might be the path C. G. Jung hoped we would take. But such symbols, and such a logical status, no longer have any reality.

In Murakami's novels, experiences of fantasies and dreams are very frequent. Mysterious happenings are also often reported. Stories are open to coincidences. What happens in dreams and visions seems to correspond to and to influence reality. "Dreaming on and on" is stressed.[23] We might conclude that we can reach the other side by way of dreaming. But, at the same time "the reality is different." "But it [the dream] doesn't last forever. Wakefulness always comes to take me back."[24] The novel suggests that our consciousness is already awake, there is no way back to the mythological world.

As the movement of the Enlightenment clearly showed, the consciousness that has awakened from the mythological world is modern consciousness. It denies the other world and fantasy. It believes only in the rational world. Is the awakened consciousness in Murakami's novel modern consciousness? In my understanding, the consciousness depicted in Murakami's novels is different from modern consciousness. Modern consciousness is characterized by the liberation of the individual from the embrace of nature, myth, and community. This liberation leads often to conflicts. A typical example is the conflict with community and family, which was originally protective, but became a burden and restriction for the independent individual. The family is a favorite battlefield for establishing modern consciousness. In this novel, however, the family does not play an

POSTMODERN CONSCIOUSNESS   *131*

important role. Sumire's mother had died when she was very young. Her father is a noble and polite but distant person. Neither Sumire nor K have conflicts or resentments against their families. Such conflicts are typical for the neurotic and hence modern consciousness. K said, "My family isn't anything special. So blandly normal, in fact, I don't know where to begin."[25] It is typical for Murakami's novels that family members are not described clearly.

In the battle against the restrictions of community, romantic love and sexuality have a symbolic meaning for modern consciousness and stand at the center of many novels. There are themes of the transgression of taboos, the restriction of individual desire within the collective value system, and secret love. But such themes are no longer an issue in Murakami's novels.

Conflict with the community leads to an internal conflict between desire and ethics within an individual, among psychic agencies. This might be an indispensable condition for psychoanalysis. Realness could be felt because of the restriction and taboo, as Lacan's theory ascertains. Or we might say that modern consciousness could be connected with the other world by way of conflict, by way of concrete negation. By denying myths, modern consciousness was still linked to the mythological world. By fighting against family and community, modern consciousness was still caught in them.

The consciousness in Murakami's novels is different from modern consciousness. K described his experience on a trip while he was still student. He met a young woman who was also traveling alone and she asked him to share a hotel room. They had a night together. She said she was getting married in two months with a man from work. "He's a very nice guy." There was no conflict—which person she loved more, rebellion against the marriage as a restriction, no guilty feeling, or so on. It is interesting that K mentioned Natsume Soseki's famous novel *Sanshiro* in comparison.[26] In the beginning of this novel Sanshiro shared a hotel room with a woman who was obviously seductive. But he did not have a sexual relationship with her. This is probably typical for the modern consciousness that has come into being in Japan after the encounter with Western culture in the Meiji era. In the case of the mythological world, it is self-evident that a man and woman fall in love immediately when they meet. In a village, a girl could have a one-night sexual experience with a visiting stranger who was regarded as a god. In modern consciousness there is an ethical conflict: one should have only one partner; there should be a continuity of personality, and so on. A direct encounter becomes impossible; the restriction enforces the ethical ideal. In this context I would like to mention that Soseki Natsume's novels describe the difficult path of establishing modern consciousness in modern Japan. He went to study in London, where he experienced a clash of two cultures and felt feelings of inferiority. He was suffering from anthropophobia, a typical Japanese symptom that shows alienation, and liberation, from the embracing community. In his novels, the theme of mysterious but unreachable women is often noticeable; this indicates that an immediate encounter and union has become impossible.

To illustrate the difference from modern consciousness, I will call the consciousness in Murakami's novels *postmodern consciousness.* There is no battle, no conflict, anymore. Nature, Gods, and community have neither protecting nor restricting power any more. Anything is possible, anything goes. It is arbitrary. Sumire loves a person who is seventeen years older—age does not count. A Korean—the country borders mean nothing. Married—social restriction is not valid. And a woman—heterosexuality, biology, is not self-evident. Because everything is possible, there is no moment of crossing a border, encountering other or otherness. In this sense there is no union with spirit, god, or other worldly beings any longer. Everyone, everything, can be united, but is, in truth, dissociated. A total affirmation leads, paradoxically, to a total negation. Immediate union on the surface is, in truth, a total dissociation.

The mythological world had, as the example of the Chinese gate shows, both vital reality and meaning. But these aspects are dissociated in postmodern consciousness. So there is a meaningful but sexless relationship on one side and a meaningless sexual relationship on the other side. This dissociation might be reflected in modern Japanese society where teenaged prostitutes and couples in sexless relationships are often reported.

According to Murakami's novels it is typical for postmodern consciousness in Japan that there is still a sense of lack and longing for that which is lost. Seen superficially, people live in a world where anything is possible and nothing is important. But in the depths, people can still feel the mythological world as missing and lost. The Japanese soul is still between postmodern consciousness and the lost mythological world. This dissociation is possible

POSTMODERN CONSCIOUSNESS

because modern consciousness, in the Western sense, has never been established in Japan. Without destroying the mythological world totally, and without establishing modern consciousness in the fullest sense, the Japanese soul has gone over to postmodern consciousness. Murakami's novels probably have such great success in Japan because they reflect, so exactly, the state of the Japanese soul today. In many ways, Murakami's novels and the postmodern consciousness of his characters reflect the emergence of a cultural complex in the Japanese collective psyche.

Union with dissociation

We have seen a dissociation that is central to postmodern consciousness in Japan. To put it more accurately, there is dissociation between the mythological world and postmodern consciousness in Japan today. The question that now arises is whether this dissociation can be overcome and united again? In the novel *Dance, Dance, Dance* the hero went over to the other side of the wall and then came back. He was united with a young woman in a hotel. The hero, who lived in a state of loss and detachment, seemed to grasp the realness again. But in many of Murakami's novels the moment of loss is stressed. In the novel *Sputnik Sweetheart*, Sumire was definitely lost. Is such a loss to be understood as failure?

It is probably a misunderstanding to try to overcome the dissociation and find literal union again. As Jung says, we should not try to overcome the dissociation, but to be taught by it.[27] The narrator K, and also Miu, had lived in compromise with the dissociation. K did not dare to declare his love to Sumire and to ask her for a sexual relationship. He was resigned from the beginning. In the case of Miu, her husband was sympathetic, had a great respect for her world, and did not request a sexual relationship. In this way, the dissociation remained. They were making compromises. But Sumire could not put up with compromises. She did not respect the dissociation, but tried to overcome it. Indeed, this commitment led to a dialectic movement.

In her dream, her mother appeared. Might we suspect that her lack of realness derived from the absence of her mother, from her mother-child relationship? A mother might be an origin for sureness and realness. Birth and death is the border to the other side. But Sumire lost her mother when she tried to approach her in her dream.

This is, however, not a question of her personal problem and life history. The realness is already lost for everyone in the present time.

134 TOSHIO KAWAI

Miu said, "Just a single mirror separates us from the other side. But I can never cross the boundary of that single pane of glass. Never."[28] It is not only Miu's personal problem. Everyone is now alienated by a pane of glass like the one experienced by Miu. Everything is virtual and encapsulated in the present world. Even the teenager prostituting herself is not a significant real experience because it costs a certain amount of money for one encounter and the act is encapsulated in an economic system. However we might try to obtain the realness (again), it only leads to a burial of the realness and a sending of the realness to the other side. It is paradoxical because we lose the raw realness by looking for it.

This was also the case for Sumire and Miu. Sumire tried to reach Miu, the Miu on the other side. In one of the discovered documents she wrote about the sacrifice. "Did you ever see anyone shot by a gun without bleeding?" "Blood must be shed. I'll sharpen my knife, ready to slit a dog's throat somewhere."[29] She looked for the realness, tried to be on the other side, and to be united with Miu on that other side.

In this way she clearly realized that she could not have an immediate, sexual relationship with Miu and so lost her. But there was no considered deception and refraining from recognizing and communicating feelings as with K toward Sumire or that of Miu's husband toward Miu. Sumire could not solve the dissociation literally, could not be united with Miu concretely, but did overcome it by being united with the dissociation itself. The dissociation was solved, not on the immediate literal level, but on the *sublated* level. I would like to analyze this in more detail.

Sumire wrote, "What I have written here is a message to myself. I toss it into the air like a boomerang."[30] She could not discover a sacrificial animal, like a dog for the ancient Chinese gate. She knew that she herself was meant as sacrifice, which is, in fact, the real meaning of sacrifice, because the one who sacrifices is also the one who is sacrificed. The sacrifice returned to herself, and she was sacrificed. That was neither why the dog, as object, was sacrificed nor Miu, as object, disappeared. She herself disappeared. She incarnated the dissociation herself. The question was not the loss of the object, as is often the case in psychoanalytic theories, but the disappearance of ego. This was an important moment in the development of postmodern consciousness.

Postmodern Consciousness

135

What Sumire had killed was herself. Because she had sacrificed herself, her ego, and disappeared, she could write two documents. Sumire who wanted to become a novelist and was not capable of it could finally write documents with true authenticity and meaning. Now she had the "something" that she needed. But this was not an acquisition of the ego, because the ego was gone.

If I follow the development of Sumire again, she had first a phase where she did not know her own other, did not know sexual desire. She could write novels, but was aware that something was lacking in her. She wrote novels without being satisfied by them. In the next phase she loved Miu and could not write anything. She said, "I don't have any confidence anymore in the act of writing itself." She was united with her own other without being aware of it. Or, she fell into a delusion of being united, of the immediacy. In the last phase it became clear for her that she could not be united with her own other by attempting to come closer to Miu. Through this trial and commitment, she made herself the sacrifice and was able to write. This was the unity with dissociation, or unity of unity and dissociation.

What Sumire had written was, so to say, a novel in a novel. This is the essence of this novel. Sumire is both author and heroine of the story. And the author and the heroine had disappeared. The two things that were left, the two documents written by Sumire, are real. In this sense there is no immediate reality anymore. But in this way, reality in postmodern consciousness was shown. It is neither the realness of the mythological world where gods appear proximately, nor the realness of modern consciousness in which the ego feels and achieves. The realness in postmodern consciousness is mediated, *sublated,* and without ego.

Afterward, Miu no longer dyed her hair. K said farewell to his girlfriend after the shoplifting incident with her son. "I'd only done what was necessary for me."[31] Miu and K did not come closer. Both felt something very close to romantic love, but they did not meet again. Everything should have been possible. But they clung to the dissociation. There is no natural, raw realness. The negation is prevailing.

If negation and dissociation are dominant, how can people be connected? In this novel, phone calls and letters are important. In Murakami's other novels, the computer plays an important role. It is not the problem of media to be understood. The point is that there is no directness. Even Miu saw herself through binoculars. But there is a

136   TOSHIO KAWAI

connection. Sumire could write documents because she was connected with the other side. It did not mean a direct relationship with Miu.

There is also connection by way of dream and vision. Like in a vision or a dream, K received a call from Sumire who said, "I really need you. You're a part of me; I'm part of you."[32] Dissociation was overcome; there was a real *conjunctio*. Despite these words, K returned to everyday reality. But these words, this recognition is real. He stared at his hands. "No scent of blood, no stiffness. The blood must have already, in its own silent way, seeped inside."[33] This seems to suggest that we do not need any immediate sacrifice and reality anymore.

His pupil, called Carrot, seemed to understand his words. There was a real encounter between them. Sputnik is a lonely metal piece in the cosmos. Each piece passes by the other without encounter. But, as the meaning of Sputnik suggests, it is a traveling companion. There is no encounter, neither in the mythological way of being as there is no God or other world anymore, nor in the modern way of life where the encounter happens between social ethics and personal desire. But we are encountering each other in an ongoing way, without producing any fixed point, neither in this world nor on the other side.

This novel shows a convincing vision of postmodern consciousness in Japan. But there is still a slight doubt that it may be attempting to stick to the old world in a very tricky way. It offers neither a nostalgic nor utopist concrete image of the lost essential. But it still preserves a topos and structure for the lost mythological world, though without presenting any concrete image or object. I would like to wait for the further development of Murakami's novels and then address this problem on another occasion.

Notes

[1] This chapter originally appeared in Thomas Singer and Samuel L. Kimbles, eds., *The Cultural Complex: Contemporary Jungian Perspectives on Psyche and Society* (Hove, East Sussex: Routledge, 2004).

[2] Haruki Murakami, *The Wind-up Bird Chronicle* (New York: Vintage International, 1997); *Norwegian Wood* (New York: Vintage International, 2000); *Sputnik Sweetheart* (New York: Vintage International, 2001); *Kafka on the Shore (Umibe no Kafka)* (Tokyo:

POSTMODERN CONSCIOUSNESS

137

Shincho-sha, 2002). *Kafka on the Shore* was published in English by Vintage International in 2006.

[3] Wolfgang Giegerich, *Der Jungsche Begriff der Neurose* (Frankfurt a.M.: Peter Lang, 1999), p. 36f.

[4] C. G. Jung, "The State of Psychotherapy Today" (1934), in *The Collected Works of C. G. Jung,* Vol. 10, ed. and trans. Gerhard Adler and R. F. C. Hull (New York: Pantheon Books, 1964), pp. 157–173, § 361.

[5] Murakami, *Sputnik Sweetheart.*

[6] *Ibid.,* p. 3.

[7] *Ibid.,* p. 177.

[8] *Ibid.,* p. 138.

[9] *Ibid.,* p. 78.

[10] *Ibid.,* p. 160.

[11] Giegerich, *Der Jungsche Begriff der Neurose,* p. 41f.

[12] Murakami, *Sputnik Sweetheart,* p. 161.

[13] Jung, CW 10, § 367.

[14] Haruki Murakami, *Dance, Dance, Dance* (New York: Vintage International, 1993).

[15] Haruki Murakami, *Hard-boiled Wonderland and the End of the World* (New York: Vintage International, 1993); *Kafka on the Shore.*

[16] Murakami, *Sputnik Sweetheart,* p. 15.

[17] *Ibid.,* p. 158.

[18] Heino Gehrts, "Initiation," *Gorgo,* 8 (4, 1985): 1-62.

[19] Murakami, *Sputnik Sweetheart,* p. 16.

[20] Haruki Murakami, *Pinball in 1973 (1973 nen no Pinball)* (Tokyo: Kodan-sha, 1983).

[21] Haruki Murakami, *A Wild Sheep Chase* (New York: Vintage International, 2002).

[22] Murakami, *The Wind-up Bird Chronicle.*

[23] Murakami, *Sputnik Sweetheart,* p. 136.

[24] *Ibid.,* p. 207.

[25] *Ibid.,* p. 55.

[26] Soseki Natsume, *Sanshiro* (Lansing, MI: University of Michigan Center, 2002). *Sanshiro* was also published by Penguin Classics in 2010.

[27] Jung, CW 10, § 361.

[28] Murakami, *Sputnik Sweetheart,* p. 157.

[29] *Ibid.*, p. 141.
[30] *Ibid.*, p. 141.
[31] *Ibid.*, p. 201.
[32] *Ibid.*, p. 209.
[33] *Ibid.*, p. 210.

6

• • • • • •

Japanese Landscape and the Subject
On the Old and New States of Consciousness

Yasuhiro Tanaka

A history of landscapes and of landscape painting reflects a particular mode of consciousness in a certain ethnic group or culture. For instance, the establishment of modern consciousness in Western Europe is closely related to the birth of the viewpoint that made it possible to draw landscape paintings. Depth psychology furthered the development of this modern consciousness—a consciousness that is also an essential premise of depth psychology.

On the other hand, in the East, there was a quite different tradition of drawing landscapes, the so-called Chinese-style landscape painting (山水画) that dates from the fourth century. Following in this tradition, the Japanese arranged Chinese-style landscape painting in a manner that is well expressed by the phrase "Japanese spirit imbued with Chinese learning" (和魂漢才), thus creating the Japanese landscape. First, after discussing the modern period in Western Europe, I will introduce the Chinese-style landscape paintings by Sesshu (雪舟; 1420–1506) in the Muromachi period (1336–1573),

---

Yasuhiro Tanaka, Prof. PhD, works for the chair of clinical psychology, Graduate School of Education, Kyoto University, and has a private practice in Tokyo. He did his training at the C. G. Jung Institute of Zürich. He is also an honorary secretary and senior analyst of the Association of Jungian Analysts, Japan.

140 YASUHIRO TANAKA

as one of the highest expressions. Then, I will discuss the general features of Japanese landscapes and how the human subject appears in them, specifically in relation to the consciousness of Autism Spectrum Disorder (ASD), which is considered to be a caricature of contemporary consciousness in Japan. This exploration will reveal "the subject *of* Japanese landscape," rather than the "Japanese landscape *and* the subject," as in the title for this chapter.

The peculiarity of the "modern" period in Western Europe

Depth psychology, on which modern psychotherapy is grounded, was established in the "modern" period, which was a special time in Western Europe. In previous eras, people and their communities were completely surrounded by Gods and Goddesses or Nature—the sun, moon, and stars; weather phenomena (rain, lightening, and thunder); and animals, plants, trees, and stones—all of which represented divine images. People expressed feelings of awe toward these objects, which deeply penetrated their lives as a whole.

To describe the presence of humans in this pre-modern world, Wolfgang Giegerich extracted the concept of "absolute in-ness."[1] This state is well symbolized by Oceanus in Greek mythology or the Midgard Serpent in Germanic mythology. This is a world in which human existence is experienced as being completely surrounded and embedded in a mythological world.

However, beginning with the modern period in the mid-nineteenth century, questions such as the "loss of meaning," "exploration of meaning," and "meaning of life" began to be discussed in the academic fields of philosophy, religious studies, and psychology. This is in stark contrast to how the world was experienced before the modern period, when an animistic state of mind filled the world with "meaning" from the beginning—that is *meaning* was already preexistent, even if nobody dared to look for it. In this context, the modern period in Western Europe was a time when people started to abandon this mode of being; in other words, it was the time when human beings tried to *truly* be born out of the "absolute in-ness." This may be the reason why the modern age required depth psychology and the psychotherapy practices that grew out of it.

Jürgen Habermas, the German philosopher, presented the concept "*Moderne*" in his article "Modernity: An Unfinished Project."[2] The origin of the word *modern* comes from the Latin word *modernus*,

JAPANESE LANDSCAPE AND THE SUBJECT

141

which is cognate with *modo,* meaning "just now." Essentially, the word *modern* does not denote a specific time, but "the expression 'modernity' repeatedly articulates the consciousness of an era that refers back to the past of classical antiquity precisely in order to comprehend itself as the result of a transition from the **old** to the **new**."[3] However, after going through the French Enlightenment,

> in the course of the nineteenth century (in which this Romanticism ceased to idealize a specific age) *this* Romanticism produced a radicalized consciousness of modernity that detached itself from all previous historical connection.[4]

After that, what remained was solely the "abstract opposition to tradition and history as a whole."[5]

In this sense, modern consciousness had to contain "this forward orientation, this anticipation of an indefinite and contingent future, the cult for the New" and thereby be characterized by unremitting "self-negating movement."[6] Such modern consciousness, which was established in the middle of the nineteenth century by detachment from history as a whole and by acquisition of its own abstractness, was a totally *new* consciousness.

Subject and landscapes in modern Western Europe

Augustin Berque, a French cultural geographer, stated, "The modern period is an extremely peculiar one in the history of Western Europe. This is especially obvious in the conception of landscape."[7]

The concept of landscape first emerged in Western Europe only in the sixteenth century. Until then, the landscape had merely been a background belonging to figures in stories. There was no word for *landscape* in ancient Greek and Latin. The closest word was *prospectus,* implying "perspective" or "view." According to Berque, the appearance of the conception of landscape was closely connected to the emergence of the modern subject—that is, the subject separating itself from its environment and taking a distance from it.

As Erwin Panofsky described in his book *Perspective as Symbolic Form,* the establishment of linear perspective in Western Europe was an essential condition for that of a subject equipped with modern individuality by creating its homogeneous and endlessly isotropic space.[8] On the other hand, as Berque described, "*modern men have believed that they were able to comprehend the reality as it was, i.e.,*

142 YASUHIRO TANAKA

objectively," with the techniques of linear perspective to represent a "rational and mathematical space."[9]

It is certain that there was such a "misconception," but it is an undeniable fact that "The arrival of modern times manifested itself as the first distance setting," and thereby, "the subject became able to objectify its environment."[10]

> However, the subject was still unable to take a distance from itself at that time. That is to say, it was unable to objectify itself. . . . *This second distance setting has first become possible only four centuries after the first one was embarked upon.*[11]

This second distance setting became possible through the psychoanalytic discovery of the existence of nonsubjective parts in the psyche—that is, objects within a subject, which means that there are "others within self (= the unconscious)." In this way, the Western European subject attempted to be born out from its own environment, as it were, in a two-stage process like the launching of a two-stage rocket. However, was the Western European subject really able to be born out from its own environment by "the second distance setting" proposed by Berque, that is to say, by the establishment of depth psychology including psychoanalysis?

"Unborn-ness" included in depth psychology

This attempt "to be born out from the environment" was accomplished *neither* by Sigmund Freud *nor* by Carl Gustav Jung, who were considered to be the great men in the depth psychology movement, beginning at the end of the nineteenth century. As a matter of course, this attempt could not be accomplished in either the psychoanalysis they inaugurated or in analytical psychology.

> Since the stars have fallen from heaven and our highest symbols have paled, a secret life holds sway in the unconscious. That is why we have a psychology today, and why we speak of the unconscious.[12]

This quote by Jung clearly indicates how his depth psychology, namely, "the psychology of the unconscious," was structured, under what kind of worldview and for which purpose. First, the *unconscious* in Jungian psychology is the internalized "another world" or "hereafter"—the Land of Gods above, in the mythological world lost in modern times. Second, after "our highest symbols have paled," the life of human

Japanese Landscape and the Subject
143

beings came to be hopelessly monotonous and dry, and then, re-infusing "a secret life" into life became a mission imposed on "the psychology of the unconscious."

Jung attempted to maintain the same attitude toward "the unconscious" or "dream" with which people looked up to "stars" and "gods" in olden days. Seen from another viewpoint, we could say that Jung needed "the unconscious" to maintain such a position. Depth psychology attempted to be modern, but it required an "internal space," that is, "the unconscious," in order to maintain a premodern mythological worldview.

In this sense, "the unconscious" was never "discovered," but rather it was "invented." Jung noted, "By becoming conscious, the individual is threatened more and more with isolation."[13] He knew well that modern men and women lived alone with themselves, "where, in the cold light of consciousness, the blank barrenness of the world reaches to the very stars."[14] Therefore, the project of "depth psychology" inaugurated by Freud and Jung and the concept of "the unconscious" that was "invented" by them enabled the following: Human beings expelled from the mythological world in which they were once embedded sought "the meaning" of mental disease or symptoms internally. This allowed the modern psyche to deny and to avoid "isolation" and "loneliness" as the outcome of the new consciousness that separated subject and object. Moreover, they were able to deny and to avoid the "emptiness" and "barrenness" that the new consciousness brought to the world. In a sense they were able to enjoy a nostalgia for their previous style of existence, of "absolute in-ness," in a manner in which people did not notice what they were really doing at first glance.

This is "the unborn-ness" that depth psychology in modern Western Europe salvaged, that is to say, "not yet being born out" or "being unable to be born out." In this sense, the establishment of "modern consciousness" in the twentieth century seemed to live in a perpetual dream, which is well shown in the state of landscape painting in modern Western Europe.

The modern Western European paradigm affected and penetrated the whole world at the end of the nineteenth century, when the subject began to see itself as an object with the "second distance setting moment" that I referred to previously. Berque suggests that this is when the modern Western European paradigm was on the verge of a crisis. This appears in the Japonism Movement at that time or in Paul Cézanne's paintings of *The Bay of Marseilles seen from L'Estaque* (1878–1879; Figure 6.1) and *Rocks at L'Estaque* (1882; Figure 6.2).[15] In these works, the linear perspective of the Renaissance is no longer maintained; rather multiple perspectives have been adopted, where plural viewpoints exist in parallel within one landscape.

Figure 6.1: Paul Cézanne, *The Bay of Marseilles seen from L'Estaque*.

Startlingly, this characteristic way of drawing can be observed in Chinese-style landscape painting established in the tenth to eleventh century in a more sophisticated and precise manner. This is what Cézanne attempted to incorporate in his works.

Multiple perspectives in Chinese-style landscape painting

In the Tang dynasty, around the third century CE, "climbing a mountain" was already regarded as a symbolic way to view the whole country *spatially,* or from the past to the future *temporally*. This may be related to a ritual called *Kuni-mi* [country inspection] in ancient Japan; when visiting a region to inspect it, the emperor looked out over the land on every side from the top of a certain mountain, thereby declaring his sovereignty over the region.

Figure 6.2: Paul Cézanne, Aix-en-Provence, França [France], 1839–1906. *Rochedos em L'Estaque* [Cliffs in L'Estaque], 1882–85. Óleo sobre tela [Oil on canvas], 73 × 92 cm. Acervo [Collection] Museu de Arte de São Paulo Assis Chateaubriand. Doação [Gift] Edward Marvin, 1953 *MASP.00087*. Foto *[Photo] João Musa.*

According to Takehiro Shindo, a Japanese researcher of Chinese-style landscape painting, "Tang poets often wrote poems when climbing mountains, hills, or lofty structures, in which 'mountains' newly took on a spiritual meaning."[16] It was Sung Ping (宗炳; 375–443), who was famous for "Preface to the Landscape Paintings," who first proposed the spiritual meanings of landscapes. By describing "smoke clouds" in a landscape, the painter could express the existence of the air therein, which also symbolized the painter's own inner reality. This kind of thought was completed by the founders of Northern Chinese landscape painting, from the Five Dynasties to the Northern Song Dynasty, such as Jing Hao (荊浩; c. 855–915) and Li Cheng (李成; 919–967) in the tenth century. In this conception of landscape, unlike that in Western Europe, the separation between the painter as the subject and landscape as the object was not emphasized as much; rather a oneness, or sharedness, was searched for as the ultimate state of mind.

146 YASUHIRO TANAKA

The most outstanding feature of the Northern Chinese-style landscape painting is that it includes a complete, or panoramic, view within itself (全景山水). Concerning this point, Seigo Matsuoka, a Japanese writer with a thorough knowledge of fine arts of all ages and countries, said, "The landscape painters attempted to contain the whole landscape therein by having, or moving, their perspective freely" and "they thought about the manners of drawing the landscape's hugeness and wideness, remoteness and deepness, in one image at the same time."[17] It was an awareness of *height* that first emerged in their drawings; they described the landscape as if looking upward at it. This is a *high distance* (高遠) that can be seen in Figure 6.3, *A Solitary Temple amid Clearing Peaks* (晴巒蕭寺図), which was drawn in the tenth century by Li Cheng, who I briefly mentioned earlier. The high distance (高遠) is well illustrated in this drawing, as the viewer looks upward from the bottom of the mountain to the top.

Landscape painters then began to draw *width* together with *height*. The sky and mountains in a far distant view, and the river and road in a near distant view, were all depicted in one picture. This is the introduction of *level distance* (平遠), which is shown in Figure 6.4, *High Pines, Level Distance* (喬松平遠図), also drawn by Li Cheng. Here, it is apparent that the width or spread toward the other side is emphasized.

Figure 6.4: Li Cheng, *High Pines, Level Distance*. (https://aras.org/spokes-of-the-wheel).

In addition, awareness of *depth* was also added, as painters attempted to depict the scenery hidden in the depth of the landscape, which was utterly invisible from their standpoint. This is the *deep distance* (深遠), also called the *Three Distances* (三遠); height, width, and depth became synchronous while also forming multiple perspectives in Northern Chinese-style landscape painting. Subsequently, in the eleventh century, these three perspectives were included in one landscape painting, as seen in the Guo Xi's *Early Spring* (早春図) (Figure 6.5).

Figure 6.5: Guo Xi, *Early Spring*. (https://aras.org/spokes-of-the-wheel).

These multiple perspectives in Chinese-style landscape painting are in considerable contrast to the perspective used in Western European-style landscape paintings, in which the viewpoint does not move.

JAPANESE LANDSCAPE AND THE SUBJECT

Figure 6.3: Attributed to Li Cheng, Chinese (919–967 C.E.). *A Solitary Temple Amid Clearing Peaks*, Northern Song Dynasty (960–1127). Hanging scroll, ink and slight color on silk, 14 × 22 inches (111.8 × 55.9 cm). The Nelson-Atkins Museum of Art, Kansas City, Missouri. Purchase: William Rockhill Nelson Trust, 47–71. Photo courtesy of Nelson-Atkins Media Services / John Lamberton.

Sesshu and the introduction of Chinese-style landscape painting

Northern Chinese-style landscape painting was imported into Japan from Southern Song with Zen Buddhism and many Zen Buddhists in the Kamakura period, around the twelfth century. As a result, Chinese-style landscape paintings were mostly drawn by artist-monks. Its ultimate expression can be seen in the work of Sesshu (雪舟; 1420–1506), who was a monk of Shokokuji, one of the five most important temples in Kyoto. Sesshu left Shokokuji when he was around fifty years old. He then journeyed to Beijing with Japanese missions to Ming China and stayed there for about two years. During this period, he drew *Four Seasons Landscape*. After his return, he established his own approach, which became the foundation for a Japanese style of Chinese-style landscape painting, as shown in *Long Scroll of Landscapes* (山水長巻) (Figure 6.6), *Splashed-Ink Style Landscape* (破墨山水図) (Figure 6.7), *Autumn* and *Winter Landscape* (秋冬山水図 (Figures 6.8 and 6.9), and *View of Ama-no-Hashidate* (天橋立図) (Figure 6.10), and other paintings.

Figure 6.6: Sesshu, *Splashed-Ink Style Landscape* (1495). (https://aras.org/spokes-of-the-wheel).

Figure 6.7: Sesshu, *Long Scroll of Landscapes* (1469). (https://aras.org/spokes-of-the-wheel).

The work in which the originality of Sesshu is most clearly shown is in *Splashed-Ink Style Landscape* (Figure 6.6). Here, the *Three Distances* are no longer explicit, but further refined to be inclusive— that is, they are highly abstracted in a more indistinct form.

Also, *Long Scroll of Landscapes* (Figure 6.7) is a scrolled painting of 0.4 m width and 16 m length. The form of "long scrolled paper" has often been used in Japan since the Heian period (794–1185/1192) as scrolled sutras dedicated to shrines or temples, or as scrolled pictures that convey the shrine's origin and history. This form, however, was not applied to landscape painting in Japan, although it was sometimes used in landscape painting in China.

The *Long Scroll of Landscapes* portrays circulating time. It begins at the end of winter. Spring comes when the flowers of the Japanese apricot trees bloom. Then comes the freshwater at the lakeside or riverside in early summer, and the village crowded with people in autumn. Next is the scene of a castle with a snowy mountain behind

Japanese Landscape and the Subject 149

it. Finally, green trees emerge that make us sense the coming of next spring. This scroll is "eternity" in a sense and an inclusive landscape *in which there is everything*. This particular long scroll painting was drawn to wish for an "eternal" reign by the feudal lord Ouchi, who Sesshu served at that time. Certainly this work was dedicated to him, but I see the "eternity" of the world also expressed in this inclusive landscape. Arata Shimao, a Japanese medieval art historian, pointed that the letters 筆受, written at the end of the scroll as a signature, were often used in the transcription of sutra.[18] Considering this, we could say that in this long scroll landscape painting, Sesshu tried to represent the eternal truth of the world itself as landscape.

Other than these features, Sesshu never drew the landscape as he saw it or as it was, as can be seen in the strong vertical lines of rock face standing out in the *Autumn Landscape* and *Winter Landscape* (Figures 6.8 and 6.9); the highly abstracted *Three Distances* in the *Splashed-Ink Style Landscape,* as mentioned previously (Figure 6.6); and the viewpoint used for *View of Ama-no-Hashidate* (Figure 6.10), which is far above the sky and never realized within this world. These landscapes are heavily tinged with the subjectivity of the painter Sesshu or with that of the Japanese people and culture via Sesshu.

> **Figure 6.8: Sesshu, *Autumn Landscape*.**
> **(https://aras.org/spokes-of-the-wheel).**
>
> **Figure 6.9: Sesshu, *Winter Landscape*.**
> **(https://aras.org/spokes-of-the-wheel).**
>
> **Figure 6.10: Sesshu, *View of Ama-no-Hashidate* (1501–1506).**
> **(https://aras.org/spokes-of-the-wheel).**

Chinese-style landscape painting was successfully digested and absorbed into Japanese culture via Sesshu, becoming Japanese-style landscape painting and the Japanese landscape itself. In addition, its essence has since been maintained by Zen Buddhism. We will discuss "the subject of Japanese landscape" again in the concluding section.

The subject remaining unborn and embedded in the landscape

Wang Yongjiang, a contemporary Chinese calligrapher and researcher of Sesshu, explained the specific aspects of Chinese-style landscape painting on seeing Sesshu's *Long Scroll of Landscapes*. He said that one of the traditional ways is not to draw a landscape as if

150 YASUHIRO TANAKA

seeing it from the outside, but for the painter to enter the landscape and to draw what the painter encounters in each place. Finally, one landscape appears on the paper.[19]

This manner of painting was described by Seigo Matsuoka. When he first looked at Fan Kuan's *Travelers Among Mountains and Streams* (渓山行旅図) (Figure 6.11), he felt with wonder, "as if I am now entering deep in the steep mountain and encountering its massiveness from various angles."[20] As discussed, this may overlap with the description by Berque of Cezanne's landscape paintings.[21] Cezanne's spatial expression nullified the central and stable position of the subject established in the linear perspective of the Renaissance, with which the relationship between man and nature completely changed. As the stratification of scenes was replaced by its juxtaposition in Cezanne's landscape paintings, the viewer's eyes move from one scene to another and thereby give each scene its own internal value defined by the object itself, not by the position of the subject. This *serpentine* eyes' movement from one scene to another, which was compared to the "undulation of a dragon's tail" in China, symbolized the subject's entering the depth of Nature.

Figure 6.11: Fan Kuan, *Travelers Among Mountains and Streams*. (https://aras.org/spokes-of-the-wheel).

Both the Chinese-style landscape painter and the viewer not only look at the landscape, but also "enter the depth" of Nature. The subject not looking at Nature from a distance, but entering the depth of Nature, was already established around the eleventh century in the East. This kind of subject achieved entry to the depth of Nature, not by being literally born from Nature, but by remaining embedded in it. Using Berque's words, the subject could enter the depth of Nature with a serpentine eyes' movement from one scene to another, which places Nature under one's eyes.

This kind of subject is completely different from that in Western European–style landscape paintings. As expressed in Cezanne's landscape paintings, at the very moment that the mode of the subject in later modern Western Europe became nearly global, it was on the verge of a crisis and could not help taking in something oriental. This phenomenon is interesting because it leads to the notion that "the subject in modern Western Europe" could not complete itself only by itself, which means that it is just one of the possible modes of the subject.

JAPANESE LANDSCAPE AND THE SUBJECT

151

In this sense, it could be said that we Japanese also need to learn other modes of the subject that differ from those in modern Western Europe, with reference to Sesshu's Japanese style of Chinese-style landscape paintings, which is regarded as one of its completed forms. Therein, the feature of "the new and old state of consciousness" in the Japanese-style is obviously included.

As is well known, Zen Buddhism finally matured in Japan after Dogen's return from Southern Song in 1228. He described this return as a "Return home with my hands empty" (空手還郷). This expression could be applied equally to Sesshu, who returned to Japan after his two-year stay in China in 1469. At that time, there was already nothing to learn "outside" Japan for Dogen and Sesshu. This may also be true for us living in contemporary Japan. Such a time has come for us, in that we not only turn our eyes to the "outside," but also look back at our "interior" carefully.

A male patient who drew a landscape like a Chinese-style landscape painting

A picture drawn by a male patient using the *Landscape Montage Technique (LMT)* motivated my research on Chinese-style landscape painting. LMT is an art therapy first devised by Hisao Nakai, an outstanding Japanese psychiatrist, to examine the possibilities and risks of using sandplay therapy in the treatment of schizophrenics who are seriously disturbed.[22] In performing LMT, the therapist draws a frame on a piece of paper and tells the patient to draw a landscape within it. The items to be drawn are stated sequentially, and the patient draws only one landscape by adding the following items in order: 1) river, 2) mountain, 3) rice field, 4) road (in far distant view), 5) house, 6) tree, 7) person (in middle distant view), 8) flower, 9) animal, and 10) stone (in near distant view). After drawing these items, the patient can add anything else and then colors the landscape to finish the drawing.

LMT is simple to administer, and the act of drawing a landscape itself fits well with the Japanese view of nature and mind. In addition, LMT is a psychological test that represents our interior quite well. Therefore, it is currently widely used as a psychological assessment tool and is often adopted to psychotherapy as one of the important techniques of art therapy. In the following discussion, I present a case in which LMT was used as a form of art therapy rather than as a tool for psychological assessment.

The patient, Mr. F, was in his late twenties when I first met him. He worried that he had not been able to throw things away for several years. All sorts of items were scattered around his room. It is important to note that he was at a loss to understand why he was repeatedly chastised by his family because he did not clean his room, rather than being upset with his own difficulty in tidying up. Mr. F went to a psychiatric clinic one year before coming to see me. Although he received antidepressant medication at the clinic, he thought that he instead had Attention Deficit Hyperactivity Disorder (ADHD).

After his mental condition calmed down owing to the medication, he started to work as a part-time foot masseur. There, he needed to take care of customers. Just after starting this work, however, he was advised by his employer that "It would be better for you to take a job dealing with things, not humans," and he was fired. He was really disappointed at his employer's words and visited me to receive psychotherapy.

When he first came to see me, his chief complaint was "I feel stuck in living my life." Around the time of his first visit to psychotherapy, he began to work for another company. However, he also left this job due to problems with interpersonal relationships within about one year. After that, he started a job to repair household electric appliances. He was good at fixing and repairing things and liked these activities. While listening to his stories about his work, I thought he did a very good job, but he also left this job because a relationship with one of the superiors went wrong.

He had poor communication skills, which made it difficult for him to continue with his work. He drifted from job to job. With a diagnosis of Autism Spectrum Disorder, not in the narrow sense but in the broader sense (corresponding to Pervasive Developmental Disorder-Not Otherwise Specified in DSM-IV), he began psychotherapy with me.

The sessions with Mr. F were based on dream analysis. He reported many dreams. As a therapist, I often could not grasp the meaning of his dreams. Moreover, even on topics other than dreams, his narratives were superficial or abstract. Therefore, I could not clearly understand his problems. In the 184th session, he reported that he had finally lost his job as a repairman and had no income. We both felt stuck. Then I spontaneously thought to myself, "I would like to ask him to draw a picture." Thus, he drew the LMT. At this time, about five and a half years had passed since his first visit to psychotherapy.

Japanese Landscape and the Subject 153

In many cases of LMT, the patient turns the drawing paper sideways. However, Mr. F used it vertically, without any hesitation, and started drawing. When I said, "Please draw a mountain" after a "river," he drew a mountain in the distance. At that moment, I had the impression that "this landscape may be seen from a really far distance."

Although Mr. F drew "persons" and "animals" (birds), they were too small to distinguish. Only when looking carefully could I see "persons" in a rice field and birds as "animals" in the upper right of the picture. His "persons" and "animals" (birds) were extremely small and dotty. As to "tree" and "flower," he did not draw a "tree" or "flower" as individual items. When instructed to draw them, he responded that "trees are in the mountains" and "flowers are in the mountains as well." In response to the last instruction, "Please complete the landscape; you can add something else if you wish," he drew a "suspension bridge" between the "mountains" in the front and back. While viewing his drawing, I could not judge whether he had really committed to draw a picture with LMT. However, I felt that something certainly shifted after I asked him to draw this picture.

In the next session, he said, "I have nothing to talk about. I felt pain in drawing the picture in the last session." In the following sessions, he said similar things: "Nothing to talk about." "Can I stop coming here?" "I am less eager to talk than before, nothing to gain from being here, as if I am desperately squeezing something…" "I have the feeling that I am like that: hard to live." Although I could see he was certainly in pain, I felt that something authentic was happening inside him.

Because Mr. F did not have a job, it became financially difficult for him to continue the sessions. Therefore, he stopped psychotherapy after the 189th session, five sessions after drawing with LMT. After that, he came to a session every few months, but he could not find a job. Finally, one year later he came to see me again and said that he wanted to restart his regular psychotherapy since he now had a new job. When restarting, he reported that he worked for a factory that made walking aids, including sticks. After that, he gradually talked about his work and his interpersonal relationships in the workplace. Because his distress and problems seemed to have become more specific and concrete, I found what he said to be understandable and less abstract.

Difference between the subject in Chinese-style landscapes and that of ASD

First, I will consider some of the distinctive features in Mr. F's LMT picture, mainly in relation to Chinese-style landscape paintings. As mentioned, he used the drawing paper vertically without hesitation. This format is similar to hanging scrolls of the Northern Chinese-style, in which high mountains and deep ravines are rendered with a round-trip viewpoint from upper to lower. With the serpentine eyes' movement finely expressed in *Three Distances,* the painter and the viewer are together able to enter the landscape's depth.

However, when viewing Mr. F's drawing, I had the impression that "This landscape may be seen from a really far distance." His perspective is merely located at a far distance—in other words, it is out of the landscape in a completely different way from the linear perspective in modern Western Europe. It did not move from one scene to another, from the upper to the lower, in the landscape, but is just floating in the air. This is well expressed in the drawings of "persons" and "animals" (birds) as very small and dotty and in the absence of "trees" and "flowers" as individual items. He never attempted to deeply penetrate the landscape.

In his case, the subject was certainly not only separated from the landscape, but also just looking at it from the air without any solid ground. The subject never entered each scene in the landscape and thus never experienced it as one world. For the subject in the drawing, there is no possibility of reflecting on itself internally and observing things externally. A subject like Mr. F could be seen as having an "incompetent sense of self," as often pointed out in regard to ASD. As Victoria Lyons and Michael Fitzgerald have said, a "sense of self" is a central aspect of human self-consciousness and refers to the experience of oneself as the agent of one's actions.[23]

Using this concept, we may understand Mr. F's difficulty in tidying his room; because of his struggle to have a sense of agency, his self was externally scattered in his disorderly room. He could not manage to create order from his scattered things, which were like fragments of his fragmented self. In addition, it was difficult for him to have a body schema as a whole person. He thus needed others' bodies externally to realize his own body internally. Although he had been fired as a part-time foot masseur just before starting psychotherapy, he later began to work for a factory making walking aids used by people to

JAPANESE LANDSCAPE AND THE SUBJECT

compensate for lost or disabled body functions. It seemed to me that, by adjusting them for each client while imagining his or her comfort, he was establishing his own body schema with which he could specifically and concretely experience each event in his workplace. He had become more active as an agent than before.

From my own clinical experience in psychotherapy with ASD patients, including Mr. F, I now believe it is more important for these patients to movably experience each event and item under their eyes with their own feeling of reality, rather than to establish the subject as a fixed, unmovable point in the modern Western European way.

Traditional Japanese landscapes and ASD today

Berque points out the three primary features of Japanese landscapes:[24]

1. *The weakness of the subject's centrality.* Bearing no relation with the linear perspective of Western European-style landscapes in modern times, the subject topologically locates itself relating to each specific and concrete place.

2. *The principle of living only for the present.* On the time axis, each moment is valued for itself. The scattered perspectives in the go-round style in landscape gardens, of which many were built in Zen temples in the Muromachi period and by the feudal lords in the Edo period, values "going-around." There is a present centering in each place. A future destination in the Christian temporal sense is not the goal.

3. *The juxtaposition.* Because the juxtaposition of nonhierarchical elements is valued, the integration of different elements under a particular governing principle is not given much thought. Instead of general order, local and fragmented orders coexist.

The *go-round* style as one of the most important styles of a traditional Japanese landscape garden is said to have been established in the Muromachi period (1336–1573) under the strong influence of Zen Buddhism. However, the gardens of nobility in the Heian period (794–1185/1192) already had this go-round style quality in the form of having a pond on the south side of the main house (*Shinden*), as shown in *Sakutei-ki* (作庭記), the oldest book on gardens in Japan. In this sense, the Japanese-style subject is historically very old and

156 YASUHIRO TANAKA

has remained unvarying in nature over many centuries, even though Japan only opened to Western countries and radically modernized in the Meiji period (1868–1912), after the national isolation in the Edo period was over. "Japanese spirit imbued with Western learning (和魂洋才)" was the characteristic attitude during this period and was derived from the concept of "Japanese spirit imbued with Chinese learning" (和魂漢才) from the middle of the Heian period. These ideas express clearly the oneness of eclecticism and syncretism that is very traditional in Japan.

Entering the twenty-first century, ASD has received remarkable attention, with increasing interest in both neuroscientific research and clinical psychology. The features of Japanese landscapes dating back to the medieval period overlap with the mentality of ASD patients' based on their "lack of subject"[25]:

1. *The weakness of the subject's centrality.* They are not active but passive, irresponsibly leaving their judgments and decisions to others, having no executing center.
2. *The principle of living only for the present.* They are not living in the flow of time—the past, the present, and the future—but only for each moment without any estimate, having difficulty remembering and storytelling their own past.
3. *The juxtaposition.* They are unable to give priority in actual life situations, leaving diverse things, tasks, and events in parallel without ordering in their mind. We might say that the Japanese psyche originally has some affinity with an ASD-like mentality.

Moreover, ordinary people in post-modern Japan, especially those in the younger generation, tend to choose an ASD-like lifestyle. They do not want to be executive or agentive in their own life, living only for each moment without consideration and estimation, without having an order of priority and thus leaving everything undecided. This is their lifestyle rather than their psychopathology or psychological problem.

In the 1960s and 1970s, there were many anthropophobic patients in Japan who suffered from disunion with themselves in attempting in vain to accommodate themselves to Western individualism. They were really neurotic in the sense that their complaints were exclusively concerned with the state of their "self-relationship" or

JAPANESE LANDSCAPE AND THE SUBJECT

157

"self-consciousness." Now, our ordinary patients do not suffer from their twisted self-consciousness; they do not choose such a way of suffering. It is not in fashion at all.

In Japan, both ordinary people and patients do not choose to be neurotic, but to be ASD-like. In this sense, I think it is possible to evaluate ASD as an "illness of *Zeitgeist*," or to say at least that it is a caricature of the post-modern consciousness in Japan.[26]

The subject of Japanese landscape: on its inclusiveness

As described in the previous section, the original Japanese psyche has not changed for a long time and has some affinity with the ASD-like mentality, which has become a hot topic today. There are, however, differences between the subject of Japanese landscape and that of ASD, as well as between the subject in Chinese-style landscapes and that of ASD. In previous sections, I stated that, when depicted from the side of the human subject, the difference should depend on whether the subject can enter the landscape, that is, go deeply into the world. But how can we describe this movement if it is being expressed from the landscape side or from the world side? In other words, how can we consider the subject of the landscape?

Berque described a peculiarity of Japanese landscapes using the concept in geography of "ecumene (inhabited areas)" in his book *Le sauvage et l'artifice: les Japonais devant la nature* (*The Savage and the L'Artifice: The Japanese in Front of Nature*).[27] He noticed a unique feature of Japanese civilization in which the Japanese people did not extend the areas they inhabited as far as possible into the wilderness compared with neighboring civilizations. For example, in China and Korea, mountainous areas were more intensively used for activities such as agriculture and stock farming, or in the Malayo-Polynesian area people more peacefully crossed the sea. Compared with these features, "Japan seems to have developed its territorial potential through dynamics directed towards the interior," where there is "an introverted development, whose logic embodies all spatiality in Japan."[28]

As a natural consequence, "dynamics directed towards the interior" did not clarify the boundary between the inhabited and uninhabited areas in the outside. In other words, it did not strengthen the dichotomy between the *ecumene* (inhabited areas) and the érème (uninhabited areas) but instead expanded the sacred uninhabited areas

158　　　　　　　　　　　　　　　　　YASUHIRO TANAKA

at the end of the cultural realm in two directions: *background* of the mountain and *offing* in the sea, or the part of the deep sea seen from the shore (in Japanese, *background* [Oku] and *offing* [*Oki*] have the same etymology). In addition, differentiation proceeded at these "boundaries" more as "the piedmont" and "rocky shore," respectively. Berque expressed this state with the words "a gradation or refinement of the relationship of nature and culture."[29]

Berque proposes the following "chorology of the relationship between nature and culture" (Table 6.1).[30]

Table 6.1. The Chorology of the Relationship between Nature and Culture

Referent	Nature		Culture		Nature
Gradient	Background (*oku*) ⟵				⟶ Offing (*oki*)
Space	The *érème* (uninhabited areas)	Limit	*Ecumene* (inhabited areas)	Limit	The *érème* (uninhabited areas)
Geographical themes	Mountain (*yama*)	Piedmont (*yama no be*)	Habitat	Shore (*iso*)	Sea (*umi*)
Mythological themes	Land of the Gods	Rocky frontier	Country of men	Marine boundary	Land of the Gods

As part of the background of Japanese people not extending their inhabited areas as far as possible, the Japanese consciousness might have an inherent tendency to emphasize "dynamics directed towards the interior." It is more likely, however, that this consciousness realized itself *there* as Japanese landscape. In addition, the Japanese landscape might be characterized by its sophisticated *inclusiveness,* equipping the unknowable sacred realm in a far-off place in the form of the background of the mountain or offing in the sea. This serves to refine the boundary between inhabited and uninhabited areas.

The introduction of Chinese-style landscapes led to an eclectic and syncretic blending with traditional Japanese landscapes, and this inclusiveness was realized in various forms in the Japanese landscapes actualized by Sesshu or via Sesshu. For example, we see this in *Long Scroll of Landscapes* as the circulating time of the four seasons mentioned previously; in *Splashed-Ink Style Landscape* and *Autumn* and *Winter Landscape* as art "regarded as" representing the "essential quality" of landscape; and in *View of Ama-no-Hashidate* as the viewpoint from far above the sky and not existing in ordinary life:

JAPANESE LANDSCAPE AND THE SUBJECT 159

going to individual places, drawing them elaborately, and including them totally.

As described in the previous section, the three features of Japanese landscapes defined by Berque certainly have similarities with ASD-like mental and behavioral traits. The definitive difference, however, is whether a landscape or a world is or is not equipped with such "inclusiveness."

Conclusion

In old Japanese landscapes equipped with inclusiveness, structured into the experience of the image, a person who stood in front of a landscape would naturally be drawn deeply within. Today's Japanese landscape, however, has lost this premise. Therefore, we cannot expect that a person who stands and gazes at a landscape goes deeply within. In our time, psychotherapy has taken on this function when it artificially seeks the experience of inclusiveness through the so-called structure of psychotherapy in terms of time, place, and fee. By so doing, it could first become the "place" to purposely do the work of going deeply within.

This is psychotherapy in postmodern times as *opus contra naturam*. Therefore, in psychotherapy for an ASD patient whose consciousness is considered to be a caricature of today, the introduction of another "landscape" or "world," such as a dream, sandplay, and drawing that is closed but open at the same time, is therapeutically significant as a way to enhance inclusiveness, in addition to the structure of psychotherapy. This is because the dream, sandplay, or drawing is not "the third" between patient and therapist in the normal Jungian sense, but it becomes the "landscape" itself in psychotherapy, in other words, "the first."

Notes

[1] Wolfgang Giegerich, "The End of Meaning and the Birth of Man," *Journal of Jungian Theory and Practice* 6 (1, 2004): 1–65.

[2] Jürgen Habermas, "Modernity: An Unfinished Project," in Maurizio Passerin d'Entrèves, and Seyla Benhabib, eds., *Habermas and the Unfinished Project of Modernity* (Cambridge: Polity Press, 1980/1996), pp. 38–55.

[3] *Ibid.,* 39.

160 YASUHIRO TANAKA

[4] *Ibid.*

[5] *Ibid.*

[6] *Ibid.*

[7] Augustine Berque, *Japanese Landscape, West European Landscape, and the Age of Landscape Design* [*Nihon no Fukei, Seiou no Keikan, soshite Zoukei no Jidai*]. Translated to Japanese by K. Shinoda (Tokyo: Kodansha, 1990), p. 53.

[8] Erwin Panofsky, *Perspective as Symbolic Form,* trans. Christopher S. Wood (New York: Zone Books, 1996). Originally published in 1927.

[9] Berque, *Japanese Landscape,* pp. 56–57. My italics.

[10] *Ibid.,* p. 170.

[11] *Ibid.,* p. 170. My italics.

[12] C. G. Jung, "Archetypes of the Collective Unconscious" (1934/1954), in *The Collected Works of C. G. Jung,* vol. 9i, ed. and trans. Gerhard Adler and R. F. C. Hull (Princeton: Princeton University Press, 1968), § 50.

[13] C. G. Jung, "The Philosophical Tree" (1945/1954), in *The Collected Works of C. G. Jung,* vol. 13, ed. and trans. Gerhard Adler and R. F. C. Hull (Princeton: Princeton University Press, 1968), § 395.

[14] Jung, CW 9i, § 29.

[15] Figure 6.2 Credit: Paul Cézanne, Aix-en-Provence, França [France],1839–1906RochedosemL'Estaque[CliffsinL'Estaque],1882–85 Óleo sobre tela [Oil on canvas], 73×92cm Coleção [Collection] Museu de Arte de São Paulo Assis Chateaubriand Doação [Gift] Edward Marvin,1953MASP.00087 Foto [Photo] João Musa.

[16] Takehiro Shindo, *What Is Chinese Landscape Painting? Nature and Art in China* [Sansuiga toha Nanika—Chugoku no Shizen to Geijutsu] (Tokyo: Fukutake Shoten, 1989).

[17] Seigo Matsuoka, *Landscape Thought—Imagination of "Negativity"* [*Sansui Shisou—"Fu" no Souzouryoku*] (Tokyo: Chikuma Shobo, 2003), p. 320.

[18] Arata Shimao, *Sesshu: His Lifetime and Works* [*Sesshu: Shogai to Sakuhin*] (Tokyo: Tokyo Bijutsu, 2012).

[19] NHK E-tele, *Revived Sesshu in China* [Chugoku de Yomigaeru Sesshu], ETV Special TV Program, 2015. Accessed Nov. 27, 2018, at http://www.nhk.or.jp/etv21c/archive/150411.html.

[20] Matsuoka, *Landscape Thought,* p. 323.

JAPANESE LANDSCAPE AND THE SUBJECT 161

[21] Berque, *Japanese Landscape*, p. 77.

[22] Y. Yamanaka, "Introduction to Landscape Montage Technique," in Y. Yamanka (ed.), *Landscape Montage Technique by H. NAKAI.* [*H. NAKAI Fukei Kosei Hou*] *Collected Works of Hisao Nakai,* vol. 1 (Tokyo: Iwasaki Gakujutsu Shuppan, 1984).

[23] Victoria Lyons and Michael Fitzgerald, "Atypical Sense of Self in Autism Spectrum Disorders: A Neuro-Cognitive Perspective," in Michael Fitzgerald, ed., *Recent Advances in Autism Spectrum Disorders,* vol. I (London: InTech, 2013). Accessed Nov. 27, 2018, at http://dx.doi.org/10.5772/53680.

[24] Berque, *Japanese Landscape.*

[25] Toshio Kawai, "Union and Separation in the Therapy of Pervasive Developmental Disorders and ADHD," *Journal of Analytical Psychology* 54 (2009): 659–675.

[26] We can find many studies to show that ASD has become an "illness of *Zeitgeist*," not only in Japan but also worldwide. Here, I would like to pick up so-called epidemiological ones among them, for example, as follows: M. Rutter, "Incidence of Autism Spectrum Disorders: Changes over Time and Their Meaning," *Acta Paediatrica* 93 (2004): 1–13; or Y. S. Kim, B. L. Leventhal, Y. J. Koh, et al. "Prevalence of Autism Spectrum Disorder in a Total Population Sample," *American Journal of Psychiatry* 168 (2011): 904–912.

[27] Augustine Berque, *Le sauvage et l'artifice: les Japonais devant la nature* (Paris: Gallimard, 1990). Or *Fûdo no Nihon,* trans. K. Shinoda (Tokyo: Chikumashobo, 1992).

[28] *Ibid.,* p. 66, 67.

[29] *Ibid.,* p. 72

[30] *Ibid.,* p. 76.

7

● ● ● ● ● ●

Agency, a Japanese Cultural Complex
Transformation of Jungian-Oriented Psychotherapy in an Age of Weaker Agency

Chihiro Hatanaka

The issue of *agency* in Japanese culture today

In this chapter, I explore the transformation of images and stories in Japan in a historical and cultural context through the perspective of *agency,* a cultural and social-psychological concept, which is at the center of controversy today. I focus on agency in Japan because Japanese people tend to show a *less agentic* attitude in this decade in comparison with previous times, although the agency of the Japanese has always been weaker than that of Westerners.

One of the biggest problems for Jungian-oriented psychotherapists in Japan is that weaker agency has led to difficulty in generating fluent stories, whereas images and stories should play a crucial role in the clinical work of analytical psychology. First, I will present a prior study and case vignettes to show the characteristics of Japanese agency in recent years. To illustrate the decline of individual agency

---

Chihiro Hatanaka, PhD, is a lecturer at the Kokoro Research Center, Kyoto University, Japan. She works as a clinical psychologist and her research focuses on the psychological features of young people in contemporary society. Her article entitled "The Apparent Lack of Agency, Empathy, and Creativity among Japanese Youth: Interpretations from Project Test Responses" was published in 2015 in *Psychologia,* vol. 58, no. 4.

in contemporary Japanese culture, I will introduce three types of individual stories with some case vignettes and examples from Japanese novels. Finally, I will discuss the possibility offered by Jungian-oriented psychotherapy in an age of loss of individual stories with another example from a Japanese novel.

Japanese weaker agency

Social-psychological research has shown that the agency of the Japanese is weaker in contrast to the independent style of agency in Western cultures. Hazel Rose Markus and Shinobu Kitayama introduced two contrasting concepts—*independent self* and *interdependent self*—to show the possibility of different types of self-construals between Western cultures and non-Western cultures.[1] They pointed out that "there is a faith in the inherent separateness of distinct persons" in many Western cultures.[2] In contrast with this, the individual is not separated from the social context but more connected to and less differentiated from others in non-Western cultures. Agency is defined in a cultural and social-psychological context as inherently personal, an element that is best characterized as a force that emanates from the inside core of the person and guides his or her actions toward the environment.[3] It is the central function that directs, regulates, and energizes a person's own thoughts, feelings, and behavior.

Takahiko Masuda and Richard Nisbett developed an interesting experiment to show the different types of self-construals between Japanese and American participants.[4] The participants were presented with vignettes of underwater scenes like the one shown in Figure 7.1, which included focal objects—three big fish and background objects like seaweed and water bubbles. When they asked participants to describe these scenes, Americans referred mainly to the features of the focal fish (large, foregrounded, rapidly moving, brightly colored), whereas Japanese referred more to context and to relationships between the focal objects and context (background objects and location of objects in relation to one another), saying things like

Figure 7.1: Underwater scene from Masuda and Nisbett's experiment.

AGENCY, A JAPANESE CULTURAL COMPLEX 165

"it was a lake or pond." Americans immediately zoomed in on the objects, whereas the Japanese paid more attention to context and tried to grasp the whole image more generally. This result clearly reflects that Japanese agency is rather weaker, based on cultural background, so the Japanese tend to adjust themselves effectively to various interpersonal contingencies.

In the clinical psychological area, Hayao Kawai pointed out that Japanese agency is weaker than that of Westerners. "The Japanese finds 'I' solely through the existence of others," for example, the Japanese language has many terms for the first person singular, such as *watakushi, boku, ore,* and *uchi*.[5] He also indicated that the character 自, which represents ego, self, I, and so on, has two paradoxical meanings, *mizukara* and *onozukara*: meaning "voluntarily, of one's own free will" and "spontaneously, of itself," respectively. The latter meaning indicates that the Japanese self is not limited to individuals. This double meaning of 自 also suggests that the agentic function is weaker in the Japanese than in Westerners.

Autism Spectrum Disorder in adults: the symbol of weaker agency

As several epidemiologic research studies have proven, the number of Autism Spectrum Disorder (ASD) patients seems to be increasing in advanced countries since around 2000.[6] Autism is seen as a severe form of neurodevelopmental disorder, which is accompanied by clearly abnormal language, as well as social and intellectual problems in the majority of cases. However, over the last decades, it has become evident that there are also many patients with high-functioning variants of ASD.

Regardless of the level of autistic tendency, their principal problem is weakness of agency, which results from the weaker boundary between self and the other. Our research project at the Kokoro Research Center, Kyoto University, aims to prove the effectiveness of special psychotherapy for children who are diagnosed as having ASD. Normal psychotherapy presupposes the existence of a subject with its reflective function. Because these children are less agentic, a special approach is needed to facilitate an emergence of a subject or to reinforce a weak subject in psychotherapy.[7]

Notably in Japan, ASD in adult patients has increased as well. As opposed to those patients with severe cases who were diagnosed

166 CHIHIRO HATANAKA

in childhood, adult ASD patients do not have strong autistic features, so their problems often rise to the surface after adolescence. Their problems concerning agency manifest in various forms; they have difficulty making decisions and choices, showing objections, and so on, even though they at least superficially have normal language abilities and above average intelligence. Many of them stumble after they have become responsible as grown-up men and women who should be agentic and subjective in social situations.

Moreover, after 2015, we have found many patients who were diagnosed as having ASD but are not to be regarded as genuine ASD patients according to our assessments and psychotherapy. They are less agentic and have had some ASD-like episodes, but they can change themselves rather more easily through psychotherapy because their symptoms and problems are not the result of an organic dysfunction. They are, as it were, in the middle between normal and ASD. In other words, the difference between normal people and people with ASD is becoming ambiguous.

Weaker agency: a general tendency in today's Japan

To illustrate that agentic function has, in general, become weaker recently, I would like to introduce my prior study in which I compared the results of Rorschach tests of university students between 2003 and 2013. In my tests, I adopted the index of an "undefined response" to investigate the style of agency of Japanese youth. This index was extracted from the Rorschach data of 147 ASD patients.[8] An *undefined response* is described as follows: 1) a response for which the core concept remains unclear; 2) a response that remains undecided even though the subject presents several concrete ideas. An example of the former is "This is some kind of animal, but I don't know what animal it is," and an example of the latter is "This is a cat or horse. I wonder which?" These are different from an abstract response like "This is an animal." As for an undefined response, the participant cannot identify the animal, even though he or she tries to focus on what kind of animal it is. The group of ASD patients presents significantly more undefined responses than neurotic patients and normal students. This result indicates that the undefined response is a sign of weakness of agency, which makes it difficult for the participant to focus on the object and to construct meaning.

AGENCY, A JAPANESE CULTURAL COMPLEX 167

The statistical comparison between the 2003 group (n = 47) and the 2013 group (n = 47) of students showed that the 2013 group presents a significantly higher number of undefined responses; the recent students group has more difficulty in being agentic. This result seems to indicate that the ability to focus on the object has become weaker. But there is a clear difference in the quality of undefined responses between the students group and that of the ASD group.

Examples from both groups follow. "Is this a panther? Panther, panther, tiger ... lion? Cat. What is this? Puma. This is not my cat." In many cases, an ASD person presents an undefined response with a feeling of confusion or puzzlement. On the other hand, there is an open-minded attitude in the examples from the students group: "This is an insect. Is it a grasshopper? Umm, but it also looks like a butterfly. Seeing only this part, it must be a snail. I think there is no exact thing. It may be this, it may be that." As shown here, students give undefined responses without confusion or perplexity. They voluntarily explain the unclearness of their responses without hesitation. Even when the tester asked them to make their response clear, many of them did not try to define their response. What these examples clarify is that the undefined responses of students are not the result of difficulty in producing a response, but rather the result of an intentionally adopted attitude. This is not to say that their agency itself is simply weak, but that they have a unique type of agency so as to avoid judging by themselves consciously. In other words, the responsibility to construct the meaning of the object is not limited within an individual agency, but is more open to the situation, which represents an interdependence-oriented relation with the object.

Weakness of agency and the loss of symbolical story

This ambiguous attitude can also be observed in clinical cases today. Kawai pointed out that consciousness is changing toward a new variation from modern consciousness, which is characterized by the self-reflective viewpoint and inner conflict.[9] His findings are based on clinical observations that an increasing number of patients are characterized by dissociation and acting out without the feeling of conflict, which can be thought of as weakness of central agency and subjectivity in holding one's conflict, image, and story.

After 2000, many psychotherapists began to notice that the number of patients who could not tell a story was increasing. Kyoko Takaishi, who has many years of experience in student counseling, pointed out the bipolarization of recent students.[10] There are two types of students—one being an "impatient group who are eager to know the immediate solution for their problem or how they should behave," and the other being a group "who cannot tell about themselves but have a vague uneasiness because they are not conscious of what is their own problem." Both groups can neither hold their own conflict nor construct their own story. In addition, Keiko Iwamiya, who also has experience in clinical work at schools over a long period, illustrates some recent cases that trouble psychotherapists: patients who do not recognize their problems, thinking only other people around them are distressed; patients who cannot verbalize their problems, even they are at a loss; and patients who expect that someone will solve their problems.[11]

Such tendencies have been observed not only in the young generation who easily reflect the trend of the times, but also in all generations. Kasahara, a prominent Japanese psychiatrist, indicated another example based on his sixty years of experience, that present-day patients tend to exhibit reactive depression instead of intrinsic depression.[12] The patients with the new type of depression are depressed when they are confronted by what they don't want to do, but they can feel happy when good things happen. They are directly reactive to the environment around them, which suggests that they don't have their essential story in their deeper psyche. In a sense, we Japanese might be losing the power and ability to tell the story of ourselves.

Jungian-oriented psychotherapists basically trust and rely on the power of image and story. Jung wrote that the unconscious can spontaneously produce a series of further images that unfold as a story.[13] Jung started *Memories, Dreams, Reflections* with the following sentences: "My life is a story of the self-realization of the unconscious... . Myth is more individual and expresses life more precisely than does science... . Whether or not the stories are 'true' is not the problem. The only question is whether what I tell is *my* fable, *my* truth."[14]

Hayao Kawai conveyed such ideas when he introduced Jungian-oriented psychology to Japan, so that Japanese Jungian-oriented

AGENCY, A JAPANESE CULTURAL COMPLEX 169

psychotherapists have considered the great value of listening to what their patients say as a story. However, the theoretical foundation of Jungian-oriented psychotherapy seems to be threatened and shaken in the age of loss of agency as just described.

Here, I include a clinical case vignette that illustrates the lack of a symbolic story.

Case A

The patient, in her twenties, worked at a bank. She did not have any developmental nor pathological problems. People around her thought that she was modest but reliable, and had enough ability and energy to adapt herself to the workplace. She quit her job because she couldn't stop crying in her office even though she had no special reason to cry. Soon after, she tried to get a new job and started work, but she quit that job and other jobs one after another before the first week was out. She started psychotherapy with me, but she could not say why she always quit. She said, "I don't know why, but I became too tired on my third day."

Although she clearly shows a problem when she tries to work, she cannot grasp her own problem. She cannot talk about her problem to me, but she just repeatedly tries to find a new workplace and breaks down. Her initial dream is as follows: *I am riding on a roller coaster. (When the dream started) I am already going down with great speed. The coaster comes down on the ground but keeps running round and round.* This dream clearly represents her psychological state, which has no clear structure, no starting point, no goal, so no conclusion. She cannot grasp her experience as a story or episode, although she has sufficient verbal ability; she just experiences body sensations.

This case is not a special exception. It seems to be difficult for people today to express an individual story. Based on this situation, I will describe three types of individual stories today that reflect the diminishment of agency in contemporary Japan.

Three types of individual stories today

As discussed, weaker agency makes it difficult for a person to create an individual story. But, of course, it is not that people today never make a story, but that the form of their story has changed. In the following sections, I suggest variations on how today's individual stories reflect less agency.

170 CHIHIRO HATANAKA

The attitude to avoid positive judgment and commitment

In 2014, Panda Ichiro, a mascot character from the job magazine *From A,* became a hot topic in Japan. Panda Ichiro looks like an adult man wearing a panda-like costume. He is a third-year student of "University A" and has a part-time job. He has a LINE account, so users can communicate with him through the Social Networking Service (SNS). Because Panda Ichiro can talk with his friends and is highly responsive, the number of his friends on LINE has increased greatly over these three years, reaching more than seventeen million as of the end of December 2017. For example, I sent a message to Ichiro, saying "You are cool!" Then he replied immediately, "Thank you! Today is good day." Another time he replied, "Everyone admires my black eyes, they're like sunglasses!" Originally, Panda Ichiro had the media function of giving users of *From A* information about part-time jobs. But the users rather enjoyed the daily conversations, whether or not they wanted to find a job. That is, Panda Ichiro is, first and foremost, a personal friend before he is a mascot character of a job magazine company.[15]

The reason why I take up Panda Ichiro here is that the idea of this planning project reflects the tendencies of Japanese people today. To find out the needs of their target audience, project planners asked young people about their motivations and reasons for using a job magazine when they want to find a part-time job. The answers these young people gave were "just because," "for some reason or other," "without knowing why," "by chance," and so on. Furthermore, they were not embarrassed, but sincerely gave such answers. In finding that today's young generation has no clearly stated need, the project team reversed their normal marketing method. They tried to find a way to interact with young people who are at a preliminary stage before having a clear need.[16] Panda Ichiro is not actively trying to convey information, but is just being with users to discover their latent needs by talking in attractive, sensible, and lovable way. People in this age of weaker agency prefer this kind of unassertive way, without positive judgment and commitment.

Now I introduce a young Japanese storywriter, Ryo Asai. His first work, *The Kirishima Thing,* received the Subal Best Young Writer Award in 2009.[17] In 2012, it was adapted into a movie and a comic. The movie was a big hit and swept the film awards that year in Japan. The title quoted here is the English version, but the essence of this

Agency, a Japanese Cultural Complex

novel can be better understood from a literal translation, which is "From what I hear, Kirishima seems to have quit the club."

The interesting point is that the structure of this novel, which is an omnibus of five stories narrated by classmates, focuses on the fact that Kirishima, the volleyball club captain, quit the club *for some reason*. The title character, Kirishima himself, does not appear in this story at all, and moreover, his retirement is not a main theme in the five stories. In the five small stories, the daily life and feelings of the classmates are illustrated from a first-person viewpoint. In each of the stories, the main character guesses why Kirishima quit the club and tries to think about the idea of entering into the feelings of other students, including Kirishima, but none of them take action. Even though Kirishima's retirement is a sudden and shocking event, they all maintain their distance and remain in their own position, so no one contacts Kirishima. Even an intimate teammate of Kirishima's, Fusuke Koizumi, who narrates the second story, does not approach him.

In this novel, none of the characters go deeply into the others' worlds. Instead, they go with the flow. This style of relationship is similar to the relationship between Panda Ichiro and *From A* users. Panda Ichiro and the users look like good friends, but they do not have a real relationship. They neither criticize each other nor approve anyone else's attitude, but silently guess the other's feelings in their own world. They are so sensitive about touching the other's world that they avoid a positive commitment to anyone else, which is one of the forms of relationship today. If such withdrawal from commitment progresses, it self-reproduces, as discussed in the next section.

Retreat from interaction and self-reproducing

To discuss *retreat from interaction,* the key concept of this section, I would like to introduce *botch*. The word *botch* is derived from the Japanese expression *Hitori-Botch,* which means the state of being alone. A *botch* is a person who does not have any friends to spend time with in social situations such as at the university. This is a masochistic expression concerning the person's poor relationships.

Reading *light novels* is one of the best ways to learn about a botch's mode of life. Light novels are a type of novel for young adults, many of which are easy to read because they consist of mostly conversational sentences and illustrations. Here I will introduce two leading titles that illustrate the school life of a botch: *My Youthful Romantic Comedy Is Wrong as I Expected* and *I Have Only Few Friends.* Both works are highly popular among today's young people and each has sold over seven million copies. In the former story, the main character is Hachiman, who in his second year of high school realizes that he is a botch. Every day, Hachiman mutters to himself about how he has no friends but is happy in his own way. He observes students around him and feels jealous of schoolmates who enjoy normal school life with their friends. One day, his teacher makes him join a "student service club" at his school, which consists of some botches trying to make friends. The original purpose of this club was to accept consultations from students and help them to search for solutions, but actually the members come together after school to chat. Hachiman clearly grasps the personality of both himself and the other members, so that is interesting for the readers of his self-deprecatory monologue.

From a general viewpoint, these botches are already friends at the moment of spending many afterschool hours together and enjoying cynical conversation. They often insist that they themselves have enough ability to communicate with others, to study well, and their appearances are not so bad. In other words, they know that they are sufficiently adaptive to relate well to other students. Nevertheless, they absolutely refuse to have actual relationships with others. They never approve of club members as their friends. Even when Hachiman is invited by his classmate to join a tennis club, he rejects the offer because he believes he cannot adapt himself to normal school life. After all, he doesn't want to engage in exchanges with non-botch students. Botch people avoid interacting with others and actively select to be alone. As a result, botch people never make friends, even if they actually do have some relationships.

The notable point is that botch people are simply alone; they keep their botch status while having intimate relations like friendships with the same kind of people, in the way that Hachiman belongs to the "student service club." In clinical cases, many patients who call themselves botch do not have any friends in reality, but have some relationships via the internet, as in the following case.

Case B

The patient, B, is in the third year of university. He had no problem until he entered a university. He said, "I became a *botch*, because there is no one who is *on the same stage* as me." Since entering the university, he hardly leaves his apartment, other than to attend classes solitarily. Because he is so afraid of meeting people face to face, he

AGENCY, A JAPANESE CULTURAL COMPLEX

173

always moves hastily around the campus. When he returns to his room, he immediately goes to BBS for Botch to read what other botches have posted online. (A BBS, which stands for *bulletin board system,* is a kind of online community.) BBS for Botch is the only place that creates a sense of ease for him, where botch people masochistically post typical episodes in their student life one after another: "There are too many sociable people in the cafeteria. I go straight to the library alone at lunch time." "English class. What I dread most are the words, 'Let's practice in pairs!'" "Campus Festival! It's consecutive holidays for me." B commented that the posts from other botches are a reliable and indispensable support for his mind, saying, "I can see that many students have the same troubles as me."

When the therapist asks how and why B became a *botch,* he answers, "I don't know why. No one spoke to me, that's all.... I did not feel that anyone disliked me, but I was just alone.... I always occupy the seat at the end of the first row of the classroom, because I feel more at ease when no one comes into my view." Moreover, he reported that a classmate called him *"B-chan"* in a friendly manner soon after he entered the university, but he did not know his name because B has never mentioned the classmate's name. The therapist points out that the classmate may feel somehow friendly to B. B answers, "I never have thought about what my classmates think about me."

Actually, B spends his student life as a botch. But at the same time, B is not alone. From the seat in the first row where B always sits in classes, B himself cannot see anyone, but the others can distinctly see him. He can find many persons similar to himself on BBS for Botch and feels connected to them. Furthermore, some classmates seem to have tried to build a relationship with B, but he was unaware of the classmates' interest in him, so he did not respond. Although B complains about his situation of being alone, he actually nips off relationships on his own accord.

The BBS format of BBS for Botch is finely categorized by subject. Even for the love-related category, each board has a highly detailed theme, that is, for men who don't get how to hit on girls, for available women who never find a boyfriend through dating apps, for men without girlfriends even though they are understood as being a ladies' man, and so on. Users are strictly segregated and not allowed to say anything that varies from the subject of each board. In the case of *BBS for Botch,* users' posts must be characteristically botch-like. If a user shows a hint of enjoying friendships, he or she comes under fire and is strongly pressured to move to another board. On the BBS, they refer to each other by number, that is, for the subject there is not a person but a post. Because all the posts there are *on the same stage,* users feel they are connected with others even if they do not have personal friendships. In this way, each board maintains a sterilized utopia without any differences by embracing exactly the same kind of people.

What is interesting is that botches never become friends with each other, even if they connect on the same BBS every day. In fact, they meet themselves in BBS for Botch. That is why they stick to maintaining their utopia, so as not to let any other kind of person enter it. B's words, "many students have the same troubles as me," can be translated as "there are many *me's.*" There is a bidirectional movement; one is self-reproducing, and the other is confined to oneself. In that sense, a *botch* is really alone due to constantly excluding others as alien existences. Their relationships can be said to be self-reproductive, not open to others but just a chain of the same things.

The *anthrophobia* (*Taijin-Kyofu-Sho*) that was observed mostly in the 1960s in Japanese society has been thought of as a culture-specific form of social anxiety disorder. Because the main symptom of anthrophobia is anxiety about what others think of them, patients feel a fear of being seen by others. B's condition is the same as anthrophobia in terms of feeling anxious about others, but different in that B can sit down in the front row, which is a place to be avoided at all costs by patients with anthrophobia. The fear of "others" felt by anthrophobia patients is psychological, because their anxiety arises even if they know that no one actually sees them. On the other hand, B does not feel anxious when he does not see anyone, though he actually knows others are there. In other words, it can be said that B lives in a world where only he himself lives.

In 2012, the cafeteria at Kyoto University installed "seats for botch," which was reported by newspapers. In fact, the cafeteria just made spaces for lunching solo by installing partitions on tables. But soon after, the students began calling these seats "botch seats." This term symbolizes the idea that those among the Japanese younger generation who are like B feel relieved *only* if others vanish from their view. The others can be there; they just don't want to see them. Perhaps the self-consciousness seen today among young people in Japan does

AGENCY, A JAPANESE CULTURAL COMPLEX 175

not exist independently, but arises as a reaction to the existence of other people. This is not a psychological complex but particular to the current botch culture.

Less than a story: a stack of moments

The last example of less agency among young people in Japan is of an extreme attitude, a *story less than a story*. Today, social networks are used worldwide. For instance, there are 2.1 billion monthly active users on Facebook (as of January 2018).[18] In Japan, the most popular social networks have changed. In the first decade of the 2000s, Mixi took the initiative. At that time, Mixi set up a "home" for each user, named "My Page," in which the users put up a profile to show themselves to others. "Home" worked as a central reference point for each person in that users could use the page literally as a home, so that they could arrange their "home" and "visit" the homes of their friends.

After 2012, Facebook become predominant, based on the "news feed" instead of "home." The news feed gives users a quick look at related information, including events, photos, videos, status updates, advertisements, the user's "likes," and so on. It is a mixture of data from the user himself or herself, from the user's friends, and from indirect third-party information. On Facebook, the importance of each item is automatically decided by the Facebook algorithm, that is, the unit is not a person but an article. The replacement of Mixi with Facebook has meant a transition from a character-centered style to the fragmented self.[19]

Since 2015, Instagram has increased its market penetration. Instagram is a service facilitating online mobile photo-sharing and video-sharing, whose users upload momentary images one after another. This service is rapidly gained popularity, with over 800 million monthly active users all over the world (reported by Instagram's official website as of January 2018).[20] In Japan, monthly active users have increased to over 20 million, especially among the young generation. Here, I would like to focus on Instagram's weak narrativity. Because Instagram focuses on the posting of images, users upload their pictures with hashtags rather than with sentences. A hashtag is user-generated tagging that makes it possible for others to easily find specific content more immediately and directly. Instagram users tend to pile up many short words with hashtags, for example, "#HappyNewYear #2018 #myfriends #colorful #holiday #girlpower." Differing from Mixi and Facebook, the "I" is represented by a stacking of instant images in

Instagram. The self that was fragmented by Facebook is now even more dispersed and has disintegrated, without temporality or narrativity. (Now many users use hashtags on Facebook, too.)

In this section, I take a short novel written by Kaori Fujino as an example. Fujino, who won Japan's most famous literary prize, the Akutagawa Prize in 2013, gives a cynical view of the Instagram world. The novel's translated title is *"A Challenge of Hyper Realism Pointillist School."*[21]

The story starts with the "greeting" text displayed at the entrance to the museum for the current exhibition on the Hyper Realism Pointillist School. The text explains that the Hyper Realism Pointillist artists have all died out. The artists were all members of the young generation who were physically very fit but the demands of their school were so great as to cause them all to die prematurely. The Hyper Realism Pointillist School, which was active from 2022 to 2037, created works on big screens making full use of pointillist skill.

The artists employed classic drawing methods; they set up a canvas in front of the object that they wanted to depict, and they drew it by stippling, through direct observation. The artists drew the object in detail with a pointed brush day after day. Of course, seasons and weather changed, but they tried to draw all the changes of the object on the same surface, exhaustively. The artists struggled with the canvas in front of them, but they all left this world before they finished the work. Thus, all of the works of this school are the Great Unfinished Work. A famous artist of this school remarked, "I can dedicate my life to this! What's important is now. Seize now!"

Of course, *hyper realism pointillist school* is just an image in this novel. But the concept of *hyper realism pointillist* shows us the negative aspect of the current tendency created by Instagram. The points drawn by the artists are a minimum form of life, but if the points do not unfold as a story, they are just a meaningless collection of dots. Users are so eagerly devoted to grasping the moment "now," that they lose the past and future.

Conclusion: intertwining of I and others as today's possibility of the story

The examples I have given demonstrate that contemporary Japanese people are losing a sense of individual personality. The borderline between self and others is weakening, so that their relationships in reality have become hard to make out. The loss of story means a loss of flow of time. The stack of pictures in Instagram is a symbol of the weak ability to make stories. If this is the case, is the future for Jungian-oriented psychotherapy, which relies on the power of story, hopeless?

To demonstrate the possibility of the power of story today, I introduce Tomoyuki Hoshino's novel *The Night Does Not End*, which won a famous literary award in Japan in 2014.[22] The main character, Leona, longs for her *own* story. Leona deceives many men and threatens to kill them: "If you want not to be killed, tell me a story I can be deeply satisfied by." Many men have failed to tell a sufficiently engaging story, and she killed them. She is looking for the one who can tell her true story at the risk of his life. She knows that "her true story" is nothing but an illusion. But still she wants her story to be told, even if it is a kind of a fiction.

Most of this novel consists of the stories told by Kuon, who is the last man deceived by Leona. Because each story Kuon tells is exciting, the readers become absorbed in the stories along with Leona. Moreover, all of the stories are not only completely different and independent, but also connected with each other; for instance, some characters appear in another story as a different but similar character. As Kuon tells one story and then the next, the chain of stories makes us unable to discern who the subject of each story is, what the difference is between true and false, and whether we live based on our agency. The series of stories deprives logic and consistency of its power and intertwines truth and fiction. However, in the last scene of this novel, the police come to the front door to arrest Leona. In the beginning, Leona was afraid of the police because of the murders she had committed. But in the last scene, Leona remains calm, even when confronted by the police. Leona, who has found her own story in what Kuon told her, has become unafraid of being arrested.

This story lets us and Leona know that the frame of "I" is not so important to get our *own* story. Now, there are many patients who do not tell their own stories by themselves, but find stories from another place—the internet. This might be culturally specific for Japan, but it is not essential "who" tells the story. To think clinically, we tend to think that patients should talk about themselves when they try to make their own story. Like the undefined response to the Rorschach Test, however, a personal story is not necessarily close to oneself, but can

178   CHIHIRO HATANAKA

be open to others, at least for today's Japanese. Our current individual stories can be found in what others tell. As Leona's story shows us, if a story has the power to capture us, we can find our own story within it. An individual story might no longer be limited to an individual; this is the possibility of the story in the age of loss of agency.

Notes

[1] Hazel Rose Markus and Shinobu Kitayama, "Culture and the Self: Implications for Cognition, Emotion, and Motivation," *Psychological Review* 198 (2, 1991): 224–253.

[2] *Ibid.*

[3] S. Kitayama and Y. Uchida, "Interdependent Agency: An Alternative System for Action," in R. Sorrentino, D. Cohen, J. M. Olson, and M. P. Zanna, eds., *Culture and Social Behavior: The Ontario Symposium,* vol. 10 (New Jersey: Erlbaum, 2005).

[4] Takahiko Masuda and Richard E. Nisbett, "Attending Holistically vs. Analytically: Comparing the Context Sensitivity of Japanese and Americans," *Journal of Personality and Social Psychology* 81 (2001): 922–934.

[5] Hayao Kawai, *Dreams, Myths and Fairy Tales in Japan* (Einsiedeln, Switzerland: Daimon Verlag, 1995), p. 13.

[6] H. Honda, Y. Shimizu, M. Imai, and Y. Nito, "Cumulative Incidence of Childhood Autism: A Total Population Study of Better Accuracy and Precision," *Developmental Medicine & Child Neurology* 47 (2005): 10–18; Michael D. Kogan, Stephen J. Blumberg, Laura A. Schieve, Coleen A. Boyle, James M. Perrin, Reem M. Ghandour, Gopal K. Singh, Bonnie B. Strickland, Edwin Trevathan, and Peter C. van Dyck, "Prevalence of Parent-Reported Diagnosis of Autism Spectrum Disorder among Children in the US, 2007," *Pediatrics* 124 (5, 2009): 1395–1403. Anita Pedersen, Sydney Pettygrove, F. John Meaney, Kristen Mancilla, Kathy Gotschall, Daniel B. Kessler, Theresa A. Grebe, and Christopher Cunniff, "Prevalence of Autism Spectrum Disorders in Hispanic and Non-Hispanic White Children Pediatrics," *Pediatrics* 129 (3, 2012): e629–635.

Agency, a Japanese Cultural Complex

[7] Toshio Kawai, "Union and Separation in the Therapy of Pervasive Developmental Disorders and ADHD," *Journal of Analytical Psychology* 54 (5, 2009): 659–675.

[8] Chihiro Hatanaka, "Ambiguous Image of the Patients for Autistic Spectrum Disorder: Analysis of 'Undefined Response' on Rorschach Test," *Archives of Sandplay Therapy* 26 (1, 2013): 29–40.

[9] Toshio Kawai, "Postmodern Consciousness in Psychotherapy," *Journal of Analytical Psychology* 51 (3, 2006): 437–450.

[10] Kyoko Takaishi, "Some Problems of Psychological Growth in Current Students and the Student Support Required for Higher Education," *Kyoto University Researches in Higher Education* 15 (2009): 79–89.

[11] Keiko Iwamiya, *The Puberty of "Normal" Students Today* (Tokyo: Iwanami Shoten, 2014).

[12] Y. Kasahara, *The Essence of Clinical Works on Depression* (Tokyo: Misuzu Shobo, 2009).

[13] C. G. Jung, "The Tavistock Lectures: Lecture V" (1935), in *The Collected Works of C. G. Jung,* vol. 18, ed. and trans. Gerhard Adler and R. F. C. Hull (Princeton, NJ: Princeton University Press, 1976), § 398.

[14] C. G. Jung, *Memories, Dreams, Reflections* (New York: Pantheon Books, 1963), p. 3.

[15] A mascot character is any person, animal, concrete image, or object that represents a group with a common identity. Many companies in Japan have mascots to give a sense of familiarity.

[16] See Ledge.ai, "Give Consideration to Potential Needs of Today's People! Talk of the Town, Panda-Ichiro Who Is LINE [AI]. Surprising 1 to 1 Marketing & Development System." Accessed Jan. 24, 2019, at http://bita.jp/blog/pandaichiro.

[17] Ryo Asai, *The Kirishima Thing* (*Kirishima, Bukatsu Yamerutte Yo*) (Tokyo: Shueisha, 2010).

[18] "Most Famous Social Network Sites Worldwide as of October 2018, Ranked by Number of Active Users (in millions)," Statista.com. Accessed Jan. 3, 2019, at https://www.statista.com/statistics/272014/global-social-networks-ranked-by-number-of-users/.

[19] Hatanaka, "Ambiguous Image of the Patients for Autistic Spectrum Disorder."

[20] Instagram, "Our Story." Accessed Jan. 3, 2019, at https://instagram-press.com/our-story/.

[21] Kaori Fujino, *A Challenge of Hyper-Realism Pointillist School* (*Ohanashi-shiteko-chan*) (Tokyo: Kodansha, 2013).

[22] Tomoyuki Hoshino, *The Night Does Not End* (Tokyo: Kodansha, 2014), p. 33.

8

• • • • • •

Voices from Nature and Withdrawal (*Hikikomori*) in Japanese Culture

Nanae Takenaka

To begin, I would like to introduce a clinical experience from my practice that relates to the theme of this chapter. Working as a psychotherapist in counseling services for university students, I often see students who do not attend classes for months, or even years. Typically, these young adults stay in their apartments day and night for months on end with seemingly no particular motive for this isolation. You might imagine these people have serious reasons that prevent them from having the normal life of a college student, or you might think that these students are just extremely lazy. Both can, of course, be true in certain cases. However, in most cases, neither of these factors represents a sufficient explanation for their withdrawal.

In my example, Rio, a male graduate student, stopped going to his laboratory sessions after summer vacation. One and a half months passed, and then his parents, who in the meantime had become aware of the situation, visited Rio in his apartment and

---

Nanae Takenaka, PhD, is associate professor at the Health and Counseling Center, Osaka University, and works as clinical psychotherapist at the Student Counseling Services. Her article "The Realization of Absolute Beauty: An Interpretation of the Fairytale Snow White" was published in the *Journal of Analytical Psychology* in 2016.

182   NANAE TAKENAKA

brought him to our office. After some counseling sessions and with a great amount of help from his advisor and his parents, we were able to accompany Rio to his laboratory. He was happy to see that his friends accepted him in spite of his long absence. Rio, who seemed to have retrieved his self-confidence, set a subsequent date to go to the laboratory on his own, but on that day he failed to follow through. Although he went the university, he did not go to his laboratory. Instead, according to what he told me subsequently, he had lunch alone at the canteen and then started to browse the internet on his smartphone. After a while, he went to the building where his laboratory was located but instead went into the lavatory. He shut himself in a stall and then returned to his smartphone. After a few hours he went back home. To my question about his thoughts or feelings when he was lost in his smartphone at the canteen and in the lavatory, he could only give an uncertain answer. That is, he said that he was not sure whether he decided to browse the internet because he did not feel like going to the lab, or he just engaged in this activity automatically and then his chance to get to the laboratory on his own had passed.

This type of action by students is usually called "school non-attendance (*Futōkō*)." Nationwide research estimates that the rate of university students who do not attend classes for more than six months is 0.7–2.9 percent of all university students in Japan.[1] Among various subtypes of school non-attendance such as truancy, anxiety, or apathy, the defining characteristic of cases such as Rio's is extreme isolation.[2] This phenomenon is closely connected with a widespread social problem among young adults in Japan, namely, withdrawal from all social relationships. In Japanese, this phenomenon is known as *hikikomori*. The definition of it by the Japanese Ministry of Health, Labour and Welfare reads: "the state that one does not attend work or school and stays at home continuously more than six months, having almost no communications with others except their family members."[3] Although *hikikomori* is not a situation observed solely in Japan, the fact that the Oxford Dictionary adopted the headword *hikikomori* in 2010 indicates that the phenomenon is associated with Japan in a global sense.[4] In this chapter, I would like to explore this type of social withdrawal (*hikikomori*) through the lens of the cultural complex.

VOICES FROM NATURE AND WITHDRAWAL

Statistics on *hikikomori*

Research conducted by the Cabinet Office, Government of Japan, in 2016, found that approximately 541,000 young adults between the ages of fifteen and thirty-nine could be classified as being in *hikikomori*.[5] People who begin to show signs of *hikikomori* are most frequently fifteen to nineteen years old (34.8 percent), and the next most common are ages twenty to twenty-four (25.9 percent). The most frequent length of social withdrawal is greater than seven years (34.7 percent), and then the second-most frequent is three to five years (28.6 percent). The ratio between women and men is 36.7 percent and 63.3 percent, respectively. The research also reported that about 80 percent of the people who are classified as experiencing *hikikomori* have some type of mental health disorder such as schizophrenia or developmental deficits. Other research has assumed that more than 250,000 families (about 0.5 percent of households in Japan) might have a family member in a state of *hikikomori*.[6]

The research conducted by the Cabinet Office has been subject to some criticism. A journalist who works energetically with the *hikikomori* issue, Masaki Ikegami, finds it problematic that this research limited the age of subjects to those younger than thirty-nine, and reported that severe cases of long-lasting withdrawal are seen in those older than the age of forty. Another criticism is about the high rate of those who were regarded as having mental disturbances.[7] Tamaki Saito, an expert in the psychiatric treatment of *hikikomori*, claims that too much emphasis on mental disturbance in these individuals could lead us to ignore other social and cultural factors that underlie this withdrawal.[8] Speaking on the numbers concerning *hikikomori*, Saito assumes that more than one million individuals suffer from social withdrawal. He has maintained that this remains the estimated number of *hikikomori* since he first discussed this problem in his 1998 book.[9]

On another occasion, Saito pointed out that "when one drops out of society, they live on the streets in the UK, while in Japan they can stay at home as a refuge," referring to a BBC survey that reports there are 250,000 young homeless in the UK.[10] The prevalence of *hikikomori* among Japanese young adults apparently indicates the strong ties they have to their home. Here *home* does not mean a literal home, but a symbolical one. Rio could shut himself in, wherever he was, except for the laboratory to which he was supposed to go.

184 · NANAE TAKENAKA

Thus *home* means the place where one is protected from obligations or threats coming from outside, from society. Realistically, parents may also bear some responsibility because without their support a person developing social withdrawal could not continually shut him- or herself in at home. However, these questions of being protected at the home versus homelessness, and the possible solutions to these problems, are not the focus of this chapter. My purpose is to explore psychological explanations for the difficulty expressed by young Japanese adults in leaving home and to identify the cultural complex affecting this situation.

The question of refusal

To comprehend this social withdrawal from the perspective of psychology, it is first helpful to have an overview of the historical changes in how school non-attendance has been viewed in the field of elementary education in Japan. This issue is similar to school phobia and school refusal, which have been topics of discussion in many societies. In Japan, as well as in other countries, when the rate of children who did not attend school began to rise in the 1980s, the name for this phenomenon was *school refusal.* However, *school non-attendance,* seen as a more neutral and inclusive term, has been used since the 1990s to describe pupils who do not attend classes.

When the term *school refusal* or *school phobia* is used, it is assumed that there is anxiety, depression, or physical complaints behind this condition.[11] As an example of school refusal, I refer to the experience of a twelve-year-old student named Carl Jung.[12] One day Jung was pushed over by his classmate and fell down. At that moment he hit his head against a curbstone; he heard a voice in his head saying that he did not have to go to school anymore. Jung was willing to listen to the voice, for he had already found his classes to be boring. Subsequently, Jung "plunged into the world of the mysterious."[13] Every time the idea of returning to school was raised, he suffered fainting spells. This situation continued for more than six months until Jung overheard his father complaining to a family friend about his son's incapacity. He recollected the moment as "[a] collision with reality."[14] Hearing this conversation was so shocking for him that he returned to school and became serious about his studies. In this case, although the fainting spells were not a conscious act by Jung, I assume that underlying his psychological state was a resistance to school education, which might have influenced his symptoms. He had stated he wanted to commune with nature much more than to attend classes. His fainting spells helped him realize this desire; that is, they allowed him to stay away from school. The word *refusal* thus accurately describes the psychological situation in Jung's case.

The change in terminology from *school refusal* to *school non-attendance* came about because "No stable clinical image can be captured (meaning that the actual state of students continuously changes), nor does there exist a stereotype of this phenomenon (i.e. neurotic school refusal or truancy)."[15] As the Ministry of Education, Culture, Sports, Science, and Technology has proclaimed that school non-attendance can happen to anyone, it is difficult to discern typical features of pupils who withdraw from school, and it is not uncommon to find an absence of unusual circumstances in their personal dispositions or environment.[16] Anxiety, physical difficulties, compulsive behavior, or family problems do not always accompany non-attendance. Clues for speculation on root causes or psychological dynamics behind non-attendance are often hard to find.

This ambiguity can also be seen in the term *hikikomori* itself, a word that does not have roots in medical or psychological practice. Originally it was simply used, for example, to describe the behavior of a writer who stays cooped up in a room to finish a work or a person who moves from a large city to the country to avoid the complications of urban life. Discussions of *hikikomori* have sometimes noted the well-known myth of the supreme goddess, *Amaterasu,* who hides herself in a rock cave to withdraw from the world.[17] For the Japanese, withdrawal is deeply rooted in an attitude that allows one to cope with reality. Furthermore, in what may be a difference from Western culture, the ability to hide one's own opinion is considered to be a crucial condition for adulthood. Whether an opinion is positive or negative is not the point. To show one's own individuality is not appreciated as much as the ability to assimilate oneself into society. In a sense, a withdrawal into the collective is what one needs to live in Japanese culture. Thus, as far as withdrawal is not accompanied by symptoms of psychosis or violent behavior, it is not easy to distinguish a pathological withdrawal from the commonly acceptable type; this is especially true at the beginning of social withdrawal.

186

An interpretation of the short story *"Sangetsuki"*: the image of hikikomori in Japanese literature

There are a number of stories and poems in Japanese literature we can look to in the discussion of social withdrawal in young adults.[18] In the investigation of a cultural complex, examining the art produced by a culture may allow more insight than focusing on individual cases, as these works often reflect a deeper layer of the cultural psyche. At this point, I would like to focus on the short story *"Sangetsuki,"* written by Atsushi Nakajima in 1942.[19] My reason for picking the story is that one of my male patients, Kei, who had suffered from withdrawal in the past, once identified himself with the protagonist of the short story.

The synopsis of the story is as follows:[20]

> The protagonist, Li-Cheng, was a capable civil servant who earned quick promotion. However, he felt that the urbane drudgery should not be his business forever. Instead, he had an ambition to make his name as a poet and have his work be known through many generations. In order to commit himself to writing poems, he resigned from government service and cut relationships with all his former friends and colleagues. However, he found afterward that he could not be successful as a poet. To earn a living for himself and his family, he reapplied to the civil service and was assigned to a lower position than he once had, a source of great disappointment. One night he suddenly jumped out of the window and into the dark woodland, never to reappear. When his old friend Yuan-Ts'an and his attendants, who were traveling on imperial orders, stepped into a path in the woods before dawn, they came across a huge tiger. Hearing the tiger say something behind the thicket, Yuan-Ts'an recognized the tiger was Li-Cheng. According to what the tiger told his old friend, on the night Li-Cheng jumped out of the window, he heard an unknown voice calling his name. He was urged to obey the voice. His transformation into a tiger began soon after that and the human spirit in him diminished day by day. Li-Cheng confessed that he always struggled with his timid pride and diffidence. He took this as the reason for his transformation into a tiger. Li-Cheng asked his old friend to write down the verses he composed when he was a human and to tell his family that Li-Cheng has died. Then, Yuan Ts'an left the thicket, when dawn was near.

VOICES FROM NATURE AND WITHDRAWAL

Kei said that he was exactly like the tiger in the story when he shut himself in his room at the age of sixteen. He scorned his parents and his school; at the same time he was ashamed of himself because of his withdrawal. He had no idea how to deal with himself. The tiger living alone in the woods and lamenting his alienation from human society certainly seemed to be an apt illustration of one who withdraws from his real social life and encloses himself in a space where he finds momentary comfort.

Sangetsuki is quite well known in Japan because it often appears in Japanese language textbooks for high-school students. In school the short story is basically interpreted to show that Li-Cheng's transformation into a tiger indicates his lack of humanity, as he is not satisfied with his difficulty in attaining a high position and casts this responsibility aside for his own ambition at the cost of his family's well-being.[21] Thus, the transformation is taken as a punishment for his arrogance. Particularly, Li-Cheng as a tiger says the following to himself in the story:

> My diffident pride was that of a wild beast and, despite all
> my intelligence and culture, I was in the end unable to keep
> it under control.[22]

The understanding of his transformation into a tiger as a punishment leads to the assumption that a person who has unrealistic self-expectations may risk becoming withdrawn. Based on my clinical experiences at the student counseling services, I would confirm that those who do not attend class tend to be convinced that they can and must be perfect in all senses, which causes great disappointment, both in themselves and in reality. These feelings are not applicable only to *hikikomori*, however; it is not at all unusual for young people to have similarly omnipotent fantasies, just as Li-Cheng does. The inclination to be perfect and the possible resulting disappointment do not suffice to explain a long withdrawal from reality. Moreover, from a standpoint that views *hikikomori* as a collective phenomenon in a certain culture, this explanation sounds too personalistic, whereas the cultural complex lies in a deeper layer of psyche. Psychologically, particularly in Jungian psychology, the transformation taking place in a story may indicate that something more than a human deed is in play. Such transformations may point to something important to the soul that is rising to the surface. From this perspective, we can even

188   NANAE TAKENAKA

speculate that the transformation of Li-Cheng into a tiger could be his final salvation from banal all-too-human reality. As long as he is human, his grandiosity or inflated self-esteem may cause conflicts in his life. As a tiger living in the forest, however, he is free from any human trivialities. Li-Cheng was, in fact, fully disappointed with his social life. This interpretation may suggest that *hikikomori* as a cultural phenomenon reflects a psychological impulse to return to nature.

Withdrawal with a purpose

There are two withdrawals in the story. The first is when Li-Cheng decides to leave his position as a civil servant and become a poet. It is noteworthy that what attracts Li-Cheng so much is solely the creation of poetry. His passion for it is irresistible, to the extent that he turns his back on his fame as a civil servant in society. Even if his goal was further fame as a writer, this would not negate his passion for poetry. That is, being a writer is a completely different concept of identity from being a civil servant for the government. As a civil servant, one lives in the society of humans and has to obey orders and be competitive to earn higher status. This is a world dominated by the logic of animus. On the other hand, as a poet, one must listen to the voice of soul, the anima, the home of illogical things such as emotions and feelings. A poem must be created through words that spontaneously arise from the depths. Li-Cheng abandons his course in life and seeks to connect with feelings, emotions, and moods, a compensatory movement in his psyche. A psyche that has been too greatly steeped in animus would seek to regulate the one-sidedness of itself. Furthermore, in a poem Li-Cheng's experiences concerning emotions and feelings have to be conveyed in particular language without diminishing the sensitivity of these emotions, which requires a highly sophisticated function of animus. By choosing to be a poet, Li-Cheng is on the right track in his process of individuation.

As long as the withdrawal takes place as part of Li-Cheng's own desire to be a writer, there is nothing wrong in his withdrawal. Although he could have been overly ambitious, challenging himself at the cost of losing financial or societal stability cannot always be condemned. Moreover, Li-Cheng is able to give this life up and return to society after he realizes that he cannot afford this type of life for his family. Because these actions are conducted on the basis of his conscious decisions, Li-Cheng's initial withdrawal should be distinguished from that seen in Japan's current *hikikomori* phenomenon. What is peculiar

VOICES FROM NATURE AND WITHDRAWAL

to the case of *hikikomori* is the absence of particular reasons and the persistence of the withdrawal.

Withdrawal led by a voice from darkness

It is the second withdrawal in *Sangetsuki* that more precisely illustrates what takes place in *hikikomori*. This episode occurs after Li-Cheng discovers that he cannot make a living as a poet. He returns to his former life and assumes a lower position as a civil servant, a great setback for a person who once had a very successful life in the same society. We might think he would become mentally vulnerable when faced with this unpleasant reality. Thereafter, he hears an unknown voice from the darkness, which causes a permanent and irreversible withdrawal. The crucial difference in this second withdrawal is that his will or conscious decision making is not at work. Instead, something unknown—the voice from the darkness—is now in charge and drags him into a solitary situation from which there is no return. The transformation of Li-Cheng into a tiger may imply that this withdrawal is not his own conscious decision. The Li-Cheng who, as a human being, is capable of making decisions by himself has ceased to exist. If something is not initiated through one's own will, then it cannot easily be brought to an end through individual willpower. In considering *hikikomori,* the situation may not be something the individual has consciously decided. The course of action exists beyond that of subjective decision making. To put this in Li-Cheng's terms, it is the unknown voice from the dark that determines the withdrawal, and taking into account Li-Cheng's transformation into a tiger, we can surmise that behind *hikikomori* there is an enormous power of nature that pulls these individuals into the "wilderness."

Here, again, Jung's own experience in his autobiography is helpful in highlighting the distinctiveness of *hikikomori*. During the period of his confrontation with the unconscious, Jung once heard a woman's voice within him saying that he was doing art. Jung felt "a great inner resistance" against the voice and said, "No, it is not art!"[23] The resistance Jung displays toward this voice is often missed in the case of *hikikomori,* and this lack of resistance can also be seen in the character of Li-Cheng. It is only after Li-Cheng notices that he has become a tiger that he understands what has happened. In addition to the strong influence of nature, we have to note the relative weakness of ego consciousness that is incapable of resisting the unknown voice coming from nature.

Nature and the "I" in Japanese culture

In comparison with Western culture, the "I" in Japanese culture has a unique relationship to nature. Putting aside *Sangetsuki* for a while, I will describe the differences in the conception of "I" in Japan and in the West through observations about the techniques of garden design in these very different cultures.

Among the original styles of garden design in Japan, one of the most famous is *karesansui*.[24] The very well-known *karesansui* garden at *Ryoan-ji* temple is seen in Figure 8.1, which is said to have been designed by a Zen priest around the beginning of sixteenth century. In a minimalistic way, this garden expresses nature, the passage of time, and the universe. Western European culture during the Renaissance had a major influence on garden design. As an example, consider the famous garden at *Villa d'Este,* dating from the Italian Renaissance and designed by Giacomo da Vignola, as shown in Figure 8.2. Marella Agnelli reads the symbolic meaning of the fountains in the Villa as "the water's gradual passage . . . marks and celebrates the dominance of reason over the forces of nature."[25]

Figure 8.1: Ryoan-ji Kyoto Zen garden May 2007.

Figure 8.2: Étienne Dupérac (1525–1604), bird's-eye plan view of the gardens at Villa d'Este (Tivoli) Italy between 1560 and 1575.

From the two images of these gardens we can see the differences in how each culture re-creates nature in a limited space—irregularity or regularity, simplicity or magnificence, de-centralizing or centralizing. In the Western garden, the clarity of the human mind is in the foreground, as the geometrical balance indicates the existence of a sophisticated ego-consciousness that "explores and reveals the mysteries of nature by imitating its marvels."[26] On the other hand, in the Japanese garden,

VOICES FROM NATURE AND WITHDRAWAL

an effort is made to, as much as possible, erase traces of human mind. The focus is on articulating the enigma of nature itself. The garden in *Ryoan-ji* shows us the imperfection of the human mind in a witty way: there are fifteen stones in the garden, one of which is always out of sight no matter where one may stand. In this simple feature, what can be noted is not the ego-consciousness that carries knowledge, but the unknowingness of the "I" emphasized in Japanese culture. It is similar to the Buddhist teaching of the selflessness or emptiness of self. Augustin Berque has noted that "scientific thinking in Europe made a major contribution to separating the natural from the social (by increasingly freeing the physical environment from morality and aesthetics through positive objectivization)."[27] However he described Japan as follows:

> Japanese culture saw nature as essentially good and, furthermore, as fundamentally indistinct from the self, and so could not challenge it. And so it never deliberately placed itself as subject in opposition to nature as object. Much more, in fact: it systematically tended to make nature its supreme referent, even its culmination.[28]

Traditionally, Japanese culture has not developed the idea of establishing ego-consciousness as a fixed point that constructs the world around itself. Instead, the flexibility of the "I" is of great importance. The "I" is defined by nature, by its surroundings. Because nature is beautiful and absolute, the "I" cannot help but recognize its own fragility and dependence on nature. The "I" is a part of Mother Nature.

In *Sangetsuki,* we can find Li-Cheng describing his "I":

> Until recently I used to wonder how I could have turned into a tiger. Now the question that haunts me is a different one: how could I ever have been human?[29]

This reminds us of the episode in Jung's autobiography that occurred when Jung was between seven to nine years old. During this time he sometimes wondered when he was sitting on a stone whether he was sitting on the stone, or the stone as the "I" was having Jung on its surface.[30] His "I" still vacillated between his own self and nature. This may explain his difficulty in adjusting to school: the institution where you learn to understand nature, instead of admiring its wonders. At school the separation from nature is taken for granted, and Jung with his unfixed "I" did not feel comfortable in this environment.

192   NANAE TAKENAKA

During his prolonged absence from school he "was fleeing from himself [myself]"[31] and enjoyed being immersed in nature. Thus, it was only after his fainting neurosis ended that he gained insight into his situation; "I knew all at once: now I am myself!"[32] Going back to school, or society as a whole, means gaining an ego-consciousness that carries a conviction to be one's own agent and to be able to master nature. The subjectivity this ego-consciousness entails greatly helps one adjust *oneself* to this reality. On the contrary, with a vague, unmoored sense of "I," it is apparently not easy to leave nature and integrate into society. Furthermore, because the "I" that Japanese culture has developed is not based on the idea of being separated from nature, integrating into society requires a complicated process of establishing the "I." The Japanese "I" is defined by nature, and as a result it always has to be flexible to some extent, but at the same time, the "I" has to live in reality as an independent adult.

The image of a tiger in nature

The image of the tiger in nature reveals the disappearance of Li-Cheng's ego-consciousness, which once had the clear goal of becoming a poet and was subsequently wholly dissatisfied with reality. He aimed to conquer nature through words, but what happened was quite the opposite; he was swallowed by nature and withdrew from society. Then my last questions shall be these: Why has the tiger been chosen as the vehicle of Li-Cheng's transformation in this story? What does this choice suggest about *hikikomori*?

As mentioned previously, Li-Cheng himself attributes his transformation into a tiger to a diffident pride that he could not tame. The wildness and fierceness of a tiger is regarded as an equal to the huge ego-consciousness Li-Cheng once possessed. It is not difficult to imagine that the human mind would experience its own transformation into such a beast as an awful event that would fill one's consciousness with remorse. However, the image of tiger itself is not something that would be the object of unconditional hatred.

Tigers are not native to Japan, but with the influence from the continent, primarily from China, they have been a familiar motif in Japan (Figure 8.3). In the seventh century, the Japanese government began to use the Chinese zodiac of twelve animals, which includes the tiger in the third position. The order of the twelve animals is correlated with the movement of Jupiter, which travels around the sun about once every twelve years. The tiger is in the third position and thus located at

Figure 8.3: Gunko-Zu, Tanyū Kanō, seventeenth century.

the beginning of spring. Therefore, the image of a tiger as the zodiac sign indicates birth, renewal, and growth. In focusing on its physical features such as its size, beautiful coat, dignified appearance, and elegance of movement, the tiger is regarded as a king of the animal world in Asian countries,[33] and its image was favored by military generals in the Warring States period of Japan (1467–1568). The tiger represents wisdom, vigor, and decisiveness.

If we take into account such positive images of the tiger, Li-Cheng's transformation can be seen in a quite different way from Li-Cheng's own interpretation of his becoming a tiger. Even though Li-Cheng deeply laments his transformation into a tiger, the compelling aesthetic of the image of a tiger reading poems under the moonlight is undeniable. Perhaps Li-Cheng could not become a poet, rather, he becomes a poem, a part of the aesthetic of nature itself. The choice of a tiger as the result of the transformation clearly indicates the inclination inherent in Japanese culture to romanticize a fusion with nature. Considering that nature has such a strong power over the Japanese, *hikikomori* can perhaps be understood as an extreme expression of the desire to be a part of it. Young adults who are still learning how to be the complicated "I" in Japanese culture can easily become entranced by nature, for the "I" in Japan has to simultaneously realize how to be an adult and a child of Mother Nature.

Conclusion

The reality of *hikikomori* is tragic for the withdrawn individuals and their families. As a matter of course, the "I" being dissolved in

194 NANAE TAKENAKA

nature in the cases of *hikikomori* cannot be compared with what the Buddhist tradition describes as the goal of one's spiritual nature. Whereas the latter is a highly developed status of the human mind so as to transcend mundane reality, what is observed in *hikikomori* is simply the giving up of becoming "I." Exactly like Li-Cheng, these individuals are often aware of the extraordinary situation they are in and blame themselves for their own condition. But they do not, or more precisely, cannot do anything to change it. Meanwhile, they stop thinking realistically, or the situation deprives them of the ability to think realistically. And subsequently they cease making an effort to move on. This can be seen as simply letting the "I" dissolve into nature until it ceases to be the agent of oneself. Nature pulling individuals into its domain has great strength in Japanese culture.

In the case of *hikikomori,* people often try to encourage these individuals to come out of their homes. It must be noted, however, that the Japanese in general may have an inclination for withdrawing. If this remains unconscious in the minds of those who are trying to help the withdrawn individuals, the disposition has to be constellated only on the side of those individuals suffering from *hikikomori.* This one-sidedness between the two groups of people may cause a pathologically prolonged withdrawal.

To cure pathologically prolonged withdrawal, we need to remember that the transcendent can only happen when the opposites are brought together, as Jung says.[34] So what is the opposite of "withdrawing into nature"? In Japan this is not as simple as "coming out of nature" or "conquering nature." Basho Matsuo, a nomadic poet in seventeenth-century Japan, said we should "get away from savagery, free ourselves from bestiality, follow nature, return to nature."[35] What is remarkable is that he distinguishes bestiality from the nature that we should follow. As discussed, Japanese culture places great importance on erasing ego-consciousness and following nature, which does not mean a withdrawal into the wild. The difficulty in the case of *hikikomori* seems to be that nature retains its savage or base elements. Without a poetic mind, nature cannot become nature in the true sense of beauty; the "I" who can admire the beauty is missing. As *hikikomori* has become an important social issue over the last few decades, we cannot overlook the influence of events during this period, namely, the rapid development of the economy, in general, and of information technology, in particular, as well as the large-scale

Voices from Nature and Withdrawal

destruction of nature that has taken place in Japan. It is the task not only of those who withdraw from this society, but also all of us to reconsider the aesthetic of nature and to make an effort to see beyond the brutality it can also hold.

Notes

[1] I. Mizuta, S. Ishitani, and N. Azumi, "Current Status and Future Agenda of Support Systems at Universities for Students with School Nonattendance and Social Withdrawal: Findings from a Survey of Student Counseling Centers at Japanese Universities" (in Japanese), *Japanese Journal of Student Counseling* 32 (1, 2011): 23–35. The wide range of data indicates a difficulty in grasping the actual rate of school non-attendance at universities where regular attendance is not always mandatory.

[2] *Student apathy* describes a group of students who shows no interest exclusively in studying. The first report on it was made in the United States (Paul A. Walters, "Student Apathy," in G. B. Blaine and C. C. McArthur, eds., *Emotional Problems of the Student* [New York: Appleton-Century Crofts, 1961], pp. 129–147). In Japan, it began to be reported in the 1960s. Although it was not discussed further in the United States, it has been and continues to be a big concern in secondary educational institutions in Japan (See Y. Kasahara, *Apathy Syndrome* [in Japanese] [Tokyo: Iwanami-shoten, 1984].)

[3] Japanese Ministry of Health Labour and Welfare, Hikikomori no hyōka, shien ni kansuru guidelines [Guidelines on assessment and support for the withdrawers], 2016. Accessed January 2018, at http://www.mhlw.go.jp/file/06-Seisakujouhou-12000000-Shakaiengokyoku-Shakai/0000147789.pdf.

[4] See also T. Kato, M. Tateno, N. Shinfuku, et al., "Does the 'Hikikomori' Syndrome of Social Withdrawal Exist Outside Japan? A Preliminary International Investigation," *Social Psychiatry and Psychiatric Epidemiology* 47 (7, 2012): 1061–1075. The definition reads, "(In Japan) the abnormal avoidance of social contact, typically by adolescent males." "Hikikomori," Oxford Dictionary. Accessed January 2018, at https://en.oxforddictionaries.com/definition/hikikomori.

[5] Cabinet Office, "Wakamono no seikatsu ni kansuru chousa houkokusho" [Report on the investigation of the life of young adults],

196   NANAE TAKENAKA

Government of Japan, 2016. Accessed January 2018, at http://www8. cao.go.jp/youth/kenkyu/hikikomori/h27/pdf-index.html.

[6] A. Koyama, Y. Miyake, N. Kawakami, M. Tsuchiya, H. Tachimori, and T. Takeshima, "Lifetime Prevalence, Psychiatric Comorbidity and Demographic Correlates of 'Hikikomori' in a Community Population in Japan," *Psychiatry Research* 176 (2010): 69–74.

[7] Masaki Ikegami, *Otona no Hikikomori; hontou wa 'sotoni deru riyū' wo sagashiteiru hitotachi* [Hikikomori in adulthood: those who are actually looking for "the reason for going out] (Tokyo: Kōdansha, 2014).

[8] Tamaki Saito, Appendix for the paperback edition of *Hikikomori Bunka-ron* [*The culture of* Hikikomori] (Tokyo: Chikuma-Shobō, 2016).

[9] Tamaki Saito, *Shakai-teki-hikikomori* [The social withdrawal) (Tokyo: PHP-Shinsho, 1998).

[10] Tamaki Saito in an online conversation transcribed by Masaki Ikegami (in Japanese), Diamond Online, 2010. Accessed in January 2018, at diamond.jp/articles/-/9794?page=3.

[11] See Jack H. Kahn, Jean P. Nursten, and Howard C. M. Carroll, *Unwillingly to School: School Phobia or School Refusal—A Psycho-Social Problem* (Oxford, England, UK: Pergamon Press, 1981).

[12] C. G. Jung, *Memories, Dreams, Reflections,* recorded and edited by Aniela Jaffe, trans. Richard and Clara Winston (New York: Vintage Books, 1989), pp. 30–32.

[13] *Ibid.,* p. 30.

[14] *Ibid.,* p. 31.

[15] T. Hosaka, "History, Present State, and Current Tasks of School Non-Attendance" (in Japanese), *The Annual Report of Educational Psychology in Japan* 41 (2002):157–169.

[16] The Ministry of Education, Culture, Sports, Science and Technology, "Tōkōkyohi (futōko)-mondai ni kanshite" [About the School refusal (school non-attendance)], 1990. Accessed January 2018, at http://www.mext.go.jp/b_menu/shingi/chukyo/chukyo3/siryo/06042105/001/001.htm.

[17] The myth is as follows: the supreme Goddess of the Sun, *Amaterasu,* once got angry with her younger brother *Susano-o* who had committed all sorts of violent acts in her sphere. The Goddess found these acts so awful that she hid herself inside a rock cave. Without the Sun Goddess, the world sank into darkness. In spite of all the efforts made by the gods outside the cave to entice the Goddess out, she did

VOICES FROM NATURE AND WITHDRAWAL 197

not come out. But when the goddess of dance initiated a humorous performance in front of the cave, which made the other gods laugh, Amaterasu became curious about what was happening outside and so left the cave. (Myth of *"Amano-Iwato"* written in *Kojiki*, the oldest collection of Japanese myths.) See A. Ogiwara, ed., *Kojiki* (Tokyo: Shogaku-kan, 1983), pp. 38–40.

[18] I have discussed the withdrawal of a young adult in the novel *Sorekara*, written by Soseki Natsume in 1909. See Doris Lier and Nanae Takenaka, "How Can the Individual Refer to Anima Mundi?" in Emilija Kiehl and Margaret Klenck, eds., *Proceedings of the Twentieth Congress of the International Association for Analytical Psychology: Kyoto 2016—Anima Mundi in Transition: Cultural, Clinical & Professional Challenges* (Einsiedeln: Daimon Verlag, 2017), pp. 301–309.

[19] The title *"Sangetsuki"* means, if translated into English word for word, "mountain-moon-story." The short story is based on the Chinese classic *"Jinkoden"* (*Renhuzhuang* in Chinese). Although the writer Nakajima kept the plot almost as it was in the original, he apparently added his own interpretation of the events in his version.

[20] My translation with reference to the English translation by Ivan Morris, with the story title "Tiger-Poet." (See Ivan Morris, "Tiger-Poet," in Ivan Morris, ed., *Modern Japanese Stories* [Tokyo: Tuttle Publishing, 1962], pp. 452–463.)

[21] M. Sano, *"Sangetsuki" wa naze kokumin kyokasho to nattanoka* [How has the *Sangetsuki* become to be used nationally in schools?"] (Tokyo: Taishūkan-Shoten, 2013).

[22] Quote from the text translated by Morris, "Tiger-Poet," p. 462, footnote 22.

[23] Jung, *Memories, Dreams, Reflections* (hereafter *MDR*), pp. 185–186.

[24] "Dry landscape" or "rock garden" in English. If translated word for word, *kare-san-sui* means "dry-mountain-water."

[25] Marella Agnelli, *Gardens of the Italian Villas* (New York: Rizzoli, 1987), p. 50.

[26] *Ibid.,* p. 19.

[27] Augustin Berque, *Japan: Nature, Artifice and Japanese Culture.* Trans. Ros Schwarz (Northamptonshire: Pilkington Press, 1997), p. 142.

[28] *Ibid.*

[29] Morris, "Tiger-Poet," p. 459, footnote 22.

198 NANAE TAKENAKA

[30] Jung, *MDR*, p. 20

[31] Jung, *MDR*, p. 31

[32] Jung, *MDR*, p. 32

[33] K. Minakata, *Jūnishi-ko I* [About the Chinese zodiac I] (Tokyo: Heibon-sha, 1972), p. 16.

[34] C. G. Jung, "The Transcendent Function" ([1916]/1957), in *The Collected Works of C. G. Jung*, vol. 8, ed. and trans. Gerhard Adler and R. F. C Hull (Princeton: Princeton University Press, 1969), § 145.

[35] Bashō Matsuo, *Oi no Kobumi*, 1709 [Notes of the Oi], in Berque, *Japan*, p. 144, footnote 28.

Korea

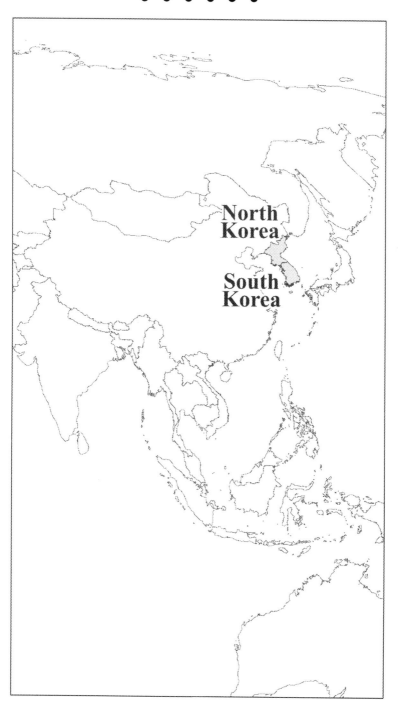

9

• • • • • •

Seeking *Hieros Gamos* on the Korean Peninsula
Understanding the Political Situations of Two Koreas from a Jungian Perspective

Nami Lee

Although dictatorships can be found everywhere—from Salazar in Portugal to Mugabe in Zimbabwe—the Kim dictatorship in North Korea has currently engrossed the world with its history of strict isolationism, aggression against the West, and the intense cultish deification of its leaders. The behaviors of its followers seem incomprehensible to Western perspectives. However, dictatorship is a product of structural failure and should not be attributed to culture or people. For example, poverty, violence, and corruption in Africa cannot be solely attributed to African tribalism but can be viewed as a byproduct of historical and political dynamics such as its history of oppression from imperialism and the slave trade. This chapter aims to clarify and explore the concept of the cultural complex by examining the nature of dictatorial politics in the Korean region through psychological reflection on the Kim family's leadership and analysis

> **Nami Lee, MD, PhD,** is a psychiatrist and Jungian analyst, currently working at Seoul National University hospital. She is teaching psychotherapy for psychiatric residents and medical students, serving as the director of the human rights center at the same hospital. She has published many articles on psychology, culture, and society, and two books, which were translated into Chinese, Thai, and Vietnamese.

202 NAMI LEE

of the unique cultural and psychological characteristics of North and South Korean society.

To contextualize North Korea's leadership, it is necessary to understand its political origins. As the founder of the current North Korean regime, Kim Il-sung based many of his ideas on the communism of Stalin and Mao. Stalin was "a secretive, paranoiac, murderous, and self-glorifying" dictator whose ideology was totalitarian Marx-Leninism.[1] To rationalize his tyranny, he resorted to Russian nationalism. Kim Il-sung devised a similar strategy by antagonizing the United States and solidifying North Korean nationalism.

The North Korean government also shadowed Maoism. Maoism is different from Marxism and traditional communism. Mao was often depicted as a godly figure who resembled the Yao/Shun emperors more than a Marxist leader. Despite the Communist Party's oppression of Confucianism, which only changed recently, Maoism stressed the authority of the government and uniformity among people. Before Deng Xiaoping's regime (1978–1989), the Chinese people had been brainwashed to believe that they should blindly defend Mao's policies and follow whatever instructions he gave. Mao claimed that he would be responsible for curing the rotten country through his benevolent, omniscient, and omnipotent leadership. Even after Mao's dictatorial regime ended, North Korea has continued to practice the idolization of its leadership to sustain its ineffective government.

Mao gained power by antagonizing "The Gang of Four" (四人幫, Sìrén bāng), a political faction composed of four extremist politicians during the Cultural Revolution (1966–1976). He claimed that he had cured the country of the ailment brought on by the Gang of Four. North Korea's dictators gained power through a similar practice. The North Korean government depicts Kim Il-sung and his children as omnipotent and flawless. Kim Il-sung has become a mythologized legend in North Korea; there is a story that he single-handedly fought against Japanese troops and he drove American imperialists and South Korean traitors out of North Korea. The North Korean people are even forced to worship the alleged historical footprints of Kim Il-sung as sacred objects. Thousands of propaganda books that strongly resemble religious scriptures have been published to hail the accomplishments of Kim's family. In contrast to other political ideologies such as liberalism, communism, socialism, and conservatism, in North Korea, Kim Il-sung, a human, is glorified as a

SEEKING HIEROS GAMOS ON THE KOREAN PENINSULA   203

god. Although the North Korean government claims to be a political organization with its own laws and regulations, North Korea in practice is more comparable to a religious cult and lawless mafia. All political and international decisions seem to be made solely by Kim Jung-un, and everyone in North Korea is expected to agree with him. When Kim Il-sung and Kim Jong-il died, people cried and lamented as if their god had died. Some North Koreans may have only acted as if their sorrow was real in order to survive, but there were also many North Koreans who were in genuine despair. For them, Kim's family and his entourage function as divine religious leaders or the shamanic elders of a primitive tribe. To reinforce the divinity of the Kim family, the North Korean Communist Party closed all churches during the earliest days of its regime. Even though there are still a few remaining Christians and Buddhists in North Korea, it has been extremely difficult for the North Korean people to participate and believe in any religion. Children and students are brainwashed from nursery school onward to worship the Kims. They have learned to revere Kim Il-sung as being above godly figures in other religions.

However, the Kim family more closely embodies archetypal images of the warrior and trickster-villain instead of those of a compassionate and benevolent god. Although the Kim family is presented as being generous and omniscient, in their impulsive violence against foreign enemies they more closely resemble *Cú Chulainn,* an Irish mythological hero who would physically transform himself into a terrifying and invincible warrior during moments of rage.[2] North Korea has committed many unpredictable acts of violence against the United States and South Korea: examples include the *Pueblo* incident in which the *USS Pueblo* was taken and eighty-three US sailors were kidnapped for eleven months in 1968; and the incidents in *Panmun-jom* in 1976, when several North Korean soldiers killed US soldiers with axes because they thought the Americans had insulted North Korea. This extreme reactivity is akin to the Irish hero whose violent spasms as a demonic/divine berserker—"a guardian totem animal deity"—often were precipitated by being shamed or having his honor assaulted by the insults of his enemies.[3] Similarly, the North Korean regime is considered one of the world's most unpredictable and is highly reactive to any form of insults or external pressures. It may not be a simple coincidence that Kim Il-sung (1912–1994) was chosen to become the ruler when he was in his thirties (circa 1946). In Korean culture, seniority is important for establishing organization. Being a political leader in one's early thirties is possible only for a king. Some historians believe that Kim Il-sung stole the persona of the real Kim Il-sung who was a legendary guerilla leader fighting the Japanese troops early in the twentieth century. But other historians think that he was a real guerilla-leader before he returned to North Korea).[4] Kim Jong-un (circa 1983–) surprisingly inherited his father's power when he was in his late twenties or early thirties in 2011.

The Kim family, in its pursuit of self-deification, may be an example of how an archetypal hero complex can devour the whole society of a country and how the hero/savior image can be used to rationalize tyranny. This archetypal identification has expressed itself in *Kim-il sung-ism*, or *Juche*. For decades, Kim Il-sung has been depicted as a godly leader in his role as the benevolent creator of the North Korean Kingdom. His embalmed corpse, which resides in a glass coffin, is worshipped as being sacred. Kim Jong-il intentionally played the role of a loyal and devoted son to Kim Il-sung and as the sacred successor to his holy Father of Kim Il-sung. Kim Jong-un has claimed the inheritance of his grandfather's great legacy. Sustaining Kim Il-sung's teachings and principles became his son's and grandson's most important mission. And *Kim Il-sung*'s fatherly dream of inheriting power was staged as Juche.

Instead of mocking such phenomena and describing North Korea as abnormal, however, we need to understand the trauma of the broken political system on the Korean peninsula during the nineteenth and twentieth centuries, which led to North Korea's current bizarre political environment. Korean history, culture, and its collective psyche all played a part in creating and sustaining the Kim family's propaganda and dictatorship and may give us some clues about both the political and psychological conflicts within North Korea. To this end, this chapter examines the psychological implications of the relationships among the major players in the region—North Korea, South Korea, and the United States. A closer look at some of North Korea's unique political ideologies and phenomena will follow, ending with a discussion of the persistent and growing cultural gap between the North and South, as well as possible paths toward integration.

The psychological meaning of "division/unification"
(분단/통일, bundan/tong-il) in Korean history

The current partition between North and South Korea is a relatively recent development in the Korean Peninsula's long history as a unified kingdom. *Go-joseon* (2333 BCE–108 CE) was the oldest unified kingdom on the Korean peninsula. After the Three Kingdoms period (57–668 CE), *Silla* (57 BCE–935 CE), annexing *Baekjae* (18 BCE–660 CE) and *Goguryo* (37 BCE–668 CE) in the seventh century, became the second unified kingdom. And *Goryo* (918–1392 CE), which defeated *Silla* and *Barhae* (698–926 CE), was the third unified kingdom. *Chosun* (1392 –1910 CE), the final unified kingdom, had sustained a centralized and unified regime until the imperialist Japanese troops invaded Korea in 1910.[5] Korea had also developed a unique culture of printing and literature. For example, Korea developed the printing press used for Buddhist scripture and other books no later than 1232.[6] Its own distinctive and ingenious writing system, *Hangul,* was invented in 1446 by King Sejong and his scholars. In addition to the pride of having developed a singular culture and history for thousands of years, the Korean people also developed a strong psychic solidarity with each other in response to the memory of having been invaded and having fought back against foreigners for thousands of years.

However, in 1945, the victors of World War II, who considered Korea a Japanese colony, divided Korea. The Soviet Union occupied North Korea, and the United States took South Korea. At first, the Korean people did not realize such a division would last for so long. Despite the expectations of unification in the near future, the Korean War broke out in 1950. The war caused several million casualties and extreme poverty all over the peninsula. Korea was full of PTSD victims, and millions of families were separated from each other.

Most Korean people view this ongoing political division between the North and the South as artificial and in need of correction, as both countries share the same language and history. Contemporary resistance to unification mostly stems from the economic burden that may come from unification and the significant numbers of young people who do not consider North Korea a part of their own country anymore. Korea now has little living memory of a time before division; this cultural history is now far from Koreans' personal experience.

Meanwhile, in North Korea, ever since the late Kim Il-sung blamed the United States and South Korea for his nation's tragedies,

North Korea has labeled itself as a victim of the so-called imperialists' war. North Koreans have been taught to believe in Kim's version of history, and they deny the fact that Kim Il-sung initiated the Korean War. Instead, North Korean politicians often condemn South Korea and the United States for causing the Korean War and bringing about North Korea's poverty (which was, in reality, caused by international sanctions against North Korea). Such an attitude has created the rationale for North Koreans to be more violent toward the United States and South Korea in retaliation for dividing the peninsula. For seventy years, North Korea's authoritarian government has told its people that North Korea must make atomic bombs in order to prevent invasion by the United States, whereas most countries see North Korea as the perpetrator of violence as one of the world's most unpredictable and dangerous countries. On the other hand, South Korean dictators such as Park Chung-hee and Chun Doo-hwan also rationalized the oppression of their own people through propaganda against communism. Dictatorship was possible because people feared and resented war. And the Korean psyche, both in the North and in the South, has retreated to psychological defenses that have further divided the two Koreas. For example, projection onto North Korea as an evil enemy of South Korea has caused fear among the South Korean people, allowing many dictators to rationalize their corruption and violence against civil rights. In order to protect South Korea, many politicians also advocate further economic sanctions against North Korea, which has only led to North Korean civilians dying of starvation. People who advocate aid for North Koreans are seen as traitors, as those goods will eventually be used to feed soldiers and dictators.

South Korea has been in many internal disputes because of its ideological splitting between the right and left. Those citizens and politicians who advocate for political or economic equality are often labeled as Communists. Conservatives sometimes express fear that North Korea is secretly manipulating younger and progressive South Koreans. Politicians, worldwide, often become demagogues who deliberately increase anger toward the minority for the sake of sustaining their own power. Some politicians target immigrants, refugees, homosexuals, minorities, among others. In South Korea, Socialists and Communists were victims of oppression, somewhat similar to the fates of Communists or Jews during the Nazi regime

SEEKING HIEROS GAMOS ON THE KOREAN PENINSULA 207

in Germany. Traumatized South Koreans who lost their families and property and who were maimed by the North Korean Communists during the Korean War have been fearful of communism and believed the North Korean troops would kill the innocent South Korean people if unification happened. Poor and illiterate people often think their jobs will be taken by foreigners and North Korean people and South Korean people will be in danger. To some degree, discrimination grows out of psychological instability and insecurity that originates in fear of change. Similarly, refugees or foreign laborers or immigrants have already been discriminated against by some people who are afraid of losing their jobs. The rich and the powerful are also afraid of losing their prestige to Communists.

With such concerns common among conservative people, Presidents Park and Chun accused many innocent anti-government citizens of being secret spies for North Korea. These dictators and their followers have claimed that South Korean students and politicians were covertly paid to demonstrate. Some people even believed that the *Gwangju Uprising* for democracy in 1980 was secretly maneuvered by the North Korean government. Extreme rightists have declared that the *Candle Revolution*, which led to the impeachment of President Park Guen-hye, dictator-president *Park Chung-hee*'s daughter, in 2016, was also staged by Communists.

Generally, many liberal people have criticized South Korean conservatives for being too rigid and resistant to change, pointing out the similarities between South Korean conservatism and McCarthyism in the United States. The rightists claim that they strive to conserve traditional virtues and liberty; the leftists insist that they preserve and strive for human rights and justice. Fundamentally, if both their proclaimed values were actually put into practice, their agendas could contribute to a better society. But many of them present their ideologies as being perfect by devaluing the other's beliefs. Extremists accuse each other of being enemies of progress and transformation and often end up idealizing dictators as their saviors, regardless of ideologies. They also identify themselves with their leaders, which helps explain the deep grief and lamentations of common people when those dictator-leaders have died or stepped down. Many conservatives wept when dictator Park died and when his daughter was later impeached in South Korea, in a manner comparable to the North Korean people who mourned for

208   NAMI LEE

the deaths of father-*Kim Il-sung* and son-*Kim Jong-Il.* The profound identification and empathy that the public felt for the loss of their leaders may not be too different from the deep sorrow that ancient and medieval people felt when their kings died.

This political division between ideologies within South Korea and the antagonism between the North and the South are manifestations of the inner splitting and projective identification that occurs in the Korean collective psyche. But despite this psychological splitting, most Koreans still hope for unification of the Korean peninsula (North Korea may be more desperate for unification than the South due to its poverty and oppression). The hope for unification can be seen as being equivalent to the longing for restoration of original wholeness. As discussed, the Korean peninsula had been a unified nation since the Silla Kingdom, or late Silla period (668–918 CE). Thus the division between North and South Korea has been viewed as an abnormal status forced upon Korea by external superpowers. Even so, the countries on both sides of this split tend to see the other as an enemy. Some conservative politicians in South Korea voice military concerns about being invaded by North Korea when their own power is being threatened. To those who are fearful of North Korean communism, they live to fight against communism and preserve liberal democracy. The result of this sense of lost wholeness paired with the ever-present threat by the current government's ideology of choice—left versus right or North versus South—results in an unsettling ambivalence toward unification.

A psychological understanding of the political situation between Korea and the United States

In order to understand the Kim family's dictatorship, we also need to understand the relationship between Korea and the United States and the effects of the US's continued presence on the peninsula. The Kim regime has shrewdly used its citizens' pathological fear of an external superpower to sustain its political stability, identifying the United States as its imperialist enemy and as a threatening presence since 1945. Even when they were given American aid, North Korean leaders secretly planned for impending skirmishes with the United States because they were worried about being attacked first.[7] To them, the United States and the wealthy West were the sources of the world's evils and disasters. The US's presence on the peninsula and a deeply

SEEKING HIEROS GAMOS ON THE KOREAN PENINSULA   209

rooted fear in Korea's collective memory of occupation by foreign powers were influential in shaping the current North Korean regime from the start.

Initial contact between Korea and the United States was not necessarily constructive. In 1866, at the beginning of the modern era, the American schooner *Surprise* was cast ashore on the northwestern coast of Korea. The ship's captain and crew members were well-treated by the Korean government and people, but eventually they were sent back home, albeit with a warning not to come back. But a few months later, the *General Sherman*, a commercial vessel that carried treasure hunters, sailed up the *Daedong* River to *Pyongyang*. Despite the warnings by the Korean government, the *General Sherman* tried to land. This provoked the Korean army to set it on fire. Every member of the crew was killed. In 1871, a further attempt by an American minister and navy soldiers to establish a connection between the two countries failed.[8] After the *General Sherman* incident, another ship with various goods tried to negotiate a diplomatic treaty for shipwrecked sailors and trade. But the inappropriate aggressiveness of the Americans and fear of the Chosun Dynasty made a diplomatic expedition impossible. Instead, it led to an armed conflict with hundreds of casualties.[9] The official relationship between the United States and Korea began in 1882 when Korea signed a Treaty of Amity and Commerce with the US. This occurred around the same time that Japanese troops arrived on the Korean peninsula to fight Chinese troops.[10] This time, Emperor Gojong might have believed that the United States, a Western superpower, would protect Korea from China, Japan, and Russia. But diplomats and government officials who traveled to the West, including the United States and Switzerland, did not receive any political or diplomatic support from Western nations. Interestingly, about a century later in 1980, a similar situation occurred, when *Gwangju* citizens felt betrayed by the US government when the United States confirmed and supported the regime of dictatorial President Chun.

These nineteenth-century incidents helped lay the groundwork for an ongoing lack of trust between North Korea and the United States. According to the Potsdam Declaration following World War II, the United States and Soviet Russia decided to occupy the Korean peninsula with their armed forces in 1945; from the perspective of most Koreans, it did not seem to be much different from the Japanese imperial occupation (1910–1945). When Soviet Russia planted their totalitarian Stalinism in North Korea beginning in 1945, the US government could have helped establish democracy in South Korea, despite their skepticism about the capabilities of Koreans. In a 1945 letter from a political advisor in Korea to the Secretary of State of the United States, Koreans were depicted as "being indifferent to the future of their country ... and no thought is given to the future."[11] Instead, Americans who did not understand the language, psyche, and culture of Korea tried to play the role of hero and teacher by giving concrete instructions to the Koreans whom they considered to be lazy and ignorant. Or perhaps they imagined they were fighting against the totalitarianism and dictatorship of Communists. Many Americans still seem to believe that they are superior and blessed and chosen by God to lead the fight against evil and corruption in the world. Consider, for example, President George W. Bush's combative declaration against the "Axis of Evil," which originates not only from his own personal psyche, but also from the collective memory of the United States as the savior of the world against communism and dictatorship—a belief that now spans a century. After all, North Korea was one of the members of the "Axis of Evil." Along with sustaining the rescue fantasy of saving the poor and those suffering from communism and dictatorship, the United States has proudly taken on the role of hero for keeping liberty and democracy safe in the world. The situation of the poor and yet-to-be democratized Korea in 1945 may have quickened the United States' resolve to work eagerly to implant ideas of Western freedom in South Korea to fight the spread of communism that could easily infiltrate from North Korea. Americans may also have been eager to prove the superiority of Western capitalism over Russian communism and Eastern feudalism.

No matter what the motives of the US government were at the time, South Korea has become an excellent model of a newly developed liberal, democratic, and Westernized capitalist country since 1987, when President Chun stepped down. Concurrently, North Korea has become a failed Communist and isolationist country. North Korea's old proclamation that they do not envy any other country may reflect their hidden jealousy of and anxiety toward the much more prosperous South Korea and United States. In other words, North Korean nationalism may, in fact, be a defensive demagoguery covering up their feeling of inferiority. But such a nationalism cannot

SEEKING HIEROS GAMOS ON THE KOREAN PENINSULA   211

last forever, primarily because of the inevitable economic hardship that ensues from dictatorships. As a result, politicians in North Korea have tried to ignite the anger of the North Korean people against the United States as their ongoing oppressor and impending attacker in order to intensify nationalism and national cohesion.

The Communist ideal, which in reality proved to be too ambiguous or too abstract to be practically implemented, can be more persuasive to common people if it is set beneath the powerful and convincing umbrella of nationalism.[12] The North Korean government offers a good example of how to use a nationalist posture against the United States as a means of controlling the oppressed. But, in an increasingly globalized world, it is hard to believe that this kind of nationalism against the United States will work over the long term in oppressing the economic desires of common people in North Korea. Although the North Korean government only allows intranet for most people, news and cultural resources have been secretly disseminated throughout the years.[13]

In addition to the use of anti-American sentiment and fear as a tool of psychological manipulation, North Korean politicians have quite convincing reasons to be afraid of being invaded and annihilated. In particular, the vast inequality of economic power between the South and the North has deepened since the 1980s, after President Park Jung-hee died. North Koreans may be fearful that, if unification happens, the assimilation of North Korean into South Korean and/or American culture would occur inevitably and unfavorably. The persecutory fear of richer and stronger countries overpowering them may perpetuate North Korean dictatorial oppression.

South Korea is also not free from the misuse of nationalism against the foreign dangers of communism, perceived as threats from the superpowers of Russia and China. In contrast to South Korean Presidents Kim Dae-jung (1998–2003), Ro Mu-hyun (2003–2008), and current president Moon Jae-in (2017–), conservative South Korean governments have initiated little significant dialogue with North Korea due to the fear of being invaded.[14] The possibility of North Korea using its atomic bombs feeds the sense of danger of being destroyed by a Communist power. And the American flag and anthem, by which some conservatives make themselves known in the streets in demonstrations against the progressive South Korean government

212   NAMI LEE

and North Korea, are often used as symbols of their opposition to communism. They believe that the United States has protected democracy from North Korean communism.

Despite the long history of mistrust and hatred between North Korea and the United States, it has recently become apparent that the North seeks to establish a new relationship with the US. Furthermore, since taking office, South Korean President Moon has actively played the role of mediating between North Korea and the United States. However, rightist politicians and their supporters often accuse the more progressive Presidents Kim, Ro, and Moon of wanting the South to become a Communist country and of having paid huge bribes to the North Koreans. The more conservative South Korean Presidents Lee Myung-bak and Park Geun-hye were not interested in reconstructing the broken relationship between the United States and North Korea. To those of the extreme right in South Korea, North Korea can never be a reliable counterpart with whom to engage in dialogue. From a Jungian perspective, the right's and left's extremists function as shadows of each other.

Referring to Jung's idea on the shadow complex, analyst Marie-Louise von Franz explained the concept of shadow in political situations as follows:

> The contemporary division of society into a right wing and a left wing is nothing but a neurotic dissociation, reflecting on the world stage what is happening in the individual modern man; a division within himself, which causes *the shadow*—that is, what is unacceptable to consciousness—to be projected onto an opponent, while he identifies with a fictitious self-image and with the abstract picture of the world offered by scientific rationalism ... and especially to the loss of caritas, the love of one's neighbor.[15]

Jung's concept of the "shadow" can be applied precisely to the oppositional stances between South and North Korea, and between the United States and North Korea. For example, just as nationalism in the United States has influenced its brave upholding of freedom and human rights around the world, it can also instigate reckless participation in wars such as those in Vietnam, Iraq, and Afghanistan. South Korean extreme rightists often use the ideology of nationalism as a rationale to be violent and destructive. They repeatedly state that they are not afraid of war and should attack

SEEKING HIEROS GAMOS ON THE KOREAN PENINSULA   213

North Korea to kill its dictators, free the oppressed, and execute the traitors in South Korea. At the same time, North Korean people are encouraged to become heroic fighters against Western imperialism.[16] Furthermore, North Korean nationalism fueled the development of a nuclear weapon, despite poverty and oppression. To them, the atomic bomb is a symbol of their independence. They needed their own ideology since their isolationism stems from the fear of being invaded and the feeling of inferiority. And the ideology of Juche provided the resolution with which to justify the country's isolationism and over-militarization.

Juche: mask of psychological and financial default status

Kim Jong-il emphasized three fundamental principles of Juche: sociopolitical independence, economic self-sustenance, and self-reliance in defense.[17] Presented in understandable language for a public that had never been exposed to democracy, North Korean scholars who advocate Juche have described North Korea as a self-contained and self-sustaining nation, analogical to the notion of a happy family that lives independently and without external influences.[18] Although decorated with gaudy words, this propaganda functions primarily to justify the Kim family's oppressive dictatorship and isolationist stance. The underlying governing principle is to resist all external influences, especially from enemies such as the United States, South Korea, and Japan. Although Juche followers proclaim that they are too proud to be influenced by any external forces, their propaganda seems to be related to wounded narcissism: a mixture of fear and pride. Narcissistic wounds associated with the feeling of inferiority may be hidden behind a boastful presentation. Jung once clarified that pride was often only a reaction covering up a secret fear.[19]

Although Juche has been the Kim family's enduring legacy, under Kim Jong-un the North Korean regime has formed a new version of Juche—the *Byung-jin*—which means dual-track development of the economy and the military.[20] The collapse of communism in Russia and Eastern Europe and the rise of capitalism in China, Russia, and Eastern Europe threatens the stability of the North Korean regime. Furthermore, propaganda emphasizing North Korean supremacy without significant economic improvement is starting to wear out the trust of North Korean citizens. The common people in North Korea could revolt against their young and inexperienced leader if they

214   NAMI LEE

continue to starve, regardless of persistent brainwashing and being deeply engrained by Juche.

The caste system that Kim Il-sung instituted also seems to be changing. For example, decades ago, only pure proletarians, or families of so-called truthful revolutionaries against the US and the Japanese, were allowed contact with people outside of North Korea. Now, commoners who have relatives outside the country or who work in foreign countries or do business with foreigners are beginning to become richer and more powerful than the truthful proletarians. Economic power through a free market economy and independent merchandising skills are also building up newly rich families. Since the mid-1990s, *Jang-madang* (meaning market grounds functioning as free markets) have been spontaneously formed by people bringing and selling goods in order to survive. The government could not offer enough food or clothes because the state rationing system no longer functioned after continued famine and financial failures.[21] These markets arose spontaneously to overcome starvation at the time of great famine in 1990s. According to more recent defectors, most North Koreans began to realize that South Korea is much wealthier, especially since the 1988 summer Olympics in Seoul. Various electronic devices have been secretly smuggled into North Korea and have exposed people to a capitalistic lifestyle. Significant numbers of North Korean people, having heard about free countries, may envy South Koreans' freedom and prosperity. Political manipulation is not as persuasive in this era of digital modernism. Hopefully, the era of religious devotion to the Kim family will come to an end with the rise of capitalism in North Korea.

In contrast to the secretive and reserved Kim Jong-il, Kim Jong-un appears more outgoing and confident—possibly a more humanized version of the Kim family. He has partially adopted his grandfather's image by imitating his hair style and outfits. At the same time, he also highlights his own value system and spontaneous esthetic tastes, such as emphasizing theme parks and sports resorts. To some degree, he does not just exist to sustain his family's legacy but claims his own authority as a modern, capable, and progressive leader. He is willing to do away with some aspects of his father and grandfather. For instance, his wife is permitted to wear Western products in public and refers to Kim Jong-un as her husband like a common citizen. This was unacceptable in his father's and grandfather's era. In addition

Seeking Hieros Gamos on the Korean Peninsula   215

to separating his own identity from that of his father and his deified grandfather, Kim Jong-un seems to want to be more innovative, but practical. Although the Kim family dictatorship is a cultish combination of communism, Confucianism, and nationalism, it is changing, partly as a result of external forces and partly dictated by internal necessity and desperate demand for change.

The cultural gap between North Korea and South Korea

Even though the cultural history of a united Korean peninsula is much longer and older than the period of its partition, various recent pressures have aggravated the political split into a deep cultural one. When the Kim family gained control of North Korea in 1945, lands and assets were confiscated by the government and redistributed to the so-called proletariat. But step by step, especially after their ideology was transformed from communism/Stalinism into *Kimilsung-ism* (Juche), in the 1960s, North Korea has become more and more isolated and impoverished. The Kim family's amoral paternalism became the most important decision-making force, analogous to how ancient feudal kings governed their lands. The Kim family's regime has become something that is beyond rational debate or systematic reflection. Nobody is ever allowed to question its moral fortitude or to point out apparent corruptions. The economy deteriorated after Kim Il-sung died. The famines and floods, due mainly to poor agricultural policy, lack of productivity, and low motivation, caused the unimaginable starvation of millions of people. Since 1990, Kim Jong-il and his successor, Kim Jong-un, have been estranged even from Russia and China. The *Perestroika* of Gorbachev and *Dengism* of Deng Xiaopin contributed to the normalizing of relations between those countries and South Korea, but North Korea has clung to its own old ideology.[22] The North Korean economy has failed not just because of communism, but also because of its corrupt dictatorship, isolationism, and blindly forced loyalty to its tyrants. The oppressors have been unaware of their egocentric greediness, and the oppressed have been uninformed and unaware of what happens inside and outside of North Korea for several decades.

Lévy-Bruhl's term *participation mystique* may be useful in understanding such an undifferentiated and underdeveloped state of consciousness in a totalitarian society. Totalitarian dictators persuade and coerce their people into believing that their value system and attitudes are the most efficient and, in fact, necessary. Perfect conformity with the leader is the highest virtue. When such a crude and harsh conformity has been imposed on a society by a tyrannical leader, there is no room for diverse perspectives or debates on what is right or wrong. Both politically and psychologically, one person decides everything for everyone. A harsh and forceful demagoguery prevails by claiming to be the absolute truth, just as kings did in the medieval era. In modern North Korea, primitive despotism has gripped the country.[23] Its citizens have been brainwashed to worship Kim Il-sung's teachings, and the Kim family has become even more totalitarian than the monarchs of the old Korean kingdoms.[24]

Communism was originally conceived to remedy the hopeless gap between the classes. Although poor people around the world had hoped for a better life through communism in the twentieth century, most discovered its limitations and considered it a deceptive and failed system. Meanwhile, the gap between the rich and the poor in capitalist countries grows even wider. The Occupy Wall Street movement and the Umbrella Revolution in Hong Kong are signs of people's dissatisfaction with such inequality. But even though financial injustice and political dissatisfaction exist in capitalist societies, the quality of life in South Korea is, in general, far better than that of North Korea. The widening economic gap between the two Koreas is splitting Koreas' cultures even further apart, weakening their desire for consolidation.

Individuals who have experienced both Koreas have a difficult time adjusting to the widening gap. Defectors usually become frustrated in the process of adapting to life in South Korea. They do not know how to handle money and survive in highly competitive working conditions; they sometimes feel inferior to South Koreans since they do not understand English and lack other information and knowledge fundamental to basic life in South Korea. As refugees and immigrants, they feel marginalized, isolated, lonely, incompetent, and confused about their identity. Trauma caused by famine and the life-threatening exodus from North Korea may make the adaptation process in South Korea even more difficult and painful.[25]

Therefore, even if the political conditions for unification were present, the psychological connectedness between North and South, on both individual and collective levels, must solidify in order to overcome the cultural differences between the current national

SEEKING HIEROS GAMOS ON THE KOREAN PENINSULA 217

identities of North and South Korea. The irreconcilable disputes between the right and the left in South Korea pose a challenge as well. Without proper and mature psychological consideration of the feelings and positions of "Others"—as in between the two Koreas and their two dominant ideologies—unification will not be successful. Furthermore, subsequent psychological instability may give rise to a new cultural complex that would mainly be related to the fear of a severe devaluation of the old way of living and thinking, as happened in Russia after the collapse of the Soviet Union. For example, older and conservative people in South Korea have been increasingly angry at and repulsed by President Moon, simply because he is willing to communicate with North Korea and try to establish a positive relationship between the two Koreas. To some, fighting against North Korean communism is not only moral, but also an existential concern about life and death. Although C. G. Jung said, "The Communist revolution has debased man far lower than democratic collective psychology has done, because it robs him of his freedom not only in the social but in the moral and spiritual sphere," democratic capitalism does not seem to have the power to enlighten the darker side of the collective psyche.[26]

Under the umbrella of consumerism, materialism, and capitalism, it is true that individual desire and determination have been respected in South Korea since 1988. Freedom of the press allows internet users to criticize their presidents without being censored, which has never been possible in North Korea. In addition, a citizen's national identity as a Korean in the South is not as intense as it once was, owing to the rapid development of individualism and globalization, and certainly not as intense as it is in the North. Globalization in South Korea tends to make people less nationalistic, which may in turn hinder the unification process as the motivation for solidarity decreases. For example, South Korean people now feel closer to Americans than they do to North Koreans. Most South Korean people identify themselves with people in advanced countries and are losing the ability to sympathize with the citizens of North Korea. The cultural and psychological differences between the two Koreas and possible hatred and disdain for each other will be a most challenging task when or if political unification is accomplished.

Since 1945, the two Koreas have been afflicted by excessive emotional hatred for one another. These powerful negative emotions

218 NAMI LEE

have been fanned and manipulated by dictators using Cold-War ideology. Von Franz wrote, "whenever we suffered from excessive emotional fascination, whether of love or hate, there is always at bottom a projection ... as a universal psychological phenomenon of ... archaic identity (denoting psychological conformity)."[27] Thus, if there is to be a successful reunification of North and South Korea, the people will need to withdraw their projections onto the other, replacing deep antipathy with empathy. In addition to the hard psychological work of withdrawing negative projections, military and economic reconciliation will also have to occur for a wholesome unification between the two Koreas, and even between North Korea and the United States. The reunification of East and West Germany may provide something of a template for such a process.

My personal response to my chapter

The day I started this project, brooding over the Kims, I had a dream: *Many medical students, all wearing the same old Korean student uniforms, gathered in a huge plaza. Only a few, including myself wore sweat suits. I was perplexed and a bit ashamed as I was not wearing a uniform, and I was also the only one who did not finish vacation homework. I was searching for the room of an important patient in a big training hospital for my medical practicum. While I had difficulties in finding him, my friend, a medical college professor, appeared wearing a white gown to let me know that she already finished her homework. She was one of the most successful professors in the medical field.*

My dream ego seems to be envious of the uniform, a sign of the collective psyche and its persona, as embodied by the eminent professor. No person or country is immune to the alluring power of the collective psyche and jealous feeling toward the superior. In the West, consumerism and materialism may subtly and cunningly influence people as its own kind of totalitarian ideology, causing them to worship material wealth and its power. In North Korea, Juche embodies the totalitarian attitude of the Kim family. In South Korea, many varied ideologies, such as socialism, nationalism, materialism, capitalism, and Confucianism, can converge to function as totalitarian ideologies that drive people to conform to the collective psyche instead of toward individuation, "being one's true Self."

Seeking Hieros Gamos on the Korean Peninsula   219

In order to understand our own personal shadows, we can think of the Kim family and the North Korean psyche as being a shadow of the West, South Korea, and, on a finer level, ourselves. South Korea has emphasized materialistic success and prosperity while often disregarding cultural traditions and identity. On the other hand, North Korea has tried to achieve mental independence from stronger countries and to preserve national pride, despite their poverty and underdevelopment. We need to understand the minds of "others" to clarify our own dark sides. North Koreans will have to do the same.

In my dream, I felt envious toward the medical students wearing white gowns and the professors wearing nametags. This may not be too different from the envy of North Koreans toward South Koreans and the West. But, interpreting it in another way, I was not fully aware of my jealousy toward conforming people, who appear to be not aware of alienation and isolation. My lack of confidence and feeling of being alone in my dream is related to the human fear of being rejected, ostracized, and lonely. Perhaps my hesitancy of pursuing the solitary and toilsome path of individuation is not so different from the common people's stubborn loyalty to the collective psyche that results from the fear of being rejected and left out.

Being acknowledged and included by others and superiors has been an important issue in the Korean group psyche. For example, trying not to lose one's so-called face (that is, making an effort not to cause any shameful episodes) and striving for a good reputation have been important social tasks for most Koreans since Confucianism became the main cultural ideology during the Chosun Dynasty (1392–1897). Korean people, including myself, seem to be more sensitive to and highly perceptive of being looked down on or humiliated by others, partly due to the traditional-shame culture and partly due to the highly competitive society that has taken hold in South Korea. To some degree, the overly exaggerated expression of the superiority of the North Korean regime is compensatory for the shame and humiliation they have likely experienced for the last several decades.

Possible integration of North and South

A South Korean man in his forties brought me an interesting dream related to the hopes for a unification process in Korea. He had not experienced the significant hardships endured by North Koreans

220

NAMI LEE

in the aftermath of the Korean War. His attitude toward North Koreans was quite positive, in contrast to the older generation, who directly experienced the Korean War. His dream was as follows:

I was trying to persuade my judges in order to get good grades. A spy from North Korea met a Japanese female agent. They were not suspicious of each other but fell in deep love with each other. When she became pregnant, blue jeans were delivered as a gift for her from North Korea. Then the lovers decorated their room by setting up a light ball. It was beautiful and glamorous. His thoughts flashed back to the days they concealed their true identities for their deep love.

Some aspects of this short, puzzling dream can be explained by considering the notion of the cultural complex as it applies to the Korean people. Sam Kimbles, a Jungian analyst, defines cultural complexes as "expressions of a dynamic system of relations that serve the basic individual need for belonging and identity through linking personal experiences and group expectations, mediated by race, ethnicity, religion, and gender processes."[28] Another Jungian analyst, Thomas Singer, explains that "some cultural complexes originate in traumatic events that happen sometimes centuries, even millennia, ago."[29] Building on Singer, the trauma that the North Korean people experienced during and after the Korean War resulted in profound hopelessness and resentment, possibly contributing to the creation of the paranoid and totalitarian psyche of North Koreans.

In this young man's dream, however, the historical enemies of South Korea—North Korea and Japan—seem to have a chance of reconciliation. Marriage can be a symbol of unification and coalition. The image of a Japanese woman wearing American clothing may allude to the Korean psyche, mixed up with memories of being occupied by the Japanese and Americans. Korea as a whole was wounded by Japanese imperialism, and North Korea also claims to have suffered for decades from Japanese annexation, US bombs during the Korean War, and threats from South Korea and Western countries.

In unifying the North and the South, Korea needs to find a secure place to integrate its traditional heritage in tandem with technological development. As a possible compensation for the long history of emphasis on spiritualism against materialism, some Korean people have become too materialistic to be connected with their own psyche. Korean Jungian analyst Rhi wrote that "the East has become more

SEEKING HIEROS GAMOS ON THE KOREAN PENINSULA 221

extraverted, aggressive, materialistic, and more collective than the West."[30] On the other hand, communism in North Korea has denied most of the spiritual traditions of Korean history, such as shamanism, Confucianism, Buddhism, and Taoism, whereas consumerism in the South has made most people slaves to money and success. The two Koreas have been too focused on becoming "winners" as nationalistic Communists or globalized capitalists, respectively.

Until very recently, Asian values such as paternalism— emphasizing solidarity of family, kinship, and country in contrast to Western individualism or scientific rationalism—has been criticized as obstructing the path toward modernity, although South Korea has followed the Western model by forfeiting its own traditions. Averse to the West, North Korea has been possessed by Juche ideology, traditional values of filial piety, blind loyalty to the leader, and paternalism. It is paradoxical that North Korea has tried to erase Confucian ideology by emphasizing their own filial piety and loyalty toward the Kim family. The two Koreas may be similar to each other in that both lost their psychological and spiritual heritage and confidence without fully developing rational modernity, which may have created barriers against unification.

Our own inferiority and paranoid ideation as well as our fear of the bigger, the powerful, and the richer need to be delved into. Understanding the North Korean Kim family may reveal clues to South Korea's own power and money complex. North Korea's isolationism is a manifestation of a lack of self-confidence and envy, as is the extremists' psyche in the South. If both Koreas become more aware of and more compassionate about each other's traumas and fears, we may have a better chance of having meaningful dialog and finally accomplishing unification. Jung wrote as follows:

> We completely forget that the reason mankind believes in the daemon was due to ... the inner effect of autonomous fragmentary systems. This effect is not abolished by criticizing... . [The autonomous systems] become an inexplicable source of disturbance which we finally assume must exist somewhere outside ourselves. The resultant projection creates a dangerous situation in that the disturbing effects are now attributed to a wicked will outside ourselves, which is our neighbor ... This leads to collective delusions, incidents, war, and to destructive mass psychoses.[31]

Communism differs from capitalism in many ways and has been criticized as a social delusion, as has the ideology of Juche. But in terms of being manipulated by a superpower and collective ideology, communism and capitalism share common phenomena: communism rationalizes the dictatorship of the Communist Party, whereas capitalism rationalizes the uncontrollable power of capital and the rich. Von Franz said,

> Concealed religio-mythical motivations lie behind the communist ideology ... the archetypal Anthropos-image found in the Gnosis and the Kabbala reappears in Karl Marx, namely the myth of the light-man sunk in darkness, who must be freed ... The myth is projected onto society. Capitalists, revisionists, imperialists and so on.[32]

I argue that capitalism is *not* absolutely free from religio-mythical motivations if money and fame are worshipped and sanctified instead of divine beings like Buddha or God.

Without mutual understanding of the deep-rooted origin of the disputes between capitalism and communism or between South and North Korea, there can be no real understanding of the opposites. Without awareness of our inner autonomous system, which makes projections onto others instead of reflecting our own complex, there is no *hieros gamos,* or unity of the opposites, no peace between enemies and opponents, on the Korean peninsula or any place else in the world.

Acknowledgments

I'd like to express my appreciation to Korean analyst Bou-young Rhi, American analyst Thomas Singer, Ms. Hillary Hansen, and my son Wonho Lee, all of whom have been willing to read my drafts several times and have given me various insightful comments with sincerity. Thanks to their considerate reviews of my paper, I could finish my article on the Korean psyche, the root of my own.

Notes

[1] Oleg V. Khlevniuk, *Stalin: New Biography of a Dictator,* trans. Nora S. Favorov (New Haven and London: Yale University Press, 2015), pp. 12, 190.

[2] *Cú Chulainn* was "an old, Irish version of the Incredible Hulk, terrifying, with superhuman rage" (http://www.bbc.co.uk/legacies/myths_legends/northern_ireland/ni_7/article_1). Irish nationalists and unionists used the image of Cú Chulainn as a nationalist symbol. See Charles Townshend, *Easter 1916: The Irish Rebellion,* London: Penguin Books Ltd., 2006, p. 36.

[3] Sylvia Brinton Perera, *Queen Maeve and Her Lovers: A Celtic Archetype of Ecstasy, Addiction, and Healing* (New York: Carrowmore Books, 1999), pp. 72–73.

[4] Michael E. Robinson, *Korea's Twentieth-Century Odyssey* (Honolulu, HI: University of Hawaii Press, 2007), pp. 87, 155.

[5] Andrew C. Nahm, *Introduction to Korean History and Culture* (Seoul: Hollym, 1993), pp. 68–73.

[6] Wanne J. Joe, *Traditional Korea: A Cultural History,* ed. and revised Hongkyo A. Choe (Seoul: Hollym, 1997), p. 176.

[7] Don Oberdorfer and Robert Carlin, *The Two Koreas: A Contemporary History* (New York: Basic Books, 2014), pp. 284–285.

[8] Joe, *Traditional Korea,* p. 361.

[9] Andrew Nahm, *Korea: A History of the Korean People,* 2nd ed. (Seoul: Hollym, 1996).

[10] Oberdorfer and Carlin, *The Two Koreas,* pp. 2–3.

[11] United States Department of State, Foreign Relations of the United States 1945,6,[a] the British Commonwealth, the Far East, 1050. Quoted in Ji Eun Park, "In Search for Democracy: The Korean Provisional Government," BA thesis, Wesleyan University, 2009.

[12] Robert Zuzowski, "The Left and Nationalism in Eastern Europe," *East European Quarterly* 41 (4, 2008). Accessed Jan. 10, 2019, at https://www.questia.com/library/p4214/east-european-quarterly.

[13] An *intranet* is a private network that operates like the internet, or World Wide Web, but is used internally by a group and may or may not allow access to the internet.

[14] Bradley K. Martin, *Under the Loving Care of the Fatherly Leader* (New York: Thomas Dunne Books, 2006), p. 675.

[15] Marie-Louise Von Franz, *C. G. Jung: His Myth in Our Time* (Toronto: Inner City Books, 1975), p. 264.

[16] Martin, *Under the Loving Care,* pp. 512–542.

[17] G. Shin, *Ethnic Nationalism in Korea: Genealogy, Politics, and Legacy* (Palo Alto, CA: Stanford University Press, 2006), pp. 91–92.

[18] C. K. Armstrong, "Familism, Socialism and Political Religion in North Korea," *Politics, Religions & Ideology* 6 (3, 2005): 383–394.

[19] C. G. Jung, *Psychology and Religion: West and East,* vol. 11, *The Collected Works of C. G. Jung,* ed. and trans. Gerhard Adler and R. F. C. Hull (Princeton, NJ: Princeton University Press, 1977), §§ 274–276.

[20] Zach Beauchamp, "Juche: The State Ideology That Makes North Koreans Revere Kim Jong Un, Explained," *Vox,* June 18, 2018. Accessed Jan. 10, 2019, at https://www.vox.com/world/2018/6/18/17441296/north-korea-propaganda-ideology-juche.

[21] Jang Jin-Sung, "The Market Shall Set North Korea Free," *The New York Times,* April 26, 2013. Accessed Jan. 10, 2019, at https://www.nytimes.com/2013/04/27/opinion/global/The-Market-Shall-Set-North-Korea-Free.html.

[22] Oberdorfer and Carlin, *The Two Koreas,* p. 203.

[23] *Ibid.,* p. 17.

[24] Before the medieval era, Korea had its own rationally organized political system that balanced the king's power with that of the aristocrats.

[25] Colleen K. Vesely, Bethany L. Letiecq, and Rachael D. Goodman, "Immigrant Family Resilience in Context: Using a Community–Based Approach to Build a New Conceptual Model," *Journal of Family Theory and Review* 9 (1, 2017).

[26] C. G. Jung, "The Undiscovered Self" (1957), in *The Collected Works of C. G. Jung,* vol. 10, ed. and trans. Gerhard Adler and R. F. C. Hull (Princeton, NJ: Princeton University Press, 1970), § 559.

[27] Von Franz, *C. G. Jung,* p. 77.

[28] Samuel Kimbles, "Cultural Complex: Myth of Invisibility," in Thomas Singer, ed., *The Vision Thing: Myth, Politics and Psyche in the World* (New York: Routledge, 2000), p. 161.

[29] Thomas Singer, Introduction, in Pilar Amezaga, Gustavo Barcellos, Áxel Capriles, Jacqueline Gerson, and Denise Ramos, eds., *Listening to Latin America: Exploring Cultural Complexes in Brazil, Chile, Colombia, Mexico, Uruguay, and Venezuela* (New Orleans, LA: Spring Journal Books, 2012), pp. 5–6.

SEEKING HIEROS GAMOS ON THE KOREAN PENINSULA   225

[30] Bou-young Rhi, "Human Mind within and beyond the Culture—Toward a Better Encounter between East and West," *Shim-Song-Yon-Gu* 28 (2, 2013): 135 (In Korean).

[31] C. G. Jung, "Commentary on 'The Secret of the Golden Flower'" (1929), in *The Collected Works of C. G. Jung,* vol. 13, ed. and trans. Gerhard Adler and R. F. C. Hull (Princeton, NJ: Princeton University Press, 1978), §§ 51–52.

[32] Von Franz, *C. G. Jung,* pp. 134–135.

10

· · · · · ·

The *Kimchi*-Bitch Cultural Complex
Modern Misogyny, Memes, and Millennial Men in South Korea

Amalya Layla Ashman

On May 19, 2016, Exit 10 of Gangnam Station in Seoul, South Korea, was unrecognizable under a thick carpet of Post-It Notes and flowers.[1] Journalists and protestors wearing masks and carrying signs jostled around the entrance. The protestors were split into two camps—male and female—and had congregated to debate the existence of misogynistic violence in South Korea, in the wake of the murder of a twenty-three-year-old woman near the station. On May 17, 2016, a thirty-four-year-old man, surnamed Kim, left the station through Exit 10, made his way to a nearby building filled with bars, and hid in the bathroom. He waited for almost an hour as six men came and went from the bathroom. When a woman entered, he stabbed her repeatedly with a 32.5 cm sushi knife he had stolen from the restaurant where he worked.[2] When he was arrested, he said he did it because

---

Amalya Layla Ashman specializes in the study of emotion, gender, and identity in South Korean media, drawing on perspectives from analytical psychology and the history of emotions. Previous to this, her doctoral thesis, supervised by Dr. Terrie Waddell, examined the Korean feeling of *han* as a post-Jungian cultural complex. The research for this contribution was supported by the Kyujanggak Institute for Korean Studies at Seoul National University, where she was a postdoctoral research fellow from 2017 to 2018.

he "hated women for belittling him."[3] The comment provoked major debate in the media and inspired a memorial of hundreds of Post-It Notes expressing nihilistic messages, mainly from young women: "I know I could've been you, you could've been me," and "She died on the seventeenth of May, by coincidence and luck, I #survived."[4] The police argued that the crime was not premeditated but "accidental" because the perpetrator was a homeless schizophrenic who had gone off his medication.[5] Despite these assurances, public sentiment lingered that the murder was not the act of "a mentally disturbed man attacking a specific woman, but [was] a symbolic example of what happens in a misogynistic society."[6]

This chapter will explore one specific symbol of misogyny in South Korean culture, which *The Economist* and *The Korea Herald* alluded to in their articles pondering the murder: that of the *kimchi-nyeon,* or in English, the *"kimchi*-bitch."[7] The *kimchi*-bitch is a pejorative internet meme that has entered common parlance in the last five years. It describes shallow, entitled, materialistic South Korean women in their twenties and thirties who look down on men.[8] This chapter will argue that the *kimchi*-bitch is a symbol of a Jungian cultural complex that emerged in online discussion boards populated by young men and filled with offensive, misogynistic humor. The chapter will trace the origins of the term *kimchi-nyeon* in South Korean cyberspace, as well as the rise of the misogynistic internet culture that incubated the symbol. I suggest that the *kimchi*-bitch is a uniquely South Korean representation of global trends of online misogyny and post-feminism. Further, I argue the *kimchi*-bitch is a shadow projection on the part of young Korean men that reveals intense insecurities about their social status (and future) in a highly competitive, neoliberal economy, and is compounded by their conscious (and unconscious) identification with "loser culture." Despite the degree to which the *kimchi*-bitch cultural complex appears to be embedded in contemporary online youth culture, many of the negative feelings and ideas about women caught up in the complex have historical bases. The chapter will explore perspectives on Korean women's virtues and vices in the premodern and early twentieth century, with special emphasis on the *Modern Girls* of the 1920s and 1930s who were objects of contempt, much like *kimchi*-bitches. Both terms reveal, I argue, the precarious status of women in South Korean society, whose rights as citizens are repeatedly

THE KIMCHI-*BITCH* CULTURAL COMPLEX

demonstrated to be dependent on men's approval of their moral character vis-à-vis resisting greed and Western influence.

Emotions, the internet, and the unconscious

Nods toward potential Jungian perspectives on the internet began with Luke Hockley's chapter in *Frames of Mind: A Post-Jungian Look at Film, Television and Technology* (2007), in which he remarks that the internet "is a collective object that is external to the psyche" but also a virtual, or *phantasy,* world "invested and appropriated in a manner that is highly personal and individual."[9] Hockley explores points of contact between the structure of the internet and that of the Jungian psyche to discuss how online avatars develop psychological identity and by what means unconscious behaviors are expressed online.[10] Ten years on, we increasingly recognize the internet as heterogenous: comprising multiple platforms, each with specific functions, agendas, and cultures; encompassing commercial, financial, scientific, and military uses of the deep web, along with the anarchic and criminal activities of the dark web.[11] This refined view of the internet requires a focused application of analytical psychology, like that of Greg Singh (2016), whose article on YouTube vlogger stardom concentrates specifically on post-Jungian constructs of self and persona in self-commodification.[12] Singh's article appeared in a special issue of *Media and Communication* dedicated to the idea of the unconscious in digital media. Steffen Krüger and Jacob Johanssen, editors of *Digital Media, Psychoanalysis and the Subject,* remark that research into online users is predicated on a rational subjectivity that ignores the "contradiction, incoherence, ambiguity, resistance and enjoyment in media texts and mediums as well as our responses to them."[13] They argue that media technologies are "moving ever closer to the body"; hence, "unconscious processes" must be acknowledged.[14] As the contributors to *Digital Media, Psychoanalysis and the Subject* demonstrate, there is a place for the unconscious in the study of our online selves. This chapter seeks to establish the concept of the Jungian cultural complex as a tool to interrogate the psychic behavior (in this case, the imagery and emotions) of the collective, as opposed to the individual, psyche.

The internet is no longer just a tool, write Tova Benski and Eran Fisher, but an emotional environment where "new emotional practices emerge, new emotional feedback loops are built, and new emotional language and manifestations crystallize."[15] "Why Pass on

230 AMALYA LAYLA ASHMAN

Viral Messages? Because They Connect Emotionally," "What Makes a Video Go Viral? An Analysis of Emotional Contagion and Internet Memes," and "To Share or Not To Share: The Role of Content and Emotion in Viral Marketing" lay the message bare: online virality of image- or video-based posts, memes, or marketing ploys is intrinsically linked to emotion.[16] Both the terms *meme* and *virality* are neologisms adapted from the biological sciences to describe online behaviors. *Viral* refers to the behavior of viruses, which replicate themselves in a host organism; whereas, *meme* first appeared in Richard Dawkins' book *The Selfish Gene,* in 1976, to describe the transmission of cultural ideas as akin to an evolutionary process:

> We need a name for the new replicator, a noun that conveys the idea of a unit of cultural transmission, or a unit of *imitation.* "Mimeme" comes from a suitable Greek root, but I want a monosyllable that sounds a bit like "gene." I hope my classicist friends will forgive me if I abbreviate mimeme to *meme.* If it is any consolation, it could alternatively be thought of as being related to "memory," or the French word *même.* It should be pronounced to rhyme with "cream." Examples of memes are tunes, ideas, catch-phrases, clothes fashions, ways of making pots or of building arches. Just as genes propagate themselves in the gene pool by leaping from body to body via sperms or eggs, so memes propagate themselves in the meme pool by leaping from brain to brain via a process which, in the broad sense, can be called imitation.[17]

For Dawkins, memes, like the Grecian gods, are propagated (to continue the allusions to biology) by music, art, and literature that pass the concepts from one generation to another.[18] However, Dawkins is more interested in a meme's evolutionary survival than its characteristics (emotional, psychic, or otherwise) and judges a good meme to be one that is not only psychologically appealing but also evolutionarily useful.[19] At this point, I think a line should be drawn under neo-Darwinian parallels, and we should instead turn to the social functions of memes compared to cultural complexes.[20]

From the pre-internet age to Web 2.0's social era, the discourse on memes continues to lend itself to comparison with the cultural complex. Dan Sperber's intuitions about the psychosocial potential of the visual culture of the internet, which was still in its infancy when *Explaining Culture: A Naturalistic Approach* was published in 1996, is one such example. Sperber, a cognitive scientist, suggests that

THE KIMCHI-*BITCH* CULTURAL COMPLEX 231

internet memes are synonymous with "cultural replicators," which are representations of psychic symbols and associations.[21] Sperber split memes into two groups: "mental representations" that are personal to the individual and "public representations" such as circulated works of art.[22] Sitting between Sperber's personal "mental representations" and "public representations" are "cultural representations," which combine the symbols of the personal unconscious with cultural products in ways particular to a social group.[23] As visual images imbued with personal and cultural meaning, Sperber's "cultural representations" are strikingly similar to the function of Jungian cultural complexes; however, it is not clear what kind of "author" Sperber is imagining in 1996 before Web 2.0 user content took over the internet.[24] Viral content can be any rapidly popularized online image, video, or phrase created by anyone from a multimillion-dollar corporate marketing department to an angsty thirteen-year-old on Tumblr. Jean Burgess attempts to embrace both these extremes when he asserts that viral content is not comprised of purely "messages" or "products" but "the mediating mechanisms through which cultural *practices* are originated, adopted and (sometimes) retained *within* social networks."[25] In short, all memes are viral content, but not all viral content are memes. Memes retain a certain anti-establishment (even counterculture) flair that is reflected in their low-fidelity (low-fi), do-it-yourself (DIY) aesthetics. And, moreover, an even smaller fraction of memes tap into the deep cultural undercurrents indicative of a cultural complex.

The cultural complex: young men and their shadow

Henry Jenkins calls the value of viral content like memes "spreadability," which is to say the ways they are reused, reworked, and redistributed "gains greater resonance in the culture, taking on new meanings, finding new audiences, attracting new markets, and generating new values."[26] By clicking to share a meme, then, internet users participate in a superficial form of "meaning making" and identify (even unconsciously) with a group. Like memes, a cultural complex gathers ideas around a central image that is endlessly reworked according to the contributions of a wide group of individuals. But unlike memes, cultural complexes are organized by a specific emotional response to that image, which is, in its totality, unknowable because it fuses conscious and unconscious materials. Memes are notorious for their postmodern flippancy, irony, and mild "relatability,"

232   AMALYA LAYLA ASHMAN

such that the majority do not engage the depths of distracted internet users' unconscious as they scroll past videos of cats surprised by cucumbers. Thomas Singer and Samuel L. Kimbles established the study of cultural complexes in 2004 by defining cultural complexes as "frequently repeated historical experiences that have taken root in the collective psyche of a group and in the psyches of the individual members of a group, and they express the archetypal values for the group."[27] More specifically, cultural complexes are a bridge between the individual's personal experiences and the expectations of the group, which "is mediated by unconscious assumptions about ethnicity, race, gender and the processes of social identity."[28] Cultural complexes are often concerned with historical memory and national identities, which surfaces in this discussion, but here gender defines the culture (the group) and the projections (the *kimchi*-bitch) of this complex.

Young South Korean men who identify with "loser culture," or the more extreme right-wing political opinions of the satirical online website Ilbe, have influenced the male millennial experience in the country. I argue that this group of men have developed an inferiority complex from an identification with the shadow archetype, which has produced the *kimchi*-bitch as a symbol. This sense of archetypal inferiority is performed online through sarcasm, self-parody, and engaging in outrageous, morally wrong acts, which range from telling sexist and racist jokes online to public demonstrations mocking parents who lost their children in the 2014 Sewol ferry disaster, by holding a "pizza party" in front of the grieving relatives on a hunger strike.[29] Jung comments that it is "rare" for "the positive qualities of the personality [to be] repressed" by ego identification with the shadow archetype, but that the projection of the individual's unacknowledged negative qualities onto the Other as the shadow is common.[30] As John Weir Perry describes it, complexes are so dominant within the psyche that the ego is temporarily usurped by the "affect-ego" (the ego under the influence of the emotional force of the complex).[31] The "affect ego" gives rise to the "affect object," which is the projection of the complex's archetypal opposite, which warps the individual's sense of reality.[32] At a collective level, cultural complexes scale up these fault lines by "imposing constraints on the perception of differences or accentuating them; emphasizing identification with or differentiation from the group; defining enemies; and allow for feelings of belonging or alienation from the group."[33]

THE KIMCHI-*BITCH* CULTURAL COMPLEX

In this case, angry, cynical young men identify as shadowy figures: poor, lonely, powerless, worthless victims. In counterbalance, they project the image of the *kimchi*-bitch onto young women, casting them as their (hated) opposite: overtly self-confident, vain (plastic surgery because "I'm worth it"), coveting riches (designer handbags), spending irresponsibly, snubbing Korean men by choosing foreign boyfriends, and entering jobs in these tough economic times "reserved" for women, out of a new culture of positive discrimination. Jung warns that when unconscious shadow qualities are projected, "uncontrolled or scarcely controlled emotions" abound.[34] As such, the *kimchi*-bitch reveals a virulent new stream of misogyny online and offline. Jung remarks that the shadow is often personified as the opposite sex (a theory he takes to further conclusions as part of his work on the *animus* and *anima*) as a symbol of binary oppositions.[35] Although there may be a persuasive reasoning to this conclusion, I am inclined to interpret the fact that young men in South Korea project their inferiorities onto women for two reasons: first, because gender roles in South Korean society continue to be starkly defined categories of experience and identity, which still organizes psychosocial behavior; and second, because women often signify a repressed sense of national shame in the South Korean imagination, as I will explore later.

The *kimchi*-bitch

The first task is to understand the evolution of the *kimchi*-bitch caricature in comments and memes and the online environment that cultivated it. In Korean, *mo-mo* is used when you cannot quite remember the word for something, like *thingamabob* in English, or to indicate missing information, similar to saying "something, something." As a result, much of name-calling in the misogynist discourse online in South Korea follows the formula of the *mo-mo-nyeo*, "something-something-girl."[36] The insults switch between *nyeo* for "girl" and *nyeon* for "bitch"; however, the pejorative tone persuades me to translate both *nyeo* and *nyeon* as "bitch." To give an example of how this formula works, women are often reduced to sexual organs on websites like Ilbe. The slang for vulva is *boji* (similar to "pussy") in Korean, which is combined with *nyeon* to coin the common insult, *boji-nyeon*, or "pussy-bitch."[37] According to In-Kyoung Chung, this type of name-calling began online in 2005 with a viral news story about a young woman who refused to clean up after her dog, which

234   *AMALYA LAYLA ASHMAN*

had defecated on the floor of the underground train she was traveling on.[38] A fellow commuter who witnessed the woman's unwillingness to clean up the mess, uploaded her photo, and that of an elderly man picking up the feces himself, to the DC Inside website.[39] Netizens dubbed her *gae-ddong-nyeon* ("dog-shit bitch") and harassed her and her family by making their personal details public online.[40] The crux of the matter for many outraged users was the perceived snobbish attitude of the woman who shirked responsibility because cleaning up dog shit was beneath her. This hateful profiling of the woman online as disdainful, selfish, and conceited was likely an early iteration of what would become the *kimchi*-bitch.

After the "dog-shit bitch" incident, two slurs appeared in 2006 that used the *mo-mo-nyeo* formula: *doenjang-nyeo* ("beanpaste girl") and *kimchi-nyeo* ("*kimchi*-bitch").[41] *Doenjang* and *kimchi* are two everyday affordable foods that typify South Korean cuisine. *Doenjang* is a thick, brown, fermented bean paste used as a stock to make a simple soup (not unlike Japanese *miso* paste). It is usually made at home or served at a modest eatery for just over US$2, with a portion of rice and a free dish of *kimchi*. *Kimchi* is essentially pickled vegetables, but usually refers to bright red, spicy, fermented cabbage. As insults, there is little that separates *doenjang*-bitch and *kimchi*-bitch, except that *doenjang*-bitch may have preceded *kimchi*-bitch slightly and that *kimchi*-bitch is more closely associated with Ilbe and is more prevalent today. The key to this slight is that *kimchi* and *doenjang* are extremely cheap, quintessentially Korean foods, so those who eat them exclusively are poor and/or very Korean in their tastes. *Kimchi*-bitches are accused of eating these dishes in secret in order to hide the fact that they are so miserly and unshakably Korean; meanwhile, publicly, they portray themselves (and think of themselves) very differently. This type of woman is "consumed with the thought of consuming," and she spends all her money on branded Western goods.[42] The South Korean artist Kim Hyun Jung captures the contradiction of the *kimchi*-bitch in her painting entitled *Oops* (2012). In it, a young woman eats *ramyeon* (instant noodles) from the lid of a cheap pot, cooking on a gas burner, the type used by poor people living alone in a room that lacks basic kitchen facilities. While she stoically eats her budget meal, her gaze is fixed firmly on her open Louis Vuitton bag with an empty Starbucks paper cup inside. The irony is clear: the Starbucks coffee she bought earlier in the day

THE KIMCHI-BITCH CULTURAL COMPLEX

cost at least twice that of a bowl of *doenjang* stew and four times that of the *kimchi ramyeon* she is eating now.[43]

A recurring theme in the characterization of the *kimchi*-bitch is her two-faced attitude: a Western girl on the outside and a Korean girl on the inside. A satirical image, shown in Figure 10.1, by a cartoonist operating under the pseudonym *I am a Patriot (Na-neun Aegukja)*, which was first posted on Ilbe on January 15, 2013, illustrates some of these contradictions.

> **Figure 10.1: Meme of the *kimchi*-bitch by a cartoonist under the pseudonym Na-neun Aegukja (I am a Patriot). (https://aras.org/spokes-of-the-wheel).**

The willowy figure in the middle of the image represents the *kimchi*-bitch. Her legs are demurely crossed, and she wears a figure-hugging dress, on her way to work or a date, and carries a designer handbag. She is surrounded by memes and emoticons that depict her consumer choices and aesthetic, or perhaps even moral, values. She has undergone plastic surgery to shave her jawbone, raise her nose, augment her breasts, and enlarge her eyes, yet she praises celebrities, like 2NE1 (labeled "good"), for circulating pictures of themselves makeup free and ungroomed, and criticizes others, like HyunA (labeled "bad") for her over-sexualized music persona. Money makes her happy, as do expensive foreign brands, suggests the artist. Korean-made products are "shit," just like Ilbe itself. The *kimchi*-bitch's disdain for local merchandise is not only a snub to the domestic economy but also extends to Korean men who she refuses to date.[44] *Kimchi*-bitches are accused of feigning higher social status. This "out of your league" attitude is considered unfair to men, who are left partnerless because of women's "false advertising." However, the illustrator predicts, the future is bleak for the image-obsessed *kimchi*-bitch. She may become the lonely old woman in a trench coat, who heads to McDonald's alone to join the throngs of impoverished, depressed elderly who wile away their days in the warmth of fast-food restaurants.[45] Or, worse yet, her obsession for plastic surgery may transform her into another Hang Mioku. Hang was discovered by her elderly parents—and later by a salacious media—with a grotesquely swollen face, after her addiction to plastic surgery, which began during her modeling career when she was twenty-eight years old, led her to inject her face repeatedly with silicone and, eventually, cooking oil.[46] The internet

236 AMALYA LAYLA ASHMAN

brims with criticisms of the *kimchi*-bitch beyond this one meme: that they evade military conscription by virtue of their sex; they jump the queue and jostle everyone around in public places; they leave work unfinished because of sick days for menstruation; and they attend language schools to become "sluts" to foreign men.[47]

Trolls, conservatives, and Ilbe Storehouse

Now that you are familiar with the image of the *kimchi*-bitch at the heart of the cultural complex, I will examine the group in the grip of this emotive symbol: young, male, right-wing online users. Much of the hate speech surrounding women who carry the image of the *kimchi*-bitch is driven by the website Ilbe Storehouse.[48] The website was established in 2010 and consists of discussion boards where anonymous users can post and comment. Popular posts are ranked by "humor" and are predominantly extreme, offensive takes on topics of popular culture, society, and politics. Owing to the anonymity of the site, Ilbe's user demographics are hard to gauge specifically, but it is believed to be comprised of men (almost exclusively if the ban on female members is to be believed) in their teens, twenties, and thirties, with 35 percent self-reporting to be between twenty-one and twenty-five years of age.[49] A history of Ilbe's founding was provided by a South Korean netizen claiming to be a knowledgeable member of the group. The user's account was published, with English translation, by the blog *KoreaBANG* in December 2012. The community of users that went on to establish the Ilbe website in April 2010 first emerged on DC Inside, a website with multiple discussion boards that allows users to sign in anonymously.[50] When a new user entered the scene under the moniker "The Holy Father of Fucks," the atmosphere changed on boards like CoGall to include more *banmal* ("low-register, colloquial Korean"), swearing, and crude humor.[51] From 2007 to 2010, CoGall was populated by users in their teens and twenties, who popularized new insults that entered mainstream culture and created a *cyber tailing* culture (internet trolling) among South Korean netizens.[52]

A popular feature of the DC Inside website was a menu of the top posts of the day, the *ilgan beseuteu* ("daily best"), but popular posts from CoGall and other forums were removed from the list because of profanity or pornography.[53] Ilbe was launched by Moe-Myungsoo as a mirror to allow the banned material from DC Inside's "daily best" list to circulate.[54] The inspiration for the website's name, Ilbe, came

THE KIMCHI-*BITCH* CULTURAL COMPLEX 237

from the abbreviation of DC Inside's *ilgan beseuteu* that they wished to restore. A motivating force to contribute to Ilbe was the wish to rise to the top of the list of most shocking or humorous memes and posts. At first, much of the material on Ilbe was direct copies of popular, but censored, memes and comments from DC Inside, but the environment began to form its own unique culture when the discussion group admins, SAD and Saebu, prohibited cliques or women "coming out" (revealing their true gender), which essentially banned women.[55] In some sense Ilbe is demographically typical of many South Korean online spaces, which are, for the most part, male-dominated, with message boards often containing misogynist material.[56] During the liberal presidency of Roh Moo-hyun, DC Inside was a relatively politically balanced, even pro-left platform. In contrast, Ilbe became a hotbed of pro-conservative voices, especially during the election of the conservative president Lee Myung-bak. This was compounded by events in 2010, when North Korea sank a South Korean navy ship and shelled a military base on the small island of Yeonpyeong.[57] Right-wing opinions have traditionally been the purview of the older generation, from their forties upward, who grew up in the staunchly anti-Communist post-war society. Whereas Ilbe's demographic is judged to include teenagers and men in their twenties and thirties, ideologically, Ilbe has singled out women, "lefties," people from the Jeolla province, and foreign migrant workers as their "enemies."[58] Yoon Bora goes so far as to say that the defining feature of Ilbe users is their pathological hatred of women.[59]

Ilbe's manifesto for misogyny

A manifesto, of sorts, exists online, which was posted by a person claiming to be deeply embedded in Ilbe. Allegedly, the manifesto began as an essay that the Ilbe user submitted as part of his university coursework and was singled out for praise by his professor. In it, he outlines a number of historical and social conditions that have resulted in an "imbalance" in gender roles in South Korea, and he links these conditions to the demographic and psychological makeup of Ilbe users to justify their hatred of women. The following comes from material lifted originally from the Ilbe website (original posts were not archived) and translated into English by the *KoreaBANG* blog. The writer begins by asserting that women have been biologically and socially conditioned to become "gold-diggers" because women are

238 AMALYA LAYLA ASHMAN

obligated to leave employment and raise children at home, which is only possible by attaching themselves to financially successful men.[60] He views the relationship between men and women (or husband and wife, more specifically) to be transactional: men share their wealth with women and, in return, women provide sex and children.[61] In this formula, women (and men) garnered respect for fulfilling their responsibilities and roles. The implication that women do not possess basic rights, and that these must be earned through their behavior in familial relationships, dates back to the neo-Confucian society of the Joseon Dynasty (1392–1897). This is truncated into the formula that first of all men have the majority of wealth, so women marry for wealth, which leads to the writer's second assertion that a man shares his wealth with his wife so that she will care for him.[62] However, this arrangement is under threat, according to the user, because women have become so entitled that they no longer perform their role (providing for their men), while men continue to shoulder the responsibility of paying for women's lifestyles.

This writer advocates for a "reasoned," "historical" understanding of the rise of the *kimchi*-bitch and not "pure misogyny." Using the analogy of the Japanese economic boom and the *dankai* generation (post-WWII baby boomer generation), he describes how birth control and sexual preference for boys created an acute gender imbalance with more men than women.[63] In this regard, the user is accurate. The South Korean government has been spending billions of dollars in recent years in an attempt to avert a demographic crisis leading to a rapidly aging population.[64] This crisis is heightened by the statistical gender imbalance between men and women. In the 1980s, around 117 boys were born per 100 girls in South Korea, at odds with the worldwide balance of 104 to 107 boys to 100 girls, which usually evens out due to the higher mortality of male babies.[65] Some media outlets report that by 2028, there will be between 120 to 123 men to every 100 women in their late twenties and early thirties, prompting the Korean press to lament that 530,000 men will be unable to find a bride.[66] According to the Ilbe commentator, this created the right conditions for women's exploitation of men. Because women are "premium" and "in demand," they can dictate how society, or at least their generation, behaves.[67] Feedback from other users on Ilbe highlighted other factors that "created" the *kimchi*-bitch, not stressed by the writer's focus on demographics. These factors included

THE KIMCHI-*BITCH* CULTURAL COMPLEX 239

- Confucian teachings that women must be protected by men
- A victim complex that was being transferred onto young women from women of the previous generation
- The perception that popular media is consumed and controlled by women in South Korea, which is chillingly similar to anti-Semitic rhetoric

The original author of the Ilbe "manifesto" acknowledges that all of these factors also contribute to the presence of these problematic women, but he continues with his pseudo–Social Darwinist analysis of the situation. He pinpoints the Asian Financial Crisis of 1997 as the critical point when the "bubble" (by which he means a strongly patriarchal society enjoying prosperous economic circumstances) burst, and men were dismissed en masse and forced to open small businesses, like fried chicken restaurants, to survive.[68] This economic humiliation to male hegemonic power in society, and individual pride, was the reckoning that cast men as feeble in the eyes of women and, therefore, inferior to foreign men and to women themselves.[69] But it is not just an abstract sense of defeat brought about by the 1997 crash, men (and women, although this is glossed over) struggle to secure jobs post-university. Company loyalty to employees, and therefore any financial security, has vanished, whereas exploitative worker contracts and unpaid internships flourish. Adding to this, the fact that the state promotes positive discrimination in favor of women seems like a cruel joke to these struggling young men.

"Na-do rujeo"—"I'm a loser, too"

The *kimchi*-bitch phenomenon was an act of retribution on behalf of the *rujeo-eui nan* (loser uprising), according to the Ilbe insider.[70] This uprising refers to the (ironic) celebration of *rujeo munhwa* (loser culture), which is not confined to the internet and has been widely referenced in popular culture in South Korea for over a decade.[71] This label is more inclusive (and less extreme) than the identity offered by Ilbe and pertains to the wider malaise affecting South Korean youth. "Loser culture" is not the only buzzword in South Korea to describe the worthlessness experienced by a generation of unemployable, unmarriageable new university graduates. They are also known as the *sampo* generation, who are said to have given up on three (*sam*) aspirations—courtship, marriage, and childbirth—because of their

240 AMALYA LAYLA ASHMAN

unstable job and living situations.[72] Another moniker, popularized by the 2007 book of the same name, *Palsipalman-won Sedae* (*The 880,000 Won Generation*), refers to the average monthly salary of a twenty-something worker who is on casual or irregular contracts of 880,000 *won,* which is just over US$800.[73] Young-Do Yun writes that the term *loser,* which was ubiquitous in the Anglophone grunge counterculture of the 1990s, was first translated as *paebaeja* and later absorbed as the Konglish, *rujeo.*[74] The South Korean indie band Kahi & The Faces, like the Western grunge bands Nirvana and Radiohead, described these disaffected youths in their lyrics.[75] In November 2009, one of the foreign female guests of *Global Talk Show* (*Minyeodeuleu suda*) stated on air that men who were less than 180cm in height were "losers," which prompted an online retaliation (mentioned above as *rujeo-eui nan*) from men, who spread her personal details online out of revenge.[76] This jocular remark on the part of a TV personality was met with a disproportionate emotional response by young men who immediately identified as "losers," and unconsciously with the cultural complex of the *kimchi*-bitch. The internet trolling that followed was also an intensified, emotional reaction toward a (foreign) woman "looking down" on South Korean men (both literally and figuratively). Such heightened affectivity or emotional reactivity is characteristic of an activated cultural complex.

Evidence of how deeply engrained the cultural complex surrounding the *kimchi*-bitch is with young South Korean men can be found by comparing socioeconomic conditions in the region. In East Asia, this subculture movement has direct parallels to *diaosi* culture in China and could be compared to the "strawberry generation" of Taiwan or perhaps with some aspects of *otaku* (geek) culture in Japan. The Korean *rujeo* and Chinese *diaosi* share the greatest resemblance, yet the Chinese movement has a playful, light-hearted online appeal that differs significantly from the bitterness spawned in South Korean internet circles. *Diaosi* literally translates from Chinese to mean "penis" (*diao*) "hair" (*si*) and is perhaps best expressed as "pube."[77] Like many internet terms, it is the product of a chain of abbreviated in-jokes, which began with users mocking fans of Li Yi, a mediocre Chinese footballer, at the end of 2011. By 2013, cyber commentators and journalists were defining *diaosi* as a new male youth identity that "calls to mind a young graduate working a dead-end job, with little prospect of saving enough to buy a house and a car—basic

THE KIMCHI-*BITCH* CULTURAL COMPLEX 241

trappings of middle-class life that are widely seen as essential prerequisites to finding a girlfriend and marriage."[78] However, more importantly, and definitely more analogous to the situation in South Korea, *diaosi* taps into a profound issue of social stratification in contemporary China. "China's *fait accompli* embracing of capitalist mass consumerism," write Yang, Tang, and Wang, "together with the highly unequal distribution of wealth makes for a society of conspicuous consumption, money-worship, pride and haughtiness of the 'haves' and envy and discontent in the 'have-nots.'"[79] They argue that the hyperconnectivity of the internet is one catalyst for acute awareness of wealth, or a lack thereof.

Feminism in South Korea

The hyper-awareness of class and money, suggested in the example of the Chinese response to youth unemployment and disillusionment, is at odds with the emotions and negative slander online in South Korea, where many male netizens are in the grip of a cultural complex that has created the *kimchi*-bitch. Instead of disdain toward those with money and connections, opportunities perceived to be "gifted" unfairly to women in South Korean society have become the focus of their ire.[80] After the first democratically elected governments took power in the 1990s, feminists in South Korea began to wield real influence in the country. In 1998, President Kim Dae-Jung (1998–2003) brought the policy of "gender mainstreaming" to the fore in the appointment of new roles protecting the rights of women, such as the Ministry of Gender Equality, which committed to promoting gender equality, women's welfare, and participation in society.[81] Moreover, the ratification of the Gender Equality Act, the Gender Discrimination Prevention and Relief Act, and the Framework Act for Women's Development all contributed to affirmative action on gender parity.[82] Under Roh Moo-hyun (2003–2008) many prominent leaders from women's civil rights groups were employed by government to undertake the administration's "national tasks," which included abolishing the patriarchal "family-head system" and preventing prostitution.[83] The decade of left-wing government was replaced by a return to right-wing politics with the election of Lee Myung-bak in 2008 and continued under Park Geun-hye (daughter of dictator Park Chung-hee) from 2013 to March 2017. Lee Myung-bak scaled back the scope and powers of the Ministry

242 AMALYA LAYLA ASHMAN

of Gender Equality and Family, filling it with loyal bureaucrats, and discontinued government focus on gender mainstreaming.[84]

Post-feminism

A decade of raising the profile of feminist causes in South Korea resulted in certain backlash. With women's basic rights asserted in society, resentment grew that women were receiving preferential treatment in hiring during a period of intense competition for graduate jobs. Modern misogyny, writes Kristin J. Anderson in her book of the same title, is the notion that, for the most part, feminism's mission has been achieved; women's rights have been asserted; and the movement is a subject for the history books.[85] Another criticism is that young girls were becoming "entitled." The perception that feminism has empowered women to the point where men are being left behind and marginalized has been dubbed the "boy crisis" by Anderson.[86] It ties into the belief that feminism is obsolete due to women's (supposed) attainment of equality in society; therefore, those who continue to pursue a feminist agenda are guilty of trying to "surpass" men, which Anderson considers a new strain of anti-feminism.[87] This anti-feminism is described as *post-feminism* in Western societies. Post-feminism assumes that the feminist movement is now defunct because women's *material* needs have been fulfilled.[88] Words like *empowerment* and *choice* continue to be employed to positively reinforce women's subjectivity, but this is a pernicious font of social validity.[89] As Anderson explains, "consumerism" and "lifestyle choice has replaced the earlier political and intellectual work of feminism."[90] The shift away from political agency to consumer choice in the rhetoric of post-feminism refocuses women's empowerment on "*self-transformation*" instead of "*social* transformation."[91] Anderson is quite clear that post-feminism speaks to white, Western, middle-class women.[92] In the case of South Korea, some level of consumerism may be equated with empowerment; however, as the *kimchi*-bitch cultural complex demonstrates, there is a very strong (male) cultural resistance to Korean women consuming or coveting wealth, particularly Western goods, which represents "lifestyle," or the rights of the individual.

Premodern perspectives on Korean women

The fear that the *kimchi*-bitch is a Korean woman "consumed by consuming" is a cultural anxiety that predates the modern era.

THE KIMCHI-*BITCH* CULTURAL COMPLEX

243

These historical attitudes often survive unacknowledged, and thus unconsciously, through cultural complexes. A good Korean woman was often remembered on her tombstone by the line "all her life, she did not covet riches" during the Joseon Dynasty (1392–1897).[93] Women are largely absent from Korean historiography, and what little remains concerns the moral education of upper-class women to conform to Confucian society.[94] In 1885, an American attaché and visitor to the kingdom wrote of the Korean woman: "Materially, physically, she is a fact; but mentally, morally, socially, she is a cipher."[95] Within the family, a woman's role was tied to a hierarchy of relationships known as the "Three Obeys" (*samgang oryo*): first was to obey the rule of her father, then that of her husband, and if her husband were to die, she was to obey her son.[96] Along with the Three Obeys, women were also compelled to aspire to the Four Virtues: wifely virtue, speech, appearance, and work.[97] Cultural complexes, like personal complexes, often "absorb the values of the family" since the family is the nucleus of wider culture.[98] Neo-Confucianists of the Joseon Dynasty examined female nature to identify its "deficiencies" and concluded that women suffered from *ki,* or "turbid mind-matter," which left them vulnerable to evil and material desires.[99] Daughters-in-law were considered the boom or bust of the family's fortune because they controlled the purse strings, whereas their husbands devoted themselves to loftier affairs.[100] Thus, frugality was considered an important virtue for women who were entrusted with economizing, inventory, debt, and ancestral property.[101] For every word of praise heaped upon a wise and frugal women, there were as many admonishments of the *nangbu* (an "extravagant woman").[102] Fathers and husbands were mindful of women's wicked "inclinations" toward greed and frequently reminded their women to beware of lending or borrowing money in fear that they become a gambling *nangbu.*[103] At the other extreme, a woman who stoically endured poverty was considered another virtuous blessing to the family.[104]

Modernity and the New Woman

Korean Confucian views of women were profoundly challenged by those of Western modernity. Prior to the establishment of the South Korean state in 1948, the Korean peninsula was a colony of the Japanese Empire from 1910 to 1945. As a result, many ideas of

244 AMALYA LAYLA ASHMAN

Western modernity arrived in Korea via Japan. In the early twentieth century, affluent women who had been university-educated overseas returned to Japan and Korea inspired by the feminist ideals of the "New Woman" movement.[105] The term *New Woman* was coined in 1894 by Sarah Grand to describe women in Europe and North America who were educated feminists challenging society's patriarchal values by adopting new styles of dress, jobs, and activities.[106] The notion of the New Woman arrived in Korea along with Western ideas of enlightenment and modernity from the mid-1880s to the early 1900s, which revolutionized the notion of subjectivity as well as women's autonomy in society.[107] New concepts arose like *min* (to denote a "person") during the Joseon Dynasty, which were expanded to *sinmin, inmin,* or *kungmin* to refer, for the first time, to someone's identity as part of a political entity, in other words, as a "subject," in the modern sense, of the state who requires a modern education.[108] Suddenly, schools for girls were on the agenda to enlighten and civilize Korea, as reflected by newspaper editorials, like this one from *Tongnip sinmun* (*Independence News,* 1896): "Girls are necessarily the children of Korea 'people' ... Girls will be the wives of men, and if they are as knowledgeable as their husbands, the family will be prosperous."[109] According to Jiyoung Suh, these voices for educational reform viewed Korean women as "a signifier of national inferiority and a reason for Korea falling behind the West."[110] As a result, Suh argues, these discourses "fixed" and "othered" East Asian women as "unenlightened and shadowy" vis-à-vis women of the West.[111] Underneath the progressive overtures to allow women access to education lay the presumption that *mingweon*—the new *Taehan* (1897–1910) concept of "national rights"—had to be *earned* by women through education and were not *innate* like those of men.[112] Echoes of this exist in the *kimchi*-bitch complex, which denies that women have "earned" their consumer freedoms because they have not performed their duty in relation to marrying, and caring for, men.

Korea's silky, but shallow, "Modern Girls"

Jiyoung Suh writes that the evolution of the New Woman discourse in Korea began with Korean aspirations toward a modern nation-state in the 1900s and 1910s, but was then caught up in the image of the "wise mother and good wife" in the 1920s.[113] This

THE KIMCHI-*BITCH* CULTURAL COMPLEX

was followed by the emergence of the "Modern Girl" in Korea in the 1930s, and the backlash against that stereotype informed a "composite" image of the Korean New Woman before the Pacific War gathered momentum.[114] In Korea of the 1920s views on the New Woman sharply polarized as the image of the Modern Girl formed from both positive and negative stereotypes around emancipated young Korean women.[115] The term *Modern Girl* was borrowed from English, first in Japan (*modan gāru*) and later in Korea (*modeongeol*).[116] From the 1900s onward, women in Japan took up careers in new urban service industries. Likewise, in Korea, Modern Girls were often employed as "shop girls," "department store girls," "elevator girls," "hello girls" (phone operators), "bus girls" (ticket officers), and "typist girls."[117] Visually, Modern Girls stood out on the streets of Seoul in the 1920s and 1930s with their alluring, colorful Western silk garments, cloche hats, red lipstick, and bobbed haircuts.[118] In the media, these peculiarly dressed women were presented as somewhat exotic because of the mystery they exuded.[119]

Their foreign fashion masked their family background and social status and suggested a strong eroticism.[120] This very same "social chameleonism," assumed by *kimchi*-bitches adorned in designer labels, is a source of indignation in contemporary times. In a similar vein, the fascination with Modern Girls in the press soon turned critical by the mid-1920s.[121] Newspapers began to report the "frivolity, shallowness, [and] careless[ness] of New Women" (*Tonga Ilbo*, 1925), accusing them of "extravagance" and being "easily tempted" (*Sinyeoseong,* 1924; 1925).[122] Socialist male intellectuals, like Yu Kwang-nyeol (1898–1981), Pak Yeong-heui (1901–?), Pak Pal-yang (1905–1988), and Cheo Hak-song (1901–1933), joined the debate to defame Modern Girls as a type of prostitute who used the upper-class sons of capitalists for their money.[123] These Modern Girls, they opined, were pleasure-seekers, enthralled by urban decadence, and reveling in the most trivial aspects of modernity, devoid of knowledge, vision, or ethical sense.[124] Excessive consumerism and sexual promiscuity characterized the negative stereotype of the Modern Girl, who they also referred to as "man's concubine," "citizen of vanity," or simply "bad girl."[125] Interestingly, the Modern Girl was also marked as a fake—that the *real* Modern Girls were yet to materialize in Korea of the 1920s.[126]

246   AMALYA LAYLA ASHMAN

Commodified bodies, neoliberal disillusionment

The most provocative symbol of the Modern Girl in Korea was her corporeality—public, sensual, materialist, and foreign—that modernists wished to control and invalidate as an "other."[127] Fake, vain, materialist *kimchi*-bitches who are too corporeal (via the spectacle of plastic surgery) and too visible (in their flashy luxury brands) are clearly the daughters, in a figurative sense, of the Modern Girl of the 1920s and 1930s. Cultural complexes, like the one described here, facilitate the "continuous movement of affect and images," according to Samuel Kimbles, which pass legacies of emotion and symbolism from one generation to the next.[128] The anxieties of a society in flux are often gendered, it seems in Korean culture, and have settled with particular rancor around the figure of the young woman in the early twentieth and twenty-first centuries. According to Jiyoung Suh, when the New Woman (who became the Modern Girl) first emerged in the early twentieth century, she signified a rupture in the way in which Korean women were perceived in society:

> This representation of the Korean woman as an "inferior other" was the projection of the Eastern or Korean traditions and was diametrically opposed to Western modernity at the time. Consequently, the eye of the "Other," which negated the status of Korean women as social beings, became the ideological scaffolding around the drastically changing life of women in Korea.[129]

I would argue that New Women, Modern Girls, and *kimchi*-bitches (and many others in between) have been Othered and designated "inferior" because they are projections of a cultural complex influenced, in some part, by the archetypal energies of the shadow. These stereotypes reveal the extent to which the South Korean cultural psyche reflects the hegemony of male heteronormativity, which projects national shame, "fragile masculinity," or millennial angst (as the occasion dictates) upon women as criticisms of lack of education, consumer patterns, or plain sexual rejection of South Korean men. Although Suh and I draw on different language (the unconscious and the subconscious, respectively), we agree on the origin of these negative portrayals. Suh describes

> the antipathy against the visualization of female sexuality in the public sphere and the excessive consumption of women reflected the consciousness of male intellectuals

THE KIMCHI-BITCH CULTURAL COMPLEX 247

regarding capitalistic modernity. The libidinal, fetishized, and commodified female body was the manifestation of "the repressed other."[130]

Equally, the *kimchi*-bitch represents the epitome of a "commodified female body" in contemporary South Korea: she only drinks Starbucks, wears Chanel, carries a Louis Vuitton handbag, speaks English, and modifies her body for bigger eyes, bigger breasts, and even a bigger butt. In the 1920s and 1930s, male critics of the Modern Girl considered themselves to be "autonomous and rational individuals," and by Othering the Modern Girl's body, they positioned her as the antithesis of the pursuit of a socialist Korean nation-state.[131] Suh takes this analogy further by adding that the figure of the Modern Girl was a symbol of "the deformity and decadence of modernity itself, as well as the superficial and pathological modernism of Chosŏn Korea and its lack of material and cultural substance."[132] Ultimately, this discourse around the moral failure and excess of the Korean Modern Girl revealed

> the multi-layered anxieties existing between the rifts of colonial modernity, including the anxiety of men towards women who made themselves visible in the public sphere, the anxiety of male intellectuals toward the capitalistic modernity occupying everyday life, as well as the instability and deficiency of the colonial state.[133]

The intellectual critics of the Modern Girl, who were influenced (to differing degrees) by Cultural Nationalist or Socialist movements, were also engaged in an ideological battle to locate Korean-ness in the midst of (or in opposition to) Japanese colonization and Western modernity. The overt adoption of the consumer trappings of Western modernity by the Modern Girls made them a conspicuous target for the identity (and, in some senses, moral) crisis that the (male) Korean intelligentsia faced. The angry young men behind the memes satirizing *kimchi*-bitches on discussion boards like Ilbe do not have such lofty ideals, yet they share a similar sense of existential threat from modern South Korean women. It is not modernity itself, although the issue of women's rights pertains to this still, that threatens young Korean men, but the neoliberal market logic, most keenly associated with the opening of the domestic South Korean market and globalization in the 1990s, which has made victims of these young men. Anxieties and inadequacies are induced by the

248   AMALYA LAYLA ASHMAN

intense competition for jobs, accommodation, and "women." Yet, all of this is masked by the neoliberalist rhetoric of individual consumer responsibility that denies social mechanisms of discrimination, such as systemic classism, regionalism, and nepotism, and instead highlights the *kimchi*-bitch as a product of this consumer paradise. The *kimchi*-bitch complex, therefore, is a millennial cultural complex, born of economic downturn, and inflamed by alt-right tendencies, which is nonetheless deeply embedded in the Korean cultural psyche and its historical Othering of Korean women.

Notes

[1] I would like to extend my thanks to Thomas Singer, Hyun Kyung Lee, and Gang Sung Un for their assistance in writing this article.

[2] The Economist, "Why South Korea Is Worrying about the Position of Women," *The Economist,* May 31, 2016. Accessed Nov. 19, 2018, at https://www.economist.com/blogs/economist-explains/2016/05/economist-explains-22; Seohoi Stephanie Park, "Murder at Gangnam Station: A Year Later," *Korea Exposé* (blog), May 18, 2017. Accessed Nov. 19, 2018, at https://koreaexpose.com/murder-gangnam-station-year-later/.

[3] The Economist, "Why South Korea Is Worrying about the Position of Women."

[4] Su-ji Park, Soo-jin Park, and Jae-uk Lee, "Gangnam Murderer Says He Killed 'Because Women Have Always Ignored Me,'" *The Hankyoreh,* May 20, 2016. Accessed Nov. 19, 2018, at http://english.hani.co.kr/arti/english_edition/e_national/744756.html; Claire Lee, "[FROM THE SCENE] Korean Women Respond to Gangnam Murder Case," *The Korea Herald,* May 19, 2016. Accessed Nov. 19, 2018, at http://www.koreaherald.com/view.php?ud=20160519000691.

[5] Park, "Murder at Gangnam Station."

[6] Quoted in Erik Thurman, "Misogyny in South Korea, Part I: Gangnam Murder," *Korea Exposé* (blog), November 22, 2016. Accessed Nov. 19, 2018, at https://koreaexpose.com/misogyny-korea-gangnam-murder/.

[7] *Kimchi-nyeo* (literally *kimchi*-girl) and *kimchi-nyeon* (literally *kimchi*-bitch) are used interchangeably in Korean. Whereas *nyeo* carries the same derisive weight when combined with *kimchi,* I opt to translate the name as "*kimchi*-bitch" to underline the offensive

THE KIMCHI-*BITCH* CULTURAL COMPLEX   249

nature of this slur for those coming across this term for the first time in English. See The Economist, "Why South Korea Is Worrying about the Position of Women"; and Lee, "[FROM THE SCENE] Korean Women Respond to Gangnam Murder Case."

[8] Most internet memes begin as a (humorous) remark or image that users react to (adding comments or "likes"), share to their own social media feeds, or adapt. The success of a meme could be measured quantitively by its longevity or global reach online, or qualitatively based on its humor, ironic pastiche of popular culture, "relatability," or its emotional resonance.

[9] Luke Hockley, *Frames of Mind: A Post-Jungian Look at Film, Television and Technology* (Chicago: Intellect Books, University of Chicago Press, 2007), p. 125.

[10] *Ibid.*

[11] *Deep web* refers to all sites not indexed by mainstream search engines. The deep web is anecdotally estimated to be 90 percent of the internet, whereas *dark web* is a fraction of the deep web that is involved in illicit activities, such as trade in drugs, weapons, child pornography, and counterfeit documents. Andy Greenberg, "Hacker Lexicon: What Is the Dark Web?," WIRED, November 19, 2014. Accessed Nov. 19, 2018, at https://www.wired.com/2014/11/hacker-lexicon-whats-dark-web/.

[12] Greg Singh, "YouTubers, Online Selves and the Performance Principle: Notes from a Post-Jungian Perspective," *Digital Media, Psychoanalysis and the Subject, Communication and Media* 38 (11, 2016): 189–216.

[13] Steffen Krüger and Jacob Johanssen, "Thinking (with) the Unconscious in Media and Communication Studies: Introduction to the Special Issue," *Digital Media, Psychoanalysis and the Subject, Communication and Media* 11 (38, 2016): 8.

[14] *Ibid.*, p. 15.

[15] Tova Benski and Eran Fisher, eds., *Internet and Emotions* (London and New York: Routledge, 2013), p. 1.

[16] Angela Dobele, Adam Lindgreen, and Michael Beverland, "Why Pass on Viral Messages? Because They Connect Emotionally," *Business Horizons* 50 (4, 2007): 291–304; Rosanna E. Guadagno, Daniel M. Rampala, and Bradley M. Okdie, "What Makes a Video Go Viral? An Analysis of Emotional Contagion and Internet Memes," *Computers in Human Behavior* 29 (6, 2013): 2312–2319; and

Elsamari Bortha and Mignon Reyneke, "To Share Or Not To Share: The Role of Content and Emotion in Viral Marketing," *2013* 13 (12, 2013): 160–71.

[17] Richard Dawkins, *The Selfish Gene* (Oxford: Oxford University Press, 1976), p. 192.

[18] *Ibid.*, p. 193.

[19] *Ibid.*

[20] Looking for the evolutionary biology of archetypal ideas, which seems very close to the description of Dawkins' meme, is a messy business that has been exhausted (one hopes) by Andrew Samuels in *Jung and the Post-Jungians* (London and Boston: Routledge & K. Paul, 1985).

[21] Dan Sperber, *Explaining Culture: A Naturalistic Approach* (Cambridge, MA: Blackwell Pub., 1996), p. 24.

[22] *Ibid.*

[23] *Ibid.*, p. 33.

[24] Web 2.0 was coined by Tim O'Reilly in 2005 to refer to the reorientation of online services around user experience and content, by promoting user interaction and input and harvesting the collective intelligence and data. Tim O'Reilly, "What Is Web 2.0: Design Patterns and Business Models for the Next Generation of Software," *Communication and Strategies* 65 (1, 2007): 17–37.

[25] Jean Burgess, "'All Your Chocolate Rain Are Belong To Us?' Viral Video, YouTube and the Dynamics of Participatory Culture," in Nikos Papastergiadis and Victoria Lynn, eds., *Art in the Global Present* (Sydney: UTSe Express, 2014), p. 87.

[26] Henry Jenkins, "Slash Me, Mash Me, Spread Me ...," *Henry Jenkins* (blog), April 23, 2007. Accessed Nov. 19, 2018, at http://henryjenkins.org/2007/04/slash_me_mash_me_but_please_sp.html.

[27] Thomas Singer and Samuel L. Kimbles, eds., *The Cultural Complex: Contemporary Jungian Perspectives on Psyche and Society* (Hove and New York: Brunner-Routledge, 2004), p. 4.

[28] Samuel L. Kimbles, "Cultural Complexes and the Transmission of Group Traumas in Everyday Life," *Psychological Perspectives* 49 (1, 2006): 97.

[29] Jae-wook Lee, "Conservatives Protest Sewol Families by Gorging on Pizza and Kimbap," *The Hankyoreh*, September 10, 2014. Accessed on Nov. 19, 2018, at http://english.hani.co.kr/arti/english_edition/e_national/654589.html.

THE KIMCHI-BITCH CULTURAL COMPLEX

251

[30] C. G Jung, *Aion: Researches into the Phenomenology of the Self,* vol. 9ii, *The Collected Works of C. G. Jung,* ed. and trans. R. F. C. Hull (London: Routledge, 1959), § 13.

[31] John Weir Perry, "Emotions and Object Relations," *Journal of Analytical Psychology* 15 (1, 1970): 1–12.

[32] *Ibid.,* p. 4.

[33] Kimbles, "Cultural Complexes and the Transmission of Group Traumas," p. 99.

[34] Jung, CW 9ii, § 15.

[35] *Ibid.,* § 19.

[36] In-Kyoung Chung, "Internet Misogyny in a Post-Feminist Era," *Issues in Feminism* 16 (1, 2016): 185–221, p. 196. Accessed on Nov. 19, 2018, at http://www.dbpia.co.kr.

[37] Another insult is *boseurachi,* which combines *boji* with the word for government official, *byeoseurachi,* to suggest a woman who mandates (like a government) that men fulfill her (material) demands. "Boseurachi," Namuwiki, September 24, 2017. Accessed on Nov. 19, 2018, at https://namu.wiki/w/%EB%B3%B4%EC%8A%AC%EC%9 5%84%EC%B9%98.

[38] Chung, "Internet Misogyny," p. 196.

[39] Jonathan Krim, "Subway Fracas Escalates into Test of the Internet's Power to Shame," *Washington Post,* July 7, 2005. Accessed on Nov. 19, 2018, at http://www.washingtonpost.com/wp-dyn/content/article/2005/07/06/AR2005070601953.html.

[40] *Netizen* is the word used in Korean for the generic English term *internet user.* Although they are interchangeable, *netizen* also implies a politicized commentator and possibly an online harasser. Krim, "Subway Fracas Escalates."

[41] Chung, "Internet Misogyny," p. 196.

[42] Dana, "Korean Through K-Pop 101: The Bean Paste Girl," *Seoul Beats* (blog), December 14, 2012. Accessed on Nov. 19, 2018, at http://seoulbeats.com/2012/12/korean-through-k-pop-101-the-bean-paste-girl/.

[43] A fascinating point of comparison to Kim Hyun Jung's painting is the cartoon on page 50 of the women's magazine *New Home* [*Sin Gajeong*] published in June 1933. It depicts a young woman in *hanbok* peering through a cafe window at men being served ice cream by a waitress. The woman is depicted as salivating over this scene of consuming (literally) Western modernity, and the

cartoonist is brusque, saying this is the ugliest sight imaginable. See my argument regarding the Modern Girl. My gratitude to Gang Sung Un for this reference.

[44] My thanks to Thomas Singer for pointing out the connection between the derision toward domestic consumerism in the *kimchi-bitch* complex and *malinchismo* in Mexico, described by Jacqueline Gerson in "Malinchismo: Betraying One's Own," in Thomas Singer and Samuel L. Kimbles, eds., *The Cultural Complex: Contemporary Jungian Perspectives on Psyche and Society* (Hove and New York: Brunner-Routledge, 2004).

[45] Michael Kimmelman, "Lessons from McDonald's Clash with Older Koreans," *The New York Times,* January 28, 2014, Art & Design. Accessed on Nov. 19, 2018, at https://www.nytimes.com/2014/01/29/arts/design/lessons-from-mcdonalds-clash-with-older-koreans.html.

[46] "Cosmetic Surgery Addict Injected Cooking Oil into Her Own Face," *The Telegraph,* November 11, 2008, News. Accessed on Nov. 19, 2018, at http://www.telegraph.co.uk/news/newstopics/howaboutthat/3439638/Cosmetic-surgery-addict-injected-cooking-oil-into-her-own-face.html.

[47] Chung, "Internet Misogyny," p. 196.

[48] *Ibid.*, p. 190.

[49] James Pearson, "(Yonhap Feature) Conservatives Go on the Online Offensive," *Yonhap News Agency,* April 30, 2013. Accessed on Nov. 19, 2018, at http://english.yonhapnews.co.kr/n_feature/2013/04/29/45/4901000000AEN20130429006500315F.HTML.

[50] In South Korea, almost all user platforms require full name, email address, identity card number, and phone number to join.

[51] In Korean, the moniker is *Ssibeol-gyohwang,* which is purposely misspelled to pass censorship; it literally reads as "fuck pope." GoCall is an abbreviation for "Comedy Program Gallery." Jay H., "Netizen Explains Roots of Korean Conservative Online Community," *KoreaBANG* (blog), December 28, 2012. Accessed on Nov. 19, 2018, at https://www.koreabang.com/2012/features/netizen-explains-roots-of-korean-conservative-online-community.html.

[52] *Cyber tailing* is a collective action to expose the personal details of victims or perpetrators of crimes or perceived wrongdoings (which can include being obnoxiously wealthy or successful), including their addresses, work places, and contact details, and then to proceed to harass the targets online and offline at home or at work. See "'Cyber

THE KIMCHI-*BITCH* CULTURAL COMPLEX 253

Tailing' Becoming a Social Problem," *The Korea Times,* November 20, 2012. Accessed on Nov. 19, 2018, at http://www.koreatimes. co.kr/www/news/nation/2012/02/113_103546.html; Jay H., "Netizen Explains Roots."

[53] Jay H., "Netizen Explains Roots.

[54] *Ibid.*

[55] *Ibid.*

[56] Chung, "Internet Misogyny."

[57] Jay H., "Netizen Explains Roots."

[58] Bora Yoon, "Ilbe and Misogyny: Ilbe Is Everywhere and Nowhere" [*Ilbewa Yeoseong Hyeomo: Ilbeneun Eodiena Itgo Eodiedo Eopda*], *The Radical Review* 57 (2013): 34.

[59] Yoon, "Ilbe and Misogyny," 35.

[60] Jay H., "Ilbe Presents: The Uniquely Korean '*Kimchi*-Bitch,'" *KoreaBANG* (blog), February 10, 2014, https://www.koreabang. com/2014/stories/ilbe-presents-the-uniquely-korean-*kimchi*-bitch.html.

[61] *Ibid.*

[62] *Ibid.*

[63] *Ibid.*

[64] Boram Kim, "Gov't Proposes 2017 Budget in Excess of Record 400 Trillion Won," *Yonhap News Agency,* August 30, 2016. Accessed Nov. 19, 2018, at https://en.yna.co.kr/view/AEN20160829009300320.

[65] The preference for male offspring is starkly portrayed in statistics on the sex of the family's third child. In the 1990s, the desire for at least one male child led parents with daughters to consistently abort female fetuses until they conceived a male child. As a consequence, the sex ratio for "the third child" is skewed to over 300 men to women in cities like Daegu and Busan. Seo-hwan Kim, "The Past is Unimaginable Now: Third Child Sex Ratio" [*Jigeumeun sangsanghagi himdeun gwageo 'setjjae ai seongbi'*], *Joongang Ilbo,* February 2, 2017. Accessed Nov. 19, 2018, at http:// news.joins.com/article/21203954. My thanks again to Gang Sung Un for making this connection. See also Mo-deum Yang, "Korean Men to Run Short of Brides Soon," *The Chosun Ilbo,* October 7, 2017. Accessed Nov. 19, 2018, at http://english.chosun.com/site/data/html_ dir/2017/01/07/2017010700379.html.

[66] Yang, "Korean Men to Run Short of Brides Soon."

[67] Jay H., "Ilbe Presents."

[68] *Ibid.*

254   AMALYA LAYLA ASHMAN

[69] *Ibid.*

[70] Jay H., "Netizen Explains Roots."

[71] *Rujeo* comes from the English word *loser* transliterated into Korean. *Gag Concert,* the long-running comedy sketch show, lampooned "the loser" in their 2006 series called "Modern Life Menagerie" [*Hyeondae saenghwal beaksu*]. Loser culture also inspired the graphic novel-turned-MBC television drama *Merry Mary* [*Meri Daegu gongbangjeon,* 2007] and the 2015 TvN comedy series *Choinshidae* (popularly translated as *The Superman Age,* but *The Age of the Übermensch* is more fitting).

[72] Jeong-in Yoo, "(Discussing the Welfare State) Volvo, a Large Lay-off, and No Strike [*Bokjigukgareul Malhanda. Bolbo, Daeryanghaegoedo Paeobeun Eopseotda*]," *The Kyunghyang Shinmun,* June 7, 2011. Accessed April 8, 2019, at http://news.khan.co.kr/kh_news/khan_art_view.html?artid=201106072127345&code=940702.

[73] Seokhun U and Gwonil Park, *The 880,000 Won Generation: The Economic Science of Hope for a Generation of Despair [88-Manweon Sedae: Cheolmang-Eui Sidae-e Sseuneun Heuimang Eui Kyeongjehak]* (Seoul: Rediang Midieo, 2007).

[74] The term *rujeo* joins other jargon that also translates into *loser*: *wangdda* (literally *king turned,* meaning "bullied into a corner"), *nakoja* (literally *fallen soldier*), *jjijili* (*worthless*), *rumpen* (abbreviated from *lumpenproletariat,* a Marxist term for the socially useless working classes), *ingyeoingan* (*surplus human-being*), *beaksu* (literally white hand, meaning "empty-handed, or penniless"), *neuteajok* (derived from *NEET,* meaning "not in employment, education, or training"). See Young do Yun, "A Study of the Loser Culture in the New Age Media Age—Focus on the Phenomenon of 'Loser' in Korean and Diaosi in China" [Nyumidieosidae rujeomunhwa sltam—hanguk-eu rujeo-wa chungguk-eu diaoseu hyeonsang-eul chungslm-euro], *The Journal of Chinese Language, Literature and Translation in Korea* 37 (2015): 217–246, p. 222.

[75] *Ibid.*

[76] *Ibid.,* p. 224.

[77] Peidong Yang, Lijun Tang, and Xuan Wang, "*Diaosi* as Infrapolitics: Scatological Tropes, Identity-Making and Cultural Intimacy on China's Internet," *Media, Culture & Society* 37 (2, 2015): 201–202.

THE KIMCHI-BITCH CULTURAL COMPLEX 255

[78] *Ibid,* p. 202; David Cohen, "Could This Be China's Youth Movement?" *The Diplomat,* March 30, 2013. Accessed Nov. 19, 2018, at https://thediplomat.com/2013/03/could-this-be-chinas-youth-movement/.

[79] Yang, Tang, and Wang, *"Diaosi* as Infrapolitics," p. 208.

[80] Interestingly, there is some similar gender-based resentment expressed toward single women in their thirties in Japan, who are pejoratively called *makeinu,* meaning "loser dog." They are derided for not contributing children to society in the face of historically low birthrates. See Tomomi Yamaguchi, "'Loser Dogs' and 'Demon Hags': Single Women in Japan and the Declining Birth Rate," *Social Science Japan Journal* 9 (1, 2006): 109–114.

[81] Seung-kyung Kim and Kyounghee Kim, "Mapping a Hundred Years of Activism," in Mina Roces and Louise Edwards, eds., *Women's Movements in Asia: Feminisms and Transnational Activism* (London and New York: Routledge, 2010), p. 200.

[82] *Ibid.,* pp. 200–201.

[83] *Ibid.,* p. 201.

[84] *Ibid.,* p. 202.

[85] Kristin J. Anderson, *Modern Misogyny: Anti-Feminism in a Post-Feminist Era* (New York: Oxford University Press, 2015), p. xii.

[86] *Ibid.,* p. 75.

[87] *Ibid.,* p. 51.

[88] *Ibid.,* p. 1.

[89] *Ibid.*

[90] *Ibid.*

[91] *Ibid.*

[92] *Ibid.*

[93] Martina Deuchler, "Propagating Female Virtues in Chosōn Korea," in Dorothy Ko, Jahyun Kim Haboush, and Joan R. Piggott, eds., *Women and Confucian Cultures in Premodern China Korea, and Japan* (Berkeley, CA: University of California Press, 2003), p. 158.

[94] Deuchler, "Propagating Female Virtues," p. 142.

[95] Lowell Percival, *Chosōn, The Land of the Morning Calm: A Sketch of Korea* (Boston: Ticknor and Co., 1888), p. 143.

[96] M. Theresa Kelleher, *The Illustrated Encyclopedia of Confucianism,* ed. Rodney Leon Taylor and Howard Yeun Fung Choy, vol. 2 (New York: Rosen Publishing Group, 2005), p. 497.

256 AMALYA LAYLA ASHMAN

[97] *Ibid.*, p. 497.

[98] Jules Cashford, "Britain: Autonomy and Insularity in an Island Race," in Joerg Rasche and Thomas Singer, eds., *Europe's Many Souls: Exploring Cultural Complexes and Identities* (New Orleans: Spring Journal Books, 2016), p. 46.

[99] Deuchler, "Propagating Female Virtues in Chosŏn Korea," p. 148.

[100] *Ibid.*, p. 156.

[101] *Ibid.*

[102] *Ibid.*, p. 157.

[103] *Ibid.*

[104] *Ibid.*

[105] Theodore Jun Yoo, *The Politics of Gender in Colonial Korea: Education, Labor, and Health, 1910–1945* (Berkeley, CA: University of California Press, 2008), ebook.

[106] Sarah Grand, "The New Aspect of the Woman Question," in Carolyn Christensen Nelson, ed., *A New Woman Reader: Fiction, Articles and Drama of the 1890s* (Peterborough, ON, Canada: Broadview Press, 2008), p. 141.

[107] Jiyoung Suh, "The 'New Woman' and the Topography of Modernity in Colonial Korea," *Korean Studies* 37 (2014): 13.

[108] So-young Kim, "'The Nation' in the Textbooks in the Kabo Reforms Period," *The Society for the Studies of Korean History* 29 (11, 2007): 171–208.

[109] Quoted in Suh, "The 'New Woman,'" p. 15.

[110] *Ibid.*, p. 16.

[111] *Ibid.*, p. 15–16.

[112] *Ibid.*, p. 16.

[113] *Ibid.*, p. 14.

[114] *Ibid.*

[115] I use the term *emancipation* in a broad sense to denote a gain in social status and implied rights, not legally or politically, given that universal suffrage and political autonomy for women did not begin on the peninsula until 1946 in North Korea and 1948 in South Korea. Suh, "The 'New Woman,'" p. 20

[116] *Ibid.*, p. 22.

[117] *Ibid.*, p. 23.

[118] Although men had been formally released from the obligation to wear their hair in a topknot in deference to the king or to wear traditional clothing, women had not been included and, instead,

THE KIMCHI-*BITCH* CULTURAL COMPLEX

were expected to eschew foreign clothes. Beverly Chico, *Hats and Headwear around the World: A Cultural Encyclopedia* (Santa Barbara: ABC-CLIO, 2015), p. 25; Suh, "The 'New Woman'" pp. 21, 24.

[119] Suh, "The 'New Woman'" p. 22.

[120] *Ibid.*

[121] *Ibid.*, p. 20.

[122] *Ibid.*, pp. 22–21.

[123] *Ibid.*, p. 21.

[124] *Ibid.*

[125] *Ibid.*, pp. 21, 22.

[126] *Ibid.*, p. 21.

[127] *Ibid.*, p. 24.

[128] Thomas Singer and Samuel L. Kimbles, "The Emerging Theory of Cultural Complexes," in Joseph Cambray and Linda Carter, eds., *Analytical Psychology: Contemporary Perspectives in Jungian Analysis* (Hove & New York: Brunner-Routledge, 2004), p. 188.

[129] Suh, "The 'New Woman,'" p. 13.

[130] *Ibid.*, p. 27.

[131] *Ibid.*, p. 24.

[132] *Ibid.*, p. 25.

[133] *Ibid.*

Taiwan

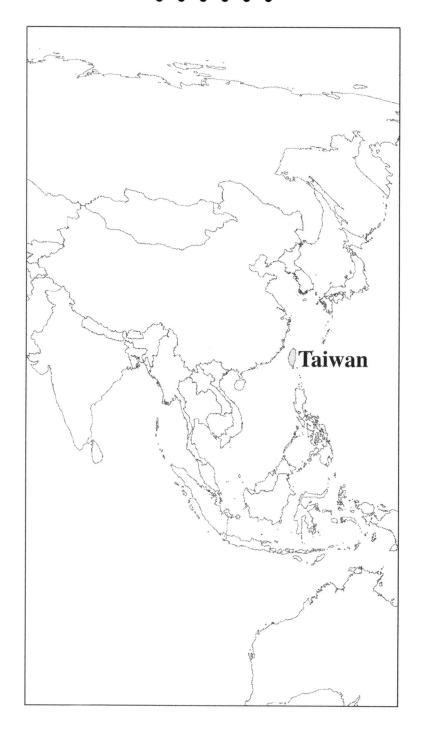

11

• • • • • •

The History of the
Search for the Father in Taiwan
A Cultural Complex

Hao-Wei Wang

Understanding the complexity of Taiwanese national identity is difficult enough for the Taiwanese people; it is even harder for people outside of Taiwan. Historically, the various groups in Taiwan have suffered numerous collective traumas, all of which have contributed to what I call the search for the father and for the fatherland along with the betrayal and abandonment by many of the fathers who have come and gone. As a result, the Taiwanese have been forced to transition from one national identity to another many times. Taiwan's collective or national identity is based as much on cultural trauma and the resultant cultural complex as on ethnicity or blood relations. This national identity complex is not only a political and social issue, but also a clinical issue.

Hao-Wei Wang is a psychiatrist, a child psychiatrist, and a Jungian analyst of the Taiwan Association of Analytical Psychology. He lives and practices in Taipei, Taiwan, where he is the director of the Taiwan Institute of Psychotherapy and vice-president of the Asian Academy of Family Therapy. Dr. Wang has written more than ten books on psychotherapy and popular psychology in Mandarin. His research themes include cultural issues in psychology, psychotherapy, and psychiatry as well as historical issues in psychoanalysis and analytical psychology.

Case example

Tim was thirty-four years old when he was referred by a psychiatrist for further dynamic psychotherapy. He had been a physician in California. Two years previous, with the urging of his father, he decided to migrate back to Taiwan to join the family. As an American-born Taiwanese with a rudimentary level of Mandarin, he found it hard to adapt to such a big change. Not only did he need to adjust to a new environment, to building a new practice and collegial relationships, and to learning a new language, but also he had to face the challenge of developing a new relationship with his parents. Six months after returning to Taiwan, his wife, an American-born Korean, and his two children also moved back, without knowing any Chinese dialect. Long-standing conflicts between Tim and his parents did not improve. When Tim became more depressed, he decided to seek help from a psychiatrist who suggested that, in addition to taking medication, he should seek psychotherapy at the same time. This was what led to our meeting.

After three months of individual psychotherapy, I suggested that we arrange a joint interview with his parents. Tim agreed. At first, Mr. Chen, Tim's father, absolutely refused such a meeting. He would not accept any psychological help, which he thought was only for weak people. Only when Tim, his only son, threatened to move back to the United States did the father consent to a family session, which seemed helpful for Tim. His mother seemed much more understanding and supportive of the difficulty in adjusting that Tim and his family faced. Surprisingly, two days after the initial family meeting, Tim's father asked to meet me individually. After discussing this request with Tim and obtaining his permission, I agreed to meet with Mr. Chen.

****

Mr. Chen arrived at my clinic, accompanied by his bodyguard who remained outside the office. Mr. Chen was anxious to explain what had happened in our initial family session and why Tim had called him selfish and snobby. During the family session, Tim had tried to make his parents understand how much moving back to Taiwan had impacted him and his family. However, Mr. Chen had remained mostly silent, dumbfounded and disbelieving of what his son said.

In the individual session, Mr. Chen tried to answer, from his perspective, the criticisms that Tim had leveled against his

SEARCH FOR THE FATHER IN TAIWAN

fatherhood. Simply put, he considered the father's role to be strict and not to spoil the child.

I asked him why he thought this way and whether his own father had treated him like that. He shook his head immediately. He said his father had been a hedonistic master, living on a huge family property that he had inherited from his father's grandfather who was a Qing Dynasty Imperial Examination Scholar (秀才). His father was so lax that his mother, who was unbelievably competent, actually managed and maintained the whole family.

While talking about the origins of his ideal father figures, he mentioned a junior high school teacher who he and his classmates had admired. This teacher had graduated from the Normal School during the Japanese colonization of Taiwan. Mr. Chen still remembered the stories that this teacher shared about his own teachers who were young men from Japan who had an inspirational attitude toward life. Those young teachers became role models, just as the teacher would later become a role model for Mr. Chen. In recalling these memories, Mr. Chen couldn't help but reflect: "What a respectable generation! They were always full of *the spirit of Japanese education!*"

The Japanese-style father

"Fathers of Japanese education spirit" (日本教育的爸爸) or "Fathers of Japanese style" (日本式的爸爸) is a familiar term to those born between 1930 and 1965. It symbolizes men who were rigorous, serious, and taciturn with their children. Even long after the end of Japanese colonization, Taiwanese people still used to call their fathers *TouSan* (多桑), a pronunciation simulating the word *father* in Japanese (父さん, とうさん).

Wu Nien-jen (吳念真, born 1952) is a famed Taiwanese scriptwriter, director of drama and film, and novelist. In 1994 he directed a film about his own father. His father became a miner when his education was interrupted because of the defeat of the Japanese Empire. At that point, the language used in schools was changed from Japanese to Mandarin. The only wish in his father's frustrated life was to see Mount Fuji and to visit the Japanese Royal Palace. In the film the father was usually silent, never showing any happiness, even when his son successfully entered the university, which was a glorious achievement at that time. The children in the film were always fearful and respectful of their father. Director Wu titled his

264 HAO-WEI WANG

film *TouSan* (*A Borrowed Life* in English). From the name *TouSan*, every Taiwanese understood that the film told the story of a typical Japanese-style father.

Wen-Shing Tseng (1935–2012) was the first Taiwanese to obtain full psychiatric residency training in a Western country. He trained at the Massachusetts Mental Health Center at Harvard Medical School in Boston (1965–1968), and after his residency, he trained in psychiatry at the National Taiwan University (1961–1965). Later he specialized in psychotherapy and cultural psychiatry. He was on the faculty of the Department of Psychiatry at the University of Hawaii, a World Health Organization consultant, chairman of the Transcultural Psychiatry Section of the World Psychiatric Association, and founder and president of the World Association of Cultural Psychiatry. In his autobiography, he wrote about his father:

> After graduating from elementary school, he wished to study further in Normal School … After entering the Normal School, he received the Japanese education. He was used to Japanese cuisine, preferring Miso soup. I guess he was influenced by the life style of the Japanese dorm. He disciplined his children strictly, perhaps also from the same influence.[1]

During our sessions, Tim told me more about his impressions of his father: "In my memory, my father was always at work. When I was born, he was still struggling with his doctoral thesis, and my mother took care of me all by herself. Then he entered a famous company as an engineer, later also as a part-time faculty member at a university not far away from home. Every Sunday my parents went to see the houses for sale. They would buy and remodel houses by themselves to make a good profit. To facilitate that, my mother got a real-estate license. They always worried that their income was not enough for our family. Every weekend my younger sister and I studied at home or went to learn Chinese. As for the weekdays, my mother looked after us, and my father always worked hard and came home late. I studied cello, my sister piano. When we performed at school or community concerts, our parents rarely showed up, unlike the parents of other classmates whose moms and dads were always there. Later, I was selected as a member of the middle school basketball team. At that age, it was an achievement of which I was proud, but my parents did not attend a single game. Even more, they actually opposed my joining a sports team from the very beginning. They were afraid that I would get hurt,

SEARCH FOR THE FATHER IN TAIWAN 265

and it would harm my academic performance. At home, my father was so silent that it was if he didn't have a voice. However my mother was always respectful to him, which made us very nervous because we couldn't tell if her attitude was out of fear or respect. In my first year of high school, my grandfather asked my father to return to Taiwan to take over the family business. Mother was left in America to look after us. Although I felt a sense of loss and sadness, I was also very happy that he did not live with us. When we went to the airport to send our father back to Taiwan, there were other Taiwanese families saying goodbye to one another. They shared hugs, laughter, tears, and kisses. In comparison, we were so quiet, with just a few tears falling down slowly from my mother's eyes."

Tim knew his father loved him very much. His father just never expressed his emotions. But when conflicts arose between Tim and his father, Tim would lose control and roar at his father for being the one who had failed. Tim had not grown up in Taiwan. He didn't know the term "Japanese-style father." However, the way he described his father was similar to what we called the "Japanese-style father."

The characteristics of the Japanese-style father

What are the characteristic of the "Japanese-style father" in Taiwan?

- *Hard working.* These fathers always work so hard that taking any break from their jobs would make them feel guilty, even if they have achieved considerable wealth. Collectively they became the locomotive of Taiwan, creating the so-called Taiwan Economic Miracle, joining with Singapore, South Korea, and Hong Kong to become known as one of the "Four Asian Tigers" between the early 1960s and 1990s.[2]
- *High standards of self-discipline, morality, and responsibility.* They not only are very strict with themselves but also demand the same high standards from the people around them, including children and colleagues. If their careers don't go well, they suffer intense self-blame. They use their anger, sometimes along with alcohol, to isolate themselves from their own family members. They exile themselves on a psychological level. Clinically they may have some depressive symptoms, but most of the time any depression they suffer is masked and can easily go unrecognized or ignored by the people around them.

- *Taciturn, emotionally flat.* They rarely show their feelings, whether positive or negative; to do so is seen as a sign of weakness. Emotional expression is so infrequent that they lose any ability to express their feelings. Clinically they can be described as *alexithymic*, which is a marked dysfunction in emotional awareness, social attachment, and interpersonal relating.
- *Authoritarian and/or authoritative.* Maintaining their dignity in every situation is of high value, as is upholding their own principles and beliefs. In this context, compromise is painful and can be experienced as a loss of dignity, resulting in depression.

These are the main characteristics of the Japanese-style father in Taiwanese men. Can we fathom the origins of the Japanese style-father, delving deeper than these outward characteristics? C. G. Jung gave a clue from his own autobiography of how we might go about understanding this phenomenon:

> When I was working on the stone table, I became aware of the fateful links between me and my ancestors. I feel very strongly that I am under the influence of things and questions which were left incomplete and unanswered by my parents and grandparents and distant ancestors. It often seems as if there was an impersonal karma within a family which is passed on from parents to children.[3]

As psychologists we have our own archaeology to do.

People with changing identities

As a 36,000 km² (approximately 13,900 square miles) island lying at the western edge of the Pacific Ocean, 130 km (80 miles) from China and 111 km (69 miles) from the Yonaguni-Jima island of Japan, Taiwan has a complicated history. In multiple public statements, the government of the People's Republic of China and its president, Xi Jinping, strongly insist that Taiwan is a part of China. In contrast, most Taiwanese people do not agree with this, according to public-opinion polling conducted over the past two decades, as shown in Figure 11.1.[4] Even more, a majority, believe that Taiwan is an independent country. The polar opposite opinions held by the leader of Mainland China on one end and the people of Taiwan on the other originate in a complicated historical context.

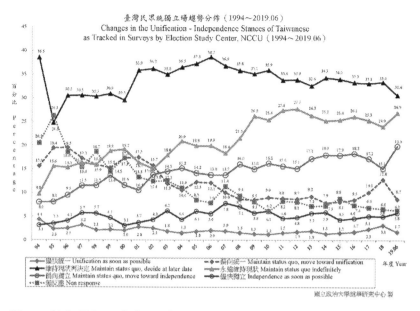

Figure 11.1: Taiwan independence versus unification with the mainland.

For people living on Taiwan, Taiwanese identity has shifted from one generation to the next, from one decade to the next: Who are you? Chinese or Taiwanese? Even within each choice, there are several variations. For example, in choosing to identify as Chinese, one could mean Chinese as in the People's Republic of China, which was founded in 1945; or Chinese as in the Republic of China, which was founded in 1911; or as overseas Chinese; or as Chinese culturally but Taiwanese politically. For people outside Taiwan, understanding the multiple transitions of national identity in the history of the Taiwanese people is difficult. A brief history of Taiwan might help orient the reader.

How the island became Chinese

According to the research of linguists, archeologists, and cultural anthropologists, there is significant evidence of people having settled on different parts of the island of Taiwan at least eight thousand years ago. The ancestors of contemporary Taiwanese aboriginal people spoke various Austronesian languages.[5]

During the Age of Discovery (from approximately the fifteenth to eighteenth centuries), the Portuguese were the first Europeans to reach the island off the southern coast of China in 1544. They named it *Formosa* (Portuguese for "beautiful") because of its beautiful landscape as seen from the sea.

First a Portuguese colony, Taiwan became a Spanish colony after 1580 when the Spanish and Portuguese crowns were unified. As a Spanish colony, Taiwan was a small fortress meant to protect the regional trade with the Philippines. There was no active colonization before the arrival of the Dutch in 1624. From 1624 to 1662, the southern part of Taiwan was under colonial rule by the Dutch Republic. The Dutch East India Company established its presence on Formosa not only to trade with China (Ming Empire) and Japan but also to prevent Portuguese and Spanish trade and colonial activities in East Asia.[6]

At the same time, from 1626 to 1642, the Spanish Empire established itself on the northern tip of the island to protect their enterprises and named it *Spanish Formosa* (*Formosa Española*). The small colony was conquered in 1642 by the Dutch Republic during the Eighty Years' War (1568–1648).[7] From that time, the Dutch controlled much of the island.[8]

The timing of the Han people's immigration from China to Taiwan is quite controversial. Scholars agree that the Han had immigrated to Taiwan earlier than the Western colonizers, but there were no official Chinese organizations in Taiwan before 1642. What remains unclear is when the Han immigration started, how many people immigrated, and whether the Han settled in established communities.

From 1644 the Qing people become the main threat to the Ming Dynasty, which was established in 1368. The Ming were slowly forced to withdraw to southern China. In 1661, under the leadership of Zheng Chenggong, or Koxinga (1624–1662), one of last Ming generals, Ming troops attacked the Dutch colonists in Dutch Formosa and took over Taiwan, using it as a base for retaking China from the Qing.[9] Zheng Chenggong, who died that same year, was the first Chinese to defeat Western colonizers. He took Taiwan from the Dutch, made it part of China, and built the government. He is still seen as a national hero by all Chinese.

The Qing Dynasty took Taiwan back from the Ming in 1683. At that time the Han population on Taiwan totaled more than 120,000 people. At first, Qing policy toward Taiwan was quite passive, although they prohibited further immigration from Mainland China.

SEARCH FOR THE FATHER IN TAIWAN

269

But on Taiwan itself, the Han population increased rapidly, from 666,000 in 1764, to 1.9 million in 1811, to 2.5 million in 1840.[10] Only in the mid-nineteenth century did the Qing Dynasty take a much more active role in Taiwan when Western countries and Japan invaded. In 1885, the Qing Dynasty formally established Taiwan as a province of China. In 1895, however, the Qing Dynasty of China ceded Taiwan to Japan after being defeated in the Sino-Japanese War.

From Chinese to Japanese

In 1683, when the Qing Dynasty took over Taiwan, many thought that Chinese culture had been annihilated forever. The Qing Dynasty was founded by the Manchu Aisin Gioro clan in Manchuria; they were seen as barbarians by the Chinese or Han people at that time. Gu Yanwu (顧炎武) (1613–1682) was a Chinese philologist and geographer and, most importantly, a well-respected intellectual. In learning that the last Ming troops had surrendered to the Qing, he wrote:

> While the names changed and the dynasty was replaced, it means more than that the country is dead. The world had been full of benevolence and righteousness. Now people drive beasts to eat people, people are forced to eat each other. It is more than the death of a country, it is the annihilation of a culture.[11]

The change of identity from being Ming people to being Qing people occurred in stages. Just as Elisabeth Kübler-Ross has described the psychological stages of death (denial, anger, bargaining, depression, and acceptance) for individuals, groups of people who are forced to change their identity experience the same grief process collectively.[12] During the transition of Taiwanese identity from Ming to Qing, we can trace the process over decades of suffering and struggling, from the formation of a resistance movement (denial and anger), to negotiations with a new government for the preservation of traditional values (bargaining), to desperately leaving the island or isolating themselves (depression), to the formation and acceptance of a new identity (acceptance).

The same forced transition of identity has happened two more times in recent Taiwanese history. In 1895, Taiwanese peoples transitioned from Qing Chinese to Japanese, and in 1945, they transitioned again from Japanese to Chinese of the Republic of China (ROC). Such

270 HAO-WEI WANG

changes in identity not only are traumatic for individuals; they also wound whole groups of people and lead to the creation of cultural complexes. As Thomas Singer writes:

> Cultural complexes structure emotional experience and operate in the personal and collective psyche in much the same way as individual complexes, although their content might be quite different. Like individual complexes, cultural complexes tend to be repetitive, autonomous, resist consciousness, and collect experience that confirms their historical point of view.[13]

When a cultural complex is activated, people have difficulty accepting their current reality while in the grips of profound emotional turmoil. In the case of the Taiwanese people, they have developed an *orphan complex* as a result of the multiple changes in collective identity. When the Qing Dynasty was defeated by Japan in the first Sino-Japanese War (1895), Li Hongzhang (李鴻章) represented the Qing Dynasty in the negotiations. Li insisted on the integrity of the Chinese territory, especially Taiwan. For Li, Taiwan was China's frontier in its encounter with Westerners. On the one hand, there is some evidence that Li was the champion of Taiwan being essential to China. On the other hand, the Taiwanese people believe that it was Li who accepted the treaty to cede Taiwan and other territories to Japan. Supposedly Li devalued Taiwan in front of Qing Empress Dowager Cixi (慈禧太后) by saying that Taiwan was a burden to China and that "the birds are silent, the flowers are not fragrant, the men are ruthless, and the women are not righteous (鳥不語，花不香，男無情，女無義)."

These words are well known among the people of Taiwan. Although there is no reliable evidence that Li uttered these words, they are quoted again and again by local historians and politicians. They reflect what I call the "orphan complex," or the "abandonment complex," of Taiwan, reflecting the deep emotional suffering the Taiwanese people endured as a result of the disintegration of previous identities and the inevitable necessity of integrating new ones. Eventually, the grief felt by the people of Taiwan in shedding their old Chinese identity was replaced with acceptance of their new Japanese identity. Although many forgot what happened during the painful transition of identities, the emotion of the orphan complex has remained deep in the cultural unconscious, easily activated with any threat to the sense of belonging.

SEARCH FOR THE FATHER IN TAIWAN 271

The Japanese government in Taiwan was essentially colonial. In his book *Taiwan under Imperialism* (1929), Tadao Yanaihara (矢原內忠雄), a professor of economics at Tokyo Imperial University, examined the structure of the colonial economy of Taiwan based on the results of his tour of Taiwan from March 23 to April 27, 1927. In addition, he discussed Taiwan's educational policies. He found that educational standards were high at the upper levels, such as in medical schools. However, primary education in Taiwan was judged to be quite poor in comparison with Japan at that time. The focus on higher education at the expense of elementary-school education was based on the demands of educated people, who were in control of a colonial system that had little regard for the Taiwanese people themselves. During the Taisho period (1912–1926), the political situation in Taiwan gradually stabilized as the democratic atmosphere in Japan became more mainstream and spread to Taiwan. The Japanese ruling authorities changed their policies then and applied fewer colonial and militaristic rules. They began to treat Taiwan more as an extension of the Japanese homeland than as a conquered land. Following the criticism of people like Professor Tadao Yanaihara, the Japanese government assigned governors from the Japanese civil service to replace the ruling military officers and promoted the same primary educational system as they had in Japan.[14] As Japanese colonial governing policy shifted from a martial colonization policy to an acculturation colonization policy, the attitude toward Taiwan, Japan's first colony, changed drastically. Kaohsiung (高雄), a southern city on Taiwan, was presumed to be the capital of the Japanese Southern Pacific territory, especially during the Pacific War beginning in 1941, when the Japanese invaded Thailand, Malaya, Singapore, and Hong Kong.[15] In some ways, Taiwan became a new province of Japan, and even more importantly, the Taiwanese saw themselves as Japanese and representative of Japan's new colonies.

Becoming Chinese again

Fifty years after being colonized by Japan in 1895, Taiwan was returned to China in 1945 in fulfillment of the 1943 Cairo Declaration, which had outlined the Allies position on post–World War II Japan. From the broader sweep of human history, this transfer of Taiwan from Japan to China may be viewed as being of negligible significance. But for the Taiwanese people, it came as an unbelievable shock. Fifty years in the span of ordinary people's collective memory is a long time; it stretches back to the era of grandparents and even great grandparents, which can seem like the ancient past.

Before the end of WWII, most of the younger generations in Taiwan thought of themselves as Japanese. Taiwanese novelist Ouyang Tzu (歐陽子, b. 1939) has reminisced about the time when she was six years old: "Younger uncle rushed back from the street and said excitedly that we can become Chinese now. But I was shocked and confused in that moment: Are we not Japanese?"

This response was quite common at the time. In Wen-Shing Tseng's autobiography, we find his account of a similar experience when he was ten years old:

> After escaping to the Taiwanese country for five months, on a night in August the head of the local school announced that Nagasaki and Hiroshima had been bombed by the US military with the "atomic bomb." The entire city was destroyed and Japan decided to surrender. This was unbelievable news. Although the city had been bombarded by air raids before, we still believed in our young minds that we must prepare for the final battle, determined to fight to the last soldier. People were full of doubts about this news of the atomic bomb. We were all familiar with the saying: I would rather be a broken jade than an intact tile (寧為玉碎，不為瓦全). It was impossible for us as Japanese to surrender. Unexpectedly, however, the Japanese emperor announced on a radio broadcast that Japan would surrender unconditionally. I could hardly believe it. I asked my father if we needed to commit harakiri (腹切り). My father told me that the Japanese emperor urged the people to endure the unendurable and to accept the fact of surrender. But, we did not have to commit suicide. At the same time, my father told me that after Japan surrendered, Taiwan would be returned to China, and we must celebrate this reunion.[16]

Before 1895, the year that the Japanese took over Taiwan, the people of Taiwan thought they were Qing Dynasty Chinese, and before that, they were Ming Dynasty Chinese who had followed Koxinga (Zheng Chenggong, 鄭成功, 1624–1662) to Taiwan with the goal of preparing for the anti-Qing movement that they hoped would result in the restoration of the Ming Dynasty. And much earlier, even before the Han Chinese had to come to Taiwan, there were aboriginal residents who belonged to different tribes speaking various Austronesian languages.[17]

Search for the Father in Taiwan

Several different group identities have been predominant at various times in the history of Taiwan: from the aboriginal people, to the Ming Han people, to the Qing Han people, to the Japanese, to the Chinese, to the Taiwanese. At times the change in national identity was so radical that it occurred in one day, as Ouyang Tzu experienced. Over the past centuries, this changing sense of identity has become quite complicated. The only identity that has never changed during these transitions is *Taiwanese*. Deep inside their psyches, either consciously or unconsciously, people have thought of themselves as Taiwanese—and also either as Chinese or Japanese depending on the era. That's why the Taiwanese people have tended to see themselves as children of Chinese or Japanese parents.

The destructive power of changing or losing identity

Under the influence of the idea of *liquid modernity* in late modernity, as introduced by Zygmunt Bauman, the Taiwanese, like many other peoples around the world, have increasingly experienced a condition in which identity has shifted from stable to fluid.[18] A sense of identity has traditionally implied an intrinsic, essential content as defined by a common origin or a common structure of experience, and often, both. But the very notion of identity itself seems to be in transition, to be fluid. As Fred Davis writes, "Identity ... is a concept that neither imprisons (as does much in sociology) nor detaches (as does much in philosophy and psychology) persons from their social and symbolic universes, [so] it has over the years retained a generic force that few concepts in our field have."[19] When identity struggles arise, however, they generally take the form of redefining negative images as positive or of deciphering the myth of "authentic" identity. An alternative approach to the notion of identity emphasizes the impossibility of authentic identities based on a universally shared experience or origin. "Identity is never a priori, nor a finished product; it is only ever the problematic process of access to an image of totality."[20]

In terms of Jungian psychology, what sociologists or political scientists discuss about identity is a kind of *persona*. As Jung defined it, "persona is ... a functional complex that comes into existence for reasons of adaptation or personal convenience";[21] and "persona is that which in reality one is not, but which oneself as well as others think one is."[22]

Identities or persona are relational, defined by their difference from something else. They emerge out of an ongoing process and can be multiple, that is, fluid. The theory of fluid identity is based on the social realities of postmodernity, or late capitalism. However, for the psyches of those people who have lived in the modern or premodern era, the changing of identities (persona), or the sense of fluid identities, can cause them to fall into an abyss of suffering. When people are forced or fated to give up their identity, they experience it as destructive. "The dread and resistance which every natural human being experiences when it comes to delving too deeply into himself is, at bottom, the fear of the journey to Hades."[23] Personal accounts of the loss of identity describe it as an endless darkness, such as in William Styron's *Darkness Visible* (1990).[24]

Loss of identity can be experienced as a "soul attack," or, as with patients who suffer a "heart attack," it can feel as though they are under a destructive attack. David H. Rose sees a "soul attack" and a "heart attack" as parallel assaults on the integrity of one's being. During a heart attack, a part of the heart dies and a regeneration process takes place. In a "soul attack," part of the psyche dies, with a possibility of a rebirth of the true self.[25] People who suffer from a loss of identity can suffer depression and then a transformation. Positive changes can occur, although no one knows if and when it will happen. As Martin Buber emphasized, individuals must heal themselves first: "Everything depends on inner change: when this has taken place, and only then, does the world change."[26]

But the painful experience of the loss of identity before transformation can be quite intolerable for those who are forced to face it. In the real world, such a loss can become a life-long trauma that takes the shape of a complex that can be passed on from generation to generation. And this painful fact is often ignored by sociologists, psychologists, scholars of cultural studies, mental health professionals, and even Jungian analysts.

Wu Zhuoliu (吳濁流, 1900–1976) was a famous Taiwanese journalist and novelist of Hakka Chinese ancestry. His masterpiece *Orphan of Asia* was written in Japanese between 1944 and 1945, the final years of World War II.[27] The central character in this autobiographical novel, Hu Taiming, is a man fated both by his Chinese cultural heritage and the opportunities for education and advancement that adoption of the Japanese language allowed.

Search for the Father in Taiwan

This situation was not unusual. Taiwan was a Japanese colony between 1895 and 1945, and *Orphan of Asia* spans the entire Japanese colonial period, following Taiming's life from birth through the final days of World War II.

As an outstanding Taiwanese student of Japanese education, the character Taiming takes advantage of the system, becoming the first one of his village to advance far in his schooling. He becomes a teacher, which makes him well-respected, but he is disillusioned after being humiliated by a Japanese superior, leading him to take a radical step: "I can study abroad. Yes, I'll forget the past, everything of the past, and start over in Japan, from page one."[28]

He wants to be a "true" Japanese. But one's history, whether personal, familial, or national, is never easily overcome, and Japan, the so-called fatherland, never embraces him fully. Despite speaking the Japanese language fluently, he is still an outsider as a student in Japan. He has the same experience when he is among the students from China. Coming to Japan as a young Hakka student who is good at the Japanese language but poor at Mandarin, he is advised "not to tell anyone you're from Taiwan."[29] After he mistakenly tells a Chinese student that he comes from Taiwan, Taiming's friend is so anxious that he shouts at him:

> "Stupid! Don't you know Japan's spy policy. In Xiamen of Southern China, there are many Taiwanese who like to be the stooges of Japan government for the privilege to exploit local Chinese people?"[30]

Taiming's confusing national identity conflict is the main theme of this novel. It is so disastrous that, as the name of novel *Orphan of Asia* implies, this man of confused identity is broken and on the verge of insanity by the end of the story.

Madness as a way of sanity

National identity, as the political scientist Benedict Anderson suggested, "is imagined because the members of even the smallest nation will never know most of their fellow-members, meet them, or even hear of them, yet in the minds of each lives the image of their communion."[31] A nation is a socially constructed community, imagined by the people who perceive themselves as part of that group.

The thinking of many scholars in the humanities or natural sciences is based on the facts of the rational world. As an outstanding

276   *HAO-WEI WANG*

scholar of the social sciences, Anderson's argument is no exception. National identity is something imagined in his theory, however, so it is quite unlikely that Anderson himself could imagine that a conflict around national identity might have such an overwhelming power as to drive someone like Hu Taiming crazy.

In 1912, Einstein introduced his theory of special relativity. In the same year, in the seminal *Wandlungen und Symbole der Libido* (later revised and published as *Psychology of the Unconscious* in 1916), C. G. Jung introduced his theory of psychic energy, perhaps as an analogy or in parallel to Einstein's physical discoveries. It was a turning point for Jung. Against Freud, he argued that "we were deceiving ourselves when we believed that we could make the libido sexualis the vehicle of an energetic perception of psychic life," and we needed "a new conception of libido" which was purely "energetic."[32]

Before his correspondence with Sigmund Freud, Jung, as an outstanding young psychiatrist mentored by the famed Eugen Bleuler at Burghölzli, had published his own research. In a 1904 paper, "The Associations of the Normal Subjects," Jung detailed the experimental procedure used in the Word Association tests. In this procedure, he examined "the reactions [time of subjects] to see whether they are at all subject to any law; and next, to discovering whether individual patterns occur, i.e., whether any definite reaction-types are to be found."[33] Jung noted there were disruptions in the subjects' responses to the Word Association tests. He referred to these disruptions in the responses to some stimulus words as "personal matter." He found the disruptions referred to a symbolic situation that was troubling the subject or indicated some problematic psychic contents. For these responses, in a 1911 paper, "On the Doctrine of Complexes," he used the term *complex* "because such a 'personal matter' is always a collection of various ideas, held together by an emotional tone common to all."[34]

Although the overt aim of the experiment was to determine average reaction speed, years later he used the term *constellation* to describe the recognition that the outward situation released a psychic process in which certain contents gather together and prepare for action.

> When we say that a person is "constellated" we mean that he has taken up a position from which he can be expected to react in an adequate definite way. But the constellation is an automatic process which happens involuntarily and which no one can stop of his own accord.[35]

SEARCH FOR THE FATHER IN TAIWAN

Jung's studies of complexes again had remarkable similarities to the concepts of the emerging field of modern physics. The mass, or value, of a complex of ideas determines the gravitational effects of an instinctual function. The more vital the function, the more its energy draws psychic material to it, creating a complex of emotionally charged associations. Though the function itself is common to all, its subjective value is relative to the individual, his or her own subjective factor borne out by experience, that is, "constellated."

One can read *Orphan of Asia*, Zhuoliu's novel about Taiming, as an example of a "constellated" cultural complex. At the end of *Orphan of Asia*, Taiming, who has gone mad, disappears from his village. Taiming's madness, a breakdown after a series of losses of identity, could be diagnosed by psychiatrists as *Hysterical Psychosis* or, according to DSM-5, *Brief Psychotic Disorder.*

> This rumor [that he took a boat to the Chinese Mainland] has not disappeared, and it is said that Taiming spread broadcast talks from the radio station in Kunming [which was one of the last cities not yet fallen in China] to Japan. However, whether he took the boat to the other side, or he was in Kunming, the truth was unknown to the villagers.[36]

Madness "can feel like a soulless thing that terrifies subject and object by its very absence of form and clear affect and by the void of experience that is part of it."[37] For people like Taiming, whose mentality is not fluid in the way described by postmodern theorists, identities are formed by multiple complexes, giving rise to a persona that crosses between conscious and unconscious. When an identity in a person like Taiming is subverted and disintegrates, the energy constellated around a complex is released suddenly, like a bomb.

Jung identified at least four aspects of the unconscious functioning of a complex—autonomy, dissociability, emotional activation (constellation), and the image "of a certain psychic situation."[38] At the personal level, complexes tend to express both deeper levels of psychic functioning and early developmental/familial relationships. "Everyone knows nowadays that people 'have complexes.' What is not so well known, though far more important theoretically, is that complexes can have us."[39]

When complexes seize Taiming, madness becomes a way of being, a kind of persona adaptation to protect his soul while Taiming's villagers still identify themselves as Japanese. The villagers, like the

278   HAO-WEI WANG

Taiwanese people of that time, are proud of being Japanese. They seem to be possessed by a collective shadow.

> Taiming suddenly went crazy, and this rumor spreads out. His insanity could be confirmed by some facts. First of all, on the second day of Zhinan's death, in front of the Ancestors' shrine table in Hu's Family Temple, Taiming painted his own face like Guan Gong's red face. There was also some handwritings on the wall, and the written ink marks were still fresh:
>> Man who determined to be the intellectual for the world,
>> Absolutely not willing to be humble slaves.
>> …
>> However, be immortal the Han spirit,
>> Rather sacrificed the flesh.
>> …
>> Although the words and deeds of Taiming are strange,
> it still cannot be asserted that he was really mad… .[40]

When people are constantly forced to change their identity, they can get trapped between their previous identity and the next one. Taiming is a man trapped at the borderline. Madness becomes the persona for this man without any recognizable identity. As Jung noted, "In all chaos there is a cosmos, in all disorder a secret order, in all caprice a fixed law, for everything that works is grounded on its opposite."[41]

Trauma of being collectively possessed

Most of the time the gods of the land, including those of the fatherland, are compassionate, but sometimes they behave in the manner described in the following Chinese sayings: "The emotion of the gods is always unpredictable (天威不可測)," or "Heaven and earth are indifferent to all the creatures, seeing them as straw dogs (天地不仁，以萬物為芻狗)." The gods are irrational and emotional, sometimes as ruthless as innocent infants.

At the beginning of his 1936 essay "Wotan," Jung described the irrationality of the Germans with the rise of Nazism:

> But what is more than curious—indeed, piquant to a degree—is that an ancient god of storm and frenzy, the long quiescent Wotan, should awake, like an extinct volcano, to new activity, in a civilized country that had long been supposed to have outgrown the Middle Ages … Wotan is a restless wanderer who creates unrest and stirs up strife,

SEARCH FOR THE FATHER IN TAIWAN   279

> now here, now there, and works magic. He was soon
> changed by Christianity into the devil, and only lived on
> in fading local traditions as a ghostly hunter who was seen
> with his retinue, flickering like a will o' the wisp through
> the stormy night.[42]

In *Orphan of Asia* Taiming was also driven crazy by the war gods. Like the Germans, human beings around the world during times of radical transition of identities are prone to becoming insane.

> (Days later) Taiming suddenly stood up and looked at the
> air with an empty gaze. He said:
> Oh! Hey!
> They are all tigers.
> These men are mad. They like a barbarian eating
> human flesh. And your father, husband, brother, and son
> all followed him. Why he shouted that everything is for the
> country, for the country.
> This shouting guy actually is a real bad guy.
> Leverage the power of the country to be the glory
> of his own.
> This is an immoral man, a bandit in disguise of a
> nice guy.
> People who killed people should be executed. But
> the guy killed so many people but cheered by people as
> a hero! Hero! Why?
> Bastard!
> He shouted it out loud, as if there was someone directly
> in front of his eyesight: Hey! Bastard! He is roaring, and
> the spirit of Taiming is completely in a state of confusion.
> Since then, Taiming has become a complete madman.
> …
> Not long after that, as the villagers were busy, they
> pay no more attention to him. No one was aware of how
> Taiming disappeared from the village.[43]

The collective shadow becomes the collective persona for the people of Taiming's village. Jung described this kind of seizure in the following way: "Every civilized human being, whatever his conscious development, is still an archaic man at the deeper levels of his psyche."[44] For Jung, the old god Wotan is experienced as a force all its own, a "personification of psychic forces" that moved through the German people "towards the end of the Weimar Republic"—through the "thousands of unemployed," who by 1933 "marched in their hundreds of thousands." The gods of the land can also be the terminators of the land. Wotan "is the god of storm and frenzy, the unleasher of passions and the lust for battle; moreover he is a superlative magician and artist in illusion who is versed in all the secrets of the occult nature."[45] About Wotan, who became the personification of the "German psyche" as possessed by a furious god, Jung wrote, "We who stand outside judge the Germans far too much as if they were responsible agents, but perhaps it would be nearer the truth to regard them also as victims." Under Adolf Hitler's National Socialist Movement, most Germans had been possessed. "These are decent and well-meaning people who honestly admit their *Ergriffenheit* and try to come to terms with this new and undeniable fact."[46]

Likewise, after Taiming finds that most of the ordinary people of his village have "come to terms with this new and undeniable fact," he can't help but shout that "They are all tigers./ These men are mad. They are like a barbarian eating human flesh. And your father, husband, brother, and son all followed him. Why he shouted that everything is for the country, for the country./ This shouting guy actually is a real bad guy."[47]

For Taiming, to be mad is the only way to keep from being insane. For most ordinary people, to survive is the first and only goal when threatened by a power like Wotan, even at the cost of becoming possessed themselves. We are faced with the paradox that possession by collective evil could be the choice for temporary healing. To avoid the psychic pain of a soul attack through the loss of identity, people can forget their history.

Alexander and Margarete Mitscherlich confronted the collective psyche of post-war Germany in their 1967 book, *The Inability to Mourn*. Germans, they wrote, were indifferent and lethargic; they lacked empathy for the victims of the Nazi genocide and were caught up in "nationalist self-centeredness."[48] Guilt, shame, and, in particular, grief over the loss were dismissed. The overwhelming majority of Germans regarded the Nazi era as a kind of "infectious childhood disease," and suddenly, only Adolf Hitler and a few leading figures were to blame. The Mitscherlichs came to the conclusion that post-war Germans saw rebuilding a functioning economy as their first priority, much more so than building a democratic state after the years of dictatorship and terror.

This is not unusual for people who have being possessed collectively. Like the collective madness of the German people

Search for the Father in Taiwan

during the Third Reich, the people of Taiming's village experienced a similar *Ergriffenheit.*

For the novelist Wu Zhuoliu, Taiming's village is the symbolic representative of all of Taiwan. In the period of a major transition from an old era to a new era, many people may suffer and try to resist. For example, when people became aware that the power of a Wotan was too strong to resist, one by one people accepted the change. The remaining few who resisted were like scapegoats to be sacrificed at the end of the old history. Taiwan has seen such changes from the Ming Han people, to the Qing Han people, to the Japanese people, to the Chinese people, and even now to the Taiwanese people. As each new identity replaced the old one during such transitions, there was always a similar experience of being possessed collectively. On the surface, the suffering of the people who had been sacrificed during the transition appeared to disappear—at least at the conscious level. However, the toll on the soul has lasted in the psyche of both individuals and groups.

Dori Laub and Daniel Podell have pointed out that when people were forced to live through extreme cumulative and collective trauma, their "primary empathic bond" was destroyed deliberately and an abyss between these sufferers and the human community was created.[49] Jungian analyst Angela Connolly has also emphasized that people after such trauma can develop symptoms like the death of time, a wound to memory, and the death of language.[50] For Taiming the villagers became disconnected from their souls to protect themselves from suffering.

From collective trauma to cultural trauma

The relationship between trauma and mental illness has been studied since the late nineteenth century. One of the major areas of interest for Jean-Martin Charcot was hysteria, a disorder commonly diagnosed in women of that era. Although he was not interested in the inner lives of his female patients, Charcot was the first to understand that the origin of hysterical symptoms was not physiological but rather psychological in nature. He "described both the problems of suggestibility in these patients, and the fact that hysterical attacks are dissociative problems—the results of having endured unbearable experiences."[51] Following his lead, Pierre Janet, Sigmund Freud, C. G. Jung, and others made note of the concept of trauma through

282   HAO-WEI WANG

their different perspectives. However it wasn't until the 1970s that psychological trauma reemerged as a major area of concern. Individual trauma had been neglected for a long time, and the notion of collective trauma had hardly been mentioned at all. Jung had introduced the concepts of the collective unconscious and the collective shadow, which implied the idea of collective trauma, as in his essay "After the Catastrophe."[52] But he did not explicitly explore the notion or reality of collective trauma or cultural complexes. The Holocaust became the primal tragedy of Western human history, but certainly was not the first, last, or only such massive example of collective trauma.

Kai Erikson, a sociologist, was among the first social scientists to develop a theory regarding trauma and its social dimensions.[53] The prime focus of his study were the consequences of the 1972 Buffalo Creek flood disaster in West Virginia. Erikson spent years performing a field study, observing the persistent destructive effects of this disaster that he documented in his 1978 book *Everything in Its Path: Destruction of Community in the Buffalo Creek Flood.*[54] His book, partly influenced by his father Erik Erikson, the famed German-born psychoanalyst, proposed the term "collective trauma" to describe group or community trauma:

> By collective trauma ... I mean a blow to the basic tissues of social life that damages the bonds attaching people together and impairs the prevailing sense of communality. The collective trauma works its way slowly and even insidiously into the awareness of those who suffer from it, so it does not have the quality of suddenness normally associated with "trauma." But it is a form of shock all the same, a gradual realization that the community no longer exists as an effective source of support and that an important part of the self has disappeared... . "I" continue to exist, though damaged and maybe even permanently changed. "You" continue to exist, though distant and hard to relate to. But "we" no longer exist as a connected pair or as linked cells in a larger communal body.[55]

With the understanding that individual psychological and physical traumas often arise out of painful, long-term events, such as "a continuing pattern of abuse," or shocking, short-term events, such as "a single searing assault," Erikson documented that social trauma can occur at the community level just as it does at the individual level: "Sometimes the tissues of community can be damaged in much the same way as the tissues of the mind and body."[56]

SEARCH FOR THE FATHER IN TAIWAN

283

Ron Eyerman, also a sociologist from Yale University, followed Kai Erikson by applying and extending the theory of collective trauma to the institution of slavery in the United States and its role in the formation of African American identity. Integrating the research on collective memory, Eyerman argued that the cultural "trauma in question is slavery, not as an institution or even an experience, but as a collective memory, a form of remembrance that grounded the identity-formation of a people."[57]

Ron Eyerman, Neil Smelser, and Piotr Sztompka, under the lead of Jeffrey Alexander, published an edited collection of essays titled *Cultural Trauma and Collective Identity* to elaborate the theories of collective and cultural trauma.[58] They used the term *cultural trauma* instead of *collective trauma* to emphasize that the sufferers have shared the same language, customs, communality, rituals, and memories.

In the field of psychology, sociopsychologists Dan Bar-On and psychoanalyst Vamik Volkan paved the way for a better understanding of how and why traumas are historically (and, hence, collectively) transmitted in the context of mass atrocities and warfare. Looking at the Holocaust legacy, Bar-On explored how the first and second generations of victims and perpetrators struggled to deal with the legacy of war and trauma in a rather similar fashion: through denial and silencing of the "indescribable" and "undiscussable."[59] Bar-On was one of the first to develop the idea of historically transmitted or intergenerational trauma—but he did not speak of collective trauma as such. To varying degrees, all research and work with the families of the perpetrators and the survivors/victims of the Holocaust stressed the great need for healing and relationship-building on individual and collective levels.[60] Finally, from the Jungian tradition Thomas Singer and Sam Kimbles have contributed the notion of cultural complexes originating in the cultural unconscious and shaping group identity. These complexes can be formed by group trauma as well as by nontraumatic sources such as group ideas of exceptionalism or even group habits such as consumerism.

> Intense collective emotion is the hallmark of an activated cultural complex at the core of which is an archetypal pattern. Cultural complexes structure emotional experience and operate in the personal and collective psyche in much the same way as individual complexes, although their content might be quite different. Like individual complexes, cultural complexes tend to be repetitive, autonomous, resist

consciousness, and collect experience that confirms their historical point of view ... Individuals and groups in the grips of a particular cultural complex automatically take on a shared body language or postures or express their distress in similar somatic complaints. Finally, like personal complexes, cultural complexes can provide those caught in their potent web of stories and emotions a simplistic certainty about the group's place in the world in the face of otherwise conflicting and ambiguous uncertainties.[61]

It does not require a big leap of the psychological imagination to see how this applies to the multiple crises of national identity faced by the Taiwanese over generations and how these crises have contributed to the Taiwanese cultural complex of being orphans, repetitively abandoned by their many fathers of diverse identity.

Fathers as orphans

In his discussion of Ulysses in the book *The Father,* Luigi Zoja connects father, fatherland, and national identity. Underlying these three interrelated concepts is the same archetype of the father. "We use the word 'fatherland'—*patria*—without really remembering what it means. The Greek *pater* means father (from the root *pa-* which means to possess, nourish, or command). *Patra* or *patrias gaia* doesn't mean 'my land,' but 'the land of my fathers.'"[62]

Where is my land then? What am I supposed to be? For people who have lived in Taiwan over the these last several hundred years, these silent questions are buried in the deepest unconscious.

Zoja furthers his exploration of the Greek *pater*: "My fatherland that doesn't belong to me, but to my fathers. I myself, in turn, am a part of my fatherland only insofar as I am truly a member of the class of fathers."[63] Hu Taiming grew up in a Taiwanese village. He studied and worked hard to satisfy the unconscious urge to be accepted by the Japanese fathers and become one of them.

> My land and my individual being are united by a metaphysical link: the idea of the father.
> Ulysses doesn't voyage toward the place of his wife, but to the place of the father, ... to his fatherland, to the place where his fathers have always lived and where he himself will always be remembered as a father. The whole *Odyssey* is permeated with this warning and appeal: woe to those who forget the name of the fathers![64]

SEARCH FOR THE FATHER IN TAIWAN   285

However, where can Taiming and other Taiwanese journey to the "fatherland," as Ulysses journeyed back to his land of the father?

> The archetype of the father has enormous meaning for our lives. For Jung, [t]he archetype of the Mother is the most immediate one for the child. But with the development of consciousness the father also enters his field of vision, and activates the archetype whose nature is in many ways opposed to that of the mother. Just as the mother archetype corresponds to the Chinese *ying*, so the father archetype to the *yang*.[65]

The father archetype is determinative of "our relation to man, to the law and the state, to reason and spirit, and the dynamism of nature.[66]

Mr. Chen, my client's father, showed his confusion about being a father. He tried so hard to be a good father, and yet his son saw him as a failure in that role. The dilemma for Mr. Chen is common for Taiwanese fathers of his generation, even to those of different generations in Taiwan. They are fathers. They are orphans also. They are searching for their fathers while simultaneously trying to be good fathers according to their ideas about "that which moves the world, like wind; the guide and creator of invisible thoughts and airy images."[67]

The Taiwanese have always searched for their fathers in the past generations. They projected their father image onto the Ming Dynasty, or the Qing Dynasty, or the Japanese, or the Republic of China, or even the People's Republic of China. And a disillusionment with the fathers occurred over and over again. Taiwanese national identity has emerged out of these multiple disillusionments.

Notes

[1] Wen-Shing Tseng (曾文星) *One Life, Three Cultures: The Impact of Japanese, Chinese, and American Cultures on My Personality Formation* [一個人生，三種文化：中國、日本、美國文化對人格形成的自我分析] (Taipei: Psychological, 三つの文化を生きた一人の精神科医　日本、中国、そして米国の各文化による性格形成への影響; and Tokyo: Sheila Shoten, 2010), p. 26.

[2] Wikipedia, s.v. "Four Asian Tigers." Accessed Oct. 30. 2019, at https://en.m.wikipedia.org/wiki/Four_Asian_Tigers.

[3] C. G. Jung, *Memories, Dreams, Reflections,* ed. Aniela Jaffé (Toronto: Random House, 1961/1989), p. 233.

[4] Election Research Center of National Taiwan Chengchi University, "The Trend Distribution of Taiwan People on the Issue of Reunification or Independence (from 1994.12 to 2019.06)" ("臺灣民眾統獨立場趨勢分佈 [1994年12月~2019年06月]"). Accessed July 10, 2019, at https://esc.nccu.edu.tw/app/news.php?Sn=167.

[5] According to the limited historical record, the first well-planned immigration of the Han to Taiwan was led by Gân Su-chê (顏思齊, 1586–1625). He was among the most activ e pirate leaders who roamed from Japan to the Philippines until 1624 when he was defeated by Japanese troops (黃阿有, 2003). See A. Huang (黃阿有), "The Research of the Emigration of Gân Su-chê and Zheng Zhilong to Taiwan" [〈顏思齊鄭芝龍入墾臺灣之研究〉《臺灣文獻》]，54 [卷] 4 [期]，2003 [年] 3 [月]. Robert Blust, "Subgrouping, Circularity and Extinction: Some Issues in Austronesian Comparative Linguistics," in Elizabeth Zeitoun and Paul Jen-kuei Li, eds., *Selected Papers from the Eighth International Conference on Austronesian Linguistics* (Taipei, Taiwan: Academia Sinica, 1999), pp. 31–94.

[6] Wikipedia, s.v. "Dutch East India Company." Accessed Nov. 4, 2019, at https://en.m.wikipedia.org/wiki/Dutch_East_India_Company.

[7] Wikipedia, s.v. "Eighty Years' War." Accessed Oct. 30, 2019, at https://en.m.wikipedia.org/wiki/Eighty_Years%27_War.

[8] Tonio Andrade, *How Taiwan Became Chinese: Dutch, Spanish, and Han Colonization in the Seventeenth Century* (New York: Columbia University Press, 2008). (歐陽泰 [Tonio Andrade]《福爾摩沙如何變成臺灣府？》, 臺北市: 遠流出版, 2007年.)

[9] William Campbell, *Formosa Under the Dutch: Described from Contemporary Records, with Explanatory Notes and a Bibliography of the Island* (London: Kegan Paul, 1903).

[10] Kongli Chen, 清代台灣移民社會研究 [*Studies on the Immigrant Society of Taiwan under the Ching Dynasty*]. (Xiamen: Xiamen University Press, 1990)

[11] Y. Gu (顧炎武), *What I Know in Everyday* [《原抄本日知錄•正始》] (台北:明倫出版社，1970), 卷 [17], 頁 [379].

[12] Elisabeth Kübler-Ross, *On Death and Dying* (London: Routledge, 1969).

[13] Thomas Singer, Introduction to Thomas Singer and Samuel L. Kimbles, eds., *The Cultural Complex: Contemporary Jungian Perspectives on Psyche and Society* (New York: Routledge, 2004), p. 6.

SEARCH FOR THE FATHER IN TAIWAN

[14] Tadao Yanaihara (矢内原忠雄), 帝国主義下の台湾 [*Taiwan under Imperialism*] (東京：岩波書店, 1929), trans. into Chinese by 周憲文,《日本帝國主義下之臺灣》(台北：海峽學術出版社, 1999 [年]).

[15] T. Nakamura (中村孝志), *Taiwan in the Era of Southern Advantage in Tashio Era* [〈大正南進期與臺灣〉],(《台北文獻》第132期,2000).

[16] Tseng, *One Life, Three Cultures,* p. 19.

[17] The *Austronesian languages* (/ˌɔːstroʊˈniːʒən/) are a *language family* widely spoken throughout Maritime Southeast Asia, Madagascar, and the islands of the Pacific Ocean. There are also a few speakers in continental Asia. These languages are spoken by about 386 million people (4.9 percent of the world's population). See Wikipedia, s.v. "Austronesian Language." Accessed Oct. 30, 2019, at https://en.wikipedia.org/wiki/Austronesian_languages.

[18] Zygmunt Bauman, *Liquid Modernity* (Cambridge, UK: Polity Press, 2000).

[19] Fred Davis, "Identity Ambivalence in Clothing: The Dialectic of the Erotic and the Chaste," in David R. Maines, ed., *Social Organization and Social Processes: Essays in Honor of Anselm Strauss,* pp. 105–116 (New York: Aldine de Gruytre), p. 105.

[20] Homi Bhabha, *The Location of Culture* (London, Routledge, 1994), p. 51.

[21] C. G. Jung, *Psychological Types,* vol. 6, *The Collected Works of C. G. Jung,* ed. and trans. Gerhard Adler and R. F. C. Hull (Princeton, NJ: Princeton University Press, 1971), § 801.

[22] C. G. Jung, "Concerning Rebirth," in *The Collected Works of C. G. Jung,* vol. 9i, ed. and trans. Gerhard Adler and R. F. C. Hull (Princeton, NJ: Princeton University Press, 1968), § 221.

[23] C. G Jung, "The Philosophical Tree," in *The Collected Works of C. G. Jung,* vol. 12, ed. and trans. Gerhard Adler and R. F. C. Hull (Princeton, NJ: Princeton University Press, 1970), § 439.

[24] William Styron, *Darkness Visible* (New York: Random House, 1990).

[25] David H. Rosen, *Transforming Depression: Healing the Soul Through Creativity* (York Beach, ME: Nicolas-Hays, 2002).

[26] Martin Buber, *Good and Evil: Two Interpretations. I. Right and Wrong II. Images of Good and Evil* (Charles Scribner's Sons, 1953), p. 6.

288   HAO-WEI WANG

[27] Wu Zhuoliu, *Orphan of Asia* (New York: Columbia University Press, 2006).

[28] *Ibid.*, p. 62.

[29] *Ibid.*, p. 69.

[30] *Ibid.*, p. 78.

[31] Benedict Anderson, *Imagined Communities: Reflections on the Origin and Spread of Nationalism* (London: Verso, 1983, 2006), pp. 6–7.

[32] C. G. Jung, *Psychology of the Unconscious* (New York: Moffat, Yar'd, and Company, 1916), p. 37.

[33] C. G. Jung, "The Associations of the Normal Subjects," in *The Collected Works of C. G. Jung,* vol. 2, ed. and trans. Leopold Stein with Diana Riviere (Princeton, NJ: Princeton University Press, 1973/1990), § 2.

[34] C. G. Jung, "On the Doctrine of Complexes," in *The Collected Works of C. G. Jung,* vol. 2, ed. and trans. Leopold Stein with Diana Riviere (Princeton, NJ: Princeton University Press, 1973/1990), §1350.

[35] C. G. Jung, "A Review of the Complex Theory" in *The Collected Works of C. G. Jung,* vol. 8, ed. and trans. Gerhard Adler and R. F. C. Hull (Princeton, NJ: Princeton University Press, 1969), § 198.

[36] Zhuoliu, *Orphan of Asia,* pp. 281–282.

[37] Nathan Schwartz-Salant, "The Borderline Personality: Vision and Healing," in Andrew Samuels, ed., *Psychopathology: Contemporary Jungian Perspectives* (London: Karnac, 1989), p. 190.

[38] Jung, CW 8, § 201.

[39] *Ibid.*, § 200.

[40] Zhuoliu, *Orphan of Asia,* pp. 278–279.

[41] C. G. Jung, "Archetypes of the Collective Unconscious," in *The Collected Works of C. G. Jung,* vol. 9i, ed. and trans. Gerhard Adler and R. F. C. Hull (Princeton, NJ: Princeton University Press, 1968), § 66.

[42] C. G. Jung, "Wotan," in *The Collected Works of C. G. Jung,* vol. 10, ed. and trans. Gerhard Adler and R. F. C. Hull (Princeton, NJ: Princeton University Press, 1968).

[43] Zhuoliu, *Orphan of Asia,* pp. 280–281.

[44] C. G. Jung, *Modern Man in Search of a Soul* (New York: Harcourt 1933), p. 128.

[45] Jung, CW 10, § 375.

SEARCH FOR THE FATHER IN TAIWAN 289

[46] *Ibid.*, § 397.

[47] Zhuoliu, *Orphan of Asia,* p. 280.

[48] Alexander Mitscherlich and Margarete Mitscherlich, *The Inability to Mourn: Principles of Collective Behavior,* trans. Beverly Placzek (New York: Grove Press, 1967).

[49] Dori Laub and Daniel Podell, "Art and Trauma," *The International Journal of Psychanalysis* 76 (5, 1995), 991–1005.

[50] Angela Connolly, "Healing the Wounds of Our Fathers: Intergenerational Trauma, Memory, Symbolization and Narrative," *Journal of Analytical Psychology* 56 (5, 2011), 607–626.

[51] Bessel van der Kolk, Lars Weisaeth, and Onno van der Hart, "History of Trauma in Psychiatry," in Bessel van der Kolk, Alexander McFarlane, and Lars Weisaeth, eds., *Traumatic Stress: The Effects of Overwhelming Experience on Mind, Body and Society* (New York: Guilford, 1996), pp. 47–76, p. 50.

[52] C. G. Jung, "After the Catastrophe," in *The Collected Works of C. G. Jung,* vol. 10, ed. and trans. Gerhard Adler and R. F. C. Hull (Princeton, NJ: Princeton University Press, 1968).

[53] Angela Onwuachi-Willig, "The Trauma of the Routine: Lessons on Cultural Trauma from the Emmett Till Verdict," *Sociological Theory* 34 (4, 2016), 335–357.

[54] Kai Erikson, *Everything in Its Path: Destruction of Community in the Buffalo Creek Flood* (New York: Simon and Schuster, 1976).

[55] *Ibid.*, p. 154.

[56] Kai Erikson, "Notes on Trauma and Community," in Cathy Caruth, ed., *Trauma: Explorations in Memory* (Baltimore, MD: Johns Hopkins University Press, 1995), p. 185.

[57] Ron Eyerman, "Cultural Trauma: Slavery and the Formation of African American Identity," in Jeffrey Alexander, Ron Eyerman, Bernard Giesen, Neil J. Smelser, and Piotr Sztompka, eds., *Cultural Trauma and Collective Identity* (Berkeley: University of California Press, 2004), p. 60.

[58] Jeffrey Alexander, "Toward a Theory of Cultural Trauma," in Jeffrey Alexander, Ron Eyerman, Bernard Giesen, Neil J. Smelser, and Piotr Sztompka, eds., *Cultural Trauma and Collective Identity* (Berkeley: University of California Press, 2004), pp. 1–30.

[59] Dan Bar-On, *The Indescribably and Undiscussable: Reconstructing Human Discourse After Trauma* (Budapest, Hungary: Central European University Press, 1999).

290 HAO-WEI WANG

[60] See, for example, Dan Bar-On, *The Indescribable and the Undiscussable: Reconstructing Human Discourse After Trauma* (Budapest, Hungary: Central European University Press, 1999); and "The Silence of Psychologists," *Journal of Political Psychology* 22 (2, 2001), 331–345.

[61] Singer, *The Cultural Complex*, p. 6.

[62] Luigi Zoja, *The Father: Historical, Psychological and Cultural Perspectives* (London: Brunner-Routledge, 2001), p.106.

[63] *Ibid.,* 107.

[64] *Ibid.*

[65] C. G. Jung, "Mind and Earth," in *The Collected Works of C. G. Jung,* vol. 10, ed. and trans. Gerhard Adler and R. F. C. Hull (Princeton, NJ: Princeton University Press, 1968), § 65

[66] *Ibid.*

[67] *Ibid.*

12
● ● ● ● ● ●

An Orphan of the Patriarchy
A Cultural Complex in Taiwanese History

Su-chen Hung and Hung-Chin Wei

A patriarchal region

The father archetype has been identified as a main force in creating a culture's law-giving function.[1] As described by Eli Weisstub and Esti Galili-Weisstub, "In patriarchal cultures, the father archetype is the source of the culture's superego. A culture and its values are threatened when its superego is weakened by attacks on its authority."[2] Throughout Taiwan's long history, patriarchal regimes have formed the core of a cultural complex as a result of the many attacks on the various patriarchal authorities.

In the nineteenth century, nationalism became an expression of ethnic identity and a way to control the libido of large groups of people. Today's postmodern globalization may well be the source of disintegration in many nation states. The politicization of a country facilitates the implementation of ideology and governing, whereas

---

Su-chen Hung, a member of the International Association of Analytical Psychology (IAAP), is a Jungian analyst and associate professor in the Department of Psychology and Counseling at the National Taipei University of Education in Taiwan.

Hung-Chin Wei, PhD, graduated from the Department of Philosophy at Peking University in China. He is a member of the Taiwan Developing Group of the IAAP.

292   SU-CHEN HUNG AND HUNG-CHIN WEI

depoliticization tends to invalidate the functions of a state, which then turns to a management style of government rather than relying on political process. As styles of leadership, both nationalism and management are based on the masculine principle. By channeling its libido through a more masculine style of government, a nation's symbols—its flag, anthem, leaders, laws, and elections (or lack thereof)—express its identity. These symbols tend to embody the principles of patriarchal rationality. Taiwan has a complex political history, moving from a totalitarian and nationalistic style of leadership to a management or more democratic style of leadership. This chapter explores the Taiwanese cultural complexes that have developed as a result of these historical processes.

Taiwanese mentality is similar to that of an adopted child who lacks the recognition of its adoptive parents. Such an adoptive child seeks to discover who its father is. At the same time, this child carries an idealized image of a father from whom it is seeking recognition and love. The child wants to win the approval of an uncertain adoptive father, creating frequent tension and conflict within the child and family. Taiwan is this adoptive child.

Although the cultural Self can be thought of as having both a "feminine spirit" and a "masculine spirit," a cultural consciousness dominated by a patriarchal superego tends to admire power and look down on weakness.[3] Chinese history and culture has had a dominant influence on Taiwanese society because so many of its citizens are ethnic Chinese. As such the Emperor was the Son of God and the Father of the Land with his dominant "masculine spirit." Throughout its history Taiwan has had many rulers and, as a result, has the experience of having been abandoned by different Father regimes. At the same time, just as in China, the Mother image is a powerful force in Taiwan. With these intertwining threads, Taiwan has long had a conflict between its cultural identity and its regime or political identity.

To take the analogy of Taiwan being an adoptive child one step further, we can say that Taiwan as an adopted child has been abandoned multiple times. As a result, it has suffered intense emotional trauma and shows extreme distrust toward its father and/or mother or any parental figures. This mistrust can distort and transform the positive father and mother functions of parenting into negatives. As a result, discipline becomes fetters; regularity is equated with rigidity; rationality is viewed as old-fashioned; and love is distrusted as conspiracy. Under such circumstances, the father as a positive symbol

An Orphan of the Patriarchy

of authority is severely undermined. In a more normal sequence of events, authority may initially be regarded by the child as power. Later in the child's development, authority may be experienced and incorporated as reputation and prestige. Finally, legitimate authority can be internalized as a symbol of knowledge and wisdom. But for children who have gone through multiple traumas of having been abandoned and/or abused by their parents, authority can live in the collective psyche as a symbol of power that is identified with violence and which is experienced in an endless, repetitive cycle of either being oppressed or as imposing oppression on others.

Throughout much of Taiwanese history, the experience of its people has not moved beyond the initial stage of authority being experienced as "violence and power." From the early rule of the Chinese Qing Dynasty (1684–1895), the first father to abandon Taiwan, to the era of Japan colonization (1895–1945), and then to the rule of the Republic of China (1945–), trauma has been a constant in Taiwanese society, which has never experienced the positive recognition of its "father" country (Republic of China government).

Singer and Kimbles point out five key elements to consider in the formation and functioning of culture complexes:[4]

1. function at the group level of the individual psyche and within the group;
2. function autonomously;
3. organize group life;
4. facilitate the individual's relationship to the group and functioning of the individual;
5. and can provide for a sense of belonging, identity and historical continuity.

If we apply their formulation of the way in which cultural complexes can operate, it becomes clear why Taiwanese society is full of conflicts, contradictions, and mutually unfriendly projections between different ethnic groups. The country and its citizens' sense of belonging, identity, and historical continuity are complicated and fragmented, their psyches fragile and prone to extreme fluctuations.

The fantasy of cultural and political relations in the East

There are fundamental differences between Eastern and Western cultures in their philosophical ideas about existence and the interactions between mind and matter in the universe. Western philosophy established a dual mind-matter relationship during the time of Plato, whereas Eastern philosophy, whether derived from the Sanskrit of Indian philosophy or the Taoism of Chinese culture, embraced a *holistic* philosophy based on the One, which did not split the mind-matter relationship. This is drastically different from the universe as perceived by Western philosophy, with its established plan and scientific rationality. In the cultural and political relations in the East fostered by his disciple Zeng, Confucius emphasized that all his teachings are linked by one consistent principle—the *Tao,* with its basic values of "loyalty and forgiveness." *Loyalty* is a kind of commitment based on one's own heart. If someone wants to achieve something, they would, at the same time, also help others to achieve what they want. The value of *forgiveness* leads to the understanding of others. Therefore, both "loyalty and forgiveness" are equivalent to *benevolence,* which has been translated by German philosophers as *Diastole und Systole.* Those who are familiar with Jungian psychology understand that this is akin to the process of individuation in which neither self-pride (inflation) nor inferiority are the way to follow or fulfill the essentials of the Tao. The ethics that grow out of Chinese Confucianism include the principles of cultivating relationships between people, relationships between people and the existing authority (for example, with the political authority), and the relationship with one's self. Confucius's Tao emphasizes the law of being in synch with the universe and the "One."

The fundamental nature of the universe is that it is "unknown." Awe and reverence are two essential attitudes for appreciating the basic unknowability of the universe. Although essentially a religious attitude, it is not a religion. In the Confucian realm of East Asia, which is composed of China, Korea, Japan, and Taiwan, culture is dominant and politics are subordinate; cultural identity supersedes political identity. The individual who achieves cultural heights becomes part of the essential core of the ongoing society. For example, Sakuma Taika, a Confucian scholar of eighteenth-century Japan, believed that Japan was more qualified to be called "China" in the context of cultural achievement.[5] Taiwan was once the most direct inheritor of Confucian culture after the establishment of the People's Republic of China on the mainland in 1949. In recent years, the *de-Sinicization* of Taiwan has come to be the dominant ideology. However, drawing a line between politics and culture in Taiwanese society and psyche

AN ORPHAN OF THE PATRIARCHY

is difficult, creating great distress as the role of Chinese culture in Taiwanese society is highly uncertain. In Taiwan, the conflict between Chinese cultural identity and Taiwanese political identity has become a potent cultural complex in the minds and hearts of its population.

The shadow and cultural complexes from Taiwan's history

In 1945, Jung gave a simple definition of the *shadow:* the shadow is "what a person does not want to be."[6] According to this definition, the shadow of Taiwan has varied from one period to another, especially when there was a conflict with the dominant cultural psychology of a particular era. Such a conflict between the shadow and the prevailing cultural psychology could produce a cultural complex. Perry pointed out that "the everyday ego" is quite different

> from the ego which has been taken over by a complex. When a complex is activated, its potent affect and frequently one-sided perceptions of the world take hold of the everyday ego and create "the affect-ego." The other part of the bipolar pair is projected onto the person with whom one is caught in the complex and they, in turn, become an "affect-object."[7]

The same can apply to a group as well as an individual. When a cultural complex takes hold of a group, "the everyday cultural identity of the group can be overtaken by the affect of the cultural complex, often built up over centuries of repetitive traumatic experiences."[8] At that point, the psyche of the group is in the territory of an "affect-ego" and "affect-object" with the powerful emotions and simplistic black-and-white ideas of the cultural complex dominating the mood and attitudes of opposing large groups of people who can view one another as enemies, causing injury to each other at both the physical and psychic level.[9]

The following narrative describes Taiwan's history prior to 1945, exploring some of the cultural complexes that have developed over that time.

The rule of the Qing Dynasty

Taiwan was ruled by the Qing Dynasty for 212 years, beginning in 1684, when Shi Lang was sent by the Qing Dynasty from China to eliminate the remaining military of the Kingdom of Tungning in Taiwan. The Qing Dynasty lasted until 1895, when the Treaty of Shimonoseki was signed and Taiwan was ceded to Japan.

After the Qing Dynasty incorporated Taiwan into its territory, it was initially classified as a part of Fujian Province. At the beginning, the Qing Dynasty did not actively govern Taiwan because the country was a wilderness area only used for exiled people. In other words, Taiwan was considered an inferior area, and the Qing Dynasty prohibited immigration to Taiwan. Nevertheless many of those who found it difficult to survive in Zhangzhou and Quanzhou provinces on Mainland China immigrated to Taiwan through the dangerous "Black Ditch" and many died in the ocean on the way. The currents in the Taiwan Strait flow northward year round along the coast of Taiwan, and the Penghu waterway is the most turbulent part in the strait. When the rushing tides take away the sediments and debris in the water, sunlight can penetrate deep into the depths, reflecting a blue so dark it's like black ink. These immigrants from Zhangzhou and Quanzhou provinces became the most significant contributors to the social foundations of the Han ethnic group in Taiwan. During this time, the indigenous plains peoples (*Pengpu*) of Taiwan suffered from compulsory Sinicization.

The Qing Dynasty failed to form a modern relationship of state governance with the people of Taiwan. The Mudan incident, which forever changed the destiny of Taiwan and marked the entry of China into the rules of modern international law, illustrates this failure (see Figure 12.1). The Ryukyu Kingdom was an independent kingdom that ruled most of the Ryukyu Islands from the fifteenth to the nineteenth centuries. In December 1871, sixty-nine Ryukyu crew members took two boats from Kume Island, which belonged to Japan, to Ryukyu Naba, an island between Taiwan and Japan. The island had been annexed by the Qing Dynasty. Japan, however, had always wanted to annex Ryukyu.

On their journey, the Ryukyu crew members encountered a typhoon. Three sailors drowned, however, the remaining sixty-six drifted to Langjiao Bayao Bay in Taiwan (the current Jiupeng Village of Manchuria in Taiwan). They then continued their journey to Gaoshifo Society (the current Gaoshi Village in Taiwan) for food, but fifty-four of them were killed. The twelve survivors fled to Shuangxikou (currently located opposite the government office of Mudan Township in Taiwan) and were taken by businessman Tien-bo Teng to the house of Yu-wang Yang, the richest man in Baoli, for shelter. They reported the incident to county officials who managed

An Orphan of the Patriarchy

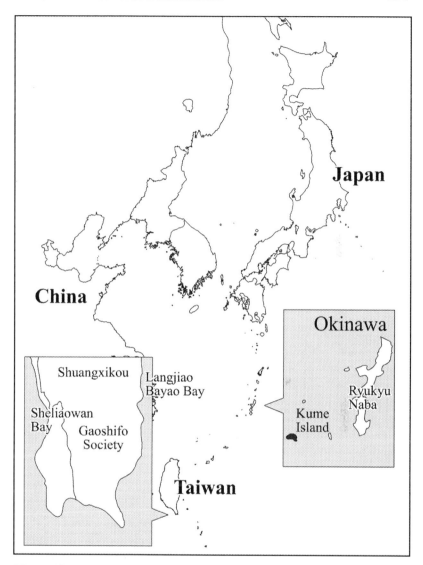

Figure 12.1: Mudan incident map.

to send the survivors back to their hometown. In 1874, Japan raised a serious diplomatic protest against the Qing Dynasty when they heard that there was a Japanese citizen among the survivors. Japan claimed that the incident involved the slaughter of Japanese nationals. Despite the fact that Ryukyu remained under the jurisdiction of the Qing Dynasty, the Qing government avoided taking responsibility for

298 SU-CHEN HUNG AND HUNG-CHIN WEI

the killing by claiming that the murderers were not citizens of the Qing Dynasty. In response, Japan launched an attack and landed at Sheliaowan Bay in Taiwan. Their first target was the Mudan Society. As a result, Alu and his son, the heads of the Mudan Society, died in the battle. This was the Mudan incident.[10]

After the Mudan incident, the Qing government began to realize the importance of Taiwan. They began to create more prefectures and counties to modernize the economy and officially established Taiwan Province in 1885. After the Mudan incident, the Qing Dynasty formally became the father of Taiwan Island. The defeat of the Chinese in the first Sino-Japanese War of 1894–1895 forced the Qing Dynasty to sign the Treaty of Shimonoseki with Japan in April 1895. At that point, Taiwan was ceded to Japan. After a short resistance by the Taiwan Democratic State was put down, the Japanese began their fifty-year rule of Taiwan in June 1895.

The Mudan incident involved multiple parties, including the Qing government in China, the Japanese government, the Han ethnic group in Taiwan (including the Hakka), and the indigenous people of Taiwan (the Mudan Society and Gaoshifo Society). In terms of international relations and law, the Qing Dynasty could not claim national sovereignty over Taiwan. It not only lost Ryukyu island; it also abandoned the right to rule Taiwan. The Qing Dynasty's recognition of "national territory" was primarily a cultural one. From its perspective, only those ethnic groups who accepted and recognized the Han culture were its people. Thus, the indigenous people (the Mudan Society and Gaoshifo Society) were not considered Chinese citizens. Even if the members of the Han ethnic group, who shared the same culture with the Qing Dynasty, were regarded as citizens by China, their relationship with the local government, which had been dispatched by the imperial court in China, seemed to be that of governor and governed. In reality, it was a relationship of mutual-interest. This was not unique in ancient China. For example, although the salaries of local officials during the Qing Dynasty were too low to support their basic needs, these officials were entitled to set the local tax rates. With part of the taxes returned to the treasury of the imperial court in China, the remainder was left in the hands of local officials, becoming their private income. In many places, as long as most of the people would tolerate it, officials levied taxes at will and fed their private pockets.

AN ORPHAN OF THE PATRIARCHY

The relationship between the state and the people during the Qing Dynasty was not like that of father and son. Rather they were like cronies who took what they needed from each other. When confronting foreign forces, Taiwan was not protected by the Qing Dynasty. Thus, a father's most fundamental and symbolic role was absent in the relationship between the Qing Dynasty in China as governor of Taiwan and the Taiwanese as the governed. If the Qing Dynasty was Taiwan's first father, then this father failed to fulfill his responsibility, leaving Taiwan in the shadow of being abandoned and inferior when compared with Mainland China.

Japanese rule

The Japanese showed Taiwan how a modern state could function. However, Japanese governance in Taiwan was that of a colonial power, and thus the relationship between the government and the governed was unequal, further contributing to the Taiwanese sense of living in the shadow of greater powers—first the Qing Dynasty of China and then the Japanese. During Japanese rule, Taiwan was modernized in terms of infrastructure, educational facilities, public health, agriculture, and industry. Taiwan had its first experience of rationality and the laws of modern governance through Japanese colonialism. But "the father" of Japanese governance in Taiwan was that of a harsh old man who was strict and without benevolence or kindness. Because Taiwan had never had a responsible father, especially with the backward and incompetent traumatic memory left by the "father" of the Qing Dynasty, the country developed a "shadow identity" of being inferior to Japan, which further damaged the collective soul of the Taiwanese people.

If a shadow has a positive force and we embrace it, it can actually transform life; by contrast, if we fall into the shadow of our ego identity, then we are in peril. This is also true for the collective ego of a group of people—even for a country. Taiwan suffered trauma under the rule of the Qing Dynasty, which gave rise to its shadow. This shadow centered around a self-image of inferiority and backwardness, which people were unwilling to face and admit to. Under the colonial rule of Japan when Taiwan was modernized, the Taiwanese people identified with modernization as a way to compensate for the shadow identity of inferiority and backwardness. But the power of Japanese colonialism only complicated and intensified the Taiwanese shadow.

300 SU-CHEN HUNG AND HUNG-CHIN WEI

This was the first time in Taiwan's history that the Taiwanese people encountered a conflict between their cultural identity and political reality. For a Han-dominated society originating in China, cultural and political identity had always been inseparable. The sudden change from Chinese to Japanese rule created a split between cultural and political identity. The case of Li Chun-sheng (1813–1924) is a good example. He was the richest man in Taiwan. After the ceding of Taiwan to Japan by China in 1895, Li Chun-sheng visited Japan in 1896 at the invitation of the Japanese colonial authorities. After his return to Taiwan, he wrote a travel essay declaring that "despite the new generous kindness [of Japan], the previous attachment [to China] is unforgettable."[11] He also defined himself as "the abandoned" several times in the essay.[12] During the Japanese occupation of Taiwan (1895–1945), Lian Heng (Yatang, 1878–1936), the author of the *General History of Taiwan*, also called himself "the abandoned in an abandoned place."[13]

The rule of the Republic of China

As a colonial ruler, Japan never intended to be a loving father, or perhaps never really wanted to be the father of Taiwan, an abandoned child. However, from the Taiwanese standpoint, Japan was a role model of what a father should be—stern and without the embrace of love. After the end of World War II, Taiwan was returned to the Republic of China in 1945. The Taiwanese people expected the government of the Republic of China to restore them to the care of "the biological father" and the embrace of Chinese culture as opposed to the colonial rule of Japan. However, the government of the Republic of China repeated what the colonialists of Japan did during their initial stage of governance on the island. The new government of the Republic of China adopted a policy of discrimination against the people of Taiwan. "The dog is gone, but a pig arrives," is how the Taiwanese characterized the government of the Republic of China after the end of the Japanese rule.

Even worse, the modernization of the Taiwanese government advocated by the Republic of China was far inferior to that of the Japanese. Disappointed and frustrated, some people in Taiwan (including the Han Chinese, the Hakkas, and the indigenous people) felt numb and turned their desire for a "good" father into a nihilistic attitude by abandoning politics altogether. On one hand, some Taiwanese showed antagonism toward the Republic of China, fearing

AN ORPHAN OF THE PATRIARCHY

the return of Japanese colonial terror. On the other hand, the Taiwanese also hoped to regain the experience that Japanese modernization had brought to Taiwan. The shadow side of Taiwanese cultural and political identity, already quite layered by the previous administrative rules of the Qing Dynasty and the Japanese colonialists, was further complicated by contempt for the new government after World War II.

"Culture complexes are based on repetitive, historical group experiences which have taken root in the cultural unconscious of the group experience."[14] Throughout its long history with both the Chinese and the Japanese, the Taiwanese people have carried an unconscious collective fear of being swallowed by the negative father archetype. At the same time they also have a deep unfulfilled yearning for both the positive father and mother archetypes to come alive in the collective group psyche as experienced in communal and individual life.

Understanding the cultural complex in Taiwanese society

This section will explore the Taiwanese cultural complex from the following perspectives:

- From the perspective of the history of trauma and the Ego-Self axis in Taiwan
- From the perspective of the archetypes of the hero and the orphan in Taiwan
- From the perspective of the shadow of Taiwan

The history of trauma and the Ego-Self axis in Taiwan

Based on the definitions of the Self and the ego, Edward Edinger formulated development in the following way: "the process of alternation between Ego-Self union and Ego-Self separation seems to occur repeatedly throughout the life of the individual both in childhood and maturity."[15] Additionally, "the process of psychotherapy and psychic development in general seems to alternate between: (i) manifestations of Ego-Self identity, which require reductive criticism, and (ii) the need for enhancing or repairing the Ego-Self axis, which calls for a synthetic supporting approach."[16] The same may be true of the development of an Ego-Self axis in the identity of a group or nation, such as Taiwan.

In considering the development of an Ego-Self axis in the psyche of the Taiwanese people, we have to add significant trauma to the equation. We know that significant trauma can fracture the inner world of an individual and the same is undoubtedly true of a nation.

Without adequate inner resources to "mourn" the injury and losses suffered as a result of trauma, neither an individual nor a group can fully heal.[17] As Wilfred Bion and Melanie Klein have noted, even after the individual self (ego) has achieved healthy development, when the individual loses a good object but has no opportunity to mourn the loss of the good object, then the individual's personality will gradually deteriorate as a result.[18] Therefore, to help those who are traumatized, it is necessary to "work through" the emotional sequelae of trauma instead of using a "walled-off" approach.[19] The response of Taiwan to its long history of trauma has become a crucial topic that requires a "working through" rather than a "walling off." Such "working through" will necessitate three interrelated abilities: 1) a collective ego function with the capacity to become fully aware of the historical trauma; 2) the psychic "space" in Taiwanese society to mourn the reality that Taiwan has had no "ideal founding father" in its history; and 3) the ability to hold open the potential space to discover the meanings in the trauma as a way to strengthen the Ego-Self axis.

The archetypes of the hero and the orphan in Taiwan
Although Taiwan had been seen as a remote region since the Qing Dynasty, exiled ancestors have been crossing the dangerous "Black Ditch" (Taiwan Strait) from Mainland China to Taiwan to reclaim land for over a thousand years. The hero archetype has been alive and well within Taiwanese society for a long time. The journey of this hero has not yet finished. This hero has also gradually become aware that he is an orphan when he goes through the journey. It is a historical reality that the cultural and ethnic roots of the Han and Hakka peoples living in Taiwan are deeply linked to Mainland China as they migrated from China to Taiwan.

These roots were established long before Chiang Kai-shek moved the Republic of China to Taiwan in 1949 when Mao seized power on the mainland. The people who moved to Taiwan with Chiang Kai-shek after 1945 are strongly identified culturally with Mainland China. Since the time of the Qing Dynasty, the Taiwanese have had no sense of having been protected by their kin from the mainland. This history contributes to the sense of Taiwan being an orphan. This archetypal identification with the orphan contributes to the widespread feeling of being alone and without an identity (Punnett 2014). The sense of being an orphan was captured dramatically in a stone that Jung carved with the following Latin inscription:[20]

An Orphan of the Patriarchy

303

*I am an orphan, alone; nevertheless I am found everywhere.
I am one, but opposed to myself. I am youth and old man
at one and the same time. I have known neither father nor
mother, because I have had to be fetched out of the deep like
a fish, or fell like a white stone from heaven. In woods and
mountains I roam, but I am hidden in the innermost soul of
man. I am mortal for everyone, yet I am not touched by the
cycle of aeons.*

There are many stories of orphan girls and boys in the aboriginal
myths of Taiwan's indigenous peoples. Often they have been
transformed into birds by the end of the stories. Birds symbolize
freedom, the sacred, love, wisdom, rebirth, death, and bravery. The
Tsou (one of indigenous groups in Taiwan) have another myth:

*A long time ago, there were two suns and they came out
at the same time so the weather was very hot. There was a
girl who was an orphan. She lived alone in the border area
of the village. Her name was Nai. Nai had a very hard life
since she was little. Men from the village went to hunt in the
forest to provide food for their wives and children. However,
none of these men would take care of Nai. She had to go fish
by the river under the two suns to support herself. One day
she caught no fish but carried home some driftwood from
the shore. Nai said to herself that at least she had firewood
for the night. The driftwood disappeared after she returned
home. A few days later Nai discovered that she was pregnant.
Then, she gave birth to a baby boy. Nai called her baby Bala.
It meant "son of the driftwood." He was clever and had a
mysterious ability. Whenever Bala pointed at a creature with
his finger, it would die. For example, if he pointed at a bird,
then the bird died; if he pointed at a deer, then the deer died.
People called him a Grim Reaper. When Bala became a young
boy he took all his companions out of the village to share an
adventure. They suggested that Bala should point at one of
the suns, hoping that it would die so that the weather not be
too hot. Bala pointed at one of the suns and it died. The other
sun was so scared that it went into hiding. The village became
very cold and dark. At the end of the story, the wise old men
of the village had to prepare offerings in order to convince the*

second sun to come out. The negotiation was successful and the sun came out again. The weather became warmer and the light came back.[21]

In the myth, the orphan girl gives birth to an orphan boy. Both of them are looked down on by society. Archetypally, they are the orphan, the hero, and the divine child all at the same time. They have the capability to survive and create with few resources. They are also able to deal with being excluded. The orphan boy is courageous and has supernatural abilities. He is able to leave the village on his own and to risk the adventure of shooting one of the suns. The wise old man in the village cooperates with the orphan boy in order to create day and night. The archetypes in this myth resonate with Jung's carving about the orphan. This myth also reflects the history of Taiwan. Before the Ming Dynasty (1368–1644), Taiwan has no clear history. Taiwan became a border area during the Qing Dynasty. Then Taiwan was a Japanese colony for fifty years. Now Taiwan exists in a precarious situation in which its international status remains in limbo. This requires maintaining an adventurous attitude such as recently voting to legalize gay marriage. Like the village in the myth, Taiwan continually needs a "wise old man" to cooperate with the orphan.

The archetype of the shadow of Taiwan

It is worth repeating Jung's simple 1945 definition of the shadow: "the thing a person has no wish to be."[22] In other words, the shadow is "the negative side of the personality." We all have unpleasant characteristics we would like to hide from others as well as insufficiently developed functions of the psyche that fall into the shadow.[23] Andrew Samuels quotes Jung in *A Critical Dictionary of Jungian Analysis:*

> Everyone carries a shadow, and the less it is embodied in the individual's conscious life, the blacker and denser it is. If an inferiority is conscious, then one always has a chance to address it; but if it is repressed from consciousness, then it never gets addressed and is likely to burst forth suddenly in a moment of unawareness. It can form an unconscious obstruction, thwarting our most well intentioned thoughts and actions.[24]

The history of Taiwan is marked by a shadow identification with a deep sense of inferiority. However, today the people of Taiwan have much greater awareness of this shadow.

AN ORPHAN OF THE PATRIARCHY

Conclusion: a way out of the orphan cultural complex

Audrey Punnett states that "when the orphan within us is activated, there is an opportunity to get to know it and discover its meaning for our life."[25] This task is not easy, but it is an important one if we are to be in touch with our true nature. This is the case not only for an individual, but also for a nation that has become identified with the archetype of the orphan through its repetitive history of being abandoned by its leaders. In considering how Taiwan might better integrate its orphan status and its feeling of inferiority, we see several paths that Taiwan could follow on its way to individuation based on its long-standing orphan status.[26]

Developing diverse and multiethnic group cultures

Bion used the term "a thinking breast" to describe how the infant/mother relationship could enhance a communicative and empathetic relationship.[27] Through the mysterious activity of the mother's *reverie*, the infant's split-off anxieties can be contained, detoxified, and returned to the infant who introjects them, but now in a modified form. Through the mother's reverie or what Bion termed the "alpha function," "unthinkable anxiety" and "nameless dread" can become bearable.[28] Extending this psychoanalytic notion to more collective group situations, a "diverse culture" could become a "thinking breast" in which the differences between people could be contained and detoxified. In fact, Taiwan's history has contributed to the possible creation of a diverse culture. Before the Dutch occupation, there were twelve distinct aboriginal groups in Taiwan. In addition, the Han and Hakka people emigrated from Mainland China before 1945. And, finally, many come people came from Mainland China with the Kuomintang party of the Republic of China in 1945. Developing a truly diverse culture is not just a matter of political identity; it remains an important task for the people of Taiwan.

Developing diverse relationships between the people and the ruler apart from the father/son relationship

Samuels has suggested that the primal scene could be seen as a metaphor for the political process itself because the emotional tone of the primal scene moves between conflict and harmony, harmony and conflict.[29] The experience of primal scene imagery may additionally be understood as expressing an individual's inner psychological approach to political functioning. In this model, the person's diverse, even conflicting psychic elements and agencies have the potential to couple into a unified whole without losing their separate identity. Perhaps it touches the great conundrum of universalism versus multiculturalism on the psycho/political level.[30] Mother and father are often at odds and quite different from each other in all sorts of ways. Yet coming together and reconciling can be found in the symbolic primal scene. By thinking of primal scene imagery in terms of political process, the psyche can be imagined as expressing citizens' capacity to cope with the unity and the diversity of the political situation they are in.[31] Samuels comments imply that both citizens and cultures have the capacity to keep their independent identity in order to be able to digest the dynamics between conflict and harmony, unity and diversity without being swallowed by a "Great Father" or a "Great Mother" culturally and politically. If a diverse culture could serve as a transitional space, it might be possible for Taiwan to develop new political forms that are not based exclusively on the Father-Son relationship originating in the patriarchy.[32]

Making the unconscious cultural complexes conscious

Taiwan must mourn the ideal Father who never came and accept the resultant feelings of being an adoptive child with deep feelings of inferiority. As Freud so wisely explored, "mourning" is an essential task for survivors who have suffered loss—whether the loss is belief itself and/or cultural and political identity.[33] To help those who have been traumatized by loss and abandonment, it is necessary to "work through" the trauma rather than to "wall it off."[34] Taiwan has a long history of trauma that requires such "working through." It is a task for the people of Taiwan and the ruling party to create the psychic space to allow the trauma of the past to surface in the collective memory of the Taiwanese in order to explore its meaning and presence in the present day and even the future. The goal is the awareness obtained through suffering through the repetitive pain of an entrenched cultural complex until its meaning and energy can be released to consciousness.[35]

Don Sandner eloquently described this process as it occurs in the psychic life of individuals. What if we extended and applied his insights to the collective psyche of the Taiwanese people?

> Death and rebirth are the mythological symbol for a psychological event: loss of conscious control, and submission to an influx of symbolic material from the unconscious. Personality growth is usually thought of

AN ORPHAN OF THE PATRIARCHY

as cumulative, a gradual expansion through time as ego consciousness gains experience and wisdom. But often it turns out to be only a pursuit of illusory ideals. Then there is cessation of growth, stultifying depression, or, more ominously, severe illness. At that point no halfway measures will do; a thoroughgoing transformation is necessary for the individual's survival. Like the sun, the ego must prepare itself for a plunge into the darkness of the unconscious underworld, there to experience rejuvenation.[36]

Individuals and diverse groups within Taiwan are under the influence of the archetypal energies of the orphan, the hero/heroine, and the wise old man. As Singer and Kimbles note

cultivating an attitude toward archetypes and cultural complexes, whenever they manifest, has the potential to develop a personality capable of consciously utilizing the connectedness of group and individual identity.[37] ...

In the broader Jungian tradition of archetypal and culture commentary, it is of enormous potential benefit to begin to make clearer distinctions between an individual complex and a cultural complex. It offers both the individual and groups the opportunity of not having to telescope or condense everything into personal or archetypal realm—but to recognize the legitimate (and illegitimate) culture and group contributions to their struggles, suffering and meaning.[38]

Taiwan is home to multiple cultures. There have been numerous marriages to Southeast Asians in the past twenty years. Those women are like the people of Zhangzhou and Quanzhou provinces on Mainland China who immigrated to Taiwan during the Qing Dynasty. They are modern-day heroines in Taiwan. They have brought a spirit of adventure, courage, and creativity into Taiwan. Taiwan originally had a rich diversity of Aboriginal cultures. Although we have lost many of these cultures, the government has assisted different indigenous groups in reestablishing their culture over the past decade, for example, through the use of policies that encourage the new generation to return to tribal development and transform their cultural spirit. This is how the hero returns home. Taiwan also has a long history of Chinese culture, rooted in the senex archetype. We cannot deny this ancient culture either. Denying one's own culture results in the formation of a cultural complex and the shadow of the orphan archetype comes into play. The foundation of culture is to transcend the rotation of power. This is the Taiwan's current challenge.

Notes

[1] Eli Weisstub and Esti Galili-Weisstub, "Collective Trauma and Cultural Complexes," in Thomas Singer and Samuel L. Kimbles, eds., *The Culture Complex: Contemporary Jungian Perspectives on Psyche and Society* (New York: Routledge, 2004), pp. 147–170.

[2] *Ibid.,* p. 161.

[3] *Ibid.*

[4] Thomas Singer and Samuel L. Kimbles, "The Emerging Theory of Cultural Complexes," in Joseph Cambray and Linda Carter, eds., *Analytical Psychology: Contemporary Perspectives in Jungian Analysis* (New York: Routledge, 2004), pp. 176–203, pp. 187–188.

[5] Junjie Huang, "The Meaning of the Concept of 'China' in Chinese Classics and Its Transformation in Modern Japan and Modern Taiwan," *Taiwan Journal of East Asian Civilization Studies* 3 (2, 2006): pp. 91–100.

[6] C. G. Jung, "The Psychology of the Transference" (1946), in *The Collected Works of C. G. Jung,* vol. 16, ed. and trans. Gerhard Adler and R. F. C. Hull (London: Routledge and Kegan Paul, 1966), § 470.

[7] John Weir Perry, "Emotions and Object Relations," *Journal of Analytical Psychology* 15 (1, 1970): 1–12. Quoted in Singer and Kimbles, "The Emerging Theory of Cultural Complexes," p. 186.

[8] *Ibid.,* p. 186.

[9] *Ibid.*

[10] Just four years before the Mudan incident, on March 12, 1867, the *Rover* Incident (羅發號事件) occurred when the American merchant ship *Rover* was wrecked off the coast of Formosa (Taiwan under Qing rule). The ship drifted into the area of Kenting, Taiwan (墾丁), where thirteen American sailors were killed by Taiwanese indigenous peoples. The Koxinga (國姓爺鄭成功), established by the Han Chinese in 1662 after their defeat of the Dutch who had colonized a small part of the southwest of Taiwan island, considered indigenous peoples to be barbarians, rather than civilized subjects, and regarded those indigenous peoples who did not accept the rule of the regime as non–human beings by setting up a boundary to block them off. The Chinese Qing Dynasty authority followed this same attitude toward indigenous peoples and thus divided them into "plains aborigines" (*mature barbarians,* 熟蕃) and "mountain aborigines" (*raw barbarians,* 生蕃). The mountain aborigines did not accept

AN ORPHAN OF THE PATRIARCHY

the rule of the government, but the plains aborigines did. So the government said the mountain aborigines are "out of the (Chinese) Culture." In the Rover Incident, the Americans eventually signed an effective treaty (南岬之盟) guaranteeing the safety of shipwrecked American and European sailors with the chief of eighteen Paiwan (排灣族) aboriginal tribes in the area where the *Rover* had gone ashore. Another shipwreck triggered the Mudan incident, which the Empire of Japan used as justification to invade and occupy a part of Taiwan in 1874. Because the Qing Dynasty denied that the mountain aborigines were citizens of the country, the Japanese Empire followed the advice of Charles W. Le Gendre who was an American consultant of the Japanese Ministry of Foreign Affairs to use the Mudan incident as a reason to build a military base. Cf. Wikipedia, "*Rover* Incident," "Mudan Incident," "Charles W. Le Gendre"; and Tay-Sheng Wang, "Indigenous Peoples in the Legal History of Taiwan: Being a Special Ethnic Group, Territory and Legal Culture," *National Taiwan University Law Journal* 44 (4, 2015): 1639–1704

[11] T. S. Lee, *Random Notes of a Sixty-Four Day Journey East* (Fuzhou: Meihua Press, 1896), p. 51.

[12] Lee, *Random Notes of a Sixty-Four Day Journey East,* pp. 9, 51, 82.

[13] Lian Heng, "Letter to Mr. Lin Zichao," in *Collection of Yatang Articles* (Nantou: The Historical Research Commission of Taiwan Province, 1964), p. 127.

[14] Singer and Kimbles, "The Emerging Theory of Cultural Complexes," p. 186.

[15] Edward Edinger, *Ego and Archetype* (New York: Putnam, 1972), pp. 3–5.

[16] Edward Edinger, "The Ego-Self Paradox," *Journal of Analytical Psychology* 5 (1, 1960): 3–18.

[17] Caroline Garland, *Understanding Trauma: A Psychoanalytical Approach* (The Tavistock Clinic Series) (London: Karnac Books, 2002).

[18] Wilfred R. Bion, "A Theory of Thinking," *International Journal of Psycho-Analysis* 43 (1962). Reprinted in Wilfred R. Bion, *Second Thoughts: Selected Papers on Psycho-Analysis* (London: Karnac Books, 1967). Melanie Klein, "Mourning and Its Relation to Manic-Depressive States," *International Journal of Psychoanalysis* 21 (1940): 125–153.

[19] Garland, *Understanding Trauma.*

310 SU-CHEN HUNG AND HUNG-CHIN WEI

[20] Audrey Punnett, *The Orphan: A Journey to Wholeness* (Sheriden, WY: Fisher King Press, 2014).

[21] B. Riftin, *From Myths to Ghost Stories: Comparative Studies on Taiwan Aboriginal Tales* (Taichung: Star Press, 1998).

[22] Jung, CW 16, § 470.

[23] C. G. Jung, "On the Psychology of the Unconscious" (1943), in *The Collected Works of C. G. Jung,* vol. 7, ed. and trans. Gerhard Adler and R. F. C. Hull (London: Routledge and Kegan Paul, 1969).

[24] Andrew Samuels, *A Critical Dictionary of Jungian Analysis* (London: Routledge, 1986); C. G. Jung, "Psychology and Religion (The Terry Lectures) (1938/1940), in *The Collected Works of C. G. Jung,* vol. 11, ed. and trans. Gerhard Adler and R. F. C. Hull (London: Routledge and Kegan Paul, 1970), § 131.

[25] Punnett, *The Orphan.*

[26] *Ibid.*

[27] Bion, "A Theory of Thinking."

[28] Wilfred R. Bion, *Elements of Psycho-Analysis* (London: William Heinemann, 1963).

[29] Andrew Samuels, *Politics on the Couch: Citizenship and the Internal Life* (London: Routledge 2001).

[30] *Ibid.,* p. 48.

[31] *Ibid.*

[32] Samuels, *Politics on the Couch.*

[33] Freud, cited in Garland, *Understanding Trauma.*

[34] Garland, *Understanding Trauma.*

[35] Thomas Singer, "The Cultural Complex and Archetypal Defenses of the Collective Spirit: Baby Zeus, Elian Gonzales, Constantine's sword, and Other Holy Wars," *The San Francisco Jung Institute Library Journal* 20 (4, 2002): 5–28.

[36] Donald Sandner, *Navaho Symbols of Healing: A Jungian Exploration of Ritual, Image, and Medicine* (Rochester, VT: Healing Arts Press, 1979).

[37] Singer and Kimbles, "The Emerging Theory of Cultural Complexes," p. 201.

[38] *Ibid.,* p. 187.

13
• • • • • •

The Wounded Feminine in Chinese Culture

Liza J. Ravitz

> Cultural complexes are based on frequently repeated historical experiences that have taken root in the collective psyche of a group and in the psyches of the individual members of a group, and they express archetypal values for the group.
>
> —Thomas Singer with Catherine Kaplinsky[1]

My first connection with Chinese culture came to me as a child. I vividly remember being five years old and on my father's shoulders in New York City's Chinatown, watching the Chinese New Year Dragon dance. The dragon undulated down the crowd-lined street, firecrackers popping off, drums beating, confetti flying. Noise, sparkle, and color surrounded me; a magical fairy tale had come alive. This beginning connection with Chinese culture was

---

Liza J. Ravitz, PhD, is a Jungian psychoanalyst and clinical psychologist. She is a teaching faculty member at the C. G. Jung Institute of San Francisco, a seminar faculty member at Sonoma State University, and a teaching member of the International Society of Sandplay Therapists (ISST). She lived in Taiwan for two years (2013–2015), where she practiced Jungian psychoanalysis, trained psychotherapists, and taught at the university. Liza presently continues her psychoanalytic practice in Asia and teaches and trains psychotherapists internationally.

312 LIZA J. RAVITZ

reinforced every Sunday when my family would go out to dinner for Chinese food. In my family, Chinese food was among our favorite foods. When my mother and I spent time together, she would playfully say she was a Chinese princess in another life. From these early childhood experiences I came to understand China as familiar, for I had eaten her food, yet at the same time, China was a faraway magical place—exotic, mysterious, and other to me.

In college during the 1960s, I began my love affair with Far Eastern religions and learned to meditate. Through the influence of cultural icons of the times, interest in Eastern philosophy flourished on American college campuses. I dove into courses on Buddhism, Taoism, and Hinduism. At the same time that my consciousness was expanding in relation to the Far East, the women's movement was developing tremendous momentum on college campuses. Gender bias became an issue. Marches and protests, consciousness-raising women's groups, and a new curriculum, Women's Studies, preoccupied my time and set me on my life's path. The impact on America's social fabric was revolutionary, reverberating still today.

In graduate school, I continued my meditation practice and channeled my interest in the woman's movement into my academics. Both my master's thesis and PhD dissertation were on gender bias. I developed a specialty—the psychology of women—which my male professors discouraged me from pursuing. They felt that specialty would ruin my career because academics would not take me seriously. Since that time, however, this specialty has grown and thrived, producing research that has helped to create more gender equality. Yet, even today, gender bias persists. In the United States, in recent years, gender bias has received significant attention. It has been scrutinized as being a factor in the treatment of presidential candidates, the lower pay of Hollywood actresses, and the dearth of female chief executives. The #metoo movement in the United States recently erupted out of the cultural unconscious, bringing to light the "acceptable" sexual harassment that women still endure. Today, almost fifty years since the birth of the modern women's movement in the US, a teenage analysand told me that she was afraid to be smart in front of her boyfriend, so she had stopped raising her hand in class; hiding oneself is safest.

My interest in the psychology of women has remained with me throughout my professional career. In a parallel manner, my interest in the Far East continued into my professional years,

THE WOUNDED FEMININE 313

leading me to Jung. Interested in meditation, I picked up a copy of *The Secret of the Golden Flower,* a Taoist text on meditation.[2] When I read Jung's commentary on the connection between analytical psychology and Eastern philosophy I had an epiphany that set me on the path to becoming a Jungian analyst. For me, Jung and the East were forever connected.

As synchronicity and fate would have it, thirty years later, in 2010, when under the auspices of the International Association of Analytical Psychology (IAAP), I was asked to be the visiting analyst for the Jungian Developing Group of Taiwan, I gladly accepted. This acceptance evolved over time into a deeper commitment, and I moved to Taiwan, where I lived and worked for two years, from 2012–2014. I had a full-time practice doing analysis and supervision, teaching in a master's counseling program at the university, and conducting workshops and trainings throughout Asia. My analysands and consultees were males and females, between the ages of thirty-six and sixty-five, from Taiwan, Hong Kong, Macau, and mainland China. They were seen at various frequencies, from one to three sessions per week; those farther away came monthly for longer sessions. All spoke English as a second language. Upon embarking on this venture, I wondered how I would be impacted and changed by an immersion in Chinese culture. Unbeknownst to me, Chinese culture, Jung, and gender bias would all come together during this experience.

A universal value inherent in cultures throughout the world is the idea that men are superior and more valued than women and, in turn, that the masculine principle of striving and achievement is more highly regarded than the feminine principle of relating and cooperation. This universal value lives in the collective unconscious and has serious negative consequences, not only for men and women but also for the planet. From this gender bias, a universal psychological complex has developed, referred to as the *wounded feminine.*[3] Within this complex, the hierarchical masculine becomes the dominant value of the culture, and its opposite, the wounded feminine, goes into the collective shadow. The word *feminine* here is used to indicate the archetypal feminine aspect that exists within both men and women as well as on earth and in all of creation. In the Chinese tradition it is known as *Yin,* in the Native American tradition as *Mother Earth,* and in Judaism as the *Shekinah.* In Jungian psychology it is known as the feminine in women, the anima in men,

314   LIZA J. RAVITZ

and the anima mundi in the universe. The hierarchical ground created by this complex is clothed uniquely in each culture, resulting in a cultural complex that becomes part of the cultural unconscious. This chapter is an attempt to examine how this complex has unfolded, specifically, in the Chinese cultural unconscious.

Living and working in a foreign country allows for a depth immersion in a culture. My experience not only afforded me an immersion in Chinese culture, but also gave me the opportunity to learn about the culture through the dreams, sandplays, and intimate accounts of my patients, supervisees, and students. Early in my experience, I became aware of the dichotomy of the privileged status of males and the masculine principle versus the devalued status of females and the feminine principle. This dichotomy permeates the culture, impacting the people I worked with both consciously and unconsciously. This discovery was a déjà vu for me. I was quite familiar with these issues, having wrestled with them all my life. I was not familiar, however, with the cultural issues around gender bias, but I could relate to the wounding my analysands had experienced at the hands of the culture. As my work progressed, I became more aware of the suffering this cultural complex inflicted on the emotional development of both men and women. This manifested in a deep wounding of the feminine in growing girls and women, a stunted anima or feminine part in boys and men, and the destruction and pollution of the environment. Women lived with an inferiority complex, feeling like second-class citizens, devalued and discardable. Men were cut off from their emotions and inspirational source, sacrificing relationships for social status. The environment was unstable, pollution a leading cause of death and disease. One of the most radical, and more recent, manifestations of this cultural complex appeared in China during the time of the one-child policy, when began in 1979 and ended in 2015. During this time girl babies, having little or no value, were often killed or abandoned. This continues even today with China's present two-child policy.

> In parts of Asia—especially India and China—baby girls are undesirable, even unacceptable. In China, if you're allowed only two children, and you already have one girl … well, in a culture where males are valued much more highly than females, it's not hard to imagine what follows. Baby girls are stuck in sacks and thrown in rivers and down wells, even dumped upside-down in buckets of water.[4]

THE WOUNDED FEMININE

In parts of China, the use of sex-selection abortions has thrown the ratio of boys to girls completely out of kilter, having ramifications for future family and societal life.

Footbinding, a more ancient practice, is another example of how this complex can wreak havoc. Shirley Ma speaks of this in her book *Footbinding:*

> When feminine qualities and women are devalued, footbinding becomes a powerful metaphor for the suppression of the feminine ..., this binding may take different forms: Struggling to achieve outward success at the cost of all else, following someone else's dreams rather than our own, desperately trying to mold our bodies into the shape that society and men consider desirable ... are but a few.[5]

In her ground-breaking book, Jean Baker Miller examines women's difficulties in claiming their "full personhood" and in valuing themselves and their strengths, which are viewed as inferior by the dominant culture.

> A dominant group, inevitably, has the greatest influence in determining a culture's overall outlook—its philosophy, morality, social theory, and even its science. The dominant group, thus, legitimizes the unequal relationship and incorporates it into society's guiding concepts.[6]

The dominant group is the model for what is considered normal.

In speaking to my patients, supervisees, and students, I learned that many women have deep wounds from childhood when they were given the message that sons were more valued than daughters. As a result, women have adopted the masculine value of achievement and striving and become disconnected from their bodies and feminine values of relating, holding, and being. Men have been pressured to achieve the highest pinnacle that their gender status expects, creating enormous stress and fear of shame. The expression of emotion is suppressed, resulting in an inward feeling of alienation and disconnection from one's deepest source. Value is placed on achieving, not relating. The anima, or feminine aspect, of men becomes wounded, just as the feminine in females is wounded. The female's animus, or masculine part, adopts the values of the dominant culture, sending internal messages of devaluation and degradation. Identifying with the dominant ruling culture is often a way that women cope with subjugation.[7] Marie-Louise von Franz held the opinion that this

316 LIZA J. RAVITZ

negative animus problem is partially rooted in culture, which values rationality and thinking over feeling and intuition. This hierarchical valuing harms the instinctual life of people and makes it incumbent on society to change.[8]

Gender bias not only injures people but also has consequences for the planet. Marion Woodman speaks to this:

> We are not only talking about women. We are talking about our own dying mother Earth, her very pulse, her trees and water poisoned by demonic patriarchal power. We are talking about the patriarchal rage that binds the feminine standpoint and poisons her soil... . The voices of the feminine in men and woman must take on the responsibility of learning to walk firmly, both feet on the ground, confident in the values that can save Mother Earth and allow her daughters—women and men—to speak and love their own reality.[9]

Confucius

Looking at Chinese culture through a Confucian lens can help us understand the historical and sociological development of "the wounded feminine" cultural complex. Born in 551 BCE, Confucius, the founder of Confucianism, was a great thinker and educator who lived seventy-two years. His philosophy about family relationships and the concept of filial piety was written down by his disciples and put into a book *The Analects. The Analects,* an enduring classic of Chinese culture, is essentially a system of ethics and morality. This classic, which continued to evolve over time, has had a large influence on writers, thinkers, and politicians throughout China's history.

Confucius was concerned with both the cosmic order comprised of Heaven and Earth and the human order comprised of humans. In his view, humans were closely connected to Heaven and Earth, were to learn from Heaven and Earth, and form a human order based on the cosmic order. In the cosmic order valued by Confucians, Heaven and Earth were seen as life giving and everything in life was relational. Creation and nurturance did not come into being in isolation, but depended on the coming together of two different elements in a relationship, thus Heaven and Earth were in relation to each other, although they observed a hierarchy. Heaven was a creative, superior element placed high above, and Earth was a receptive, inferior element positioned below. Another aspect of the cosmic order was concerned

THE WOUNDED FEMININE

317

with the harmonious and orderly interaction of its parts. These ideas formed the cornerstone of Confucian philosophy. To establish the correct ordering of human society, humans were to honor the life-giving energy of the cosmos in a parallel way, through the honoring of the life-giving energy of the ancestors and of marriage and progeny.

Family relationships were seen as an expression of moral law in addition to carrying out a biological function. The human order was to parallel the cosmic order and thus contained the same hierarchy. Different hierarchical relationships existed: Superior positions were held by parents, rulers, husbands, and older siblings; inferior positions were held by children, subjects, wives, and younger siblings. Children were taught to be filial to their parents; subjects loyal to their rulers; wives submissive to their husbands; and younger siblings respectful of their older siblings. Just as Heaven was to Earth, men were superior and women were inferior. To promote human order and harmony as in the cosmos, Confucius devised various rituals and behaviors for these hierarchical relationships. Appropriate behaviors were spelled out in quite specific terms. This central concept of the parallels between the cosmic order and the human order put an archetypal layer on woman's inferiority to men. The strength of this hierarchical dichotomy remains deeply embedded in the unconscious, as according to Confucianism, a woman accepts her inferior status not because she is told to but because the "authority of the cosmic order demands it."[10]

This inequality between the genders in Chinese culture can be traced from prehistoric times onward. Evidence from archaeology shows that inequality between men and women was already present during the Neolithic period.[11] Confucianism, a patriarchal religious tradition, evaluated women's nature as lowly. In the Five Classics, the texts of early Confucianism, "the female was inferior by nature, she was dark as the moon and changeable as water, jealous, narrow minded and insinuating. She was indiscreet, unintelligent and dominated by emotion."[12]

As time evolved, new interpretations initiated by neo-Confucian scholars further rigidified rules and regulations concerning women's roles and behaviors, instilling a stronger stance on the superiority of men over women.[13] Dong Zhong-Shu (179–104 BCE), the Han Confucian master, maintained that between the two principles that governed the universe, the *Yang* and *Yin, Yang* was superior and *Yin* inferior. In turn, on the human level, the husband was *Yang* and superior,

318   LIZA J. RAVITZ

and the wife was *Yin* and inferior. Through his influence the practice of footbinding was instituted. This degrading attitude toward women became extreme during the period of Song-Ming neo-Confucianism. Zhu Xi (1130–1200 CE), the prominent neo-Confucian, advocated the *Three Bonds,* which asserted the ruler's authority over the minister, the father over the son, and the husband over the wife.[14] In the human order, men functioned out in the world, in the wider sociopolitical order; women functioned only in the context of the family. In the family, women were to follow the *Three Obediences:* daughter to father, wife to husband, and, when older, to her son.[15] The focal point of a woman's life was marriage, regarded as a sacred event. The roles of wife, daughter-in-law, and mother defined her identity. Men could divorce but not women. Grounds for divorce could be failure to bear a male child and disobedience to her husband's parents. Women had no grounds for divorce and, even after her husband's death, were supposed to remain loyal to him and never remarry. Her allegiance was first and foremost to his family; no attention was given to her individual wishes or strivings.

By the late nineteenth and twentieth centuries, China was in decline. Reformers saw Confucianism as one of the main reasons for the country's problems. The position of women was also at an all-time low, exampled by the widespread practices of female infanticide, the buying and selling of women, and footbinding. Women, as well as male reformers, began to turn against the tradition.[16] Questions have been raised about Confucian attitudes toward women at recent conferences on Confucianism. Even though scholars agree that there is a gender inequality in present-day Confucianism, very few attempts have been made to deal with or to correct this inequity. Chenyang Li has labeled this issue in Confucianism, "The Gender Complex."[17]

In my experience working in Asia, women and men are rejecting the patriarchal system, the system of inferiority and obedience, with a new consciousness. I have found, however, that unconsciously this hierarchy lives on in the culture, continuing to cause a host of problems in the psyches of both men and women.

Analytical psychology

Jung used an ancient Greek term coined by the philosopher Heraclitus, *enantiodromia,* to indicate that an "unconscious opposite" would "always occur when an extreme, one-sided tendency dominates

THE WOUNDED FEMININE

conscious life."[18] With the conscious one-sided view of the superiority of the masculine, the devalued feminine falls into the unconscious shadow. Seen from the one-sided point of view of the conscious attitude, the shadow, considered to hold negative and inferior aspects of the personality, is repressed. If the shadow does not become conscious, it expresses itself indirectly and all the more destructively by being projected out onto others. In order to become a more whole human being, the repressed shadow material must be made conscious. This process produces a tension of opposites in the psyche, which is necessary for any forward movement and development. Without this consciousness of both sides within, stagnation results for "life is born only of the spark of opposites.[19]

Jung postulated that each sex has a contrasexual element within the psyche. In the male, the feminine aspect is called the *anima*. *Anima* can be defined as "soul." The anima development of males is influenced by the culture's view of the feminine, by the father's anima, and by important females in their early life—mother, grandmother, aunt, sister. As these females suffer from a wounded feminine caused by the devaluation of females in the culture, so, too, the anima of the male will incorporate this wounding. The souls of men carry this wound in the unconscious, resulting in a disconnection from their emotional life, including their vitality, creativity, and flexibility.

The masculine aspect of a female is called the *animus*. This is the part of the female that helps her to navigate the world, to succeed in life, to take charge, to move forward. The development of the animus is mainly influenced by important men in her early life—father, grandfather, uncle, and brother—as well as by the animus of the important women in her early life. The internalized patriarchal view of girls and women will be transmitted to the girl child's developing animus. In its negative aspect, the animus will sabotage successful attempts to function in the world by internally whispering attacking, devaluing messages to the developing girl child, often resulting in conflict, guilt, and low self-esteem. This dynamic continues into adulthood as the internal critic, either consciously or unconsciously paralleling the cultural value, transmits the message of inferiority and lack of value. For individuals to become more conscious and whole, they must become conscious of the anima and animus that live in the unconscious.

Clinical material

The wounded feminine complex, created by the overvaluation of the masculine and the devaluation of the feminine, effects the development of a sense of self in both males and females, causing an alienation from the feminine and a disconnection from their inner source of aliveness. This complex appeared in my analysands', supervisees', and students' material in various ways. I will explore six areas in which this complex was activated: daughters versus sons, women's roles, the mothers, the daughter-in-law, achievement, and the body.

Daughters vs. Sons

> If you get your ears pierced you will come back as a girl.
> —Chinese Proverb
> Raising a girl is like plowing someone else's field.
> —Chinese Proverb

The majority of my female patients who had brothers talked about the preferential treatment their brothers received and the resulting pain and fury this engendered. One analysand spent many sessions talking about her painful feelings at the difference in how she and her brother were treated by her parents, especially her mother. She felt her brother, as the boy, was always favored over her. He was urged to develop and pursue education; she was not. He was showered with gifts and birthday celebrations; she was not. Her feeling was that her mother smiled when she saw her brother and frowned when she appeared. This attitude toward her from both parents had an injurious impact on her development, resulting in an internalized self-devaluation. The majority of my female patients who had brothers told me variations on these themes.

When analysands talked about the possibility of starting a family, their issues about having a girl child emerged. Comments indicating an internalized negative view of girls were often expressed. Some analysands wondered how they would feel if they had a girl child, for being a daughter was not a good thing. They expressed fear about bringing up a girl child, feeling their own wounding would be passed down to her unconsciously. One patient talked about her mother's difficult childhood; her mother had been given away at birth, for a girl child was undesirable. This initial abandonment of my patient's

THE WOUNDED FEMININE   321

mother was reenacted with my patient, and she, in turn, was fearful she would reenact this with her girl child. These exchanges gave me some ideas about how the negative attitude toward girls was transmitted throughout the generations. Even in modern Chinese women, who are aware of feminism, who embrace equality, an unconscious bias may persist and be transmitted unconsciously to their female children.

Themes of envy and competition were often explored. In discussing the preference paid to their brothers, several female analysands told of their envy and intense competition with their brothers, especially for their mother's attention and for family resources. This dynamic seemed to follow these women into adult life. Envy came in the form of social status, income, jobs, and over male babies born to friends. These two things—envy and competition—were major motivating factors in life decisions and behaviors. The feeling expressed was "If I want to be seen, I must be the best."

This theme of striving to be the best was repeated over and over again by many women. Interestingly, envy would come up in the transference. They envied me for my higher social status as a teacher, professor, and analyst, and for my intellect and professional achievements. These are all things that might fit into the masculine principle, developed by my animus or masculine aspect of my psyche. No envy of a more feminine nature was apparent or ever expressed.

At times, a negative transference would develop; upsets aimed at me—"I did not value them; I did not see their achievements; I did not acknowledge their efforts; I acted like I was smarter than them; I talked down to them"—really seemed to express projected feelings they had about themselves. On the other side of the complex were comments such as "You are worthless; you have nothing to offer; you do not know anything." This projected depreciation gave me a strong flavor of what they were feeling. Inside I myself heard the voice of the culture telling me I was deficient.

Women's role

Female analysands told me they were raised to suppress their needs and to serve the needs of others, especially fathers and husbands. They told me this was the role of women. They were not expected to have needs or to pursue their passion but to ignore their inner voice. Often higher education was discouraged, encouraged only for boys. Their role in life was to marry and have sons. If this did not happen, they did not pass the "life test"; they did not hit the standard for a woman. Marrying was an absolute must, the lack of which caused much pressure, not only from parents but from relatives and the culture at large. In their experience, becoming highly educated was against the cultural norm, which dictated that women give attention to the home, not to the outside world. I heard this dynamic many times from high-achieving, bright, educated women who felt guilty at their success, for behaving differently from the norm, and thus breaking the cultural imperative to serve the patriarchy. This pervasive guilt left them feeling unloved, unseen, unvalued, and nonexistent. In an ironic way, it was often the mothers, as the agents of culture, who transmitted this attitude to their girl children.

The mothers

The devaluation of the feminine and females has left women feeling both consciously and unconsciously devalued. Traditional culture dictates that the only way to have value as a female is to marry well and to bear a son. This brings great status. If a woman births only girls, her status is lower, and, at times, she is rejected and devalued further for not fulfilling her role and promise. This has implications for how a mother feels about her girl child. The mother may reject the child outright or unconsciously harbor negative feelings toward her. She may feel angry or resentful that the girl child deprived her of the only way to obtain status, that is, to bear a son. A lack of mirroring, emotional neglect, or abandonment may result. These mothers may expect their children to fill the void in their own mirroring process. When childhood is sacrificed to meeting a parents' needs, the child loses the possibility of developing a living connection to the Self.[20]

One of my patients talked about her grandmother who made delicious food for her daughter-in-law who had had a son, but for my patient's mother, also a daughter-in-law, the grandmother did not make any special food, for she had only born a girl child. The grandmother did not give her mother any extra care after birthing, as is traditionally done, for her child had no value and did not add anything to the family. This difference in treatment continued as my patient grew, causing her much pain, for in her mind it was her fault that her mother was not treated well. This dynamic caused enormous guilt for causing the suffering of her mother, for not contributing to the development of the family, for being an inferior human being. Several of my female analysands felt very guilty in relation to their mothers yet could not identify why they felt this way or where this feeling may have come

THE WOUNDED FEMININE 323

from. As compensation, these women, as girls, tried everything to get approval, yet nothing was ever good enough. Some of them reported that something was missing in their relationship with their mother, either in the connection between them or in the lack of valuing or admiring. This feeling was internalized, resulting in the women not valuing or admiring themselves. They were left feeling inadequate, with the deep knowledge that something integral was wrong with them. This phenomenon can lead to low self-esteem and a lifetime of guilty feelings of not measuring up to others. It also contributes to intense lifelong striving and competition for approval.

The resulting low self-esteem continues unconsciously as these women bear children and have contact with grandchildren. One place where women can feel some status and power is in relation to their daughters-in-law. All the emotional abuse and devaluation they received as a result of being girls is now heaped on their daughters-in-law. Stories of the difficulties and sufferings of daughters-in-law are rather legendary in traditional Chinese families.

The daughter-in-law

The daughter-in-law's job is to take care of her husband and husband's family, especially his parents, and to bear sons to increase the status of the family. I have heard terrible stories of treatment by mothers-in-law. In the traditional family, one of the only places a woman can have any power is over her daughter-in-law who, in the adult family hierarchy, is on the lowest rung. The mother-in-law can ask or order the daughter-in-law to do whatever she desires. The only place the daughter-in-law has power is over her children. If she bears a son, eventually he will gain more status than her, though her girl child will not. These dynamics continue through the generations as the daughter-in-law, in turn, deals with her daughter-in-law in a similar manner, having finally arrived at a more powerful position.

One analysand was in the position of being the daughter-in-law in a very traditional family. The burdens and demands put on her, the total lack of power, the devaluation she suffered for bearing a girl child, all left her feeling inferior, defeated, resentful, and unhappy. The preferential treatment her sister-in-law received for having born a son was especially painful. Her husband did not seem to have any insight into her dilemma as he supported traditional values and saw everything in its right order as it stood. Other analysands were able to live separately from their husband's family and were less compliant with the demands from their mother-in-law. However, this caused tension in the family, resulting in guilty feelings. An internalized patriarchal judge condemned them for not following the rules of their station and keeping harmony in the family. One woman could not understand why she felt so deeply depressed around this tension. She came to understand how her guilt from unconscious holding of supposedly rejected patriarchal values was impacting her psyche. After working with this for some time, she was able to soften the inner judge and to reduce the intense inner conflict she had suffered.

After marriage, at a time when men begin to develop their careers, to come into their full power as adult men, their wives are subjected to the lowering of their status in regard to the mother-in-law who can even make decisions about her work. As an anecdote, my manicurist, a young woman in her early twenties, married with two young children, was working happily at her job. One day her mother-in-law decided she no longer wanted to care for the children and that my manicurist had to quit her job immediately and return home to do childcare. Finding some other childcare person was not an option and the grandmother wanted more free time. This young lady was very upset about this change in her life plan but felt powerless to alter the outcome. Perhaps, if she had been older she may have been able to push back, but with no support from her husband she had to comply with her mother-in-law's demands.

Some women suffer such a lack of control over their lives that it leads to anxiety and depression. As their self-strivings are repressed further, a feeling of hopelessness and powerlessness sets in. This has implications not only for a woman's emotional well-being, but also for her children. A depressed, overworked, resentful mother cannot always be emotionally available to her children.

Achievement
Achievement was a major issue for all of my patients, both men and women. Women seemed to strive for achievement to fulfill a cultural demand and also to establish some form of self-esteem. The dominant culture values the masculine principle of achievement, moving forward, producing, and gaining material resources. The qualities of the feminine principle, being, holding, and relating, are relegated to the back of the line and tend to fall into the unconscious. The price paid for striving to meet the patriarchal demands of high achievement leaves both men and women disconnected from their

THE WOUNDED FEMININE

feminine sides, as they choose the material over the soul. A dream of a female patient reflects this devaluing of the feminine and the valuing of achievement at any price:

My husband and I have a newborn child. We are professional tennis players. Someone takes the baby away because they have to train it to be a professional tennis player.

In exploring the dream, my patient explained that the baby must sacrifice the parents' caring to become a professional. The parents must sacrifice their relationship to the baby so their child can become a successful professional. She then asserted that, in the dream, she accepted this situation without a doubt. The ensuing conversation centered on her feelings of being devalued as a female and the cultural value placed on education and achievement. Any emphasis on relationship, or on connection with oneself, with her more vulnerable and needy parts, in her mind, was considered indulgent and a sign of a lazy person. In addition, she felt split off from her body, as she had to "become a man" to be successful, leaving a deep scar within her feminine self.

Several of my female analysands constantly had conflicts about achievement, first fearing they were not good enough to pursue an education, and second, feeling guilty about pursuing higher education as it was against their cultural values. In an ironic way, even though females have adopted the dominant value of the culture to strive for achievement, culturally it was neither expected nor encouraged or appreciated. Patients talked about hiding their true self, especially with men, around their intelligence and achievements. I was told that the culture does not encourage girls to express themselves, nor to work toward reaching their potential. More importantly, a girl should be polite and cooperative, quiet, obedient, and not talk too much. Another admonition was not to show one's intelligence too much for this may offend a man. One patient had reached the highest pinnacle in her profession, with an extremely coveted higher degree. When she told the head of her family about her hard-earned accomplishment, she was told that her achievement was no honor to her family as she was a girl who will marry and belong to another family. My patient was devastated by this response, understanding, once again, it was not valued for a female to shine intellectually; her role was to marry and bear sons. Much of the analysis centered on allowing her true self to come out of hiding.

326   LIZA J. RAVITZ

Here are some of the messages I repeatedly heard from analysands expressing conflictual feelings about achievement:

"A stupid woman is much better than a smart woman. So best to hide your smart side."

"If I do nothing and think nothing I am acceptable; if I think something and do something, that is not good; it is against the cultural norm."

"As a child I was believed unintelligent because I was a girl, even though I was much smarter than my brothers; they were encouraged to succeed and get education, but not me."

"No matter how much education you have, it is not as important as marrying and having a boy child. Then you really are a woman."

"If you marry and have a boy you have achieved 100% and can feel confident as a woman; if you did not achieve these things, the culture sees you as a failure."

"I'm a loser because men are superior."

"I cannot do well because I am a girl."

"If I am not married and I work, I must be a man inside."

Conflicting attitudes about achievement were revealed in dream material. While teaching in a master's program at the university, it was our custom to talk about dreams from the class. A female student had the following dream:

My father is teaching class in my hometown. I sit in his classroom and I tell my father, "I will go to Liza's class." He responds by asking if I have a boyfriend yet.

As we discussed this dream in class, many girls spoke to the feeling of being degraded as a girl, feeling not good enough. The dreamer was angry that the dream father asked about her boyfriend and not about her interests or knowledge. In class this led to a discussion of the power of the patriarchy over girls: A woman is man's possession and a girl child is someone to mold to one's own image. The boys brought up feelings of being controlled by the patriarchy and having to fulfill high expectations in a role that causes much stress, shame, and guilt. Many students talked about not being able to be their true selves. This

THE WOUNDED FEMININE

was a very emotional discussion, quite out of the ordinary for a usually reserved group of students.

Women are not the only ones who suffer. Men are cut off from their feminine parts for the same reason as women. It is from the anima that emotion, inspiration, and soul emanate. Disconnection from one's feminine part, or anima, results in a partially lived life, one disconnected from one's source and from the aliveness of feeling. Men are under terrible pressure to succeed and to prosper materially. This is the cultural expectation of their role. If they achieve below expectations, they experience a deep feeling of shame. This leaves little room for an inner receptive space to develop, for a man's role is to be out in the world working. In talking with my analysands and in case consultations about children, invariably, there was the absent father who worked most of the time, spent little time with the children, and was never able to make parent sessions with the child therapist because he was always working. The absence of the fathers has created a father hunger in the culture. *Father hunger* is the void experienced by women whose fathers were physically or emotionally absent—an emptiness that leads to disordered eating, constant dieting, and an unrealistic body image.[21] The emotional isolation of men masks a hunger for fathering and male mentoring. Father hunger is an injury that comes from not seeing your father when you are small, never being with him, having an absent father, a workaholic father, or a remote father.[22] Fathers themselves have been deprived of contact with their fathers, and so this dynamic gets reenacted with the younger generation.

In regard to achievement, females felt it was important to develop a masculine style to be accepted. To be successful, they had to devalue the feminine, including the female body, and develop their masculine side according to the dictates of the patriarchy. From this situation, a split results in the psyche between the mind and the body, energy goes into developing the mind and cutting off any connection to the body. This disconnection between mind and body is an integral aspect of the wounded feminine complex.

The body

Many of my female analysands were disconnected from their bodies but were unaware of this phenomenon. As discussions evolved, it became clear that the devaluation of girls also carried with it the devaluation of the female body in general. Within this

328   LIZA J. RAVITZ

general devaluation of the female body, a further devaluation resulted, depending on how well one fit the patriarchal criteria for a good body—big breasts, big butt, skinny torso, and so on. In talking about the onset of menses, there were no stories of celebrations, just practical teachings. Often the menses arrived as a surprise. Mothers did not prepare their girls for this important event. No one could recall ever having had a discussion with their mother about their body or sex. This was a topic that seemed to live underground. Many women felt a need to hide their bodies and dress in a more masculine style. They felt this would bring them more success. The lack of reverence for the female body has left women with a feeling of self-loathing, cut off from their very essence.

When there is a split between mind and body the psyche is unable to connect with its deepest source. The ego becomes disconnected from the self, living in a head space without contact with the rich, fertile soil of a woman's being. There is an internal feeling that something is missing. This split causes depression, dissociation, and a feeling of shallowness. Healing comes from working on this shadow material and bringing this complex to consciousness. Even though there is a conscious awareness of this hierarchy in the culture, its negative impact on the psyche of men and women remains hidden in the unconscious.

The future

This chapter is focused on the shadow complex of the hierarchical patriarchy—the wounded feminine—and how it manifests in the Chinese cultural unconscious. This complex develops from gender bias, when a culture values the masculine and men over the feminine and women. This phenomenon can negatively impact self-esteem, self-agency, and self-image in both women and men. There are many variations of how this complex manifests in other cultures and continues to reverberate throughout the world. More awareness is emerging in the world psyche about gender inequality. There are several examples of a new consciousness emerging regarding the treatment of women. One example is the recent permission (September 2017) given to Saudi women allowing them to drive, offering them more freedom and power within an oppressive patriarchal system. Another is the global spread of the #metoo movement raising worldwide consciousness of rampant sexual harassment. The United Nations sat aside November 26, 2018, as a day to protest violence against women. Thousands of

THE WOUNDED FEMININE

people around the globe took to the streets to protest gender-based violence.[23] A new paradigm is emerging out of the world collective and cultural unconscious, shifting humanity, albeit very slowly, toward the day Yin and Yang sit equally upon the throne of human interaction.

> The more women can experience their own initiation into womanhood as being as valid as the initiation of men into manhood, the less there will be to interfere with the growth and development of true and equal relationships. Initiation above all means transition, which affects not only individuals but also groups, families …[24]

and culture.

Notes

[1] Thomas Singer, with Catherine Kaplinsky, "Cultural Complexes in Analysis," in Murray Stein, ed., *Jungian Psychoanalysis: Working in the Spirit of C.G. Jung* (Chicago: Open Court Publishing Company, 2010), pp. 22–37.

[2] Richard Wilhelm, trans., *Secret of the Golden Flower: A Chinese Book of Life,* with a Commentary by C. G. Jung (New York: Harcourt Brace Jovanovich, 1962).

[3] Jean Baker Miller, *Toward a New Psychology of Women* (Boston: Beacon Press, 1976); Marion Woodman, *Leaving My Father's House: A Journey to Conscious Femininity* (Boston, Shambhala, 1976).

[4] Kristen Walker-Hatten, "200 Million Girls Killed in China," Lifenews.com, Nov. 2, 2012.

[5] Shirley See Yan Ma, *Footbinding: A Jungian Engagement with Chinese Culture and Psychology* (New York: Routledge, 2010), p. 10.

[6] Miller, *Toward a New Psychology of Women,* p. 8.

[7] *Ibid.*

[8] Fraser Boa, trans. and prod., "The Animus," *The Way of the Dream: Conversations on Dream Interpretation with Dr. Marie-Louise von Franz,* Marion Woodman Foundation, Disc 3.

[9] Marian Woodman, Foreword to *Footbinding: A Jungian Engagement with Chinese Culture and Psychology* (New York: Routledge, 2010), p. xiv.

[10] Theresa Kelleher, "Confucianism," in Arvind Sharma, ed., *Women in World Religions* (Albany, NY: State University of New York Press, 1987), p. 147.

330   *LIZA J. RAVITZ*

[11] David N. Keightley, "The Shang: China's First Historical Dynasty," in Michael Loewe and Edward L. Shaughnessy, eds., *The Cambridge History of Ancient China: From the Origins of Civilization to 221 BC* (Cambridge: Cambridge University Press, 1999), Ch. 4, p. 263.

[12] Richard Guisso, "'Thunder over the Lake': The Five Classics and the Perception of Women in Early China," in Richard W. Guisso and Stanley Johannesen, eds., *Women in China: Current Directions in Historical Scholarship* (New York: Philo Press, 1981), p. 59.

[13] Ye Lang and Zhu Liangzhi, *Insights into Chinese Culture* (Beijing: Foreign Language Teaching and Research Press, 2008), p. 3.

[14] *Ibid,* p. 188.

[15] *Ibid.,* p.140.

[16] *Ibid,* p. 158.

[17] Chenyang Li, "Confucianism and Feminist Concerns: Overcoming the Confucian 'Gender Complex,'" *Journal of Chinese Philosophy* 27 (2, 2000): 187–199, p. 187.

[18] C. G. Jung, *Psychological Types,* vol. 6, *The Collected Works of C. G. Jung,* ed. and trans. Gerhard Adler and R. F. C. Hull (Princeton, NJ: Princeton University Press, 1971), § 709.

[19] C. G. Jung, "On the Psychology of the Unconscious" (1943), in *The Collected Works of C. G. Jung,* vol. 7, ed. and trans. Gerhard Adler and R. F. C. Hull (Princeton NJ: Princeton University Press, 1953), § 78).

[20] Alice Miller, *The Drama of the Gifted Child,* trans. R. Ward (New York: Basic Books, 1981).

[21] Margo Maine, *Father Hunger: Fathers, Daughters, and the Pursuit of Thinness* (Carlsbad, NM: Gurze Books, 2004).

[22] Robert Bly, *Iron John: A Book about Men* (Philadelphia: DaCapa Press, 2004), p. 32.

[23] Raphael Minder, Yonette Joseph, and Iliana Magra, "Marching to End Violence Against Women," *New York Times,* Nov. 26, 2018, A6.

[24] Joe Henderson, *Shadow and Self: Selected Papers in Analytical Psychology* (Wilmette, IL: Chiron Publications, 1990), p. 12.

Index

●●●●●●●●

Note: Page numbers in *italic* indicate a figure and page numbers in **bold** indicate a table on the corresponding page.

achievement 320–321, 324–327
affect 16, 18, 232, 246, 277, 295
agency: and autistic spectrum disorder 165–166; and individual stories today 169–176; intertwining of I and others 176–178; in Japanese culture today 163–164; Japanese weaker agency 164–165, 166–167; and symbolical story 167–169
Amaterasu 185, 197–197
analytical psychology 1–2, 7–8, 313, 318–319; clinical material 320–329
ancestor, Chinese word for 50–54
ancestral worship 49–50, **66**; and Chinese nationalism 54–58; and the Grand Chinese Scholar Tree 70–74; and the imperial hereditary system 58–65; and the "Sacred Ancestral Tree" culture 66–69; significance of the words *root* and *ancestor* 50–54
animus archetype 97–98; and compensation through education 111–114; forming the Chinese animus 98–103; negative cultural animus 105–107;

positive cultural animus 103–105; and the White Snake 114–119; wounded cultural animus 107–111
anxiety *see* displacement
archetype 301; of femininity 26–35, 46; and the Garden of the Heart & Soul 42, 44, 46; hero and orphan 302–305; of love *45*; and missing women of China 36; shadow 304; *see also* animus archetype
ASD 154–155, 155–157; *see also* Autism Spectrum Disorder
Ashman, Amalya Layla 20, 227
Autism Spectrum Disorder (ASD) 19, 140, 152, 154–157, 159, 161n26, 165–167
autonomy 15, 221–222

ballads 70–74
beatings 79–80, 109–110, *109*, 117
Beebe, John 1
Beebe Model of Typology 26
bipolarity 17–18, 168, 295
Bixia Yuanjun 27, *28*, 33, 36; temple for *29*
black and white thinking 16
bodies 31–32, 37, 40, 154, 246–248; clinical material 327–329

332

Book of Changes (I Ching) 2, 9, 43–45, 51, 61, 100–102
Buddhism 2, 9; China 104; Japan 148–149, 151, 155, 191, 194; Korea 203, 205

capitalism 210, 213–214, 216–218, 221–222
Cezanne, Paul 150; *The Bay of Marseilles seen from L'Estaque 144*; *Rochedos em L'Estaque 145*
chaos 107–112
Chiang Kai-shek 302
Chihiro Hatanaka 19–20, 163
China 18–19, 23; and analytical psychology 318–319; ancestral worship in 49–74; animus archetype in 97–119; archetypes of femininity in 26–35; clinical material 320–329; compensation through education 111–114; and Confucius 316–320; femininity in Chinese culture 25–47; forming the Chinese animus 98–103; the Garden of the Heart & Soul 41–47; the Grand Chinese Scholar Tree 70–74; the imperial hereditary system 58–65; missing women of 35–41; nationalism 54–58; negative cultural animus 105–107; positive cultural animus 103–105; the "Sacred Ancestral Tree" culture 66–69; significance of the words *root* and *ancestor* 50–54; and Taiwan 300–301; the White Snake 114–119; wounded

cultural animus 107–111; wounded feminine 311–329
Chinese Scholar Trees 66, 69–72, *70*, 76n27
chorology: relationship between nature and culture 158, **158**
Ci-bei (empathetic grief) 42, 44–45, *44*
city dwellers 110, *110*
collective psyche 7–8, 10–13, 218–219
colonization 247, 263, 268, 271, 293, 308
commodification 229, 246–248
communism 202, 206–213, 215–217, 221–222
Communist Party 108, 202–203, 222
compassion *see Ci-bei*
compensation 111–114
Confucianism 2, 9; China 55, 62–63, 75, 86, 88, 95, 103–105; Korea 202, 215, 218–219, 221, 239, 243; neo-Confucianism 104–108, 238, 317–318; Taiwan 294, 316–317
Confucius 9; and ancestral worship 62–63; and the animus archetype 103, 106–107; and femininity 36, 45; and the orphan of patriarchy 294; and the wounded feminine 316–318; *see also* Confucianism
consciousness 139–140; and inclusiveness 157–159; making unconscious cultural complexes conscious 306–307; and the "modern" period in Western Europe

INDEX

140–141; subject and the landscape 141–142, 151, 154; traditional Japanese landscapes and ASD today 157; and "unbornness" in depth psychology 142–144; *see also* modern consciousness; postmodern consciousness

conservatives 206–208, 211–212, 236–237

consumerism 217–218, 221, 241–242, 245, 252n44, 283–284

cosmic egg *99*

couple separation 85–87, 94

cultural complexes 14–18; bipolarity of 17–18; cultural complex theory 8–11, 14; making the unconscious conscious 306–307; in Taiwan 295–304; *see also* agency; ancestral worship; individual complexes; *kimchi*-bitch; orphan of the patriarchy; postmodern consciousness; search for the father

cultural heritage: forming the Chinese animus 98–103; negative cultural animus 105–107; positive cultural animus 103–105; wounded cultural animus 107–111

Cultural Revolution 80; and the animus archetype 98, 108–110, *109*, 118; and femininity 26, 36; and Korea 202

culture: cultural conflicts 83–84; cultural identity 16–18, 294–295; cultural

relations 293–295; cultural unconscious 14–15, 87–88, 328–329; developing diverse and multiethnic group cultures 305; relationship between nature and **158**; *see also* cultural complexes; cultural heritage

Dao De Jing see Tao Te Ching

Daoism 25–27, 31, 33–36

daughters 92–93, 315–316; clinical material 320–321; daughter-in-law 243, 318, 320, 322–324

Dawkins, Richard 230

Dayu 42, 61, 64

default 213–215

depth psychology 34, 115–119, 139–140, 142–144

Ding (the vessel) 101–102, *102*

disillusionment 246–248

displacement 78, 86; displacement anxiety 81–85, 88, 93–94; and immigrant mothers' phenomenon 81–85; and self-identity 87–93

dissociation 127–128, 132–133; union with 133–136

diversity 305–307

division/unification (bundan/tong-il) 205–208

Dupérac, Étienne *190*

Eastern Han Dynasty (25–220 CE) 74n1, 106

education: China 83–85, 102–105, 111–114; Japan 184–185, 195–196; Korea 243–244; Taiwan 263–264, 274–275, 320–321, 325–326

Ego-Self axis 301–304
emigration 78, 86, 93, 305; history of Hongtong Dahuaishu 67–69; *see also* migration
emotion 15–16; China 44–45, 62–63, 65–66, 91–92; Korea 217–218, 229–233, 240; Taiwan 276–278, 283–284, 314–319, 324, 327
Europe *see* Western Europe

family environment 82
family names 59–60
family values 83–84
Fan Kuan: *Travelers Among Mountains and Streams* 150
fantasy 119, 130, 210, 293–295
farming culture 55; morality of 63–65
fathers: father/son relationship 305–306; Japanese-style 263–267; as orphans 284–285; *see also* search for the father
female individuation 93–94
femininity 25–26; archetypes of 26–35; and the Garden of the Heart & Soul 41–47; and the missing women of China 35–41; *see also* wounded feminine
feminism: post-feminism 228, 242; in South Korea 241–242
filial piety 55, 62–63, 73, 221, 316
footbinding 315, 318
fraternal duty 62
Freud, Sigmund 42, 142–143, 276, 281–282, 306
future 328–329
Fuxi 32–33, 43–47, 56, 60–61, 63

Gang of Four 202
Gao Lan 18–19, 25
Garden of the Heart & Soul 26, 39, 41–47
Gen hexagram 51, *51*
goddesses 46; Amaterasu 185, 197–197; Bixia Yuanjun 27, *28–29*, 33, 36; Daoist 33–35; Demeter 90; Nüwa 27, 31–33, *31*, 36, 43, 60–61; Xi Wang Mu 27–31, *30*, 33, 36, 39–40
Gong Xi 19, 77
Grand Chinese Scholar Tree 66, 69–74, *70*; *see also* Chinese Scholar Trees
Great Northern Wilderness *110*
Greek mythology 90, 140
Guo Xi: *Early Spring* 146

Han Dynasty (202 BCE–220 CE) 29–33, 45, 120n7
Han Wudi 103, 120n7
Hao-Wei Wang 20, 261
healing 42–43
Heian period (794–1185/1192) 148, 155–156
Henderson, Joseph 14, 44, 87–88
hero archetype 203–204, 302–305, 307
hexagram 43, 45, 51, *51*, 100–102, *100, 102*
hieros gamos (unity of opposites) 222
hikikomori 20, 181–182, 193–195; in Japanese literature 186–193; the question of refusal 184–185; statistics on 183–184
holy land 67, 72–74

INDEX

Hongtong Dahuaishu (ancestral tree) 50, 66–69, *67–68*, *73*; *see also* ancestral worship
Hou Yingchun 19, 49
Huainanzi 32, 47n3
Huangdi *see* Yellow Emperor
Hui (kindheartedness) 45–46, *46*
Hung-Chin Wei 20, 291

I, the: and nature 190–192; and others 176–178
I Ching *see Book of Changes*
identity 10–11, 20–21; China 114–116; cultural identity 16–18, 294–295; Korea 215–220, 232–233, 239–240; self-identity 87–93; Taiwan 266–267, 269–270, 273–281, 283–285, 291–295, 299–302, 305–307
Ilbe (website) 232–239, 247
immigrant mothers *see* single mothers in marriage
imperial hereditary system 55, 58–65
inclusiveness 157–159
individual complexes 12, 91, 270, 283, 307
individuation 11–12, 218–219; female 93–94
inheritance 55, 57, 59–60
initiating 42, 44
interaction 171–172
internet: Japan 177, 182; Korea 217, 228–232, 235–241, 249n8, 249n11
intranet 211, 223n13
Italy: Villa d'Este (Tivoli) *190*

Japan 19–20, 121; agency in Japanese culture today 163–164; and autistic spectrum disorder 165–166; and inclusiveness 157–159; and individual stories today 169–176; intertwining of I and others 176–178; the introduction of Chinese-style landscape painting 148–149; Japanese-style father 263–267; landscape and the subject 139–159; and Landscape Montage Technique 151–153; and the subject in the landscape 149–151, 154–155; and symbolical story 167–169; and Taiwan 299–300; traditional Japanese landscapes and ASD today 155–157; and "unborn-ness" in depth psychology 142–144; weaker agency 164–165, 166–167; *see also hikikomori*; Murakami, Haruki; *Sputnik Sweetheart*
Ji 26, *26*
Jiang 26, *26*
Jin Dynasty (265–420 CE) 27
Juche (Kim-il sung-ism) 204, 213–215, 218, 221–222
Jung, C. G. 2–3, 8–14, 17; and agency 168; and ancestral worship 53; and the animus archetype 111, 119; and femininity 25–26, 33–35, 42, 44; Japanese landscape and the subject 142–143; and the *kimchi*-bitch cultural complex 232–233; nature and withdrawal 184–185, 189, 191, 194; and the orphan of

336   INDEX

patriarchy 295, 302–304; the political situation of two Koreas 212–213, 217, 221; and postmodern consciousness 124–125, 130, 133; and the search for the father 266, 273, 276–282, 285; and single mothers in marriage 88, 91–94; and the wounded feminine 313, 318–319; *see also* Jungian perspective; psychotherapy, Jungian-oriented

Jungian perspective 20, 201–204, 218–219; on the cultural gap between the two Koreas 215–218; on division/ unification in Korean history 205–208; on Juche 213–215; on the political situation between Korea and the United States 208–213; on possible integration of the two Koreas 219–222

Kim Dae-jung 211, 241
Kim Hyun Jung 234–235, 251–252
Kim Il-sung 202–206, 208, 214–216; *see also* Juche
Kim Jong-Il 203–204, 208, 213–215
Kimbles, Sam 14; and the kimchi-*bitch* cultural complex 232, 246; and the orphan of patriarchy 293, 307; and the political situation of two Koreas 220; and the search for the father 283; and single mothers in marriage 88

kimchi-bitch (*kimchi-nyeon*) 228, 232–236, 238–244, 247–248
kindheartedness 41–47; *Hui* 45–46, *46*
Kong Fuzi *see* Confucius
Korea 20, 199, 227–229; cultural gap between the two Koreas 215–218; division/unification in Korean history 205–208; emotions, the internet, and the unconscious 229–231; feminism 241–242; Ilbe's manifesto for misogyny 237–239; Juche 213–215; Jungian perspective 201–219; *kimchi*-bitch complex 233–236; "modern girls" 244–245; modernity and the new woman 243–244; neoliberal disillusionment 246–248; political situation between the United States and 208–213; possible integration of the two Koreas 219–222; post-feminism 242; premodern perspectives on women 242–243; *rujeo-eui nan* 239–241; trolls, conservatives, and the Ilbe storehouse 236–237; young men and their shadow 231–233
Kuan Tzu 51, 74n1
Kunlun Mountains 27–28, 31, 35

lack, sense of 127–128, 132
landscape 139–140; and ASD today 155–157; and inclusiveness 157–159; Landscape Montage Technique 151–153; and the

INDEX

"modern" period in Western Europe 140–141; multiple perspectives in Chinese-style landscape painting 143–147; Sesshu 148–149; the subject and 141–142, 149–151, 154–155; and "unborn-ness" in depth psychology 142–144
Landscape Montage Technique (LMT) 19, 151–154
language barrier 82–83, 85
Lao Tzu 2, 8–9, 25, 33, 53–54
Li Cheng 145–147; *High Pines, Level Distance* 146; *A Solitary Temple Amid Clearing Peaks* 146, *147*
Li Xianghui 19, 49
living environment 78, 81–82, 88
"loosen hands" 71
love 44–46, *45*; and ancestral worship 62–64; and the animus archetype 114–115; and postmodern consciousness 125–128; and single mothers in marriage 86–87, 90–91

Madame White Snake 114–119
madness 275–278, 280
Mao Zedong 110–111, 202, 302
Maoism 202
marriage: marriage crisis 83; *see also* single mothers in marriage
Marxism 202, 254n74
Marx-Leninism 202
Masuda, Takahiko 164–165, *164*
materialism 217–221, 246
Meiji period (1868–1912) 131, 156

memes 228, 230–231, 233, 235–237, 247, 249
men 231–233; *see also* fathers; millennial men; sons
migration 67–71, *70*, 76n27, 268–269, 286n5, 296; *see also* single mothers in marriage
millennial men 227–229, 234–240, 242, 244–247; and shadow 231–233
Ming Dynasty (1368–1644) 66, 68, 107, 115; Taiwan 268, 272, 285, 304
misogyny 227–228, 233, 237–238, 242
modern consciousness 19, 128–133, 135, 139–143, 167
modernity 140–141, 245–247; liquid modernity 273; and the new woman 243–244
modern period in Western Europe 139–141
Moon Jae-in 211
morality 63–65, 95n10, 191, 265, 315–316
mothers: China 33, 35–40, *38*, 45–46, 56, 112–119; Japan 125–126; mother-in-law 117, 323–324; Taiwan 262–265, 301–306, 318–324; *see also* single mothers in marriage
Mount Tai 27, *29*, 31, 35, 100
Mudan incident 20–21, 296–298, *297*, 308–309
multiethnic group cultures 305
Murakami, Haruki 19, 123–125; *see also Sputnik Sweetheart*
Muromachi period (1336–1573) 139–140, 155

338 INDEX

mythological world 128–133, 135–136, 140, 142–143

Nami Lee 20, 201
naming 42, 44
Nanae Takenaka 20, 181
Na-neun Aegukja (I am a Patriot) 235
narcissism 213
national character 17
nationalism 54–58, 211–213, 217–218, 291–292
nature: and *hikikomori* 185, 188–195; relationship between culture and 158, **158**
negative cultural animus 105–107, 112–115, 118–119
neoliberalism 228, 246–248
netizens 234, 236, 241, 251n40
Nisbett, Richard 164–165, *164*
Northern Song Dynasty (960–1127) 104, 145, *147*
nurturing 42–44
Nüwa 27, 31–33, *31*, 36, 43, 60–61

Occupy Wall Street 216
Oedipus complex 124
oracle bone script 26, 45–46, *45*, 52, 59
orphan of the patriarchy 20, 291–293; and the cultural complex in Taiwanese society 301–304; cultural and political relations 293–295; and the shadow 295–301; a way out of 305–307
orphans and orphanages 41, 44; fathers as 284–285; orphan complex 270; *see also* orphan of the patriarchy

painting *see* landscape
Pangu 60–61, 97–102, *99*, 119
patriarchy 58–65, 316–319, 322–328; *see also* orphan of the patriarchy
Peng Dehuai (Marshal) 108–109, *109*
planting trees 71–72
point of view 15–16, 124, 284, 319
political relations 293–295
positive cultural animus 97, 103–105, 114, 119
post-feminism 228, 242
postmodern consciousness 124, 128–136
psyche *see* collective psyche
psychoanalytical perspectives 85–87
psychology 123–125; clinical material 320–329; meaning of "division/unification" 205–208; and the political situation between Korea and the United States 208–213; *see also* analytical psychology; depth psychology
psychotherapy, Jungian-oriented: and agency in Japanese culture today 163–164; and autistic spectrum disorder 165–166; and individual stories today 169–176; intertwining of I and others 176–178; and Japanese weaker agency 164–165, 166–167; and symbolical story 167–169

Qing Dynasty (1840–1912 CE): China 97, 107–108; Taiwan

INDEX

263, 268–272, 285, 293, 295–302, 304, 307–309
Queen Mother of the West (Xi Wang Mu) 27–31, *30*, 33, 36, 39–40

racial discrimination 81, 84
Ravitz, Liza J. 21, 311
Red Guards 36, 109
refusal 184–185
relationships between the people and the ruler 299, 305–306
repetition 15
revolution 107–111; *see also* Cultural Revolution
ritual 41–42, 62–63, 104–105, 128–130
Roh Moo-hyun 211, 237, 241
roots 72–74, 76n27; Chinese word for 50–54
rujeo-eui nan (loser uprising) 239–241
Ryoan-ji temple 190–191, *190*

sandplay 2, *38–39*, 37–39, 41–42, 151, 159
Sangetsuki 20, 186–193, 197n19
sanity 275–278
scholars and scholar-officials 74n1, 100, 104–110, *109*, 119
sage 103–105
search for the father 261; case example 262–263; collective and cultural trauma 281–284; fathers as orphans 284–285; identity change or loss 273–275; Japanese-style father 263–267; madness as a way of sanity 275–278; how Taiwan became Chinese 267–269,

271–273; how Taiwan became Japanese 269–271; trauma of being collectively possessed 278–281
self-identity 87–93
self-improvement 55, 60–62
selfish smart fool 105–107
self-reproducing 171–172, 174
self-sacrifice 60–62
self-value 84–85, 90
Sesshu 139–140, 148–151, 158–159; *Autumn Landscape* 149; *Long Scroll of Landscapes* 148–150, 158; *Splashed-Ink Style Landscape* 148–149, 158; *View of Ama-no-Hashidate* 148–149, 158; *Winter Landscape* 148–149, 158
shadow 12, 21; Korea 212–213, 219, 228, 231–233, 246; Taiwan 278–282, 295–301, 304, 307, 313, 319, 328
Shang Dynasty (1600–1046 BCE) 52, 56–58
Shan Hai Jing 30
Shen Heyong 18–19, 25
Shennong 42–43
Shi Bo 64–65, 75
Shuowen Jiezi 51–52, 58–59, 67, 74n1
Si 26, *26*
Singer, Thomas 7, 88, 220, 252n44, 283, 293, 307
single mothers in marriage 77–81; and displacement anxiety 81–85; and female individuation 93–94; psychoanalytical perspectives 85–87; and self-identity 87–93
Song Dynasty (960–1279) 27, 104

sons 33, 92, 315, 318, 320–323, 325; *see also* fathers
Southern Song period 104–105, 148, 151
Spring and Autumn period (722–476 BCE) 62, 74n1, 103
Sputnik Sweetheart (Murakami) 125–127; consciousness 128–133; dissociation and sense of lack 127–128; union with dissociation 133–136
Stalinism 210, 215
stories: Grand Chinese Scholar Tree 70–74; intertwining of I and others 176–178; less than a story 175–176; types of 169–176; and weakness of agency 167–169; *see also Sangetsuki*; symbolical story
subject, the 139–140; and Chinese-style landscape painting 143–149; and inclusiveness 157–159; and the landscape 141–142, 149–151, 154–155; and Landscape Montage Technique 151–153; and the "modern" period in Western Europe 140–141; traditional Japanese landscapes and ASD today 155–157; and "unborn-ness" in depth psychology 142–144
Su-chen Hung 20–21, 291
surnames 26, 55, 59–60, 68, 72
symbolical story 167–169; *see also* stories

Taiwan 20–21, 259, 291–293, 305–307; case example 262–263; collective and cultural trauma 281–284; and the cultural complex 301–304; cultural and political relations 293–295; fathers as orphans 284–285; identity change or loss 273–275; independence versus unification *267*; Japanese-style father 263–267; madness as a way of sanity 275–278; search for the father in 261–281; and the shadow 295–301; how Taiwan became Chinese 267–269, 271–273; how Taiwan became Japanese 269–271; trauma of being collectively possessed 278–281
taming 42–44
Tang Dynasty (618 CE–907 CE) 85, 104, 144–145
Tao 2, 34–35, 53, 63, 100, 294
Tao Te Ching/Dao De Jing 2, 8–9, 33
temple 58–59, 148; for Bixia Yuanjun 27, *29*; *Ryoan-ji* 190, *190*
Tiananmen Square *109*
tiger 186–189, 191–193, *193*
timing 43–47
Toshio Kawai 19, 123
totem worship: of the Ancient Chinese people 55–56
transforming 42–47
trauma: China 36, 39–40, 88–91; collective 281–284; cultural 36, 40, 261, 281–284; and the Ego-Self axis 301–304; Korea 220–221; Taiwan 261, 278–284, 292–295, 299, 301–304, 306
trees *see* Chinese Scholar Trees

INDEX

trolls 236–237
Two Toenails on the Little Toe 70–74

Umbrella Revolution 216
unborn-ness 142–144, 149–151
unconscious, the 13–15; China 83–88, 92, 118–119; Japan 142–143, 168; Korea 228–233; Taiwan 276–277, 282–284, 306–307, 312–314, 317–324, 328–329; unconscious cultural complexes 306–307; *see also* cultural unconscious
unification *see* division/ unification
union 33, 132; with dissociation 133–136
United States (US) 1–2; and Korea 202–214, 218, 220; psychological understanding of 208–213; and Taiwan 262, 272, 283, 312

war 107–111; Afghanistan 212; Chinese civil war 97, 108; Cold War 218; Eighty Years' War 268; Iraq 212; Korean War 206–207, 220; Opium Wars 97, 108; Pacific War 245, 271; Sino-Japanese War 269–270, 298; Vietnam War 212; World War I 8, 12; World War II 97, 205, 209, 271, 274–275, 300–301
Warring States period (475–221 BCE) 29, 62, 75, 106, 193
weaving 33, 46, *46*
Western Europe 139, 140–145, 150–151, 154

Western Han Dynasty (202 BCE–8 CE) 64–65
Western Zhou Dynasty (1046–771 BCE) 58–59, 62–63, 75
White Snake 114–119
withdrawal *see hikikomori*
women: clinical material 321–322; female individuation 93–94; missing women of China 35–41; "modern girls" of Korea 244–245; and modernity 243–244; premodern perspectives on Korean women 242–243; *see also* daughters; female individuation; femininity; feminism; mothers; single mothers in marriage; wounded feminine
wounded cultural animus 107–111
wounded feminine 311–316; and analytical psychology 318–319; clinical material 320–329; and Confucius 316–320
Wu Zhuoliu 274, 281

Xi Wang Mu (Queen Mother of the West) 27–31, *30*, 33, 36, 39–40
Xia Dynasty (2070–1600 BCE) 57–58
Xing 26, *27*
Xu Jun 19, 97

Yang and Yin: and ancestral worship 53–54; and the animus archetype 98–100, *99*, 102;

and femininity 27, 29, 31;
and the wounded feminine
317–318, 329
Yasuhiro Tanaka 19, 139
Yellow Emperor 31, 57, 61,
97, 101
Yin *see* Yang and Yin

Yuan Dynasty (1271–1368) 27,
68, 104

Zhang Lei 19, 49
Zhou Dynasty (1046–256 BCE)
43, 56, 57, 63
Zhu Xi 105–106

Printed in the United States
By Bookmasters